8

AF774786

Limitation of Actions in England and Wales

Limitation of Actions in England and Wales

Martin Canny
BCL (Int), LLM (Comm Law) (NUI)
Barrister-at-Law of Kings Inns and Middle Temple

Bloomsbury Professional

Bloomsbury Professional Limited, Maxwelton House, 41–43 Boltro Road, Haywards Heath, West Sussex, RH16 1BJ

© Bloomsbury Professional Limited 2013

Bloomsbury Professional is an imprint of Bloomsbury Publishing Plc

All rights reserved. No part of this publication may be reproduced in any material form (including photocopying or storing it in any medium by electronic means and whether or not transiently or incidentally to some other use of this publication) without the written permission of the copyright owner except in accordance with the provisions of the Copyright, Designs and Patents Act 1988 or under the terms of a licence issued by the Copyright Licensing Agency Ltd, Saffron House, 6–10 Kirby Street, London EC1N 8TS, England. Applications for the copyright owner's written permission to reproduce any part of this publication should be addressed to the publisher.

Warning: The doing of an unauthorised act in relation to a copyright work may result in both a civil claim for damages and criminal prosecution.

Crown copyright material is reproduced with the permission of the Controller of HMSO and the Queen's Printer for Scotland. Any European material in this work which has been reproduced from EUR-lex, the official European Communities legislation website, is European Communities copyright. A CIP Catalogue record for this book is available from the British Library.

ISBN 978 1 78043 335 6

Typeset by Phoenix Photosetting, Chatham, Kent
Printed and bound in Great Britain by Martins the Printers, Berwick-upon-Tweed, Northumberland

Preface

On being informed that the Limitation Act 1980 ('LA 1980') contains the limitation periods for nearly all causes of action, in reasonably intelligible language, one might justifiably ask whether there is any need for this legal textbook. However, limitation issues frequently arise for consideration before the courts and the body of case law on limitation issues reveals that there is much by way of light and shade in the contours of the LA 1980. A tardy claimant may think himself out of time, but sometimes an argument based on an acknowledgment or part payment, deliberate concealment or his date of knowledge may avail him. The purpose of this text is to shine a light on this topic, in ease of those who are called upon to advise on a limitation point.

The ambiguities in the language used in the LA 1980, often copied from previous enactments of some antiquity, and the accepted construction of particular sections which differ from the dictionary definitions of the words used, can be striking. To give an obvious example, the standard wording used throughout the LA 1980 states that 'no action shall be brought' if the claimant's right of action is statute barred. This does not, in fact, mean what it says and a statute barred claim form may indeed be issued without any difficulty. One must instead have regard to the rules on pleading and the burden of proof in raising a limitation defence. From that starting point things get somewhat more predictable, but care must still be taken with the prevailing interpretation given to the provisions of the LA 1980. An example of this is *A v Hoare* [2008] 1 AC 844 in which the House of Lords departed from its own decision in *Stubbings v Webb* [1993] AC 498 on the issue of whether a sexual assault is a class of 'negligence, nuisance or breach of duty'. Looking to the near future, the divergent approaches evident in a number of recent decisions on the question of whether s 21(1)(a) of the LA 1980 applies to those who dishonestly assist in a breach of trust will hopefully be resolved by the Supreme Court, as a decision on an appeal from *Williams v Central Bank of Nigeria* [2012] 3 WLR 1501 is keenly awaited.

In addition to difficulties of interpretation involving the LA 1980, one must also keep abreast of amendments to that Act and changes to related limitation legislation. There has been a period of relative legislative calm in the last ten years, with only the definition of 'disability' being amended, and three sections of marginal importance being inserted into the LA 1980. Sections 27B and 27C relate to the proceeds of crime and criminals profiting from publications about their crimes, respectively. Section 33A was inserted by the Cross-Border Mediation (EU Directive) Regulations 2011 and introduces a 'pause' button on the running of time for cross-border mediations occurring near the end of the limitation period. Outside of the four corners of the LA 1980, the time limits for public procurement challenges were changed to a significant extent by the Public Procurement (Miscellaneous Amendments) Regulations 2011, which simultaneously shortened the applicable time limit and introduced a date of knowledge test.

Of all of the recent changes to the law, the criminalisation of squatting in a residential building by s 144 of the Legal Aid, Sentencing and Punishment of Offenders Act 2012 has the potential to have the most significant effect on the law in this area. The interaction between the doctrine of *ex turpi causa non oritur actio* (a wrongful act cannot be relied upon to found a claim) and the law on adverse possession, in the guise of the status of criminal acts being relied upon as acts of possession, was raised in *R (Smith) v Land Registry (Peterborough)* [2009] EWHC 328 (Admin). While an appeal to the Court of Appeal from that decision was disposed of on grounds that did not require comment on the *ex turpi causa* issue, the broader scope of criminalisation now brought about by s 144 means that this issue will quite likely arise for consideration again in the near future.

Elsewhere, the expansion of European legislation on the choice of law for contractual and non-contractual obligations (the Rome I and II Regulations), and their displacement of the rules in the Foreign Limitation Provisions Act 1984, must be borne in mind in disputes involving another EU Member State, and the continued implementation into EU law of the Conventions governing transport by air, sea and rail (the 'Carriage Statutes') requires the diligent legal adviser to double-check the source of a particular time limit or notification requirement.

Martin Casimir, Managing Director of Bloomsbury Professional, was a pleasure to deal with from the outset, as were Andy Hill, Head of Legal Publishing and Jane Bradford, Editorial Manager, the latter two taking with good humour several missed deadlines, which they characterised as inevitable wrinkles on the path towards publication and par for the course for legal authors. My copy-editor, Rebecca Cupit, has valiantly attempted to smooth out the syntactical blemishes and finesse the language in the book and I thank her for her diligence.

My brother, Niall Canny, a solicitor with Clifford Chance LLP, reviewed several chapters in their early incarnations and offered very helpful comments. My parents have supported me throughout my life and especially on my path to the Bar. Their kindness, generosity and encouragement in many ways made the writing of this book possible.

My wife, Sinéad, has just cause to complain that her agreement to my writing this book was obtained under false pretences. I now accept that she may have been right all along as to the level of dereliction of household duties this endeavour would entail, which was amplified by our decision to move house in the middle of writing the book and the demands of our respective professional careers. My two-year-old daughter Béibhinn will now have the pleasure of listening to her father regale her with interesting limitation stories as the Long Vacation draws tantalisingly close. I will take this opportunity to thank Sinéad for her support and express my love for both ladies.

I have endeavoured to state the law as at 1 May 2013; however, the principle of caveat lector applies and no legal liability is accepted for any inaccuracies contained in the text.

Martin Canny

21 June 2013
Longford Terrace
Monkstown
Co. Dublin.

Contents

Table of Statutes

All references are to paragraph number.

D

E

F

Table of Statutory Instruments

All references are to paragraph number.

Table of Cases

All references are to paragraph number.

B

C

D

E

G

I

J

K

L

M

N

O

P

Q

R

S

T

U

V

W

Y

PART I

Introduction and General

CHAPTER 1

Introduction and General Principles

INTRODUCTION

The necessity for a statute of limitations

1.01 There is a self-evident need for temporal limitations on the institution of proceedings. With the passage of time recollections fade, witnesses pass away, records are lost, insurance policies lapse and people move on with their lives. In the words of Best CJ in *A'Court v Cross*,[1] '[l]ong dormant claims have often more of cruelty than of justice in them'.[2] The Limitation Act 1980 ('LA 1980') (as amended[3] and supplemented[4]) imposes temporal limitations on the bringing of proceedings. In the case of most causes of action, the effect of the expiry of the limitation period is that, if a defendant raises a defence of limitation, a claimant will be denied a remedy by the courts.[5] By contrast, in the case of real property and chattels,[6] if a person remains in adverse possession of the property for the limitation period, the title of the dispossessed person (ie their right) to that property will be extinguished.[7] Considerations that this led to an undesirable outcome in the case of the theft of a chattel, and an unnecessary outcome in the case of registered land, have led to the rule not now applying in those two situations.[8]

1 (1825) 3 Bing 329; 130 ER 540.
2 (1825) 3 Bing 329 at 332–333; 130 ER 540 at 541.
3 See, in particular, the Latent Damage Act 1986, Consumer Protection Act 1987, Arbitration Act 1996, Defamation Act 1996 and Proceeds of Crime Act 2002.
4 See, in particular, the Foreign Limitation Periods Act 1984, Rome Regulations, Merchant Shipping Act 1995, Land Registration Act 2002 and the carriage statutes (discussed in Ch 22).
5 The fact that the claimant's right is not barred can be of significance in relation to contract debts: see paras 1.16–1.17.
6 LA 1980, s 3 refers to 'chattels', which in this context means tangible personal property such as goods.
7 LA 1980, ss 3(2) and 17; an exception exists in the case of the theft of a chattel.
8 See now the LA 1980, ss 4, 27A and 27B (for chattels) and the Land Registration Act 2002, s 96 and Sch 6 (for registered land) and the discussion in paras 15.06 and 15.07 of whether a more general exception arises in cases of criminal conduct.

1.02 In his judgment in *Abdulla v Birmingham City Council,*[9] Lord Sumption offered the following comments which relate to the status of limitation provisions generally:

> '[I]ssues of limitation are bedevilled by an unarticulated tendency to treat it as an unmeritorious procedural technicality. This is, I think, unjustified. Limitation in English law is generally procedural. But it is not a technicality, nor is it necessarily unmeritorious. It has been part of English statute law for nearly four centuries. It has generated analogous non-statutory principles in equity. Some form of limitation is a feature of almost all other systems of law. And it has been accepted in principle in the jurisprudence of both the Court of Justice of the European Union and the European Court of Human Rights. Limitation reflects a fundamental and all but universal legal policy that the litigation of stale claims is potentially a significant injustice. Delay impoverishes the evidence available to determine the claim, prolongs uncertainty, impedes the definitive settlement of the parties' mutual affairs and consumes scarce judicial resources in dealing with claims that should have been brought long ago or not at all.'[10]

The competing interests involved in limitation provisions

1.03 The LA 1980 balances the competing interests of claimants and defendants in relation to the time limits for issuing a writ. As was stated by Lord Nicholls in the House of Lords in *Haward v Fawcetts*:[11]

> 'Statutes of limitation seek to hold a balance between two competing interests: the interests of claimants in having maximum opportunity to pursue their legal claims, and the interests of defendants in not having to defend stale proceedings. Traditionally the limitation period for most claims is six years. This goes back to the Limitation Act 1623 (21 Jac 1, c 16). On its face this period, with extensions in cases of fraud and mistake, is a generous, perhaps over-generous, period within which to be able to start court proceedings in respect of a wrong.'[12]

1.04 The law on adverse possession of real property raises somewhat different issues to those that arise in relation to other causes of action. These include the need to encourage the productive use of land, and to allow for the quieting of titles where long possession has replaced paper title as the indicia of ownership. It might be argued that a squatter who extinguishes the title of a landowner at the expiration of the limitation period is thereby allowed to turn his 'wrong' into a 'right'.[13] The question of whether the limitation rules relating to real property strike the correct balance is a matter of some controversy which is discussed at greater length in Chapter 15.

9 [2012] UKSC 47, [2013] 1 All ER 649.
10 [2012] UKSC 47, [2013] 1 All ER 649 at para 41.
11 [2006] UKHL 9, [2006] 1 WLR 682.
12 [2006] UKHL 9, [2006] 1 WLR 682 at para 2.
13 See *Buckinghamshire County Council v Moran* [1990] Ch 623 at 644D, where Nourse LJ described adverse possession as 'possession as of wrong'.

A brief history of limitation provisions

1.05 Although statutes dating back to the Statute of Merton 1235[14] contained limitation provisions for actions relating to real property,[15] the Limitation Act 1623[16] was the first proper limitation act. The LA 1980 consolidates and amends the previous limitation provisions and is drafted in similar, though not identical, terms to the Limitation Act 1939. The length of the limitation periods contained in the Limitation Act 1980 are arbitrary; some have remained the same since the Limitation Act 1623 (such as the general six-year limitation period for common law actions) and some have been reduced in the intervening years (such as the periods relating to real property).[17] Case law on the equivalent provisions in the older Acts continues to be relevant in interpreting the provisions in the LA 1980, as in many cases the wording of the limitation provision has remained the same for a lengthy period. However, the relevance of the prior case law can itself give rise to disagreement, such as in *Cave v Robinson Jarvis & Rolf,*[18] where the House of Lords had to consider the effect of s 32(2) of the LA 1980 (on deliberate concealment), which had been enacted to codify the case law on fraudulent concealment under the Limitation Act 1939. As there was a gap or ambiguity in the section, the House of Lords held that it was possible to have regard to the prior case law (on a differently worded provision) to explain why parliament had used the wording contained in s 32(2).

The sources of limitation periods and actions subject to no limitation period

1.06 The LA 1980 is the primary source of limitation provisions but, as stated above, it is supplemented by numerous other statutes,[19] and those other limitation provisions are also discussed in this text. As a limitation period is a creature of statute, if no statutory limitation period applies to a cause of action, then prima facie such an action may be brought without limitation of time.[20] For example, the supervisory jurisdiction possessed by the High Court in relation to solicitors generally and undertakings given by them was held in *Bray v Stuart A West & Co*[21] not to be subject to any limitation period. In general though, even if a cause of action is not expressly dealt with by a provision in the LA 1980, the wording of an appropriate section in the Act is generally given an expansive interpretation so as to subject the claim to a limitation period. For example, this approach has been adopted for actions claiming damages from the State for breach of

14 20 Hen 3, c 4.
15 See para 15.02.
16 21 Jac 1, c 16.
17 See further the discussion of the development of the limitation periods for actions relating to real property in para 15.02.
18 [2003] 1 AC 384: see in particular the comments of Lord Millett at paras 19 and 23 and Lord Scott at paras 43–45.
19 See para 1.01, fn 4; the LA 1980, s 39 states that the Act does not apply in the case of 'any action for which a period of limitation is fixed by any other limitation enactment'.
20 See further para 1.15.
21 (1989) 139 NLJ 753.

European Union law,[22] restitutionary claims[23] and actions founded on statutory provisions even if not expressly subject to a time limit by that statute.[24] A significant exception to this principle exists in the case of actions seeking equitable relief[25] and those actions alleging breach of trust or breach of fiduciary duty for which no limitation period is prescribed by the LA 1980.[26] In those cases, the courts retain the same jurisdiction to refuse relief on grounds of *laches* or acquiescence as the courts of equity possessed historically.

Reform of the law on limitation

1.07 Limitation provisions have the ability to operate very unfairly: some aspects of this are inherent in any limitation framework but other aspects are due to the legislative provisions operating unfairly in the case of particular claimants. Reform has occurred over time both by legislative and judicial intervention. For example, the Limitation Act 1939 did not contain any provisions which expressly extended time in a case where the claimant only discovered that he had suffered personal injuries, or how it had occurred and who was at fault, after the expiration of the limitation period applicable to his cause of action. In 1963 the House of Lords in *Cartledge v E Jopling & Sons Ltd*[27] held that an action brought by a claimant who suffered a progressive lung disease from inhaling noxious dust at work was statute barred before he had any reason to believe he was injured. This was rightly considered to be grossly unfair on claimants affected by this rule and led to the passing of the Limitation Act 1963, which introduced a 'date of knowledge' test for personal injuries actions. This legislative innovation is retained in modified form in the LA 1980, which also provides, by s 33 of the Act, that the limitation period for a personal injuries action may be disapplied if it is equitable to allow the action to proceed. Other examples of legislative reform are discussed in the text; refinement of the law by judicial intervention has been more subtle and has largely involved the correction of decisions thought to be incorrect,[28] though in one notable case it was held that the erroneous view of the law was so well established that it should not be corrected.[29] In 2001 the Law Commission produced a detailed report on the limitation of actions[30] which proposed replacing the current statutory framework with a core regime containing a three-year limitation for most causes of action, which would run from the claimant's date of knowledge and be subject to a ten-year statutory long-stop. A discretion would

22 *R v Secretary of State for Transport, Ex p Factortame (No 6)* [2001] 1 WLR 942 (tort limitation period applied); see Ch 26.
23 *Kleinwort Benson Ltd v South Tyneside Metropolitan BC* [1994] 4 All ER 972 (contract limitation period applied); see Ch 9.
24 See *Hill v Spread Trustee Co Ltd* [2006] EWCA Civ 542, [2007] 1 WLR 2404, where the LA 1980, ss 8 and 9 were held to apply in such cases; see further para 24.13.
25 LA 1980, s 36(1): see Ch 18.
26 LA 1980, ss 21(1) and 36(2): see Chs 17 and 18.
27 [1963] AC 758.
28 See, for example, *A v Hoare* [2008] UKHL 6, [2008] 1 AC 844, which overruled *Stubbings v Webb* [1993] AC 498, discussed further in paras 13.06–13.08.
29 See *Lowsley v Forbes* [1999] 1 AC 329, discussed in paras 4.03–4.05.
30 Law Com No 270.

be retained to disapply the limitation period for personal injuries actions and a ten-year period would apply to adverse possession claims. Several Canadian provinces have reformed their limitation legislation along these lines but at the time of writing there does not appear to be any impetus towards implementing the recommendations in the Law Commission report.

GENERAL PRINCIPLES

An overview of the limitation periods

1.08 A comprehensive table of limitation periods is included at the end of this book, but the main limitation periods are as follows: actions for the recovery of unregistered[31] land – 12 years; actions for breach of contract – six years; actions in tort (other than personal injuries or defamation) – six years; actions claiming damages for personal injuries arising out of negligence – three years; defamation actions – one year. The limitation periods for personal injuries actions, non-personal injuries actions claiming damages for negligence and defective products claims under Pt 1 of the Consumer Protection Act 1987 are all subject to extension on date-of-knowledge grounds. The limitation periods for personal injuries and defamation claims may be disapplied if it is equitable to allow the action to proceed. Claims for damages for negligence not involving personal injuries and under Pt 1 of the Consumer Protection Act 1987 are subject to a long-stop of 15 years and ten years respectively. The LA 1980 does not contain any provisions which govern criminal prosecutions and it does not apply to customs or revenue proceedings,[32] proceedings involving the forfeiture of a ship,[33] or any claim by the Crown to any gold or silver mine,[34] but subject to those exceptions it applies to the Crown.[35]

An outline of the procedure applicable to limitation issues

1.09 The primary rule governing the limitation of actions is that time runs from the date of accrual of the cause of action until the date that proceedings are brought.[36] For personal injuries actions (and negligence actions not involving personal injuries), if the 'date of knowledge'[37] of an injured person is after the date of accrual of his cause of action, time runs from his date of knowledge. In the case of actions based on fraud and actions where a fact relevant to the right

31 The recovery of registered land now falls outside the LA 1980 altogether and is subject to its own rules contained in the Land Registration Act 2002: see Ch 15.

32 LA 1980, s 37(2)(a) and (b).

33 LA 1980, s 37(2)(c).

34 LA 1980, s 37(6).

35 LA 1980, s 37(1); see further paras 31.08–31.09.

36 The meaning of the words 'proceeding' and 'brought' and the rules governing the computation of time and other aspects of practice and procedure are discussed in Ch 2.

37 LA 1980, ss 11(4)(b) and 14 (personal injuries): see Ch 13; and s 14A(4) and (6) (non-personal injuries negligence actions): see Ch 12.

of action is deliberately concealed, time runs from the date when the fraud or the concealed fact was discoverable with the exercise of reasonable diligence.[38] In the case of an arbitration, time runs until the date on which the claimant serves a notice of arbitration on the defendant in compliance with the requirements of the arbitration clause; if no requirements are specified, until served in compliance with the provisions in the Arbitration Act 1996.[39] Where a claimant is under a disability when a cause of action accrues, the limitation period runs from the date that he ceases to be under the disability or dies.[40]

1.10 Once the limitation period starts to run, it will continue to run until it expires and a supervening disability will not affect the running of time.[41] However, if a fact relevant to a right of action is deliberately concealed after the right of action has accrued to the claimant, the limitation period will cease to run and will then only run afresh from when the concealed fact is, or by the exercise of reasonable diligence could have been, discovered.[42] If a defendant acknowledges a debt or the claimant's title to land, or makes a part payment towards a debt, the limitation period will commence afresh.[43] A rare statutory encroachment into this principle was brought about by the Cross-Border Mediation (EU Directive) Regulations 2011,[44] which suspend the expiry of the limitation period if a cross-border mediation takes place in the period of eight weeks prior to the expiration of the limitation period, in which case the limitation period shall expire instead 'at the end of eight weeks after the mediation ends'.[45]

Parties free to agree to a shorter limitation period

1.11 The LA 1980 does not impose any restrictions that prevent parties from agreeing that a shorter limitation period should govern any claim arising out of their relationship or any goods or services to be provided. This principle was applied without demur in *Inframatrix Investments Ltd v Dean Construction Ltd*,[46] where the parties had agreed that no action or proceedings under or in respect of the agreement could be brought at the expiry of one year from the date of practical completion, or if practical completion did not occur, one year from the date the contractor last performed services[47] in relation to the contract. It was held by the Court of Appeal that proceedings brought after the expiration of the period contained in the limitation clause were barred by the agreement. A somewhat

38 LA 1980, s 32(1)(a) and (b): see Ch 7.
39 Arbitration Act 1996, s 14: see para 23.02.
40 LA 1980, s 28: see Ch 5.
41 *Prideaux v Webber* (1661) 1 Lev 31.
42 *Sheldon v Outhwaite* [1996] 1 AC 102, discussed in para 7.02.
43 LA 1980, ss 29-31: see Ch 6.
44 SI 2011/1133. This Statutory Instrument implements Directive 2008/52/EC of the European Parliament and of the Council of 21 May 2008 on certain aspects of mediation in civil and commercial matters.
45 LA 1980, s 33A(3): see further para 23.16.
46 [2012] EWCA Civ 64, [2012] 2 All ER (Comm) 337.
47 An argument that an inspection and report in relation to the repairs needed, which occurred at a without prejudice meeting, constituted 'services under the contract' was also rejected.

illogical distinction exists between a clause that has the effect of imposing a short time limit on instituting any type of action and one which only limits the ability of a party to commence an arbitration. In the former situation, the clause may only be challenged under the Unfair Contract Terms Act 1977 (or under similar legislation), whereas a claimant may apply to the court under s 12 of the Arbitration Act 1996 to extend time to commence an arbitration,[48] notwithstanding the expiry of the time limit contained in the contract.

Agreements to extend the limitation period ('standstill agreements')

1.12 Individuals are free to agree that a longer period should govern any claim that may be brought by one party against the other in future. This arises most frequently after a claim has been intimated and if the parties, are in negotiations in the period leading up to the expiration of the limitation period, and is commonly referred to as a 'standstill agreement'. An example of a case where the parties agreed to extend the limitation period is *Braceforce Warehousing Ltd v Mediterranean Shipping Company (UK) Ltd*,[49] where a one-year extension was agreed while negotiations continued.

Negotiations and other acts giving rise to an estoppel

1.13 The limitation period for a cause of action will continue to run during the period that any negotiations take place between the parties, in the absence of an agreement between them to the contrary or conduct giving rise to an estoppel preventing the defendant from raising a limitation defence. The doctrine of estoppel in this context is a narrow one, although in *Lubovsky v Snelling*,[50] which is the first of the modern authorities on this point, a broader jurisdiction was suggested. The defendant in this action admitted liability in a fatal injuries matter but reserved its position on quantum. The Court of Appeal held that a writ issued outside the limitation period could not be met with a limitation defence as the defendant was estopped from raising any defence on liability by reason of its earlier promise. By contrast, in the more recent decision of *Cotterell v Leeds Day (a firm)*,[51] it was held by Buckley J that an admission of liability was not in itself sufficient to give rise to an estoppel preventing a limitation defence from being raised. Instead, the trend of the modern case law is to require a specific representation that a limitation defence will not be raised, reliance on this representation and detriment in order for an estoppel to arise, or in other words practically a complete agreement. By contrast, a second and inconsistent approach was adopted for example in *Co-operative Wholesale Society v Chester le Street District Council*.[52] This approach requires the court to ask whether there was 'unconscionable con-

48 See paras 23.06–23.09 for a discussion of the AA 1996, s 12.
49 [2009] EWHC 3839 (QB), [2009] All ER (D) 101 (Jun).
50 [1944] KB 44.
51 Unreported, 21 December 1999 (QBD), Buckley J.
52 [1996] 2 EGLR 143.

duct'[53] in deciding whether matters said in the course of negotiations should lead to a defendant being estopped from raising a limitation point. Despite the breadth of some of the language used in *Co-operative Wholesale Society*, it was distinguished in *Hillingdon London Borough Council v ARC Ltd (No 2)*[54] as being a case where the parties had a shared common assumption that the claimant was entitled to some compensation based on steps already taken by it to commence its claim. Instead, in *Hillingdon London Borough Council v ARC (No 2)*, the Court of Appeal confirmed that it is necessary to establish an unequivocal representation that the claim was valid and that the defendant would not rely upon a limitation defence for an estoppel to arise.

1.14 In *Law Society v Sephton & Co*,[55] the Court of Appeal rejected a proposition that a request that a claimant refrain from issuing proceedings until related litigation concludes could be said to carry with it an implied statement that no limitation point would be taken, as each party 'is entitled to assume that the intending claimant and its solicitors are able to look after themselves so far as Limitation Act implications are concerned',[56] although Neuberger LJ noted that the position might be different if sharp practice was involved. The same approach was adopted by the Privy Council in *Super Chem Products Ltd v American Life and General Insurance Co Ltd*,[57] where Lord Steyn held that an insurer was entitled to negotiate and investigate a claim and that this did not suspend the running of the limitation period without more; instead it was incumbent on the claimant to seek agreement to the limitation period being extended or to issue a protective writ to protect its position. The Supreme Court of Canada in *Maracle v Travellers Indemnity*[58] adopted a position broadly analogous to that adopted in *Law Society v Sephton & Co* and held that while an admission of liability was evidence from which a representation not to rely on a limitation defence could be established, it was not *per se* sufficient. A difference of emphasis is evident in the decision of the Supreme Court of Ireland in *Murphy v Grealish*,[59] where Geoghegan J held that, the defendant having admitted liability to a rear-ending road traffic accident, 'some added facts would be necessary to create an estoppel but not much addition would be required'[60] and that on the facts it would be inequitable and unconscionable for the defendant to be allowed to raise a limitation defence in the proceedings. On the present state of the case law, the decision in *Murphy v Grealish* is overly forgiving of claimant inertia and does not represent the law in England, but each case depends on its own facts and its focus on inequitable and unconscionable conduct may be explored in future case law.

53 [1996] 2 EGLR 143 at 148, per Judge Marder QC.
54 [2000] 3 EGLR 97; to similar effect is *Seechurn v Ace Insurance Sa-Nv (formerly Cigna Insurance Co of Europe Sa-Nv)* [2002] EWCA Civ 67, [2002] 2 Lloyd's Rep 390.
55 [2004] EWCA Civ 1627, [2005] 3 WLR 212, affd without reference to this point: [2006] UKHL 22, [2006] 2 AC 543.
56 [2004] EWCA Civ 1627, [2005] 3 WLR 212 at para 127, per Neuberger LJ.
57 [2004] UKPC 02, [2004] 2 All ER 358.
58 [1991] 2 SCR 50.
59 [2009] IESC 9, [2009] 3 IR 366 at 377.
60 [2009] IESC 9, [2009] 3 IR 366 at 375.

Want of prosecution and lapse of time justifying dismissal of proceedings

1.15 Prior to the commencement of the CPR, there developed a significant body of case law on when want of prosecution and delays by a claimant in progressing proceedings would justify the dismissal of his action.[61] The central role of case management in the CPR now means that this topic is of historic interest only, which is preferable to the position in other common law jurisdictions that have failed to introduce active case management, where a significant amount of court time is still taken up by applications relating to litigant delay.[62] The courts of England and Wales have not (yet) had to rule directly on whether they have jurisdiction to dismiss non-statute barred proceedings that are brought such a long time after the events under consideration that a fair trial is not possible or the defendant cannot reasonably be expected to defend himself. As this factor already features in applications to disapply the limitation period under s 33 of the LA 1980, it is only likely to arise where a date of knowledge issue or claimant disability gives rise to a lengthy period of delay not causing the applicable limitation period to expire. Although it is sometimes said that there is 'no limitation at common law',[63] the interaction between this concept and the obligation in art 6 of the European Convention on Human Rights to ensure that civil obligations are resolved within a reasonable time remains to be teased out. The Supreme Court of Ireland recognised that it had such a jurisdiction in *Toal v Duignan (Nos 1 and 2),*[64] in an action where the claimant was born in 1961 and brought non-statute barred proceedings in 1984 which alleged that treatment received by him in 1961 and 1971 had been negligent. The court dismissed the proceedings against those defendants who could point to irremediable prejudice (loss of records and deaths) but not those who were not so prejudiced, with Finlay CJ stating that the court should ask whether the delay 'would probably lead to an unjust trial and an unjust remedy'[65] and that the interest protected by the court in such circumstances was a 'defendant's basic right not to be subjected to a claim which he or she could not reasonably be expected to defend'.[66] This remains a feature of the law applied in Ireland,[67] though decisions to date in England have required a defendant to prove an additional factor such as would make the action an abuse of process in order to justify striking out non-statute barred proceedings.[68]

61 *Birkett v James* [1978] AC 297; *Grovit v Doctor* [1997] 1 WLR 640; Oughton, Merkin and Lowry, *Limitation of Actions* (2nd edn, London: LLP, 1998) at 95–100.

62 For recent Irish case law, see *Lismore Builders Ltd (in receivership) v Bank of Ireland Finance Ltd* [2013] IESC 6; *Comcast International Holdings Inc v Minister for Public Expenditure* [2012] IESC 50.

63 McGee, *Limitation Periods* (6th edn, London: Sweet & Maxwell, 2010) at para 1.052.

64 [1991] ILRM 135 (No 1) and 140 (No 2).

65 [1991] ILRM 140 at 143.

66 [1991] ILRM 140 at 143.

67 See *Kearney v McQuillan* [2010] IESC 20 and *McBrearty v North Western Health Board* [2010] IESC 27.

68 See *Hogg v Hamilton* [1992] PIQR 387; *Headford v Bristol DHA*, unreported, 17 June 1994 (QBD).

Effect of the expiration of the limitation period

1.16 Although the LA 1980 provides that 'no action shall be brought' in respect of a cause of action after the limitation period has expired, this is not interpreted literally and a claimant may still institute proceedings.[69] In most cases, the expiration of the limitation period will only bar a claimant from obtaining a remedy in respect of the wrong alleged if the defendant chooses to rely on a limitation defence. The effect of the expiration of limitation period in these cases is treated as being 'procedural' in nature. However, in the case of actions relating to estates in unregistered land or chattels, subject to two exceptions in the case of chattels,[70] the expiration of the limitation period for bringing an action will have the result that the title of the owner of the property will be extinguished.[71] A claim under Pt 1 of the Consumer Protection Act 1987[72] is subject to a ten-year longstop, a negligence action not claiming damages for personal injuries is subject to an overriding time limit of 15 years,[73] and claims under the carriage statutes are also extinguished upon the expiration of the limitation period.[74] The limitation provision is treated as having a 'substantive' effect on the rights of the parties in these situations.[75]

1.17 As there is no means of obtaining redress[76] for a tort other than by action, the fact that the expiry of a limitation period may only bar the remedy is only of relevance in relation to statute barred contract debts. If a creditor is paid a debt which is statute barred, the payment cannot subsequently be recovered on grounds that it was not due.[77] An executor may deduct from the amount of a specific or residuary legacy the amount of any statute barred debt owing from the legatee to the estate.[78] While an executor[79] and a trustee[80] may validly pay a statute barred debt, it has been held that a liquidator may not.[81] A creditor may exercise a lien over goods in his possession in order to secure payment of a statute barred

69 The language used in the LA 1980 would suggest that a court office has no jurisdiction to issue statute barred proceedings but limitation provisions have never been treated in this manner, a point adverted to by the Irish Supreme Court in *O'Domhnall v Merrick* [1984] IR 151 at 158, per Henchy J.

70 LA 1980, ss 4 (theft), 27A and 27B (Proceeds of Crime Act 2002).

71 LA 1980, ss 3(2) (chattels) and 17 (real property).

72 LA 1980, s 11A(3).

73 LA 1980, s 14B: see Ch 12.

74 See Ch 22; for example, in *Aires Tanker Corpn v Total Transport Ltd* [1977] 1 WLR 185 (HL), it was held that the expiration of a time limit under the Hague-Visby Rules extinguished the claimant's right of action.

75 *McKain v RW Miller & Co (SA) Pty Ltd* (1992) 174 CLR 1 at para 20. However, the current state of the law has been subjected to criticism: see Franks, *Limitation of Actions* (London: Eastern Press Ltd, 1959) at 37, and the comments of Lord Wilbeforce in *Black-Clawson Ltd v Papierwerke AG* [1975] AC 591 at 632.

76 The remedy of damages is only available by action: the conversion can be ended by the claimant retaking possession of his chattel.

77 The law concerning payments made towards an account where some of the debts are statute barred is discussed in para 6.28.

78 *Courtenay v Williams* (1844) 3 Hare 539.

79 *In re Rownson* (1885) 29 Ch D 358, but cf *Midgely v Midgely* [1893] 3 Ch 382.

80 *Bridgett v Bridgett* [1895] 1 Ch 202.

81 *Re General Rolling Stock Co Ltd* (1872) 7 ChApp 646.

debt,[82] as may a solicitor in respect of his lien over the subject-matter of litigation[83] or his client's papers.[84]

Limitation periods and jurisdictional time limits

1.18 A time limit for instituting proceedings which applies to an existing cause of action is a 'limitation period'. A time limit which forms part of a new statutory cause of action, which provides that the making of a claim within the time limit is a requirement of a claim being validly made, is not properly called a limitation period but is instead a jurisdictional time limit. The best examples of this are provisions in the employment legislation which use language such as the following: 'an employment tribunal shall not consider a complaint' unless it is presented within a certain period of time.[85] In a number of decisions in the 1970s,[86] which were recently followed by the Court of Appeal in *Radakovits v Abbey National Plc*,[87] it has been held that the time limits for claims before employment tribunals are jurisdictional in nature. This had the effect in *Radakovits* that, even though the employer took no issue in relation to a claim being brought one day late, the tribunal felt compelled to raise the point of its own motion and dismissed the claim. The Court of Appeal upheld this decision, with Elias LJ stating that 'a tribunal cannot exercise jurisdiction by concession',[88] although he added that a tribunal can act on a concession based on an apparently satisfactory reason to extend time and 'does not have to explore fully every case where a jurisdictional issue could potentially arise'.[89]

The necessity to plead the Statute of Limitations

1.19 In all cases where the expiry of a limitation period bars the claimant's remedy, but not his right, a defendant must specifically plead a limitation defence in order to raise this issue at trial.[90] In cases where the expiry of the limitation period extinguishes the claimant's right (as well as his remedy), while it is arguable that there is no need to plead the expiry of the limitation period, in reality it is still incumbent on the defendant to draw this fact to the attention of the court and CPR PD 16.13(1) should be read as so requiring. In cases where the time

82 *Re Lloyd* [1903] 1 Ch 385 at 401.
83 *Higgins v Scott* (1831) 2 B & Ad 413 (proceeds of execution); *Re Hepburn* (1884) 14 QBD 394 at 399–400.
84 *Curwen v Milburn* (1889) 42 Ch D 424.
85 Employment Rights Act 1996, s 111(2).
86 See *Dedman v British Building and Engineering Appliances Ltd* [1974] 1 All ER 520 (CA) and *Rogers v Bodfari (Transport) Ltd* [1973] IRLR 172.
87 [2009] EWCA Civ 1346, [2010] IRLR 307; however, see also the doubts expressed by Lord Sumption as to the correctness of this distinction in *Abdulla v Birmingham City Council* [2012] UKSC 47, [2013] 1 All ER 649 at para 42.
88 [2009] EWCA Civ 1346, [2010] IRLR 307 at para 22.
89 [2009] EWCA Civ 1346, [2010] IRLR 307 at para 22.
90 *Ketteman v Hansel Properties Ltd* [1987] AC 189 at 219.

limit goes to the jurisdiction of the court, it is not necessary to plead that the time limit has expired and the court may raise the time limit point of its own volition.[91]

There must be a claimant to sue and a defendant to be sued

1.20 It is a requirement for a limitation period to run that there must be a claimant to sue and a defendant to be sued. What is meant by this requirement is that such persons must be in existence as legal personae to occupy the positions of claimant and defendant. The fact that the claimant does not know who committed a tort, such as the car thief in *RB Policies at Lloyd's v Butler*,[92] will not prevent the limitation period from running and expiring, unless the claimant can successfully rely on one of the reasons to extend the limitation period such as fraud, concealment or a date of knowledge argument or other similar point. The first circumstance where a cause of action will not accrue because a party is not in existence is where a company has been struck off the register of companies, which is discussed in Chapter 24 as the Companies Acts contain special provisions which are not of general application. A second circumstance arises in cases involving the intestate estates of deceased persons. While an executor derives his title from the will (and the grant of probate confirms this for evidentiary purposes), an administrator obtains his title from the grant alone, which does not 'relate back' to the date of death of the deceased. Consequently, there is no competent claimant or defendant (as the case may be) in the interval between the death and the grant of letters of administration, and the cause of action cannot accrue until the latter event.[93] A statutory exception is contained in s 26 of the LA 1980, which provides that the limitation period runs during the period between death and the grant in the case of actions by administrators to recover land. A third circumstance is where a defendant has diplomatic immunity from suit in which case it was held in *Musurus Bey v Gadban*[94] that the limitation period will only start to run on any claim against him when the immunity ceases.

Same person as claimant and defendant

1.21 It has been said in a number of cases that where 'the hand to pay and the hand to receive'[95] are the same (ie they belong to the same individual), the limitation period cannot run. This can arise in at least three circumstances, which must be considered separately. First, where at the time when a cause of action would accrue in the normal way the potential claimant and potential defendant are the same person, accrual is prevented and time does not run.[96] Secondly, where the same person becomes both claimant and defendant after a cause of action has accrued, such as where a debtor is appointed administrator of the estate of

91 See para 1.18.
92 [1950] 1 KB 76; for criticism of this decision see para 7.18.
93 *Atkinson v Bradford Third Equitable Building Society* (1890) 25 QBD 377.
94 [1894] 2 QB 352.
95 *Hodgson v Salt* [1936] 1 All ER 95 at 98.
96 *Binns v Nichols* (1866) LR 2 Eq 256 (personal representative and legatee).

his creditor, has been held that the running of time is suspended.[97] In *Bowring-Hanbury Trustee v Bowring-Hanbury*,[98] it was held that time continued to run while a creditor was executor of the estate of the debtor, although this decision has been the subject of academic criticism.[99] Thirdly, in cases where the person liable to pay and the person liable to receive periodical payments are the same, such as where a person is entitled to periodical payments from land of which he is in possession, the period of such combination is disregarded, or in other words, a payment is presumed to have been made during that period.[100]

Procedural bars on instituting suit do not affect the limitation period

1.22 The rules governing the accrual of a cause of action are discussed separately in the chapter concerning the relevant cause of action. Of more general application are procedural bars which prevent a claimant from instituting suit and their effect on the limitation period. The rule in such cases is that the limitation period will continue to run even though no action could have been brought.[101] One example is the statutory bar on a solicitor suing his own client for fees for one month after delivery of a bill of costs that was originally contained in the Solicitors Act 1843,[102] which in *Coburn v Colledge*[103] was held not to delay the commencement of the limitation period during that month. In *O'Connor v Isaacs*,[104] it was held that the claimant's cause of action for false imprisonment was complete from the date of the false imprisonment and not the date when his conviction was quashed. In *Central Electricity Board v Halifax Corpn*,[105] a requirement that the plaintiff obtain a Minister's decision on a matter prior to being able to bring proceedings in respect of that matter was found to be procedural and not part of the cause of action. More recently, in *Awoyami v Radford*,[106] it was held that the limitation period for the claimant to sue the barrister who had acted for her ran from the date of the acts complained of in 1995, even though it was not until 2000 that the House of Lords in *Hall v Simons*[107] held that barristers should no longer enjoy an immunity from suit. By contrast, if the matter which precludes the bringing of proceedings is in fact part of the cause of action, time will not run until the condition precedent has been satisfied. Examples in this category include a demand for repayment of a deposit made by a bank customer

97 *Seagram v Knight* (1867) LR 2 Ch App 628.
98 [1943] Ch 104.
99 See the case note by Megarry (1943) 59 LQR 117.
100 *Topham v Booth* (1887) 35 Ch D 607 at 612; *Re England* [1895] 2 Ch 820 at 825.
101 This rule is criticised in Scanlan, 'The Chagos Islanders' Case – A Question of Limitation?' (2007) CLQ 292, discussing *Chagos Islanders v Attorney General* [2004] EWCA Civ 997.
102 See now the Solicitors Act 1974.
103 [1897] 1 QB 702.
104 [1956] 2 QB 288.
105 [1963] AC 785; see also *Sevcon Ltd v Lucas Ltd* [1986] 1 WLR 462.
106 [2007] EWHC 1671 (QB); [2008] 3 WLR 34.
107 [2002] 1 AC 615.

to their banker[108] or the expiry of a credit period allowed for making payment for goods.[109]

Amendment of the limitation period and retrospective effect

1.23 An amendment to a limitation provision can purport to have retrospective effect: it may revive a cause of action which was statute barred or shorten the limitation period for a cause of action which has already accrued. Although it relies on an artificial distinction, there exists a common law 'prima facie rule of construction'[110] which draws a distinction between an amendment to a limitation provision that has given rise to a procedural defence and one that has given rise to a substantive defence. In the former case, parliament is free to amend the limitation provision with retrospective effect, whereas in the latter case it is not, as this would be akin to an interference with a property right. This rule of construction was summarised in the following terms by Lord Brightman, giving the advice of the Privy Council in *Yew Bon Tew v Kenderaan Bas Mara*,[111] in the following terms:

> '[A]n accrued right to plead a time bar, which is acquired after the lapse of the statutory period, is in every sense a right, even though it arises under an act which is procedural. It is a right which is not to be taken away by conferring on the statute a retrospective operation, unless such a construction is unavoidable.'[112]

Similarly, it was held by the Court of Appeal in *The Ydun*[113] that a statute which reduced[114] the limitation period for a cause of action which had already accrued was a procedural amendment that did not offend against the presumption against retrospective effect, which, it held, only applied to matters of substantive law. However, this decision, though followed subsequently,[115] draws a distinction between substantive and procedural rights which later cases have criticised, such as the decision of the Privy Council in *Gangar v Espinet*,[116] where Lord Brown indicated that the case law may require examination in a future decision.[117]

1.24 This position at common law referred to in the previous paragraph is partially reflected in s 16(1) of the Interpretation Act 1978, which provides that the repeal of an enactment 'does not, unless the contrary intention appears … (c) affect any right, privilege, obligation or liability acquired, accrued or incurred

108 *Joachimson v Swiss Bank* [1921] 3 KB 110.
109 *Helps v Winterbottom* (1831) 2 B & Ad 431.
110 *Yew Bon Tew v Kenderaan Bas Mara* [1983] 1 AC 553 at 558, per Lord Brightman.
111 [1983] 1 AC 553.
112 [1983] 1 AC 553 at 563.
113 [1899] P 236.
114 The shortened limitation period had not expired on the date the amending Act came into force, which was treated as a point of importance in *Yew Bon Tew v Kenderaan Bas Mara* [1983] 1 AC 553 at 563.
115 *R v Chandra Dharma* [1905] 2 KB 335; *Jones v Trollope Colls Cementation Overseas Ltd*, *The Times*, 26 January 1990 (CA).
116 [2008] UKPC 48, [2009] 4 LRC 260.
117 See [2008] UKPC 48, [2009] 4 LRC 260 at para 18.

under that enactment'. Schedule 2, para 9(1) of the LA 1980 provides that nothing in the Act shall either:

(a) enable any action to be brought which was barred by the LA 1980 or the Limitation Act 1939 before 1 August 1980, or

(b) affect any action or arbitration commenced prior to that date.[118]

1.25 The LA 1980 only expressly states that it has no retrospective effect when a cause of action was barred by the Limitation Act 1939; its effect on a cause of action which was barred by a different enactment prior to its commencement came before the House of Lords in *Arnold v Central Electricity Generating Board*.[119] It held that the statutory provisions in question were not sufficiently clearly drafted for the court to conclude that they had been intended to deprive the defendant of an accrued limitation defence in circumstances falling outside Sch 2, para 9(2). By way of contrast, Lord Bridge in *Arnold* stated that it was:

> '[B]eyond question that the [Limitation Act] 1963 operated retrospectively when the appropriate conditions were satisfied, to deprive a defendant of an accrued time bar in respect of a claim for damages for personal injuries in which the cause of action had accrued since 4 June 1954.'[120]

However, he held that the Limitation Act 1963 did not have this effect for a cause of action which became statute barred prior to 4 June 1954 and that the LA 1980 was not sufficiently clearly drafted for the court to conclude that it had been intended to deprive the defendant of a limitation defence which had accrued to it in July 1944. The point was revisited in *McDonnell v Congregation of Christian Brothers Trustees*,[121] where the claimant sought to argue that *Arnold* was wrongly decided, or in the alternative to limit its application to causes of action formerly subject to s 21 of the Limitation Act 1939, which governed claims against public authorities. The House of Lords followed its earlier decision, with Lord Bingham finding that *Arnold* was 'not clearly wrong' and that it had general application. Despite the criticisms by McGee of *Arnold* and *McDonnell*, it would appear as if this point of statutory interpretation is now settled.[122]

118 The Latent Damage Act 1986, s 4(1) contains effectively the same clause as of LA 1980, Sch 9, para 9(2) but the Defamation Act 1996 and the Land Registration Act 2002 are more clear in stating that they do not have retrospective effect.

119 [1988] AC 228.

120 [1988] AC 228 at 268; these comments were directed in particular at a limitation defence arising under the Limitation Act 1939, s 21.

121 [2003] UKHL 63, [2004] 1 AC 1101; see also the decisions of the Supreme Court of Canada to like effect in *Martin v Perrie* [1986] 1 SCR 41 and *Angus v Sun Alliance Insurance Co* [1988] 2 SCR 256 and that of the Manitoba Court of Appeal in *Ciecierski v Fenning* (2005) 258 DLR (4th) 103 (a non-limitation case).

122 See McGee, *Limitation Periods* (6th edn, London: Sweet & Maxwell, 2010) at paras 1.022 to 1.033. His criticisms of *Arnold* in previous editions of his textbook were noted by Lord Bingham in *McDonnell* [2003] UKHL 63, [2004] 1 AC 1101 at para 24 but were found to be insufficient to justify the House departing from its earlier decision.

CHAPTER 2

Pleading, Procedure, Amendment and Calculating Time

INTRODUCTION

2.01 This chapter discusses a number of aspects of practice and procedure which arise in connection with limitation issues. These include the questions of when the limitation period stops to run, how the limitation period should be calculated and the rules governing the joinder and substitution of parties and the amendment of pleadings after the limitation period has expired. In addition, it discusses the question of who bears the burden of proof when a limitation defence is raised and issues concerning the pleading of a limitation defence and the mode of trial of limitation issues.

THE RUNNING AND COMPUTATION OF TIME

Limitation period runs from accrual until proceedings are brought

2.02 The basic rule under the Limitation Act 1980 ('LA 1980') is that time runs from the date of accrual of the cause of action until the date an action is brought and that any intervening disability on the part of the claimant does not affect the running of time.[1] The word 'action' is defined in s 38(1) of the LA 1980 as including 'any proceeding … in a court established by law'. 'Proceeding' is not defined in the LA 1980, but it is clear that it includes an originating court document issued out of the relevant court office;[2] however, it has been held not to include an application to the Land Registry.[3] The limitation period runs until the claim form (or other originating document) is issued, but it only remains in

1 *Prideaux v Webber* (1661) 1 Lev 31. However, a subsequent deliberate concealment of facts will set time running afresh until the concealed facts are, or ought to have been, discovered: *Sheldon v RHM Outhwaite (Underwriting Agencies) Ltd* [1996] AC 102.

2 See *China v Harrow Urban District Council* [1954] 1 QB 178. The law relating to the commencement of arbitrations is discussed in Ch 23.

3 *JA Pye (Oxford) Ltd v Graham* [2000] Ch 676.

force for the period allowed for service of the document.[4] If the claim form is not served during the period allowed for service, the proceedings are effectively at an end and their existence can be disregarded for limitation purposes unless the claimant obtains an extension of time to serve the claim form.[5] If time is extended and the claim form validly served then the claimant once again gains the benefit of the date of issue of the proceedings for limitation purposes. If an extension of time is refused, new proceedings must be brought and the relevant date for limitation purposes is the date of issue of the new set of proceedings (not the first).[6]

Parts of a day are ignored; first day is excluded from calculations

2.03 The limitation periods for all causes of action dealt with by the LA 1980 are framed in similar terms, and state that the action in question 'shall not be brought after the expiration of' the relevant limitation period. In calculating the limitation period, the date the accident occurred is excluded from the computation of the period of time. For example, in a case having no complicating date of knowledge issues, if a claimant suffers personal injuries in an accident which occurs on 10 May 2009 he will have until the court office closes on 10 May 2012 to issue proceedings claiming damages for negligence.[7] For a time limit expressed in a period of months, one month from 25 May will expire on 25 June.[8]

Limitation period ending on a day when court offices are closed

2.04 If the last day that a claim form could be issued which would not be statute barred is a day when the court offices are closed, the claimant has until the end of the next day when the court offices are open within which to issue proceedings.[9] In *Moulai v Deputy Public Prosecutor in Creteil, France*,[10] a case relating to the 'issuing' of a notice of appeal, Lord Neuberger appeared to suggest[11] that a claimant may also be entitled to an extension of time to the next

4 A claimant has four months from the date of issue to serve a claim form within the jurisdiction; six months if issued for service outside the jurisdiction: CPR 7.5(1) and (2).

5 Extensions of time are governed by CPR 7.6 and are not considered in this textbook. For the law on applications under CPR 7.6, see *Nanglegan v Royal Free Hampstead NHS Trust* [2001] EWCA Civ 127, [2002] 1 WLR 1043 and *Collier v Williams* [2006] EWCA Civ 20, [2007] 1 All ER 991. In exceptional circumstances the court can also dispense with service under CPR 6.9: see *Cranfield v Bridgegrove Ltd* [2003] EWCA Civ 656, [2003] 3 All ER 129.

6 See *Cia Colombiana de Seguros v Pacific Steam Navigation Co* [1965] 1 QB 101 at 126, where Roskill J stated that a limitation defence asks 'whether the action before the court, and not some other action, has been instituted within the relevant limitation period'.

7 LA 1980, s 11(4)(a); see *Marren v Dawson Bentley & Co Ltd* [1961] 2 QB 135. The example disregards any issues relating to the claimant's date of knowledge or the LA 1980, s 33.

8 *Radcliffe v Bartholomew* [1892] 1 QB 161; *Dodds v Walker* [1980] 2 All ER 507. However, the position appears to be different in relation to time limits expressed in weeks: see *Okolo v Secretary of State for the Environment* [1997] 4 All ER 242 and *R (Barker) v Hambleton District Council* [2012] EWCA Civ 610, (2013) 1 P & CR 1.

9 *Pritam Kaur v S Russell & Sons Ltd* [1973] QB 336.

10 [2009] UKHL 2, [2009] 3 All ER 1035.

11 [2009] UKHL 2, [2009] 3 All ER 1035 at para 85.

working day if the court office closes early on the last day that non-statute barred proceedings could be brought.

When are proceedings brought? Delays and errors by court staff

2.05 In a straightforward case it is obvious when proceedings are brought: proceedings are brought when the court office issues a claim form at the request of the claimant;[12] a claim form is issued on the date entered on the form by the court office.[13] However, matters are sometimes rather more complicated, as was the case in *Page v Hewetts Solicitors*[14] where the claimants' solicitor alleged he had sent the claim form, particulars of claim, fee and bundles to the court office by DX prior to the limitation period for his client's cause of action expiring. He surmised that these had been mislaid by the court office; the replacement papers he sent were received after the applicable limitation period had expired. In those proceedings, his clients sought to rely on the date the papers were or should have been received on the first occasion as the date the proceedings had been 'brought'. It was held by the Court of Appeal that 'a claim is brought when the claimant's request for the issue of a claim form (together with the court fee) is delivered to the court office'.[15] The court held that the question of when an action was 'brought' was a question of construction of the LA 1980 and is not governed by the CPR or the relevant Practice Direction, although it found sensible guidance in the latter.[16] The court held that any other construction would be unjust as the claimant would then have to take the risk that the court office would fail to process his request to issue a claim form in time. In light of these findings on the law, the court held that the defendants were not entitled to summary judgment: a full hearing was required to determine whether the claim form had in fact been delivered to the court office[17] (but lost) prior to the limitation period expiring, as it could not be said that the claimants had no reasonable prospects of success on that point.[18]

Time limits where no further action necessary by court office

2.06 For certain types of application a document simply has to be 'delivered' or 'filed' as opposed to being 'stamped' or 'issued'. In such a case, if a time

12 CPR 7.2(1).
13 CPR 7.2(2); see also PD 7A, para 5.
14 [2012] EWCA Civ 805, [2012] All ER (D) 78 (Jun).
15 [2012] EWCA Civ 805, [2012] All ER (D) 78 (Jun) at para 30, quoting from the judgment of Tuckey LJ in *Barnes v St Helen's MBC* [2006] EWCA Civ 1372, [2007] 3 All ER 525. In *Barnes*, industrial action prevented the claim form being issued on the date it was delivered, but this was still held to constitute the date the proceedings were brought.
16 See PD 7A, para 5.
17 [2012] EWCA Civ 805 at para 38.
18 To similar effect, see *Secretary of State for Trade and Industry v Vohora* [2007] EWHC 2656 (Ch) and *Riniker v University College London* [1999] All ER (D) 371 (CA), but see contra *Salford City Council v Garner* [2004] EWCA Civ 364, *The Times*, 10 March 2004; see also Willins, 'Don't blame the messenger' (2006) 156 NLJ 1826.

limit expires on a day the office is closed, there is less reason to allow the party until the next day the office is open to file the document. In *Van Aken v Camden London Borough Council*,[19] the claimant had a number of days within which to 'file' a notice of appeal. On the final day of that period his solicitors took the appeal papers to the court office, but arrived at 4:15 pm, 15 minutes after the office had closed in accordance with its normal opening hours. Later that day, the solicitors posted the papers through the court letterbox, which were processed in the ordinary way the next day. CPR 2.3(1) applied, which states that 'filing' a document means delivering it, by post or otherwise, to the court office, and the court held that the appeal had been filed in time. It held that delivery of a document to an office did not require collaboration and was a unilateral act. In all cases, care must be taken to analyse what exactly was required to be done, and what was actually done, in each case.[20]

SET-OFFS, COUNTERCLAIMS AND PT 20 CLAIMS

Set-offs and counterclaims

2.07 Section 35 of the LA 1980 provides that a set-off or counterclaim[21] shall be deemed to be a separate action and to have commenced on the same date as the action in which the set-off or counterclaim was brought. A defence, properly so called, can never become statute barred. If a defendant wishes to raise a cross-claim, he may do so either in a separate action (or arbitration), in which case the ordinary limitation period will apply to those proceedings, or as a set-off or counterclaim within the proceedings, which will then be subject to the provisions of s 35. In *Henriksens Rederi A/S v Rolimpex (THZ)*,[22] Lord Denning MR stated that a cross-claim will be considered to raise a defence if it arises out of the same transaction as the claim and goes directly in diminution or extinction of the claim, such as an allegation that the goods delivered or works carried out are worth less than the contract price by reason of the breach of contract.[23] However, if the cross-claim does not reduce the value of the goods sold or the work done, but alleges other damage, such as losses arising out of delays or damage to other property of the defendant, this does not raise a defence but instead arises as a set-off or counterclaim.[24] In *Henriksens Rederi A/S*,[25] it was held that the defendant's liquidated cross-claim arising out of short delivery of goods arose as a counterclaim to the plaintiff's action for the freight, and not as a matter of defence to their claim. This was of significance because the action for the freight was

19 [2002] EWCA Civ 1724, [2003] 1 WLR 684.

20 See also *Moulai v Deputy Public Prosecutor in Creteil, France* [2009] UKHL 2, [2009] 3 All ER 1035.

21 LA 1980, s 35(3) limits the scope of this provision to matters pleaded in an 'original set-off or an original counterclaim', ie the first such pleading delivered in the action.

22 [1974] QB 233.

23 [1974] QB 233 at 247.

24 [1974] QB 233 at 248; see also the analysis in *Chitty on Contracts* (31st edn, London: Sweet & Maxwell, 2012) at para 28-123.

25 [1974] QB 233.

subject to a six-year limitation period, whereas the counterclaim was governed by the Hague-Visby Rules, which imposed a one-year limitation period.[26] As the claim and counterclaim had both been brought over one year after the respective causes of action accrued, the result was that the counterclaim, but not the claim, was statute barred.

2.08 A number of issues relating to 'counterclaims' arose for consideration in *Law Society v Wemyss*,[27] where it was noted that 'counterclaim' in this context means 'any cause of action that might be asserted by an existing defendant against a claimant'. What was before the court in *Wemyss* was the defendants' application for liberty to amend their defence and counterclaim under CPR 17.1(2)(b). It was refused on grounds that the differences between the existing and the additional claims were sufficiently substantial for the court to take the view that 'an already complex action should not be further complicated',[28] thus leaving the defendants to pursue those claims in fresh proceedings. If the defendants in *Wemyss* had delivered the extended counterclaim at the outset (and had not needed leave to amend), the claimants could still have applied under CPR 20.9(1) to have the counterclaim dealt with separately to the claim. An order of this nature was made in *Ernst & Young v Butte Mining Plc*,[29] where the defendant's counterclaim was struck out having regard to the interests of procedural convenience as it raised issues which ought to have been tried in a separate action, even though its cause of action in those other proceedings would be statute barred.

Part 20 claims (third party proceedings)

2.09 Section 35(1)(a) of the LA 1980 provides that, for the purposes of the Act, a new claim made in third party proceedings shall be deemed to have been brought on the date on which those proceedings were commenced. 'Third party proceedings' are defined in s 35(2) as being any proceedings brought in the course of any action by any party to the action against a person not previously a party to the action, other than proceedings brought by joining any such person as defendant to any claim already made in the original action by the party bringing the proceedings. This definition includes a counterclaim against an added party, ie one not already claiming any relief against the defendant.

JOINDER AND SUBSTITUTION OF PARTIES AND AMENDMENT OF PLEADINGS AFTER LIMITATION PERIOD HAS EXPIRED

2.10 An application to amend pleadings or substitute parties after the expiration of the limitation period may only be granted if it is allowed by s 35 of the LA 1980. If it is allowed, s 35(2) has the effect that the new cause of action or the claim involving the added party relates back to the date that the proceedings

26 Article III, r 6.
27 [2008] EWHC 2515 (Ch), [2009] 1 All ER 752.
28 [2008] EWHC 2515 (Ch), [2009] 1 All ER 752 at para 24.
29 [1997] 1 WLR 1485.

were commenced. In *Welsh Development Agency v Redpath Dorman Long Ltd*,[30] it was held by the Court of Appeal that the test for whether s 35 applies, once an objection to an amendment based on limitation is raised, is whether the claimant can show that the defendant does not have a reasonably arguable case on limitation[31] which would be prejudiced by the new claim. If the claimant would have a full answer to a limitation defence to the new claims by relying on s 14A of the LA 1980, as was the case in *Chandra v Brooke North (a firm)*,[32] there is no need to have regard to s 35 in considering the amendment application. If the limitation defence remains arguable then the claimant must either satisfy s 35 or issue a new claim form containing the matters he wishes to add by amendment.

2.11 Section 35(3) of the LA 1980 provides that rules of court may allow for a party to make a new claim in any action after the expiry of the limitation period[33] for that claim, provided that the conditions set out in s 35(5)–(7) are satisfied. The relevant rules of court, which take account of the restrictions imposed by s 35 are contained in CPR 17.4 and CPR 19.5. CPR 17.4 contains the rules that permit the court to allow a party to amend his statement of case where a limitation period has expired. CPR 19.5 contains the rules that permit the court to allow a change of parties after the expiration of the limitation period, which contains two further tests common to the three circumstances it envisages, namely that an order can only be made if the limitation period was current when the proceedings were commenced[34] and that the addition or substitution of a party is necessary.[35] Taken together, these rules allow an amendment, joinder or substitution in the following circumstances:

1 In a claim for personal injuries or death where the court exercises its discretion under s 33 of the LA 1980 to disapply the limitation period under ss 11 or 12 or directs that the issue of whether those sections shall apply shall be determined at trial.[36]

2 An amendment whose effect will be to add or substitute a new cause of action that arises out of the same facts or substantially the same facts as those already advanced in the proceedings by the party applying for permission to amend may be allowed under CPR 17.4(2).

30 [1994] 4 All ER 10.

31 This should be judged at the date the amendment is actually made with leave of court and not the date the application is issued: [1994] 4 All ER 10 at 22.

32 [2013] EWHC 417 (QB).

33 The limitation period referred to here is one contained in the LA 1980, the Foreign Limitation Periods Act 1984 or any other enactment which allows such an amendment or change. Excluded, for example, are time limits contained in many of the carriages statutes discussed in Ch 22 and claims subject to the ten-year long-stop in the Consumer Protection Act 1987, s 11A(3): see *O'Byrne v Aventis Pasteur MSD Ltd* [2010] UKSC 23, [2010] 1 WLR 1412.

34 CPD 19.5(2)(a).

35 CPD 19.5(2)(b).

36 CPR 19.5(4). In *Wood v Chief Constable of the West Midlands Police* [2004] EWCA Civ 1638 at para 76, the Court of Appeal noted that it was possible that parliament had accidentally omitted to refer to s 32A (discretion to disapply limitation period for defamation claims) in s 35(3), but held that as a libel was pleaded already, adding a claim of slander on substantially the same facts was permissible under CPR 17.4(2). In addition, if the limitation period was disapplied under s 32A, there would be no need to refer to s 35 in amending the pleadings.

3 An amendment to add or substitute a party or amend their title either under CPR 17.4 –

(i) to correct a genuine mistake which did not cause reasonable doubt as to the identity of the party in question;[37]

(ii) to alter the capacity in which a party claims if the new capacity is one which that party had when the proceedings started or has since acquired;[38]

or under CPR 19.5 (see the extra hurdle, above) –

(iii) in substitution for a party who was named in the claim form by mistake;[39]

(iv) where the claim cannot properly be carried on by or against the original party unless the new party is added or substituted as claimant or defendant;[40] and

(v) where the original party has died or been made bankrupt and his interest or liability has passed to the new party.[41]

The discretion arising where s 33 of the LA 1980 is raised depends entirely on whether the claimant can successfully rely on that section and is considered in the chapter on personal injuries.[42]

Whether amendment seeks to add a 'new cause of action'

2.12 The first issue to be determined on an application under CPR 17.4(2) is whether the amendment seeks to add a new cause of action. The leading definition of a 'cause of action' is the statement of Diplock LJ in *Letang v Cooper*[43] that a cause of action is 'simply a factual situation the existence of which entitles one party to obtain from the court a remedy against another person', as distinct from 'a form of action ... used as a convenient and succinct description of a particular category of factual situation'.[44] An amendment which merely seeks to give further particulars of loss arising out of already pleaded facts does not constitute the addition of a new cause of action,[45] although some amendments can be quite close to the borderline. For example in *Aldi Stores Ltd v Holmes Buildings Plc*,[46]

37 CPR 17.4(3).
38 CPR 17.4(4).
39 CPR 19.5(3)(a).
40 CPR 19.5(3)(b).
41 CPR 19.5(3)(c).
42 See Ch 13.
43 [1965] 1 QB 232.
44 [1965] 1 QB 232 at 242–243. This definition has been followed on many occasions, including in *Lloyds Bank Plc v Rogers* [1999] 38 EG 83 at 85F, per Auld LJ and *Aldi Stores Ltd v Holmes Buildings Plc* [2003] EWCA Civ 1882, [2005] PNLR 9 at para 21, per Dyson LJ.
45 See, for example, the comments of Longmore LJ in *Berezovsky v Abrahamovich* [2011] EWCA Civ 153, [2011] 1 WLR 2290 at para 64.
46 [2003] EWCA Civ 1882, [2005] PNLR 9.

the proposed amendments sought to add new claims for loss and these were held not to involve the addition of a new cause of action, even though additional facts would have to be pleaded and proven at trial to establish causation. The crucial factor was that no new duty and no new breach of duty were sought to be added.[47] By contrast, in *Co-Operative Group Ltd v Birse Developments Ltd*,[48] a plea that a concrete slab was structurally unsound because of inadequate steel content was held by the Court of Appeal to constitute a different cause of action to the already pleaded case that the concrete was defective because it was not sufficiently thick. Similarly, in *Seele Austria GmbH v Tokio Marine Europe Insurance Ltd*,[49] an amendment to justify a claim on a different factual basis, which did not alter the sum claimed, was found to constitute the making of a new claim outside the limitation period and the amendment was refused.

2.13 In the sprawling *Berezovsky v Abrahamovich*[50] litigation, the Court of Appeal delivered a judgment on the claimant's application to amend his pleadings under CPR 17.4 to change his pleaded case despite counsel for the defendant arguing that this involved seven material amendments. These included changing an allegation that various rights held by him were trust rights to an allegation that they were contractual; removing reference to the rights having been obtained by oral declaration of trust; and amending certain factual allegations alleged to form the basis of the claim and the applicable law for the action. The Court of Appeal allowed the amendments, with Longmore LJ noting the definition of the phrase 'cause of action' and stating as follows:

> 'A new claim, according to section 35(2) of the 1980 Act, is a claim involving the addition or substitution of a new cause of action. A cause of action is that combination of facts which gives rise to a legal right. A cause of action in tort has, as its essential ingredients, a plea of duty, breach of duty and consequent damage to the claimant. If it happens to be the case that an element of one of those essential ingredients is misstated, misdescribed or omitted, it does not mean that a correct statement, description or inclusion is a new cause of action; even if the formal result of such a misstatement, misdescription or omission might technically be that an unaltered claim would have to be dismissed, that still does not mean that a corrective alteration involves or constitutes a new cause of action.'[51]

Whether new cause of action arises out of 'the same facts' or 'substantially the same facts' as those already pleaded

2.14 If the amendment seeks to add a new cause of action, it is a question of fact and degree and 'substantially a matter of impression'[52] as to whether the plea

47 [2003] EWCA Civ 1882, [2005] PNLR 9 at para 26, per Dyson LJ.

48 [2013] EWCA Civ 474; see also *D & G Cars Ltd v Essex Police Authority* [2013] EWCA Civ 514, where the Court of Appeal also considered whether the matters sought to be added to the claim by amendment could instead be pleaded in a reply to defence.

49 [2009] EWHC 2066 (TCC).

50 [2011] EWCA Civ 153, [2011] 1 WLR 2290.

51 [2011] EWCA Civ 153, [2011] 1 WLR 2290 at para 59.

52 *Welsh Development Agency v Redpath Dorman Long Ltd* [1994] 1 WLR 1409 at 1419.

sought to be introduced arises out of the same facts or substantially the same facts. In deciding on this issue it is necessary to compare the manner in which the facts constituting the cause of action in the original pleading were phrased with the wording in the proposed amended pleading, leaving out the non-essential facts.[53] An allegation of fraud was held in *Paragon Finance Plc v DB Thakerar & Co*[54] not to arise out of substantially the same facts as an allegation of negligence. By contrast, a claim by the dependents of a deceased person under the Fatal Accidents Act 1976 will usually arise out of substantially the same facts as a claim on behalf of his estate under the Law Reform (Miscellaneous Provisions) Act 1934.[55] In *Goode v Martin*,[56] the Court of Appeal held that CPR 17.4(2) should be read as referring to the facts 'already in issue' as opposed to 'already pleaded' so as to allow the claimant to amend to reflect matters pleaded in the defence which were not pleaded in his particulars of claim. This was expanded upon in *Charles Church Developments Ltd v Stent Foundation Ltd*,[57] where the claimant was allowed to amend its particulars of claim against one defendant after the expiry of the limitation period to adopt facts that had been pleaded by a different defendant in its defence in the action.

2.15 In *Mersey Docks Property Holdings Ltd v Birse Construction Ltd*,[58] the claimant brought proceedings in respect of a fire at its premises which alleged negligence and breach of contract by the defendants, including a failure to warn and the use of inadequate, inappropriate or poorly secured materials. It sought leave to amend its particulars to include more detail concerning the manner in which the fire occurred and the defendant's fault. The court held that the proposed amendments arose out of substantially the same facts and should be allowed, relying on *Goode v Martin*[59] for authority that they did not have to be pleaded already against that particular defendant, and further that it was appropriate that the court exercise its discretion in favour of allowing the amendments. Returning to two of the cases discussed above,[60] in *Co-Operative Group Ltd v Birse Developments Ltd*,[61] the court held that the plea of a different breach of duty in relation to the concrete slab did not arise out of substantially the same facts as the original plea. The reasons for this were that different expert evidence would be required to try the new issue and the loss claimed was significantly greater and included the cost of replacement and not simply the cost of repairing the concrete slab. In *Aldi Stores Ltd v Holmes Buildings Plc*,[62] the additional facts involved pleas that two parties relied on already pleaded advice given by a defendant and

53 See *Smith v Henniker-Major* [2003] Ch 182 and *P & O Nedlloyd BV v Arab Metals Co* [2006] EWCA Civ 1330, [2007] 1 WLR 2483 at para 14, per Thomas LJ.

54 [1999] 1 All ER 400 (CA); followed in *Fattal v Walbrook Trustees (Jersey) Ltd* [2010] EWHC 2767 (Ch).

55 *Booker v Associated British Ports* [1995] PIQR P375 (CA).

56 [2002] 1 All ER 620.

57 [2006] EWHC 3166 (TCC), [2007] 1 WLR 1203.

58 [2004] EWHC 3264 (TCC), (2004) 99 ConLR 122.

59 [2002] 1 All ER 620; see also *Charles Church Developments Ltd v Stent Foundations Ltd* [2006] EWHC 3158 (TCC), [2007] 1 WLR 1203, per Jackson J.

60 See para 2.12.

61 [2013] EWCA Civ 474.

62 [2003] EWCA Civ 1882, [2005] PNLR 9.

that this had caused loss. Dyson LJ held that even if the proposed amendment did seek to add a new cause of action, the facts to be added were substantially the same as those already pleaded and he would have granted liberty to amend.

Amendment to correct a genuine mistake

2.16 An amendment to add or substitute a party after the expiration of the limitation period will be allowed on grounds of mistake if it comes within the wording of CPR 17.4(3) or CPR 19.5(3)(a). The question of whether the mistake caused reasonable doubt as to identity has to be determined objectively having regard to what is said in the claim form and what was known by the defendant.[63] A description in the particulars of claim may be referred to in clarifying the identity of the person intended.[64] The case law in the area was reviewed at length in *Adelson v Associated Newspapers Ltd*,[65] in an action where the second claimant, which was described as a trading company, was named in defamation proceedings. After the expiration of the limitation period, the claimants sought to amend the description of that party to that of 'holding company' and to join the third and fourth claimants, which were described as trading companies whom it was alleged had also been defamed. The judgment of the Court of Appeal was delivered by Lord Phillips CJ, who noted that CPR 19.5(3) was 'notoriously causing problems'[66] and traced the legislative history of s 35(3) and the case law on the old RSC Ord 20, r 5 and their replacement provisions in the CPR.[67] As both rules were enacted under the power provided by s 35(6)(a) of the LA 1980, he held that CPR 17.4(3) and CPR 19.5(3)(a) should be read together, notwithstanding the differences in language in the two rules.[68] In commenting on the types of mistakes that can be corrected, he noted that 'the mistake that the rule envisages is one of nomenclature, not of identification'.[69] After detailed consideration of the issues, the court held that the claimants had not placed sufficient material before the court to establish that a genuine mistake had been made, as opposed to a strategic decision, to name the second claimant, and the application was refused. The court was clearly unimpressed that the issue had been flagged in the defendants' defence and a reply had been delivered prior to the limitation period expiring, but the application to amend was only brought some time later.

2.17 Despite the claimant(s) being unsuccessful in the application to join new parties in *Adelson v Associated Newspapers Ltd*,[70] the judgment of Lord Phillips

63 See *ABB Asea Brown Boveri Ltd v Hiscox Dedicated Corporate Member Ltd* [2007] EWHC 1150 (Comm).

64 *International Bulk Shipping and Services Ltd v Minerals and Metals Trading Corp of India* [1996] 1 All ER 1017.

65 [2007] EWCA Civ 701, [2008] 1 WLR 585.

66 [2007] EWCA Civ 701, [2008] 1 WLR 585 at para 5.

67 Particular regard was paid to the judgment of Millett LJ in *Yorkshire Regional Health Authority v Fairclough Building Ltd* [1996] 1 WLR 210 at 219.

68 [2007] EWCA Civ 701, [2008] 1 WLR 585 at para 44, per Lord Phillips CJ.

69 [2007] EWCA Civ 701, [2008] 1 WLR 585 at para 33.

70 [2007] EWCA Civ 701, [2008] 1 WLR 585.

CJ approved the use of the relatively benign '*Sardinia Sulcis* test'[71] for applications under CPR 19.5(3). This asks whether the claimant got the 'right description but wrong name'. This allows for substitution in circumstances such as those that arose in *Gregson v Channel Four Television Corpn*,[72] where 'Channel Four Television Co Ltd' (a dormant company) was sued instead of 'Channel Four Television Corpn'; in *The Insight Group Ltd v Kingston Smith (a firm)*,[73] where the defendant LLP was sued whereas it was still an ordinary partnership at the date of the acts in question; in *Parsons v George*,[74] where 'the landlord' was the respondent but the wrong name was used; and *Horne-Roberts v SmithKline Beecham plc*,[75] where the claimant sought to sue 'the manufacturer of vaccine batch No 108A41A', but named Merck rather than SmithKline, although Keene LJ noted that if the 'correct defendant' was unaware of the claim until after the expiration of the limitation period then the court would be likely to exercise its discretion against allowing the substitution.[76]

Amendment to alter capacity or substitute a party where this is necessary for the action to be maintained

2.18 The other three rules in the CPR which allow a claimant to alter the capacity in which a party is named or to substitute another party for one named in the proceedings (CPR 17.4(4), 19.5(3)(b) and (c)) were all promulgated under ss 35(6)(b) and 35(7) of the LA 1980 and so share common features. CPR 19.5(3)(c) expressly deals with situations where the original party has died or had a bankruptcy order made against him and his interest or liability has passed to the new party, which does not give rise to any difficulties. CPR 17.4(4) deals with an alteration of the capacity in which a claimant sues, which does not cover the situation that arose in *Haq v Singh*,[77] where proceedings vested in the trustee in bankruptcy were wrongly issued in the bankrupt claimant's name and she subsequently sought to amend after receiving an assignment from the trustee. It was held that she had sued in her personal capacity at all times and thus fell outside CPR 17.4(4). Arden LJ's judgment helpfully sets out some examples of what is meant by the reference to changes in the claimant's capacity, such as will be the case if they gain capacity to act as 'administrator' of an estate,[78] or litigation friend, or as representative of a club.[79] CPR 19.5(3)(b) allows the joinder of an additional party if the claim 'cannot be properly carried on without the new party'. This does not provide the court with a general discretion and has instead

71 *The Sardinia Sulcis* [1991] 1 Lloyd's Rep 201.
72 [2000] CP Rep 60.
73 [2012] EWHC 3644 (QB); to similar effect is *Quayle v Rothman Pantall & Co (a firm)* [2012] EWHC 1474 (Ch), where the wrong corporate form was used in naming the defendant in the claim form.
74 [2004] EWCA Civ 912, [2004] 1 WLR 3264.
75 [2002] 1 WLR 1662.
76 [2002] 1 WLR 1662 at para 44.
77 [2001] EWCA Civ 957, [2001] 1 WLR 1594.
78 Thus lessening the effect of *Ingall v Moran* [1944] 1 KB 160, although see also *Millburn-Snell v Evans* [2011] EWCA Civ 577, [2012] 1 WLR 41.
79 [2001] EWCA Civ 957, [2001] 1 WLR 1594 at 1600–1601.

been restrictively interpreted. An example of a situation where it was successfully invoked was *Merrett v Baab,*[80] where a cause of action was vested in the new party and the claimant jointly but not severally, thus necessitating their joinder to the action. It also covers a situation where the claimant was an equitable assignee and had omitted to join the assignor prior to the expiry of the limitation period.[81] A third situation where it applies is if proceedings should have been brought as relator proceedings in the name of the Attorney General. A fourth situation is to substitute a company in whose name a shareholder (or administrator) should have brought proceedings for that other party in whose name they were actually brought.[82] In *Roberts v Gill & Co,*[83] it was noted by Lord Collins that:

> '[T]he common factors in these examples were that (1) the claimant's action was not properly constituted unless the new party were joined; and (2) the plaintiff was not seeking any substantive relief against the new party.'[84]

2.19 The conceptually difficult wording in CPR 19.5(3)(b) and the question of whether a claim 'cannot properly be maintained' came before the Supreme Court in *Roberts v Gill & Co.*[85] The proceedings in this case had been brought by the claimant, in his capacity as beneficiary of a deceased person, against a firm of solicitors alleging negligence in the drafting of a will. He later sought to amend his title and description in the action to describe him as suing on his own behalf and on behalf of the estate (by way of a derivative action), which also required the joinder of the administrator of the estate to the action (unless special circumstances were established). The Supreme Court refused leave to join the administrator under CPR 19.5(3)(b), finding that this was not necessary for the further continuation of the action brought by the claimant as disappointed beneficiary. It also refused him leave to change the capacity in which he sued from beneficiary to suing on behalf of the estate, pursuant to CPR 17.4(4) as this required the administrator to be joined to the action for him to maintain this derivative action on behalf of the estate. The court held that it would be an abuse of process[86] for him to be granted leave to amend the capacity in which he sued, and then in a sequential step to join the administrator as a necessary party, in order to overcome the refusal to join the administrator as a primary relief. The decision in *Roberts v Gill & Co* was applied in *Nemeti v Sabre Insurance Company Ltd,*[87] where Judge Cotter QC refused the claimant leave to join the estate of a deceased driver in place of his insurance company in a foreign motor accident case brought before the English courts. He held that the joinder was not necessary for the original action to be maintained and that the jurisdiction to allow a substitution only arose in narrow circumstances, 'aimed at errors in the

80 [2001] QB 1174; see further *Roche v Sherrington* [1982] 1 WLR 599 and the Partnership Act 1890, s 9.

81 See *Roberts v Gill & Co* [2010] UKSC 22, [2011] 1 AC 2407 at paras 4 and 28, per Lord Collins; this rule reverses *Hudson v Fernyhough* (1890) 34 SJ 228.

82 *Irwin v Lynch* [2010] EWCA Civ 1153, [2011] 1 WLR 1364.

83 [2010] UKSC 22, [2011] 1 AC 2407.

84 [2010] UKSC 22, [2011] 1 AC 2407 at para 28.

85 [2010] UKSC 22, [2011] 1 AC 2407.

86 [2010] UKSC 22, [2011] 1 AC 2407 at paras 70–71 (Lord Collins) and 85 (Lord Rodger).

87 [2012] EWHC 3355 (QB).

constitution or formality of the action'.[88] As the insurance company was simultaneously arguing that it should never have been sued (and that the estate should have been the sole defendant) this decision may seem a little harsh, but in deciding on an issue where both side's arguments were not without merit, the judge was clearly unimpressed by the manner in which the claimant's legal advisers had progressed the action, noting that the problems were 'of their own making'.[89]

PLEADINGS, THE BURDEN OF PROOF AND THE MODE OF TRIAL

The necessity to plead a limitation defence

2.20 A defendant wishing to raise a limitation defence must specifically plead that the action is statute barred.[90] The approach in the CPR reflects the prior practice, such as in *Ketteman v Hansel Properties Ltd*,[91] where the House of Lords upheld the decision of a trial judge to refuse the defendant leave to amend its defence in closing arguments at the end of a two-week trial. As Lord Griffiths stated, if a defendant chooses not to raise a limitation defence but instead to defend an action on its merits:

> '[H]e should not be permitted to fall back upon a plea of limitation as a second line of defence at the end of the trial when it is apparent that he is likely to lose on the merits'.[92]

Where fraud, deliberate concealment or mistake is relied upon as postponing the limitation period, it must be sufficiently alleged in the pleading to bring the case within the appropriate statutory provision.[93] In an action where the expiry of the limitation period bars the remedy but not the substantive right, a plea of deliberate concealment can be advanced in a reply to defence,[94] as may a plea that time only ran from the date of discovery of the fraud of the defendant.[95] In *Ford & Warren v Warring-Davies*,[96] it was held by Coulson J that it was permissible for the claimant to include a plea of deliberate concealment in his particulars of claim in a case which was prima facie statute barred. Where the title is barred as well as the remedy, it is suggested in *Halsbury's Laws* that the plea must be contained in the particulars of claim as it is part of the cause of action.[97] While many of the cases cited in support of these propositions are all of some antiquity, it is submitted that they are sound in principle and continue to have effect.

88 [2012] EWHC 3355 (QB) at para 41.
89 [2012] EWHC 3355 (QB) at para 58.
90 CPR 16PD, para 13.1.
91 [1987] 1 AC 189.
92 [1987] 1 AC 189 at 219.
93 See also the more detailed discussion of pleading issues where fraud or concealment are alleged that is contained in para 7.04.
94 *Gibbs v Guild* (1881) 8 QBD 296.
95 *Lynn v Bamber* [1930] 2 KB 72.
96 [2012] EWHC 3523 (QB).
97 *Halsbury's Laws of England* (5th edn, LexisNexis 2008), vol 68, paras 942–943.

The burden of proof for limitation issues

2.21 In cases where the expiry of the limitation period does not extinguish the claimant's rights, it is not, strictly speaking, necessary for the claimant to plead and establish the date of accrual of his cause of action. However, if a defendant raises a limitation defence, despite some of the older authorities being in conflict, the view which has been accepted by the English courts is that the claimant bears the burden of proving that his cause of action accrued within the limitation period and that his claim is not statute barred,[98] although it is worth noting that a different approach is evident in other jurisdictions.[99] In *London Congregational Union v Harriss & Harriss*,[100] this led the Court of Appeal to find that the claimant's action was statute barred in circumstances where neither party was able to establish on the balance of probabilities when the cause of action accrued. If a claimant relies on a ground for extending or postponing the limitation period, he will bear the burden of proving that he is entitled to that extended limitation period. Thus, in *Haward v Fawcetts*,[101] the claimant was held to bear the burden of proving that he did not have knowledge of the facts that constituted his 'starting date' within the meaning of s 14A until less than three years prior to the proceedings being brought. However, matters become somewhat complicated at this point, as in *Nash v Eli Lilly & Co*[102] it was held that if a defendant wishes to advance a different and earlier date of accrual of the claimant's cause of action (or date of knowledge), he will bear the burden of proof on this issue. By contrast, the Court of Appeal in *Serious Organised Crime Agency v Gale*[103] held that the defendants in proceedings brought under the Proceeds of Crime Act 2002 bore the burden of proof in raising a limitation defence, which required them to prove when the SOCA cause of action accrued. This should be treated as containing a special rule for actions under the Proceeds of Crime Act 2002 limited to a type of case where, as Carnwath LJ stated 'there is nothing unreasonable in denying him a limitation defence, if his own conduct has made it practically impossible for anyone to discover the true source'.[104]

Mode of trial of limitation issues

2.22 There are four procedural routes by which a limitation plea may be dealt with by the court. The first of these is if the claimant applies under CPR 3.4 to strike out the proceedings as disclosing no reasonable grounds or being an abuse of process. This will rarely be appropriate unless the case as pleaded is prima

98 McGee, *Limitation Periods* (6th edn, London: Sweet & Maxwell, 2010) at para 21.010, referring to *Ketteman v Hansel Properties Ltd* [1985] 1 All ER 352 (CA) and, more recently, *MAC Hotels Ltd v Rider Levett Bucknall UK Ltd* [2010] EWHC 767 (TCC).

99 See *Humphrey v Fairweather* [1993] 3 NZLR 91 and *Pullen v Gutteridge, Haskins & Davey Pty Ltd* [1993] 1 VR 27, noted by Mullany (1993) 109 LQR 215.

100 [1988] 1 All ER 15.

101 [2006] UKHL 9, [2006] 1 WLR 682.

102 [1993] 4 All ER 383 at 396, per Purchas LJ.

103 [2010] EWCA Civ 759, [2010] 1 WLR 2881, CA, affd without reference to this point: [2011] UKSC 49, [2011] 1 WLR 2760.

104 [2010] EWCA Civ 759, [2010] 1 WLR 2881 at para 25.

facie statute barred and no ground to extend time is capable of being raised. Even in those circumstances, the court is unlikely without more to find that the issuing of prima facie statute barred proceedings is of itself an abuse of process. The second option is for the defendant to deliver a defence raising a limitation point and then apply for summary judgment under CPR 24.[105] The wording of CPR 24(2)(a) requires a defendant to prove that a claimant has 'no real prospect of succeeding on the claim or issue', which is a difficult test to satisfy on a summary judgment application. The application is normally heard on the pleadings and witness statements and without oral evidence. The third option is for the court, in the exercise of its general powers of case management,[106] to direct the separate trial of the limitation issue and/or that this issue be tried first. Issues the court will have regard to at a case management conference for proceedings allocated to the multi-track in relation to the trial of a separate issue include whether it will be just and will save costs to order a split trial or the trial of one or more preliminary issues.[107] The separate trial of a limitation issue is most appropriate where the limitation issues have only a limited degree of overlap with the substantive contest on liability. This may be the case in particular where the issue is whether a claimant has a 'date of knowledge' point open to him or whether he is entitled to rely on s 33 of the LA 1980. While the trial of a preliminary issue on limitation will normally be heard based on the pleadings, witness statements and disclosure,[108] in *AB v Nugent Care Society – Practice Note*[109] the Court of Appeal held that in sexual abuse cases where a claimant seeks to rely on s 33 of the LA 1980 there are likely to be many actions in which a judge will decide that oral evidence will be required in order to reach a fair decision.[110] The fourth option is for the defendant to deliver his defence containing a limitation point and then rely on the LA 1980 at the trial of the action. This will be appropriate if the issues of liability and limitation are inter-linked or for other reasons it would not lead to a saving of costs or would otherwise create a risk of injustice if the limitation issues were tried first.

105 See *Page v Hewetts Solicitors* [2012] EWCA Civ 805, [2012] All ER (D) 78 (Jun), (unsuccessful application) and *Seaton v Seddon* [2012] EWHC 735 (Ch), [2013] 1 All ER 29 (successful in large part).

106 CPR 3.1(2)(i) and (j).

107 PD 29, para 5.3(7); see to similar effect PD 60, para 8.6(3) for Technology and Construction Court proceedings.

108 *KR v Bryn Alyn Community (Holdings) Ltd* [2003] EWCA Civ 85, [2003] QB 1441.

109 [2009] EWCA Civ 827, [2010] 1 WLR 516.

110 [2009] EWCA Civ 827, [2010] 1 WLR 516 at para 21, per Lord Clarke MR.

CHAPTER 3

The Foreign Limitation Periods Act 1984 and the Rome Regulations

THE CHOICE OF LAW RULES AT COMMON LAW

3.01 Historically, limitation provisions were treated, in general, as being purely procedural in nature and thus part of the *lex fori*. This had the result that a claimant who litigated a matter having foreign elements before the English courts was subject to the English limitation provisions;[1] even if the foreign limitation provision (if applicable) would have barred the claimant's remedy, only the English limitation provisions would apply.[2] However, a limitation period which extinguished the rights of a party was treated as a matter of substantive law[3] and if the foreign limitation enactment had, by the time proceedings were brought in England, barred both the right and the remedy of the claimant, the claimant's action would fail even if he was not statute barred under the domestic limitation rules.[4] A judgment obtained abroad, on a debt which would be statute barred if it had been pursued in proceedings brought in England, is enforceable within the State.[5] The common law rules have now been superseded by the legislation discussed below.

THE CHOICE OF LAW RULES UNDER THE FOREIGN LIMITATION PERIODS ACT 1984

3.02 The law in England was amended by the Foreign Law Limitation Periods Act 1984 ('FLPA 1984'), which provides that, in general, the law governing the substantive issues in a claim will also be applied in relation to the limitation of actions.[6] An exception exists where both foreign law and English law are to be

1 Franks, *Limitation of Actions* (London: Sweet & Maxwell, 1959) at 37.
2 *Huber v Steiner* (1835) 2 Bing NC 202.
3 See *McKain v RW Miller & Co (SA) Pty Ltd* (1992) 174 CLR 1 at para 18.
4 *Harris v Quine* (1869) LR 4 QB 653; *Phillips v Eyre* (1870) LR 6 QB 1 at 29.
5 *Re Low* [1894] 1 Ch 147.
6 FLPA 1984, s 1(1). See the judgment of Moses J in *City of Gotha v Sotheby's*, unreported, 9 September 1998 (QBD), *The Times*, 8 October 1998, quoted by Gray J in *Islamic Republic of Iran v The Barakat Galleries Ltd* [2007] EWHC 705 (QB) at 14 for assistance as to how the foreign rules on limitation are to be determined and also *Intercontainer Interfrigo SC (ICF) v Balkenende Oosthuizen BV* (Case C-133/08) [2010] QB 411.

taken into account in the proceedings,[7] in which case the claim is subject to both the foreign and the English limitation provisions.[8] The provisions of this Act are considered in this chapter, including the discretion granted to the courts to deny application to a foreign limitation period if its application would infringe public policy.[9] A broad definition is given to the phrase 'law on limitation' in s 4 of the FLPA 1984, but s 4(3) provides that the rules that provide the court with a discretion to refuse equitable relief on grounds of acquiescence or otherwise shall still apply, although the court shall still have regard to the provisions of the foreign limitation law relating to the action. Section 2(3) contains a further exception to the general rule and provides that any foreign limitation period which allows for the extension or interruption of the limitation period 'in respect of the absence of a party to the action ... from any specified jurisdiction or country' shall be disregarded. Section 1A of the FLPA 1984[10] applies where a cross-border mediation ends less than eight weeks prior to the relevant limitation period under the FLPA 1984 expiring. It provides that in those circumstances the limitation period will expire instead at the end of eight weeks after the mediation ends.[11] Section 3 of the FLPA 1984 provides that the determination by a foreign court of a point relating to limitation, for the purposes of the law relating to that determination, shall be deemed to have been determined on its merits.

THE LIMITATION ASPECTS OF THE CHOICE OF LAW RULES IN THE ROME REGULATIONS

3.03 The FLPA 1984 has now been amended to make clear that it shall not apply to actions governed by either Regulation (EC) No 593/2008[12] on the law applicable to contractual obligations (the 'Rome I Regulation') or Regulation (EC) No 864/2007[13] on the law applicable to non-contractual obligations (the 'Rome II Regulation').[14] The amended s 8 of the FLPA 1984 now provides that ss 1, 2 and 4 of the Act shall not apply to an action which is subject to the Rome I Regulation or the Rome II Regulation. While these actions govern choice of law in proceedings having a European dimension generally, it should be noted that many types of proceedings are excluded from their ambit. Neither Rome Regulation applies to

7 FLPA 1984, s 1(2). The 'double actionability' rule was abolished for actions in tort other than defamation by the Private Law (Miscellaneous Provisions) Act 1995, s 10; however, in *Gotha City v Sotheby's (No 2), Germany v Sotheby's*, unreported, 9 September 1998 (QBD), *The Times*, 8 October 1998, it was held that as foreign law had to be relied upon by the claimant to prove title to goods, s 1(2) applied to the action and the limitation rules of both countries had to be considered.

8 FLPA 1984, s 1(2).

9 FLPA 1984, s 2(2): see para 3.05.

10 As inserted by the Cross-Border Mediation (EU Directive) Regulations 2011 (SI 2011/1133), reg 29.

11 FLPA 1984, s 1A(3).

12 The Rome I Regulation applies to breaches of contracts concluded after 17 December 2009: see art 28.

13 The Rome II Regulation applies to torts which occur after 11 January, 2009: see art 32.

14 FLPA 1984, s 8, as amended by the Law Applicable to Non-Contractual Obligations (England and Wales and Northern Ireland) Regulations 2008 (SI 2008/2986) and the Law Applicable to Contractual Obligations (England and Wales and Northern Ireland) Regulations 2009 (SI 2009/3064).

revenue, customs or administrative matters and nor does the Rome II Regulation apply to actions concerning the liability of the State for acts and omissions in the exercise of State authority.[15] The Rome I Regulation lists a number of additional excluded actions in art 1(2), which include actions concerning contractual obligations relating to family relationships including wills and succession; certain company law matters; arbitration contracts; bills of exchange or other negotiable instruments; agency disputes; certain trust disputes; obligations arising out of dealings prior to the conclusion of a contract; and certain insurance contracts. The Rome II Regulation lists a number of excluded types of action in art 1(2), which include actions involving non-contractual obligations arising out of family or matrimonial relationships; bills of exchange or other negotiable instruments; certain company law matters; certain trust disputes; and privacy and defamation claims. Both Rome Regulations, where they apply, provide that the limitation rules of the governing law apply to the action and both Regulations provide a framework of rules to determine this issue.[16] Both Rome Regulations permit a foreign period of limitation to be denied application if its application would be 'manifestly incompatible with the public policy of the forum'.[17]

COMMENCEMENT OF PROCEEDINGS, EXERCISE OF DISCRETIONS AND EXCLUSION OF RULES OF PRIVATE INTERNATIONAL LAW, S 1 OF THE FLPA 1984

3.04 Section 1(3) of the FLPA 1984 provides that the law of England and Wales shall determine the date on which proceedings governed by foreign limitation law were commenced and that s 35 of the LA 1980 shall apply to any such action.[18] The effect of this provision is easily understood but it may give rise to unfairness if a short foreign limitation period which runs until notification of a claim will now run until proceedings are brought. Section 1(4) is a somewhat superfluous provision which provides that in exercising any discretion conferred by the law of the foreign country, the court shall exercise that discretion in the manner in which it is exercised in comparable cases in that country. Section 1(5) provides that 'law' as referred in s 1 shall not include 'rules of private international law'.[19]

FOREIGN LIMITATION RULES CONTRARY TO PUBLIC POLICY SHALL NOT APPLY

3.05 The FLPA 1984[20] and both of the Rome Regulations[21] provide that any foreign limitation period that conflicts with public policy shall not apply.[22]

15 Rome I Regulation, art 1(1); Rome II Regulation, art 1(1).
16 Rome I Regulation, art 12(1)(d); Rome II Regulation, art 15(h).
17 Rome I Regulation, art 21; Rome II Regulation, art 26.
18 See *Naylor v Trafalgar Tours Ltd*, unreported, 12 November 1993, Mance J (QBD).
19 See Carter (1985) 101 LQR 68 at 73–74.
20 FLPA 1984, s 2(1) and (2).
21 Rome I Regulation, art 21; Rome II Regulation, art 26.
22 It is not clear what limitation period, if any, applies if the foreign period is disapplied by s 2(1): see *Hellenic Steel Co v Svolomar Shipping Co Ltd, The Komninos S* [1991] 1 Lloyd's Rep 370 at 377 (CA), per Bingham LJ; and *Arab Monetary Fund v Hashim* [1993] 1 Lloyd's Rep 543 at 593, per Evans J.

Section 2(2) provides that a foreign limitation provision shall conflict with public policy to the extent that its application would cause undue hardship to a claimant.[23] The wording of the article in the Rome Regulations only applies if the provision is 'manifestly contrary' to public policy but it is submitted that the test will be the same in either case and the provisions are discussed together in this paragraph.[24] It is matter of impression as to whether a limitation provision conflicts with public policy; what is considered fair changes over time and one must look to the decided cases for guidance. In *Connelly v Rio Tinto Plc*,[25] it was held that a foreign limitation provision which allowed a claimant three years from his date of knowledge to bring proceedings, but did not provide the court with a discretion to disapply this limitation period, did not conflict with public policy. In *City of Gotha v Sotheby's*,[26] the claimant sought the delivery up of a painting which had been looted at the end of World War II but came into the possession of the defendant auction house in 1998. While Moses J found that the claimant's action was not statute barred under =German law, he held that if German law had barred the claim he would not have applied that law as it was contrary to public policy to allow a defendant who derived title from a thief, who had secretly retained the stolen property thereafter, to rely on the limitation period. In *Harley v Smith*,[27] the Court of Appeal held that the claimant had brought proceedings within the applicable 12-month Shari'ah law time limit. It proceeded to say that if the proceedings had not been brought in time, the foreign limitation period did not conflict with public policy and the fact that any failure by the claimant's solicitors to understand the applicable time limits did not cause 'undue hardship' of a type relevant to section 2(2).[28]

23 In *Durham v T&N Plc*, unreported, 1 May 1996 (CA) at 12, Sir Thomas Bingham MR stated that a limitation provision will not conflict with public policy merely because it is less generous than the comparable English provision.

24 For confirmation of the narrow interpretation to a public policy exception, see the comments of Scarman J in *In The Estate of Fuld (deceased) (No 3)* [1965] 3 All ER 776 at 781, 'an English court will refuse to apply a law which outrages its sense of justice or decency', and the foreign limitation judgments *Arab Monetary Fund v Hashim* [1993] 1 Lloyd's Rep 543 at 592 and *City of Gotha v Sotheby's*, unreported, 9 September 1998 (QBD), *The Times,* 8 October 1998.

25 Unreported, 4 December 1998 (QBD). A Russian limitation period of three years for an action based on fraud was held not to conflict with public policy in *Yugraneft v Abramovich* [2008] EWHC 2613 (Comm) at paras 318–324, per Christopher Clarke J.

26 Unreported, 9 September 1998 (QBD), *The Times*, 8 October 1998.

27 [2010] EWCA Civ 78; see also *Jones v Trollope Colls Cementation Overseas Ltd*, *The Times*, 26 January 1990 (CA), where reliance by a defendant on a 12-month limitation period for a personal injuries action was held to cause undue hardship due to the defendant's representations during that period that it would settle the claim, the claimant's serious injuries, and its conduct in later pleading limitation.

28 The Court of Appeal reversed the decision of the trial judge on the public policy issue: see [2009] EWHC 56 (QB), Foskett J.

CHAPTER 4

Enforcement of Judgments

INTRODUCTION

4.01 Section 24 of the Limitation Act 1980 ('LA 1980') contains what the Act describes as the 'time limit for actions to enforce judgments'. While this is technically an accurate description, as a narrow interpretation has been given to the phrase 'an action upon a judgment',[1] one must also look to the case law and various other provisions in discussing the time limits for enforcement of a judgment.[2] This is because, where one is not bringing an 'action upon a judgment' nor subject to the extendable time limit for execution on a judgment,[3] as was noted by Lord Brown in *A v Hoare*, '[j]udgments, although interest-bearing for only six years, are enforceable without limit of time'.[4] An action on a foreign judgment[5] is not treated as an action upon a judgment but is instead treated as an action in debt arising upon the implied contract to pay the amount of the foreign judgment.[6] With the foregoing caveats in mind, the elegant wording of the section merits quoting in full:

> '(1) An action shall not be brought upon any judgment after the expiration of six years from the date on which the judgment became enforceable.
>
> (2) No arrears of interest in respect of any judgment debt shall be recovered after the expiration of six years from the date on which the interest became due.'

1 See para 4.06 et seq. The LA 1980, s 38(1) provides a non-exhaustive definition of 'action', and states that it 'includes any proceeding in a court of law, including an ecclesiastical court'.
2 The phrase 'enforcement of a judgment' is intended to include all means of enforcing a judgment, whether by action upon the judgment; execution on the judgment; charging order; winding up or bankruptcy petitions or third party debt orders, all of which are discussed in this chapter.
3 RSC Sch 1 Ord 46, r 2(1): see para 4.10 et seq.
4 [2008] UKHL 6; [2008] 1 AC 844 at para 88.
5 Following the passing of Council Regulation (EC) No 44/2001 of 22 December 2000 on jurisdiction and the recognition and enforcement of judgments in civil and commercial matters, actions on foreign judgments are most commonly encountered where a claimant seeks to enforce a judgment of a United States federal or State court.
6 *Grant v Easton* (1883) 13 QBD 302 at 303; see also *Berliner Industriebank Aktiengesellschaft v Jost* [1971] 2 All ER 117 at 119, per Brandon J.

Acknowledgment and part payment

4.02 The limitation period for the enforcement of a judgment will start to run again from the date of an acknowledgment[7] or part payment[8] of the judgment debt. In *Brew v Brew*,[9] it was held that monies paid to the judgment creditor following the seizure and sale of goods by the sheriff qualified as a part payment for limitation purposes.

THE HISTORY AND DEVELOPMENT OF THE LIMITATION PERIOD FOR ENFORCING A JUDGMENT

4.03 Historically, at common law there was no limitation period for the enforcement of a judgment but there were restrictions on the procedures which might be adopted to enforce a judgment.[10] Further, a presumption existed that a personal judgment was satisfied within a year and a day; if a judgment creditor failed to issue execution within that period, he could execute the order only by applying to the court to revive the judgment by issuing a writ of *scire facias*.[11] At the hearing of the writ the judgment debtor could appear and challenge the enforceability of the judgment. The Common Law Procedure Act 1852[12] altered the procedure for granting leave to enforce a judgment by abolishing the year-and-a-day rule and providing that execution could issue within six years of judgment without a *scire facias*. This rule is now contained in RSC Sch 1 Ord 46, rr 2 and 6.

4.04 As an alternative to executing on a judgment, it was formerly acceptable to bring a new action upon the judgment.[13] The first limitation period for an action on a judgment was introduced by s 40 of the Real Property Limitation Act 1833,[14] which introduced a limitation period of 20 years.[15] In his speech in *Lowsley v Forbes*,[16] Lord Lloyd commented on the changes to the law brought about by the 1833 Act, stating that:

7 *National Westminster Bank Plc v Powney* [1990] 2 All ER 416; *Good Challenger Navegante SA v Metalexportimport SA* [2003] EWCA Civ 1668, [2004] 1 Lloyd's Rep 67; see Ch 6.
8 *Good Challenger Navegante SA v Metalexportimport SA* [2003] EWCA Civ 1668; [2004] 1 Lloyd's Rep 67; *Brew v Brew* [1899] IR 163; see further Ch 6.
9 [1899] IR 163.
10 *Lowsley v Forbes* [1999] 1 AC 329 at 335.
11 This procedure had been introduced by the Statute of Westminster II (13 Edw 1 c24) in 1285.
12 15 & 16 Vict c76 s 128.
13 *Lowsley v Forbes* [1999] 1 AC 329 at 335. In most cases this would now be an abuse of process: see paras 4.08–4.09.
14 3 & 4 Will 4 c27.
15 See *Watson v Birch* (1847) 15 Sim 523.
16 [1999] 1 AC 329 at 335–336.

> '[I]n the absence of an intervening writ of *scire facias* a judgment debt became statute-barred for all purposes after 20 years.[17] It was not only too late to bring a fresh action on the judgment; it was also too late to execute.'[18]

In *Lowsley v Forbes*,[19] the claimants had obtained judgment against the defendant in February 1981. The defendant then left the jurisdiction and the judgment debt remained unpaid. In 1992 the claimants discovered that the defendant owned property and had a bank account in England. In July 1992 the claimants sought leave to issue execution on the judgment together with interest.[20] The defendant applied to set aside the execution orders, arguing that the debt was statute barred as the six-year limitation period for bringing an action on a judgment contained in s 24(1) of the LA 1980 had expired. The House of Lords held that the six-year limitation period applied only to a fresh action on a judgment and that it did not apply to an application seeking leave to execute on an existing judgment. For this latter category of proceeding, RSC Ord 46 gives the court a discretion to grant leave to allow execution on a judgment more than six years after the date of the judgment.

4.05 More interesting than the actual result in *Lowsley v Forbes*,[21] which followed *WT Lamb & Sons v Rider*,[22] is the curious reasoning of Lord Lloyd. Despite holding that *WT Lamb & Sons v Rider*[23] was wrongly decided,[24] he felt compelled to follow its outcome on grounds that parliament, in enacting the LA 1980, had assumed that it correctly represented the law[25] (as had the Law Reform Committee[26]). The law was thus exposed as having been founded on a fallacy which was too venerable to be undone, leaving several methods of enforcing a judgment without any temporal limitation whatsoever. Despite the absence of judicial criticism of the state of the law in this area, and the fact that defaulting judgment debtors generally fail to elicit much sympathy, the imposition of statu-

17 The limitation period for an action on a judgment was reduced to 12 years by the Real Property Limitation Act 1874 (37 & 38 Vict c57), s 8 and to six years by the LA 1980, s 24(1).

18 [1999] 1 AC 329 at 336. His speech continued by noting that the introduction of the 20-year limitation period was a cause of concern for some who 'left [judgments] outstanding for very long periods, apparently as a form of investment': *ibid.*

19 [1999] 1 AC 329.

20 The Master granted the claimants leave ex parte to enforce the judgment by way of a charging order nisi on the defendant's property and a garnishee order nisi over his bank account, both in a sum representing the judgment debt plus 11 and a half years' interest.

21 [1999] 1 AC 329.

22 [1948] 2 KB 331.

23 [1948] 2 KB 331.

24 See [1999] 1 AC 329 at 335–336, where Lord Lloyd noted that two relevant decisions of the House of Lords from the 1840s had not been cited in *WT Lamb & Sons v Rider* [1948] 2 KB 331, and that both were contrary to the decision reached in that case.

25 As stated by Lord Lloyd at 342, '[i]f common error can make the law, so can parliamentary error'.

26 Report of the Law Reform Committee on Limitation of Actions (1977) (Cmnd. 6923).

tory or judicially imposed[27] time limits for all methods of enforcement of a judgment would surely improve the coherence of this area of the law.[28]

ACTIONS UPON A JUDGMENT

From what date does the limitation period run?

4.06 The limitation period to bring an action upon a judgment runs from the date the judgment is enforceable.[29] A judgment or order takes effect from the day when it is given or made, or such later date as the court may specify.[30] In the event of an appeal, the limitation period runs from the date of the appeal court's judgment.[31] In *Chohan v Times Newspapers Ltd*,[32] the Court of Appeal held that a costs order is only 'enforceable' within the meaning of the LA 1980 when it is taxed and ascertained. As was stated by Aldous LJ, '[t]he word "enforceable" must mean enforceable in a practical way according to law',[33] as to hold otherwise would cause time to run at a time when any action brought to enforce the costs order would be struck out as an abuse of process.

Entitlement to bring an action upon a judgment

4.07 The practice of bringing an action upon a judgment was common when the common law presumption was that a judgment was satisfied after a year and a day if no execution had been issued. The provision is now of limited importance as the bringing of an action upon a judgment is rare, on account of the improved means now open to judgment creditors to enforce a domestic judgment. However, the older authorities[34] have been followed in a number of recent English judgments,[35] most recently in *Kuwait Oil Tanker Company SAK v Al*

27 See, for example, the jurisdiction recognised by the courts of Ireland to dismiss significantly delayed but not statute barred claims where the passage of time has prejudiced the defendant and created a fundamental unfairness: *McBrearty v North Western Health Board* [2010] IESC 27 (SC).

28 See also *Chadee v Rampersad* (2007) 73 WIR 392, where the Court of Appeal of Trinidad and Tobago, unburdened by implied parliamentary imprimatur given to a wrong turning in the law, chose to follow the logic rather than the result of Lord Lloyd's speech in *Lowsley v Forbes*.

29 Section 24(1).

30 CPR 40.7(1).

31 *Roddy v Atkinson* (1949) 3 DLR 328. This may depend on whether a stay was placed on the judgment at first instance: see *Berliner Industriebank Aktiengesellschaft v Jost* [1971] 2 All ER 117 (HC) at 116 and [1971] 2 All ER 1513 at 1518–1519 (CA).

32 [2001] 1 WLR 1859. But see also the Canadian case law: *Syed v Randhawa* (1996) 1996 CanLII 2386 (BC SC) and *Lau v Lee* (2006) 21 CBR (5th) 161, 2006 BCSC 643 (CanLII).

33 [2001] 1 WLR 1859 at 1868.

34 See *Adams v Ready* (1861) 6 H&N 261 and *Grant v Easton* (1883) 13 QBD 302.

35 *ED & F Man (Sugar) Ltd v Haryanto, The Times*, 9 August 1996 (CA); *Bennett v Bank of Scotland* [2004] EWCA Civ 988.

Bader,[36] where Teare J noted that, '[t]he juridical basis of the second action has long been explained as being an implied contract to honour the judgment in the first action'.[37] He continued, stating that, '[t]he only possible defence to such a claim is that the second action is an abuse of the process of the court. That depends upon the reasons for it'.[38]

When will an action upon a judgment not be an abuse of process?

4.08 Although it is still technically open to a litigant to bring an action upon a judgment in all cases, a court will find it to be an abuse of process if some more appropriate way of proceeding was open to the claimant.[39] In *Bank of Scotland v Bennett*,[40] the claimant obtained a judgment against the defendant which it did not enforce during the ensuing period of six years. It brought a new action on the original judgment one day inside that six-year period, which the defendant subsequently argued was an abuse of process. He claimed that the delays were the bank's fault and that the new proceedings should be struck out, as their only purpose was to deprive him of a limitation defence. These arguments were not accepted, and it was held that it was not an abuse of process per se to commence a second action with the object of preserving one's rights to take bankruptcy proceedings, absent some other factors which, in the particular circumstances of the case, render that unjustifiable. Although the principle remains applicable, the result on the facts of the case is no longer good law in light of *Ridgeway Motors (Isleworth) Ltd v ALTS Ltd*,[41] where it was held that the bringing of a bankruptcy petition was not an action upon a judgment.

4.09 In *Kuwait Oil Tanker Company SAK v Al Bader*,[42] the claimants were awarded damages for fraud of US$137 million in 1998,[43] which they managed to enforce only in part. A few days before the expiry of six years from the date of the judgment in the first action, the claimants issued new proceedings wherein they sought judgment upon the earlier judgment for the outstanding judgment debt. They contended that the action was not an abuse of process, but was instead precautionary, as the Swiss courts would only allow enforcement of a judgment which remained enforceable within the originating country. It was held that the claimants were entitled to judgment against the first defendant upon the judgment in the first action, with a stay of execution which the claimants could apply to have lifted if it transpired that they needed to activate the second judgment.

36 [2008] EWHC 2432 (Comm), [2008] All ER (D) 165 (Oct); see Hoyle, 'Out with the old' (2009) 159 NLJ 344.
37 [2008] EWHC 2432 (Comm), [2008] All ER (D) 165 (Oct) at para 8.
38 [2008] EWHC 2432 (Comm), [2008] All ER (D) 165 (Oct) at para 9.
39 *Pritchett v English and Colonial Syndicate* [1899] 2 QB 428; *ED & F Man (Sugar) Ltd v Haryanto*, *The Times*, 9 August 1996 (CA).
40 [2004] EWCA Civ 988, [2004] All ER (D) 417 (Jul).
41 [2005] EWCA Civ 92, [2005] 1 WLR 2871.
42 [2008] EWHC 2432 (Comm), [2008] All ER (D) 165 (Oct).
43 [1998] All ER (D) 785; affirmed [2000] 2 All ER (Comm) 271 (CA).

EXECUTION OF JUDGMENTS

4.10 The definition given for the phrase 'writ of execution' in RSC Sch 1 Ord 46, r 1 states that it 'includes a writ of fieri facias, a writ of possession,[44] a writ of delivery, a writ of sequestration and any further writ in aid of any of the aforementioned writs'. The common feature connecting these writs was stated by Millett LJ as being that each is 'issued by the court on the application of the [claimant] without any hearing by a judicial officer of any kind'.[45] While not subject to the six-year limitation period contained in s 24(1) of the LA 1980,[46] RSC Sch 1 Ord 46, r 2(1) provides that a writ of execution to enforce a judgment or order may not issue without the permission of the court in several circumstances, one of which is if six years or more have elapsed since the date of the judgment or order.

4.11 As discussed above, in *WT Lamb & Sons v Rider*,[47] The Court of Appeal held that no limitation period applies to execution on a judgment. The result of this case, though not the reasoning, was followed by the House of Lords in *Lowsley v Forbes*,[48] where the claimant was allowed to execute on a judgment after the limitation period applicable to an action upon a judgment had expired. The issue which has come before the courts on a number of occasions in relation to time limits for execution on a judgment concerns the circumstances in which the court will exercise its discretion to grant 'permission' to execute more than six years after the date of the judgment or order.[49]

4.12 The test to be applied in an application for leave to issue execution more than six years after the date of the judgment or order was expressed by Peter Gibson LJ in *Patel v Singh*[50] in the following terms:

> '[T]he court must start from the position that the lapse of six years may, and will ordinarily, in itself justify refusing the judgment creditor permission to issue the writ of execution, unless the judgment creditor can justify the granting of permission by showing that the circumstances of his or her case take it out of the ordinary.'[51]

Matters which may constitute exceptional reasons include delays in the court system that were not the fault of the party concerned,[52] although difficulties in

44 A writ of possession was formerly not included within the definition of a 'writ of execution': see *Lougher v Donovan* [1948] 2 All ER 11 and the comments of Lord Lloyd in *Lowsley v Forbes* [1999] 1 AC 329 at 339.
45 *Ezekiel v Orapko* [1997] 1 WLR 340 at 343–344.
46 *Lowsley v Forbes* [1999] 1 AC 329.
47 [1948] 2 KB 331, but cf *Loughner v Donovan* [1948] 2 All ER 11.
48 [1999] 1 AC 329.
49 RSC Ord 46, r 2(1).
50 [2002] EWCA Civ 1938, [2002] All ER (D) 227 (Dec), cited with approval in *Good Challenger Navegante SA v Metalexportimport SA* [2003] EWCA Civ 1668, [2004] 1 Lloyd's Rep 67 (CA).
51 [2002] EWCA Civ 1938, [2002] All ER (D) 227 (Dec) at para 21.
52 *National Westminster Bank Plc v Powney* [1991] Ch 339; see also *Society of Lloyd's v Longtin* [2005] EWHC 2491 (Comm).

locating a defendant have been found not to provide sufficient reason for the court to grant leave in a number of judgments.[53]

Shorter time limit to enforce judgment for possession of registered land

4.13 A shorter time limit than those discussed above governs the enforcement of a judgment for possession of registered land given in proceedings brought against a person entitled to make an application under Sch 6, para 1 (ie if they had been in adverse possession of the registered estate for ten years). In such a case, s 98(2) and (4) of the Land Registration Act 2002 ('LRA 2002') provides that a judgment for possession of the registered land will cease to be enforceable two years after the date of the judgment. This provision counter-balances the fact that a squatter on registered land is not entitled to be registered as owner of the land by adverse possession unless he satisfies one of the three narrowly drafted conditions set out in Sch 6, para 5 of the LRA 2002.[54] At the end of the period of two years following the obtaining of a judgment for possession, the squatter may lodge a second application for registration as owner of the registered estate by adverse possession[55] or, if sued for possession, will have a full defence[56] to the action and can counterclaim for an order that he be registered as owner of the registered estate.[57]

OTHER METHODS OF ENFORCEMENT: CHARGING ORDERS, WINDING UP AND BANKRUPTCY PETITIONS, AND ATTACHMENT OF DEBTS

Limitation treatment of charging orders

4.14 One enforcement option open to a judgment creditor is to obtain an order under the Charging Orders Act 1979 imposing a charge on the judgment debtor's property to secure the payment of any money due under a judgment or order. Millett LJ in *Ezekiel v Orapko*[58] held that charging orders fall outside s 24(1) of the LA 1980, as they do not come within the narrow definition of an 'action upon a judgment'. Accordingly, charging orders would not appear to be subject to any time limits. In *Yorkshire Bank Finance Ltd v Mulhall*,[59] it was held that no limitation period applies to the enforcement of a charging order after it

53 *Patel v Singh* [2002] EWCA Civ 1938, [2002] All ER (D) 227 (Dec); *Duer v Frazer* [2001] 1 WLR 919.
54 See paras 15.49–15.50.
55 LRA 2002, Sch 6, para 6.
56 LRA 2002, s 98(3).
57 LRA 2002, s 98(5).
58 [1997] 1 WLR 340; in *Barnett v Bradley* (1890) 26 LR Ir 209 it was held that registering a judgment mortgage (under the old procedure) was not a step in execution of a judgment.
59 [2008] EWCA Civ 1156, [2009] 2 All ER (Comm) 164; see also *Gotham v Doodes* [2006] EWCA Civ 1080, [2007] 1 WLR 86.

is obtained. The defendant here unsuccessfully sought to argue that the court should hold to the contrary by reference to the decision of the Court of Appeal in *Ashe v National Westminster Bank Plc*.[60] In *Ashe*, a mortgagor who had been in possession of a mortgaged property for in excess of 12 years without making any payments was held to have extinguished the mortgagee's title. This authority was distinguished in *Yorkshire Bank Finance Ltd v Mulhall* on grounds that a charging order merely gives security for a judgment debt, and as no limitation period applies to the enforcement of the judgment by this means (per *Ezekiel v Orapko*[61]), it is not extinguished at the expiry of 12 years in like manner as an ordinary mortgage.

Winding up petitions and bankruptcy petitions

4.15 The question of whether a winding up petition that relies on a judgment debt[62] is an action upon a judgment came before the Court of Appeal in *Ridgeway Motors (Isleworth) Ltd v ALTS Ltd*.[63] It held that the petition was neither an action upon a judgment nor execution on that judgment, and that no limitation period applies when a judgment debt is relied upon in a petition. Mummery LJ held that the correct definition of 'action' in this context means a 'fresh action' brought upon a judgment in order to obtain a second judgment, which can be executed. In discussing the juridical nature of a winding up petition, Mummery LJ said, '[i]t is sui generis, being in the nature of a wider legal proceeding available for the collective enforcement of the admitted or proved debts of the company for the benefit of the general body of creditors on a pari passu basis'.[64] While it had been held in *Re a debtor (No 50A/SD/95)*[65] that a bankruptcy petition relying on a judgment debt was an action upon that judgment, this decision is no longer good law in light of *Ridgeway Motors (Isleworth) Ltd*, albeit that it does not appear to have been formally overruled in any subsequent case.

Attachment of debts: third party debt orders

4.16 In *Westacre v Yugoimport*,[66] it was held that no limitation period applies to an application to attach a debt in satisfaction of monies due on a judgment.[67] Historically, applications of this nature were treated differently to writs of execution,[68] which issue out of the court office as a matter of course without the

60 [2008] EWCA Civ 55, [2008] 1 WLR 710.

61 [1997] 1 WLR 340.

62 A petitioning creditor relying on a seven-year-old contract debt and not a judgment debt would have no standing to petition to wind up a company as his debt would be statute barred: [2005] EWCA Civ 92, [2005] 1 WLR 2871 at para 35.

63 [2005] EWCA Civ 92, [2005] 1 WLR 2871. However, see to the contrary *Re Tynte, Ex p Tynte* (1880) 15 Ch D 125, which was not cited in *Ridgeway Motors*.

64 [2005] EWCA Civ 92, [2005] 1 WLR 2871, CA at para 29.

65 [1997] 2 All ER 789.

66 [2008] EWHC 801 (Comm), [2009] 1 All ER (Comm) 780.

67 The procedure governing applications for third party debt orders (formerly referred to as garnishee orders) is contained in CPR 72.

68 *Fellows v Thornton* (1884) 14 QBD 335.

need for a court application.[69] For this reason it was held that such an application is neither an action on a judgment (subject to s 24(1)) nor execution on a judgment (in which case leave to issue execution is required once six years have elapsed).[70]

INTEREST ON JUDGMENTS

4.17 Section 24(2) of the LA 1980 provides that:

> 'No arrears of interest in respect of any judgment debt shall be recovered after the expiration of six years from the date on which the interest became due.'

In *Lowsley v Forbes*,[71] it was held by the House of Lords that a judgment creditor who sought a garnishee order and a charging order in excess of 11 years after obtaining judgment against the defendant was limited to claiming the judgment sum together with interest for the period of six years prior to the date of the garnishee and charging orders. The result of this decision is that in relation to interest on a judgment, though not the judgment itself, the same provisions apply in case of execution of the judgment and actions on the judgment. The fact that interest is recoverable on a statute barred judgment is an exception to the rule that once the principal sum has become statute barred, the creditor also loses the right to sue for non-statute barred interest.[72]

Mortgagee or chargee may recover interest for in excess of six years

4.18 In any action by a mortgagor to redeem his mortgage, and in cases where a mortgagee sells the mortgaged property and has in his hands a surplus, he is entitled to insist on payment of the full amount of the interest due without reference to limitations of time.[73] The basis of this rule is that, whether the mortgagor is seeking to redeem or the mortgagee is accounting to the mortgagor for the surplus, the mortgagee is not bringing an action to recover interest; instead, he already has the mortgaged property or the proceeds of the security in his hands.

69 See *Ezekiel v Orakpo* [1997] 1 WLR 340 at 343–344.

70 See *Society of Lloyd's v Longtin* [2005] EWHC 2491 (Comm) at para 9; *Westacre v Yugoimport* [2008] EWHC 801 (Comm), [2009] 1 All ER (Comm) 780 at paras 22–23, where Toulson J stated that he would have required 'compelling evidence of prejudice' to refuse to make a garnishee order absolute despite the fact that the judgment giving rise to the application was over six years old.

71 [1999] 1 AC 329.

72 See *Elder v Northcott* [1930] 2 Ch 422 and McGee, *Limitation Periods* (6th edn, London: Sweet & Maxwell, 2010) at para 17.007.

73 See *Dingle v Coppen* [1899] 1 Ch 726; *Edmunds v Waugh* (1866) LR 1 Eq 418; *In re Marshfield, Marshfield v Hutchings* (1887) 34 Ch D 721; and *Holmes v Cowcher* [1970] 1 WLR 834.

In *Ezekiel v Orapko*,[74] the Court of Appeal stated that the case law on redemption actions also applies to cases where a judgment creditor obtains an order under the Charging Orders Act 1979. In such a case, all interest which accrues between the date of the charging order and the date of the sale of the property must be paid out of any monies realised in the sale of the property.

74 [1997] 1 WLR 340. Although the principle is as stated in the text, Millett LJ in fact held that the dispute concerning interest was governed by s 20(5) of the LA 1980 but that this was not engaged as the steps taken by the claimant to enforce his charging order did not constitute an 'action to recover arrears of interest' within the meaning of subs (5).

PART II

General Extensions to the Limitation Period

CHAPTER 5

Disability: Minors and Persons Lacking Capacity to Conduct Legal Proceedings

INTRODUCTION

5.01 The Limitation Act 1980 ('LA 1980') provides that a person who is 'under a disability' when a right of action accrues to him shall have an extended limitation period within which to institute suit.[1] Section 38 of the LA 1980 lists only two classes of disability: infants[2] and persons lacking capacity to conduct legal proceedings.[3] The effect of the statutory provision is that for a person who is under a disability when a right of action accrues to him, or when he first has knowledge of the facts that constitute his date of knowledge where this is relevant, time will only start to run when he ceases to be under a disability or dies, subject to exceptions discussed below.

Development of the scope of the disability provision

5.02 The categories of disability originally recognised by s 7 of the Limitation Act 1623[4] included the fact that a claimant was *feme covert* (ie a married woman), a convict or beyond the seas, although over time these categories of disability were deleted from the statutory definition. In *Chagos Islanders v Attorney General*,[5] an attempt was made to broaden the concept of disability as defined in the LA 1980 to include persons who were outside the jurisdiction of the High Court and impoverished, illiterate and ignorant as a result of the defendant's acts.

1 LA 1980, ss 28 and 29. A litigation friend must be appointed to bring or defend proceedings on behalf of the person under a disability: see CPR Pt 21.

2 See para 5.07.

3 See para 5.08 et seq.

4 21 Jac 1, c16; see Lightwood, *The Time Limits for Actions* (London: Butterworth & Co, 1905) at 250–251.

5 [2003] EWHC 2222 (QB), [2003] All ER (D) 166 (Oct) at paras 612–614; affirmed [2004] EWCA Civ 557, [2004] All ER (D) 85 (Aug). The Chagos Archipelago lies in the middle of the Indian Ocean and includes the island of Diego Garcia and the Salomon Islands. Its population was evacuated to Mauritius by the United Kingdom and United States governments in 1967–1973, to safeguard the interests of the United States naval base on Diego Garcia. The proceedings in which these judgments were delivered were brought in 2002. See further Allen, 'Return to Paradise from Realpolitik' (2006) 156 NLJ 1122 and Scanlan, 'The Chagos Islanders' Case – A Question of Limitation' (2007) CLQ 252.

These arguments were rejected by Ouseley J, who held that the definition of 'disability' in the LA 1980 was exhaustive. Although the Court of Appeal dismissed the claimants' appeal on the merits, Sedley LJ in an obiter dictum commented that there was scope for arguing that the definition was not exhaustive.[6]

LIMITATION PERIODS IN CASES OF DISABILITY

Applicable limitation period in cases of disability

5.03 Section 28(1) of the LA 1980 provides that, if a person was under a disability on the date when the right of action accrued, an action may be brought 'at any time before the expiration of six years from the date when the person ceased to be under a disability or died (whichever first occurred), notwithstanding that the limitation period has expired'. A claimant will gain an extension of time for a period of less than six years from the date when he ceases to be under a disability, or dies, for the following classes of actions:

(i) Libel and slander actions

Section 28(4A)(a) provides that an action for libel or slander must be brought within one year from the date when the claimant ceased to be under a disability.

(ii) Actions for slander of title, slander of goods or other malicious falsehood

Section 28(4A)(b) provides that these types of actions must be brought within one year from the date when the claimant ceased to be under a disability or died.

(iii) Contribution actions

Section 28(5) provides that an action claiming contribution under the Civil Liability (Contribution) Act 1978 must be brought within two years from the date when the claimant ceased to be under a disability or died.

(iv) Personal injuries actions

Section 28(6) provides that an action claiming damages for personal injuries arising out of negligence, nuisance or breach of duty must be brought within three years of the date when the person ceased to be under a disability or died.[7]

6 [2004] EWCA Civ 557, [2004] All ER (D) 85 (Aug) at para 47.
7 The reference in this subsection to actions where the injured party has died relates to actions brought on behalf of the estate of a deceased person under the Law Reform (Miscellaneous Provisions) Act 1934. Issues of disability may arise here if a party entitled to bring the proceedings was under a disability when the right of action accrued to him.

(v) Actions under the Fatal Accidents Act 1976 ('FAA 1976')

Section 28(6) also provides that an action under the FAA 1976 must be brought within three years from the date when the person to whom a right of action accrued under the FAA 1976 ceased to be under a disability or died.

(vi) Actions under Pt 1 of the Consumer Protection Act 1987 ('CPA 1987')

Section 28(7) provides that any extension to the limitation period for an action in respect of a defective product arising by virtue of the claimant being under a disability must be brought within three years from when the claimant ceased to be under a disability or died, but that any such extension shall not override the statutory long-stop of ten years contained in s 11A(3) of the LA 1980.

(vii) Action by successive owner in respect of latent damage to property

Section 3 of the Latent Damage Act 1986 ('LDA 1986') creates a new cause of action in favour of a successive owner in respect of latent damage to property. Section 3(3) of the LDA 1986 disapplies s 28 of the LA 1980 in relation to this cause of action. Instead, in such a case if the claimant is entitled to rely upon the limitation period of three years contained in s 14A(4)(b), which runs from the date when he had knowledge of the matters set out in s 14A(6)–(10), but was under a disability on that date, s 28A applies to the action. This provides that in such a case the action may be brought at any time before the expiration of three years from the date when he ceased to be under a disability or died (whichever occurs first) notwithstanding that the three-year period has expired, but subject to the overriding time limit of 15 years contained in s 14B of the LA 1980. Oddly, the section would appear to lead to a situation where a person under a disability having a cause of action under s 3 of the LDA 1986 is in a better position if they are not able to rely on s 14A(4)(b) as in such a case they would be entitled to bring an action for six years after their disability came to an end. The impenetrable wording used in s 28A has been the subject of academic criticism which asks whether the wording reflects what may have been intended by parliament.[8] While the author can see the logic in tailoring a section to deal solely with actions brought under s 3 of the LDA 1986, the language used is some distance from making it a model of clarity.

Cases where no extension of time granted to person under a disability

5.04 There are two exceptions to the rules providing for an extension to the limitation period for persons who are under a disability:

8 McGee, *Limitation Periods* (6th edn, London: Sweet & Maxwell, 2010) at para 19.030.

(i) section 28(2) provides that no extension of time on grounds of disability shall arise where the right of action first accrued to some person who is not under a disability, through whom the person under a disability claims;[9] and

(ii) section 28(3) provides that where a right of action accrues to a person who is under a disability which, on his death, accrues to another person under a disability, no further extension of time shall be allowed by reason of the disability of the second person.

Long-stop for actions to recover land or money charged on land

5.05 Section 28(4) provides that no action to recover unregistered land[10] or money charged on unregistered land shall be brought after the expiration of 30 years from the date on which the right of action accrued to that person, or to some person through whom he claims.[11] Although its effect has been lessened by the passing of the Land Registration Act 2002, this section performs a useful function in allowing for the quieting of titles. It delimits the maximum period of time during which a squatter's title may be questioned. While it could lead to a person of unsound mind having his rights extinguished without ever being in a position where he could assert those rights, it is submitted that it is a necessary provision. The absence of such a section could cause significant conveyancing difficulties, as in some cases a squatter (or the purchaser of land from a squatter) may not know the identity of the person he has dispossessed and would otherwise never have the comfort of knowing that the previous owner's title had been extinguished.

Overriding time limit for non-personal injuries negligence actions

5.06 Section 14B of the LA 1980 is described in the Act as containing an 'overriding time limit for negligence actions not involving personal injuries'. It provides that such an action shall not be brought after the expiration of 15 years from the date of the negligent act or omission (or last of a series of acts or omissions) to which the damage alleged is attributable. Although s 14B(1) is not referred to in s 28, as the latter section specifically excludes only actions governed by s 11 from its ambit it would appear to limit the maximum length of any extension to the limitation period on grounds of disability in negligence cases where the damages sought do not consist of or include damages for personal injuries.

9 The LA 1980, s 38(5) explains the concept of claiming through another person; see also *Eddis v Chichester Constable* [1969] 2 All ER 912.

10 A somewhat extended definition is given to the phrase 'right of action to recover land' by the LA 1980, s 38(7).

11 See the LA 1980, s 38(5) and *Eddis v Chichester Constable* [1969] 2 All ER 912.

MINORS

Minority as a category of disability

5.07 The most widely encountered application of the rules on disability arises in the case of actions brought on behalf of minors claiming damages for personal injuries. Section 38(2) of the LA 1980 provides that a person shall be treated as under a disability while he is an 'infant'. This language is now outdated and the words 'minor', 'minority' and 'majority' are preferred in this chapter. Section 1 of the Family Law Reform Act 1969 reduced the age of majority to 18 years and accordingly the limitation period in all cases where a minor is the claimant will only start to run on their eighteenth birthday. The extension of time afforded to minors to institute suit has not led to much litigation, presumably as it is relatively easily understood and applied. The Limitation Act 1939 contained a more nuanced statutory provision, not retained in the LA 1980, which limited the category of infants under a disability to those who were not in the custody of a parent. This clause was incorporated into the Irish Statute of Limitations 1957 until it was found to be unconstitutional by the Irish Supreme Court in *O'Brien v Keogh*[12] on account of its failure to vindicate the rights of infants whose parents failed to institute proceedings in time.

PERSONS LACKING CAPACITY TO CONDUCT LEGAL PROCEEDINGS

Capacity to conduct legal proceedings and unsoundness of mind

5.08 The second category of person treated as being 'under a disability' for limitation purposes, as defined by s 38(2) of the LA 1980, are persons who lack 'capacity (within the meaning of the Mental Capacity Act 2005) to conduct legal proceedings'. Although the wording now contained in s 38(2) is of recent origin[13] and differs from that used previously, the older case law is still relevant as the test had been applied in a flexible and conscientious manner in many of the decided cases.[14] For many years the leading case was *Kirby v Leather*,[15] in which the claimant had suffered serious head injuries in a road traffic accident but failed to institute proceedings until over four years later. In response to a limitation

12 [1972] IR 144.

13 Section 38(2) formerly referred to persons 'of unsound mind' and prior to the most recent amendment stated that 'a person is of unsound mind if he is a person who, by reason of mental disorder [as defined in the Mental Health Act 1983], is incapable of managing and administering his property and affairs'.

14 The current wording in s 38(2) applies to all causes of action which occurred on or after 1 October 2007. In *Maga v Trustees of the Birmingham Archdiocese* [2010] 1 WLR 1441 at para 16, it was held (apparently based on a concession by counsel) that the law in force when the proceedings were commenced governs the test on disability, whereas in *Seaton v Seddon* [2012] EWHC 735 (Ch), it was held by Roth J that the applicable test is that contained in the law in force when the cause of action accrued.

15 [1965] 2 QB 367.

defence, it was argued that he was of unsound mind from the date of the accident onwards. Lord Denning MR held that the phrase should be interpreted by reference to its context, namely whether his ability to institute proceedings was impaired. He said that a person was of unsound mind if he was 'by reason of mental illness incapable of managing his affairs in relation to the accident as a reasonable man would do';[16] having summarised the evidence he proceeded to find the claimant of unsound mind.[17] By contrast, in *Morley v Hunt & Co (a firm)*,[18] the evidence disclosed that the claimant had been able to instruct solicitors and to consider the question of professional negligence. Despite the fact that he displayed a lack of wisdom and some gullibility, he was found not to have demonstrated an inability to manage his own affairs and thus he was held not to be under a disability.

5.09 More recently, in *Maga v Trustees of the Birmingham Archdiocese*,[19] the Court of Appeal gave detailed consideration to whether the claimant, a man who suffered minor brain damage at birth and had a low IQ and epilepsy, was a person of unsound mind for limitation purposes. Lord Neuberger MR noted that the trial judge had applied a test of 'whether the claimant was able to conduct the instant proceedings, in the sense of being able to deal rationally with the problems that ... will arise in the course of it', but commented that he had some doubt as to whether this was 'precisely the right formulation'.[20] Notwithstanding these judicial misgivings, the Court of Appeal unanimously dismissed the appeal and upheld the trial judge's finding that the claimant was under a disability at the relevant time. It noted that the trial judge had acknowledged that the question of whether the claimant had capacity to conduct the proceedings was finely balanced and made clear that a fact-specific assessment of mental capacity is a matter best entrusted to a trial judge who had the benefit of hearing *viva voce* evidence.

The Mental Capacity Act 2005 and the new test for lack of capacity

5.10 The Mental Capacity Act 2005 ('MCA 2005') sets out a detailed framework for assessing whether an individual lacks mental capacity. The main sections relevant to the question of whether a claimant is under a disability for limitation purposes on account of a lack of capacity to conduct legal proceedings are as follows:

> '2(1) [A] person lacks capacity in relation to a matter if at the material time he is unable to make a decision for himself in relation to the matter because of an impairment of, or a disturbance in the functioning of, the mind or brain.

16 [1965] 2 QB 367 at 383.

17 [1965] 2 QB 367 at 384.

18 [2005] All ER (D) 41 (Jan). Other relevant decisions that predate the Mental Capacity Act 2005 are *Masterman-Lister v Brutton (Nos 1 & 2)* [2003] 1 WLR 1511; *Sheffield City Council v E* [2005] 2 WLR 953 and *Marsh v Sofaer* [2006] EWHC 1217 (Ch).

19 [2010] EWCA Civ 256, [2010] 1 WLR 1441 (CA).

20 [2010] 1 WLR 1441 at para 18. He also added that he was 'far from convinced that the judge adopted the wrong formulation': *ibid*.

(2) It does not matter whether the impairment or disturbance is permanent or temporary.

…

3(1) For the purposes of section 2, a person is unable to make a decision for himself if he is unable:

(a) to understand the information relevant to the decision,

(b) to retain that information,

(c) to use or weigh that information as part of the process of making the decision, or

(d) to communicate his decision (whether by talking, using sign language or any other means).

(2) A person is not to be regarded as unable to understand the information relevant to a decision if he is able to understand an explanation of it given to him in a way that is appropriate to his circumstances (using simple language, visual aids or any other means).

(3) The fact that a person is able to retain the information relevant to a decision for a short period only does not prevent him from being regarded as able to make the decision.

(4) The information relevant to a decision includes information about the reasonably foreseeable consequences of:

(a) deciding one way or another, or

(b) failing to make the decision.'

Given the detailed and fact-specific nature of the inquiry mandated by the MCA 2005, appropriate expert evidence from a psychiatrist or similar should be obtained if a claimant wishes to rely on a plea of disability.

5.11 Although the MCA 2005 has already generated a significant volume of case law,[21] the judgment of Roth J in *Seaton v Seddon*[22] would appear to be the only judgment to date where the Act was considered in a limitation context. In analysing the new approach to assessing incapacity under the MCA 2005, Roth J stated that 'the matters to be considered before finding that a person lacks what is now called mental capacity have been broadened, such that a more detailed and sensitive evaluation is required before the statutory presumption of capacity is displaced'.[23] While he accepted that the claimant suffered from a schizophrenic illness, he was not satisfied that the claimant had established that he remained

21 See Ashton, *Mental Capacity Law and Practice* (2nd edn, Bristol: Jordan Publishing Ltd, 2012) at 97–107 and *Re LT (vulnerable adult) (decision making: capacity)* [2010] EWHC 1910 (Fam); *LBL v RYJ* [2010] EWHC 2665 (COP); *In re A (capacity: refusal of contraception)* [2011] Fam 61; and *D Borough Council v AB* [2011] 3 All ER 435.

22 [2012] EWHC 735 (Ch).

23 [2012] EWHC 735 (Ch) at para 108. Roth J also commented in the same paragraph that, 'Because of the implications of a finding of mental incapacity for an individual's freedom of action, the thrust of the 2005 Act is to safeguard against a ready finding of lack of capacity.'

under a disability for the entire period since his right of action had accrued. He noted in particular that other proceedings had been brought in the name of the claimant in 2002 which had been settled without his solicitors considering it necessary to apply to court for approval of the settlement. He held that this weighed strongly against a finding that he was under a disability when the earlier proceedings were compromised.

Disability arising after the right of action accrues

5.12 Section 28(1) of the LA 1980 provides that to gain the benefit of an extension to the limitation period on grounds of disability, the person must have been under the disability 'on the date when any right of action accrued'. It is a principle of long standing that if time has begun to run, the running of time will not be suspended if the claimant later falls under a disability,[24] and this same rule applies in the case of extensions of time on grounds of disability under s 28 of the LA 1980. However, in *Kirby v Leather*,[25] it was stated by Lord Denning MR that '"[o]n the date" means, I think, at any time before the end of the day, because the law takes no account of fractions of a day'.[26]

Disability, want of prosecution and abuse of process

5.13 A limitation period of in excess of 20 years may apply to a right of action that accrues to a minor when he is very young, and no limitation period applies to a person under a permanent disability. This can give rise to problems for defendants if proceedings are brought but not progressed, or are struck out by the court but then re-issued. However, in *Tolley v Morris*,[27] the House of Lords refused to strike out proceedings for want of prosecution which had been brought on behalf of a person under a disability, noting that this would serve no purpose as new non-statute barred proceedings could be issued if the original action was struck out. This decision was followed in subsequent cases[28] but is likely to be of limited significance following the adoption of more active case management procedures under the CPR.[29] This approach should be contrasted with that adopted in *Hogg v Hamilton and Northumberland Health Authority*,[30] where the claimant was under a permanent disability and a writ had been issued in 1979 which had been struck out in January 1982 for want of prosecution and failure to serve a statement of claim. New proceedings were issued in November 1988, which the Court of Appeal struck out as an abuse of process. It is to be doubted

24 *Prideaux v Webber* (1661) 1 Lev 31; *Purnell v Roche* [1927] 2 Ch 142.

25 [1965] 2 QB 367.

26 [1965] 2 QB 367 at 383.

27 [1979] 1 WLR 592.

28 See, for example, *Headford v Bristol and District Health Authority* (1994) 24 BMLR 20 (CA).

29 For a rare recent example, see *Stacey v Joint Mission Hospital Equipment Board Ltd* [2001] All ER (D) 207 (Oct).

30 [1993] 4 Med LR 369, [1992] PIQR P387 (CA).

whether the approach adopted in *Tolley v Morris*[31] is fully consistent with art 6 of the European Convention on Human Rights and its requirement that a defendant is entitled to a determination of his civil obligations within a reasonable time. However, given the content of the CPR, the mischief which was excused by the House of Lords in *Tolley* is now less likely to arise in practice.

Disability and negative declarations

5.14 As a claimant who is under a permanent disability will never find any right of action open to him to be statute barred, the question arises as to what a defendant or insurance company can do to bring finality to their exposure to pay compensation to him. In *Eidha v Toropdar*,[32] the claimant brought proceedings in which he sought a negative declaration concerning his liability to pay damages in respect of injuries suffered by the then ten-year-old defendant in a road traffic accident which occurred on 22 June 2002. The proceedings were brought on 19 December 2006, the defendant's solicitors having sent an initial letter of claim on 27 January 2003 and thereafter having threatened to issue proceedings on several occasions but never so doing. The defendant objected and argued that the court should not entertain an application for a negative declaration. McCombe J held that the procedure was appropriate in this case by reason of delay on the injured party's side including threats of litigation which never materialised, coupled with the risk that the trial of the action would become less and less satisfactory as time went on and as witnesses' recollections faded. The application for a negative declaration was heard by Christopher Clarke J, who delivered judgment *sub nom Toropdar v D (a minor by his litigation friend)*,[33] and refused the negative declaration sought. However, he held that if it had been appropriate on the facts, he would have made the declaration,[34] noting that the defendant had obtained the services of a competent legal team (funded by legal aid) and that there was no request for time to prepare for trial or obtain further evidence. He agreed with the reasoning of McCombe J and commented that such applications were likely to be rare. Although any inequality of arms between the parties caused by an absence of legal funding for the defendant might in other cases weigh against the court entertaining an application for a negative declaration, he added that, 'The matter should not be allowed to fester forever in the hope simply that something will turn up'.[35] Although McGee comments that this decision undermines the express statutory limitation period, it is submitted that it provides a valuable procedural method to force intransigent persons who are under a disability (and their carers or guardians, as appropriate) to either prosecute or abandon a claim that is open

31 [1979] 1 WLR 592.

32 [2008] EWHC 1219 (QB), [2008] All ER (D) 07 (Jun).

33 [2009] EWHC 567 (QB), [2010] Lloyd's Rep IR 358; see also Patten, 'When is a limitation period not a limitation period?' (2010) 29 CJQ 284.

34 It is not clear why the parties were still arguing about whether the court had the power to grant a negative declaration in light of the earlier decision of McCombe J in the same action: [2008] EWHC 1219 (QB).

35 [2009] EWHC 567 (QB) at para 102, referring to the judgment of McCombe J.

to them before memories fade and witnesses become unavailable. The careful judgment of Christopher Clarke J in *Toropdar* makes clear that the courts will be vigilant to avoid an inequality of arms harming the interests of an injured party who has not rushed into litigation. It will be interesting to see how this newly recognised jurisdiction develops.

CHAPTER 6

Acknowledgment and Part Payment

INTRODUCTION

6.01 The Limitation Act 1980 ('LA 1980') provides that, once the statutory criteria are satisfied, if a defendant acknowledges a claimant's title to land (whether a right to possession, a mortgagee's interest or a mortgagor's equity of redemption), a mortgagee's title to personal property, a debt owing to the claimant or a claimant's right to a share or interest in an estate, the right of action is deemed to have accrued on the date of the acknowledgment. Similarly, if a defendant makes a payment in respect of a liquidated debt or other liquidated pecuniary claim (including a mortgage debt)[1] or a claim to a share or interest in an estate, the right of action is deemed to have accrued on the date of the payment. The concepts of acknowledgment and part payment are discussed together in this chapter as a part payment is merely a particular kind of acknowledgment. Section 96 of the Land Registration Act 2002 provides that no period of limitation for the recovery of land,[2] redemption of land[3] or the extinction of title on the expiry of the time limit[4] applies to registered land. Accordingly, all references in this chapter to acknowledgments or payments in relation to land relate only to unregistered land.

GENERAL PRINCIPLES

History and rationale

6.02 The rationale for the rules on acknowledgment and part payment is a recognition that, without such principles regulating the affairs of the population, an unscrupulous debtor could lull a claimant into a false sense of security with payments on account while waiting for the limitation period to expire. Further,

1 The debt or other liquidated pecuniary claim must arise out of a contractual or quasi-contractual obligation; a claim in tort for a specific sum in damages falls outside the definition of 'liquidated claim' for these purposes: see paras 6.09–6.10.
2 LRA 2002, s 96(1), disapplying LA 1980, s 15.
3 LRA 2002, s 96(2), disapplying LA 1980, s 16.
4 LRA 2002, s 96(3), disapplying LA 1980, s 17.

claims which have been acknowledged in writing are unlikely to lead to any serious disputes as to the existence of the debt, even after several years have passed. The first proper limitation statute, the Limitation Act 1623,[5] did not contain any provision to the effect that an acknowledgment of a debt or a title to land should extend the limitation period. However, from as early as 1699 the courts have held that if a defendant made a fresh promise to pay the debt, time began to run again from the date of the promise.[6] This rule was extended over time so that the courts asked instead whether an acknowledgment of a debt was such that a fresh promise to pay could be inferred.[7] The requirement that the acknowledgment must contain an implied promise to pay was removed by the Limitation Act 1939,[8] which is the form retained in s 29 of the Limitation Act 1980.

Requirement that acknowledgment be in writing and signed

6.03 The main formal requirements for an acknowledgment are that it must be in writing and signed by the person making it.[9] The exclusion of oral acknowledgments serves an obvious purpose, which was discussed by Lord Templeman giving the decision of the Privy Council in *Browne v Perry*,[10] where he stated as follows:

> 'If an oral acknowledgment were allowed to constitute an interruption litigation would be encouraged and litigants would dispute what was said, by whom and to whom … Once an acknowledgment has been reduced to writing, there is certainty about the words used and the court need only decide whether the words which have been written amount to an acknowledgment. There is no room for fraud, mistake or failure of memory. The written word speaks for itself.'[11]

Admission of extrinsic evidence in support of acknowledgment

6.04 In addition to the court considering the document in question, extrinsic evidence is admissible to assist in understanding a purported acknowledgment. In commenting on the extract from Lord Templeman's judgment set out above, Simon Brown LJ in *Bigden v Lambeth London Borough Council*[12] stated that, while the court will be astute not to reintroduce the risk of 'fraud, mistake or failure of memory' which the rule is designed to avoid:

> '[T]he court need not otherwise be inhibited in its inquiry … There is, in short, no reason why the court should strain against finding an acknowledgment of title (or debt) … so long only as the certainty of the writing avoids the risk of fraud or mistake.'[13]

5 21 Jac 1 c16.
6 *Hyleing v Hastings* (1699) 1 Ld Raym 389. The history of this area is well set out in *Spencer v Hummerde* [1922] 2 AC 507 and *Surrendra Overseas Ltd v Government of Sri Lanka* [1977] 1 WLR 565.
7 *Tanner v Smart* (1827) 6 B & C 603.
8 *Good v Parry* [1963] 2 WLR 846.
9 Section 30(1); see further para 6.13.
10 [1991] 1 WLR 1297.
11 [1991] 1 WLR 1297 at 1301–1302.
12 [2000] EWCA Civ 302, [2000] All ER (D) 2076.
13 [2000] EWCA Civ 302, [2000] All ER (D) 2076.

Causes of action which may be revived by acknowledgment or payment

6.05 Although, in summary, the provisions dealing with acknowledgment and part payment affect claims involving real property and debts, the full list of causes of action covered are:

1 The following claims involving land or personal property –

(a) right of action (including a foreclosure action) to recover land or any right of a mortgagee of personal property to bring a foreclosure action – acknowledgment[14] and part payment;[15] and

(b) right of action of mortgagor to redeem land in the possession of the mortgagee – acknowledgment[16] and part payment.[17]

2 In respect of debts and other liquidated pecuniary claims –

(a) right of action to recover any debt or other liquidated pecuniary claim – acknowledgment[18] and part payment;[19] and

(b) any right of action to recover any claim to the personal estate of a deceased person or to any share or interest in the estate – acknowledgment[20] and part payment.[21]

Effect of payment of part of rent or interest on principal debt

6.06 Section 29(6) provides that a payment of part of the rent or interest due at any time shall not extend the period for claiming the balance then due. In addition, the section provides that any payment of interest shall be treated as a payment in respect of the principal debt.

Statute barred claims and multiple extensions of time

6.07 The Limitation Act 1939 provided that time ran afresh if a payment was made towards, or if there was an acknowledgment of, a statute barred debt.[22] However, s 29(7) of the LA 1980 now provides that a right of action once barred by the Act cannot be revived by any subsequent acknowledgment or payment.

14 Section 29(1) and (2): acknowledgment of title by person in possession of the land or personal property. Section 29(2)(b) deals with rights of action which have accrued to a person entitled to an estate or interest taking effect on the determination of an estate in tail.
15 Section 29(3): payment in respect of the mortgage debt (principal or interest) by the person in possession of the land or personal property.
16 Section 29(4)(b): acknowledgment by mortgagee of title or equity of redemption of mortgagor.
17 Section 29(4)(a): payment to mortgagee in respect of principal or interest of mortgage debt.
18 Section 29(5)(a): acknowledgment of the claim by the person liable or accountable.
19 Section 29(5)(a): payment in respect of the claim by the person liable or accountable.
20 Section 29(5)(b): acknowledgment of the claim by the person liable or accountable.
21 Section 29(5)(b): payment in respect of the claim by the person liable or accountable.
22 See *In re Compania de Electricidad* [1980] Ch 146 at 192.

However, the section also provides that the limitation period for a non-statute barred right of action may be repeatedly extended by further acknowledgments or payments.

Debts and liquidated pecuniary claims

6.08 The LA 1980 does not require that an acknowledgment identifies the amount of the debt and it may instead acknowledge a general indebtedness, provided that the amount of the debt can be ascertained by extraneous evidence.[23] This occurred in *Dungate v Dungate*,[24] where a debtor sent a letter to his brother saying, '[k]eep a check on totals and amounts I owe you and we will have an account now and then … Sorry, I cannot do you a cheque now'.[25] It was held that this was a sufficient acknowledgment of indebtedness. The level of certainty required for a debt which may be acknowledged was stated as follows by Lord Denning MR in *Good v Parry*:[26]

> 'In order to be an acknowledgment, however, the debt must be quantified in figures or, at all events, it must be liquidated in this sense that it is capable of ascertainment by calculation, or by extrinsic evidence, without further agreement of the parties.'[27]

6.09 The question of whether a monetary claim is a 'liquidated pecuniary claim' has given rise to a considerable volume of case law. The main area of difficulty which has arisen is as to whether or not claims for payment on a *quantum meruit* basis and other claims in the law of unjust enrichment are liquidated pecuniary claims. In *Amantilla v Telefusion*,[28] it was held that a claim for the reasonable value of building works was a liquidated pecuniary claim, although academic commentators have pointed out that the defendant in *Amantilla* conceded that there was a contract in existence between the parties and questioned whether the same result would have followed in the absence of one.[29] A claim relating to a purely restitutionary cause of action came before the courts in *FJ Chalke Ltd v Revenue and Customs Commissioners*,[30] where a restitutionary claim against the Revenue for compound interest on taxes wrongly levied was held to be a claim for a liquidated amount, as, in the words of Henderson J, the claim was 'more akin to the *quantum meruit* claim in *Amantilla* than to a claim for damages in tort or contract'.[31] In light of the foregoing approach to the provision, the Court of Appeal was correct to treat a solicitor's claim for fees (as contained in

23 *Dungate v Dungate* [1965] 1 WLR 1477.
24 [1965] 1 WLR 1477.
25 [1965] 1 WLR 1477 at 1479.
26 [1963] 2 QB 418.
27 [1963] 2 QB 418 at 423–424; see also *Ross v McGrath* [2004] EWCA Civ 1054, [2004] All ER (D) (Jul) and see further the discussion at paras 6.16–6.18 below.
28 (1987) 98 ConLR 139.
29 Oughton, Lowry and Merkin, *Limitation of Actions* (London: LLP Reference Publishing, 1998) at 149.
30 [2009] EWHC 952 (Ch), [2009] STC 2027 (affd [2010] EWCA Civ 313, [2010] STC 1642).
31 [2009] EWHC 952 (Ch), [2009] STC 2027 at para 157; see also *Kleinwort Benson Ltd v South Tyneside Metropolitan Borough Council* [1994] 4 All ER 972.

his invoice but disputed by the client and not yet assessed) against his client as being a claim for a liquidated pecuniary amount in *Phillips & Co (a firm) v Bath Housing Co-Operative Ltd.*[32]

6.10 The most notable exclusions from the rights of action which may be acknowledged (or part payments made in respect of) are claims in tort and all claims in contract which seek unliquidated damages.[33] In *Dwr Cymru v Marthenshire CC*,[34] it was confirmed that claims in tort cannot be the subject of an acknowledgment. Here, the defendant county council's contractors damaged the claimant's property. Liability was admitted but the parties could not agree on the remedial works to be carried out. Proceedings were not issued during the limitation period and when they were ultimately brought, seeking damages for negligence and nuisance, the defendant raised a limitation defence. It was held that the admission of liability had no effect on the running of the limitation period, as claims in negligence and nuisance could not be acknowledged. In other cases it has been doubted whether a claim for compensation following the compulsory purchase of land is a liquidated claim.[35] Interestingly, the Canadian legislature amended the law so that a claim in tort can now be the subject of an acknowledgment.[36] In addition, the effect of admissions made in negotiations may give rise to an estoppel which prevents the defendant from later raising a limitation defence, even for causes of action which are not capable of acknowledgment.[37]

Relationship between acknowledgment, estoppel and compromise

6.11 The principles that a statute barred right of action cannot be revived by acknowledgment or payment and that certain rights of action cannot be the subject of an acknowledgment can be simply stated. However, in practice they are sometimes less easily applied, as a claimant's arguments may overlap with arguments relating to estoppel and may be raised in tandem with an argument that the acknowledgment was in fact a compromise of potential proceedings. In *Revenue and Customs Commissioners v Benchdollar Ltd*,[38] an argument of

32 [2012] EWCA Civ 1591.

33 The English Law Commission's 2001 *Report on Limitation of Actions* (Law Com No 270) has described the present distinction made between claims for specific amounts and claims for unspecific amounts as 'anomalous' (para 3.149). They have recommended that a written acknowledgment or a part payment 'irrespective of the nature of the claim, should restart the running of time': see para 3.155(1).

34 [2004] EWHC 2991 (TCC), [2004] All ER (D) 307 (Oct). Interim payments by insurance companies in personal injuries actions where liability has been admitted have not been relied on as part payments in several cases, including *Horton v Sadler* [2006] UKHL 27, [2007] 1 AC 307.

35 *BP Oil Ltd v Kent CC* [2003] EWCA Civ 798, [2004] 1 P & CR 416. In *Mehra v Shah* [2003] All ER (D) 15 (Aug) it was doubted whether acknowledgment could arise in an action for an account.

36 *Pedersen v Lehn* (1981) 126 DLR (3rd) 118.

37 See the decision of the Supreme Court of Ireland in *Murphy v Grealish* [2009] IESC 9, [2009] 3 IR 366, discussed in para 6.11.

38 [2009] EWHC 1310 (Ch), [2010] 1 All ER 174.

estoppel by convention was raised by the claimant in tandem with an alleged acknowledgment of its claim. Briggs J had no difficulty with the claimant raising these arguments in the alternative, but ultimately rejected both, finding that it was not unconscionable for the defendants to rely on a limitation defence and that no acknowledgment had been made. In *Colchester Borough Council v Smith,*[39] the defendant argued that a purported acknowledgment of the claimant's title was of no effect as it had been given after the 12-year limitation period had expired. It was held that, properly construed, this was more than a mere acknowledgment (of a title which had been extinguished) and was instead a compromise of contemplated proceedings and that the defendant was estopped by representation from resiling from that agreement. The judgment in *Colchester BC v Smith* has been criticised as giving rise to an 'undesirable method'[40] of circumventing the LA 1980. However, it provides a useful and effective means of defeating the argument of an unscrupulous party where it would be unconscionable for him to argue that an admitted or proven acknowledgment was of no effect. Although it has been stated that a party will only find himself estopped from raising a limitation point in exceptional cases,[41] a broader doctrine has been applied by the courts of Ireland in recent decisions which was discussed earlier in the book.[42] It is worth noting that the doctrine of estoppel may have a role to play in cases where the right of action is not capable of being acknowledged.

Position in cases of multiple parties

6.12 A debt may be owed by, or to, more than one person. Similarly, more than one person may be in possession of, or have an interest in, a property. In such cases the following provisions of the LA 1980 apply:

- an acknowledgment of title to any land, benefice or mortgaged personalty by any person in possession of it binds all other persons in possession during the ensuing period of limitation: s 31(1);
- a payment in respect of a mortgage debt by the mortgagor or any other person in possession of the mortgaged property shall, so far as the right of the mortgagee to foreclose or otherwise recover the property is concerned, bind all other persons in possession during the ensuing period of limitation: s 31(2);
- where two or more mortgagees are by virtue of the mortgage in possession of land, if one mortgagee acknowledges the mortgagor's title or equity of redemption, that acknowledgment shall bind *only the acknowledgor* and his successors in title: s 31(3);

39 [1992] Ch 421; see also *St Pancras and Humanist Housing Association Ltd v Leonard* [2008] EWCA Civ 1442.

40 McGee, *Limitation Periods* (6th edn, London: Sweet & Maxwell, 2010), para 18.032.

41 See *Holding and Management (Solitaire) Ltd v Ideal Homes North West Ltd* [2004] EWHC 2408 (TCC), (2004) 96 ConLR 114 at para 83, where Judge Toulson QC found that 'exceptional circumstances' had not been established in the case before him.

42 See para 1.14.

- where, in a case within s 31(3), the mortgagee by whom an acknowledgment was given is entitled to part of the mortgaged land and not to an ascertained part of the mortgage debt, the mortgagor is entitled to redeem that part of the land upon payment of a pro rata portion of the debt as reflects his share of the mortgaged land to the total land: s 31(4);
- if there are two or more mortgagors and the title or equity of redemption of one of them is acknowledged, that acknowledgment is deemed to have been made to all of the mortgagors: s 31(5);
- an acknowledgment of a debt binds the acknowledgor and his successors but not any other person: s 31(6);
- a payment in respect of a debt binds all persons liable in respect of the debt or claim: s 31(7);
- an acknowledgment by one of several personal representatives of any claim to the personal estate of a deceased person or to any share or interest therein shall bind the estate of the deceased person: s 31(8).

The word 'successor' is defined in s 31(9) in relation to any mortgagee or a person liable in respect of a debt or claim, as his personal representatives and any other person on whom the rights under the mortgage (or liability in respect of the debt or claim) devolves, whether on death or bankruptcy or the disposition of property or the determination of a limited estate or interest in settled property or otherwise. The important distinction between the effect of acknowledgments and payments towards a debt or liquidated pecuniary claim in subsections (6) and (7) should be noted. The latter, but not the former, binds the joint debtors, the reason being that since a part payment operates for the advantage of all debtors, so too does the payment affect their limitation position.[43]

ACKNOWLEDGMENT

Acknowledgment must be in writing and signed by the person making the acknowledgment

6.13 Section 30(1) of the LA 1980 provides that 'every acknowledgment shall be in writing and signed by the person making the acknowledgment'.[44] It is settled law that no special form of words need be used and that the document relied upon as constituting the acknowledgment may have been written without any intention on the acknowledgor's part to make the acknowledgment. The signature may appear at the head of the acknowledgment,[45] or be by initials.[46]

43 *Chitty on Contracts* (31st edn, Sweet & Maxwell: London, 2012) at para 28-103.

44 This requirement has been contained in the statutes of limitation since the Statute of Frauds Amendment Act 1828 (9 Geo 4, c14) (Lord Tenterden's Act).

45 *Holmes v Mackrell* (1858) 3 CBNS 789.

46 *Lord St John v Boughton* (1838) 9 Sim 219.

In *Good Challenger Navegante SA v Metalexportimport SA*,[47] it was argued by the defendant that a typed signature on a telex was not sufficient and the court noted that there had been no prior reported judgments on the meaning of 'signed' in relation to acknowledgments and the Limitation Acts. However, the court referred to a number of judgments which considered the equivalent requirement in the Statute of Frauds[48] and held that there was no reason to stipulate for stricter formal requirements for a document by which the maker acknowledges his own liability for the purpose of discontinuing a period of limitation, than for a document by which the maker assumes liability as surety for another. In a passage which was quoted with approval by the Court of Appeal, Mr Michael Crane QC sitting as a deputy judge of the Commercial Court stated that:

> 'As a matter of general principle, in my view a document is signed by the maker of it when his name or mark is attached to it in a manner which indicates, objectively, his approval of the contents. How this is done will depend upon the nature and format of the document. Thus in the case of a formal contract which prints the names of the parties and leaves a space under each name for the parties to write their names, the document will not have been signed by a party until he writes his name in the space provided. Conversely, with a telex, where there is no such facility, the typed name of the sender at the end of the telex not only identifies the maker but leads to the inference that he has approved the contents: the typed name, therefore, constitutes his signature. Thus in my judgment each of the telexes relied on by the claimant was signed by the sender typing in its name, or his name, at the foot of the document.'[49]

As technology moves from telexes to emails and text messages, the law will be called on to adapt to the times and the *Good Challenger Navegante* case indicates that the requirement of a 'signature' will be broadly interpreted in future cases. A person's signature on the counterpart to an invalid (and fraudulent) lease can constitute an acknowledgment.[50] Extrinsic evidence is admissible to link one document to another so that when read together there is an acknowledgment.[51] In *Haydon v Williams*,[52] extrinsic evidence was admitted as secondary evidence to establish the existence of a lost written acknowledgment.

Acknowledgment may be made by an agent

6.14 Section 30(2)(a) provides that an acknowledgment under s 29 may be made by the agent of the person by whom it is required to be made. The agency may be express or implied and it is irrelevant whether or not the client had given

47 [2003] EWHC 10 (Comm) at para 60, [2003] 1 Lloyd's Rep 471 at 487 (affd [2003] EWCA Civ 1668, [2004] 1 Lloyd's Rep 67).

48 See *Schneider v Norris* (1814) 2 M & S 286; *Decouvreur v Jordan*, *The Times*, 25 May 1987 (CA); and *The Anemone* [1987] 1 Lloyd's Rep 546.

49 *Good Challenger Navegante SA v Metalexportimport SA* [2003] EWHC 10 (Comm) at para 61, [2003] 1 Lloyd's Rep 471 at 487 (affd [2003] EWCA Civ 1668, [2004] 1 Lloyd's Rep 67).

50 *Rehman v Benfield* [2006] EWCA Civ 1392, (2007) 2 P & CR 317.

51 *McGuffe v Burleigh* (1898) 78 LT 264.

52 (1830) 7 Bing 163; *Read v Price* [1909] 2 KB 724.

specific authority to make the acknowledgment.[53] However, an acknowledgment made by a stranger is of no effect and an agency must be found to exist for a person to be caught by s 30(2)(a). In *Wright v Peppin*,[54] a mortgagor's solicitor wrote a letter which was alleged to constitute an acknowledgment of the mortgagee's title. Harman J held that he had implied authority on the facts of the case. However, in *Re Beavan*,[55] it was held by Neville J that a trustee appointed to manage the affairs of a person of unsound mind did not have authority to acknowledge his debts, although this decision has been the subject of cogent criticism and may not still represent the law.[56] In *In re Transplanters (Holding Company) Ltd*,[57] it was held that a company director could not rely on a balance sheet signed by him as an acknowledgment of a debt owed to him by the company as he himself was interested in the debt.[58] Nor was a certificate prepared by the company's auditors certifying the correctness of the contents of the company's balance sheet sufficient to give rise to an acknowledgment as an auditor of a company is (apart from any special contract) not an agent of the company for the purpose of being able to bind the company. Instead, his function is to make a report to the members on the accounts examined by them.[59]

Acknowledgment must be made to the person whose claim is being acknowledged

6.15 Section 30(2)(b) of the LA 1980 provides that the acknowledgment shall be made to the person or the agent of the person whose title, right, equity of redemption or claim is being acknowledged. In *Bowring-Hanbury's Trustee v Bowring-Hanbury*,[60] it was held that an admission of a debt contained in a revenue probate affidavit was not a sufficient acknowledgment as it was not made to the creditor. This requirement was elaborated upon in *Re Compania de Electrididad*,[61] where Slade J stated as follows:

> '[A] written acknowledgment cannot be said to be "made to" a creditor or his agent, within the meaning of section 24(2) [of the Limitation Act 1939] unless either:

53 *Agricultural Mortgage Corporation Plc v Williams*, unreported, 15 May 1995 (CA).
54 [1954] 1 WLR 635. Other cases focusing on the authority of solicitors include: *Newbould v Smith* (1886) 33 Ch D 127; *Curwen v Milburn* (1889) 42 Ch D 424; *Bowring-Hanbury's Trustee v Bowring-Hanbury* [1943] Ch 104.
55 [1912] 1 Ch 196.
56 *Re Beavan* is described as 'puzzling' in McGee, *Limitation Periods* (6th edn, London: Sweet & Maxwell, 2010), para.18.012, although he notes that it may be explained as an example of the lengths the courts go to protect those of unsound mind.
57 [1958] 1 WLR 822.
58 A ratification of the acknowledgment by the company in general meeting would appear to be effective, see *Re Gee & Co (Woolwich) Ltd* [1975] Ch 52.
59 [1958] 1 WLR 822 at 826.
60 [1943] 1 Ch 104, CA. This decision should be treated with care as the main finding was that the executor was not capable of acknowledging a debt purportedly owed by the estate to him, and regard should also be had to *In re Overmark Smith Warden Ltd* [1982] 1 WLR 1195.
61 [1980] Ch 146.

> (a) it is delivered to the creditor or his agent by or with the authority of the debtor or his agent, or
>
> (b) it is expressly or implicitly addressed to and is actually received by the creditor or his agent.
>
> In my judgment, in case (a) it would not matter that the acknowledgment was not, according to its terms, expressly or implicitly addressed to the recipient. In case (b) it would not matter that the acknowledgment reached the hands of the creditor otherwise than by or with the authority of the debtor. In either case, however, it would be necessary that the creditor should actually receive the acknowledgment before he could rely on it.'[62]

In *Jones v Bellgrove Properties Ltd*,[63] it was held that a company's balance sheet, signed by the company's accountants and two directors and presented to the shareholders in general meeting, containing a reference to a debt owed to a shareholder was an acknowledgment to him of that debt. This was the case even though he received the document in his capacity as shareholder and not as a creditor. Although there are a number of older authorities which hold that a statement of affairs signed by a duly authorised person in a bankruptcy, liquidation or receivership cannot constitute a sufficient acknowledgment,[64] this would appear not to still represent the law[65] and care should be taken as the law in this area remains regrettably unclear.

Sufficient acknowledgment

6.16 The LA 1980 does not contain a definition of 'acknowledgment'; no special form of words need be used and the document may have been written without any intention on the writer's part to acknowledge the right of action. The cases decided prior to the Limitation Act 1939 required the claimant to find an implied promise to pay in the acknowledgment, whereas an admission of liability is now all that is required.[66] There being no statutory definition, recourse must be had to the ordinary meaning of the word, and as was stated by Kerr J in *Surrendra (Overseas) Ltd v Government of Sri Lanka*,[67] '[t]o acknowledge a claim … signifies an admission that it is due'.[68] This will be the case even if a defendant indicates that he is either unwilling or unable to discharge the debt.[69] However, a document referring to the claim but denying its validity cannot be a

62 [1980] Ch 146 at 193.

63 [1949] 2 KB 700.

64 See *Everett v Robinson* (1858) 28 LJQB 2, *contra Barrett v Birmingham* (1842) 4 Ir Eq Rep 537, quoted with approval in *Hipworth v Maher* (1952) 87 CLR 335 (HCA).

65 Slade J in *In re Overmark Smith Warden Ltd* [1982] 1 WLR 1195 at 1205–1206 did not have to express a final decision on the point and it does not appear to have arisen for determination since that date; see also the cases referred to in *Halsbury's Laws of England* (5th edn, LexisNexis 2008), vol 68, para 1193.

66 For the older law, see *Surrendra Overseas Ltd v Government of Sri Lanka* [1977] 1 WLR 565 and *Spencer v Hemmerde* [1922] 2 AC 507.

67 [1977] 1 WLR 565.

68 [1977] 1 WLR 565 at 573.

69 *Good v Parry* [1963] 2 QB 418 at 423.

good acknowledgment.[70] Further, a document must be taken in its entirety such that an acknowledgment of a debt coupled with the assertion of a set-off or cross-claim does not amount to an acknowledgment of the creditor's claim, unless an undisputed balance is outstanding.[71] Extrinsic evidence is admissible to identify the debt to which the acknowledgment refers,[72] or to ascertain the amount of debt[73] or the date of the acknowledgment.[74] Although the decided cases are of assistance in helping to ascertain whether a particular statement does indeed contain an acknowledgment of a debt owed to the claimant or of his title to land, it is a case-specific exercise to determine whether in fact a sufficient acknowledgment was made.

6.17 In *Good v Parry*,[75] the defendant was the tenant of the claimant and owed him a sum as rent which was due for in excess of six years. The document alleged to constitute the acknowledgment of the debt contained an offer to purchase the property (offering £1,350 subject to contract), and continued, '[t]he question of outstanding rent can be settled as a separate agreement as soon as you present your account'. It was held not to constitute an acknowledgment of the landlord's claim for rent. Lord Denning MR said that the sentence meant 'there may be some rent outstanding and it can be made the subject of an agreement as soon as you present your account' and concluded:

> 'Such being the meaning of it, I am quite satisfied there is no acknowledgment, because there is no admission of any rent of a defined amount due, or of any amount that can be ascertained by calculation. The amount is uncertain altogether. Nor can I regard it as a promise to pay whatever amount may be found due on taking an account. The tenant clearly reserves the right to examine it and not to be bound except by separate agreement.'[76]

The judgment of Lord Denning MR went further, however, and said that if the debt is not quantified and is not ascertainable without further agreement, then there is no acknowledgment sufficient to satisfy the statute.[77] A different approach is evident from a differently constituted Court of Appeal in *Dungate v Dungate*,[78] where a letter sent by the defendant read as follows, 'Keep a check on totals and amounts I owe you and we will have account now and then … Sorry I cannot do you a cheque yet – terribly short at the moment.' Holding this to be an acknowledgment of the claim, Diplock LJ said that 'an acknowledgment under this Act need not identify the amount of the debt and may acknowledge a

70 *Horner v Cartwright*, unreported, 11 July 1989 (CA).

71 *Surrendra (Overseas) Ltd v Government of Sri Lanka* [1977] 1 WLR 565 at 575; see also *In re Flynn (deceased) (No 2)* [1969] 2 Ch 403.

72 *Read v Price* [1909] 2 KB 724; *Jones v Bellgrove Properties Ltd* [1949] 2 KB 700.

73 *Dungate v Dungate* [1965] 1 WLR 1477; *Kamouh v Associated Electrical Industries International Ltd* [1980] QB 199; *Re Overmark Smith Warden Ltd* [1982] 1 WLR 1195 at 1204.

74 *Edmunds v Downes* (1834) 1 Cr & M 459 at 463.

75 [1963] 2 QB 418.

76 [1963] 2 QB 418 at 424. In his concurring judgment, Davies LJ at 425 was of the view that 'the letter did not acknowledge the claim; it only acknowledged that there might be a claim'.

77 [1963] 2 QB 418 at 424.

78 [1965] 1 WLR 1477 (CA).

general indebtedness, provided that the amount of the debt can be ascertained by extraneous evidence.'[79]

6.18 In *Bradford & Bingley Plc v Rashid*,[80] Lord Brown gave some consideration to whether there was any conflict between the judgments of the Court of Appeal in *Good v Parry*[81] and *Dungate v Dungate*.[82] His conclusion was that '*Dungate v Dungate* was to my mind rightly decided. Acknowledgments are not confined to admissions of debts which are indisputable as to quantum as well as liability'.[83] This has the effect that 'any uncertainties as to the quantum of the admitted liability can be determined by 'extraneous evidence', including if necessary oral evidence to resolve any dispute'.[84] The letter which was alleged to constitute the acknowledgment in that case stated that the defendant was not in a position to pay 'the outstanding balance, owed to you'. In the words of Lord Hoffmann:

> 'It seems to me that the plain meaning of those words is that the defendant was admitting that he owed the claimants a sum of money which for the time being he was unable to pay. There could not be a clearer way of acknowledging that the defendant was under a legal liability to pay the outstanding balance. It is not disputed that the amount of the balance was capable of being determined by extrinsic evidence.'[85]

Date of acknowledgment

6.19 In several cases the question has arisen as to whether the 'date of the acknowledgment' as contained in s 29(5) of the LA 1980 should be either the date on which the document was signed or the date to which the signed document relates. For acknowledgments contained in court pleadings, the question has arisen as to whether the relevant date should be the date a pleading was issued or delivered or the last date on which it was relied upon. In *Ofulue v Bossert*,[86] a defence was delivered in 1990 in proceedings which were only determined in 2002. While accepting that an acknowledgment could 'cover a continuing state of affairs', Lord Neuberger continued by stating that, 'the more natural meaning of the word would suggest that it arises as at the date of the document – most naturally the date on which the document is provided to the person to whom the acknowledgment is made'.[87] In *Re Overmark Smith Warden Ltd*,[88] a receiver and manager was appointed over the assets of the applicant company, following which a statement of affairs listing the unsecured creditors was sworn by

79 [1965] 1 WLR 1477 (CA) at 1487.
80 [2006] UKHL 37, [2006] 1 WLR 2066.
81 [1963] 2 QB 418.
82 [1965] 1 WLR 1477 (CA).
83 [2006] UKHL 37, [2006] 1 WLR 2066 at para 66.
84 [2006] UKHL 37, [2006] 1 WLR 2066 at para 55.
85 [2006] UKHL 37, [2006] 1 WLR 2066 at para 22.
86 [2009] UKHL 16, [2009] 1 AC 990.
87 [2009] UKHL 16, [2009] 1 AC 990 at para 80.
88 [1982] 1 WLR 1195.

the company's directors in December 1971. At the end of the receivership in 1978 the company was placed into liquidation and a new statement of affairs was sworn which listed the company's assets and liabilities as of August 1971 in the same terms as the earlier statement of affairs. It later transpired (in 1979) that a surplus was available for distribution among the unsecured creditors, and the liquidator appointed to the company applied to the court for directions as to whether these debts were statute barred. It was held by Slade J that both statements of affairs and the related correspondence did not purport to do more than show the liabilities of the company to unsecured creditors as at August 1971 and did not constitute a continuing acknowledgment of liability for the debts such as could still be relied upon at the end of the period of receivership.[89]

Acknowledgments of title to unregistered land

6.20 An acknowledgment of the paper title to unregistered[90] land need only acknowledge that the landowner has a better title than the acknowledgor's title and need not acknowledge that he has a particular interest in the land. In *Edgington v Clark*,[91] a squatter wrote to the agent of the landowner (not knowing the identity of the landowner) offering to purchase the property. Even though the offer was made subject to contract, it was held that it amounted to an acknowledgment that the landowner had better title to the property such that the limitation period commenced again from the date of the letter. This approach was confirmed by the House of Lords in *Ofulue v Bossert*,[92] where an offer to purchase a freehold interest in land would have been a sufficient acknowledgment of the claimant's title if it had not been made in without prejudice communications. In *Allen v Matthews*,[93] it was held that, while the person acknowledging title does not have to know who the owner is, the acknowledgment must be by or on behalf of the person in possession. Thus, a letter sent by the solicitors acting for a company, which had been in possession of a property until it had been struck off the register of companies, did not bind the shareholder of the company who had thereafter been in possession in his personal capacity.

6.21 Whether or not a particular document contains an acknowledgment depends on the true construction of the document in all the circumstances. An admission by the person in possession that he holds the property as tenant is sufficient.[94] An offer to take a lease will ordinarily be an acknowledgment of title unless it is found instead to be an offer to compromise potential litigation.[95] An affidavit delivered in earlier proceedings between the same parties can also suf-

89 See also *In re Gee & Co (Woolwich) Ltd* [1975] Ch 52. This approach was also taken by the High Court of Australia in *The Stage Club Ltd v Millers Hotel Pty Ltd* (1982) 56 ALJR 113.

90 The Land Registration Act 2002 disapplies the provisions on adverse possession to registered land: see para 6.01.

91 [1964] 1 QB 367.

92 [2009] UKHL 16, [2009] 1 AC 990.

93 [2007] EWCA Civ 216, [2007] 2 P & CR 441.

94 *Goode v Job* (1858) 28 LJQB 1.

95 *Ofulue v Bossert* [2009] UKHL 16, [2009] 1 AC 990.

fice.[96] If, in answer to a claim for rent, the person in possession does not deny the title of the person entitled but asks for more time to pay the rent, this may be sufficient to start time running afresh,[97] as may a letter from a squatter in a local authority property asking the local authority for funds to refurbish the property.[98] A covenant to pay a mortgage debt in a deed executed subsequent to and referring to the mortgage is an acknowledgment of the existence of the relation of mortgagor and mortgagee, and therefore of the mortgagee's title.[99]

Without prejudice communications

6.22 The question of when a communication will be found to have been made on a without prejudice basis, and the admissibility of an acknowledgment of a claim contained in the communication, was reviewed by the House of Lords in *Bradford & Bingley Plc v Rashid*.[100] In this case, the defendant had borrowed money from the claimant bank in 1989. After he fell into arrears on his loan repayments, the claimant had sold his property in 1991, leaving a shortfall of £15,583. The claimant subsequently had difficulty in tracing the defendant's whereabouts, but in 2001 an advice centre wrote on his behalf to the claimant saying that 'at present he is not in a position to repay the outstanding balance, owed to you' but that once his financial situation was stable he would start to repay it. A second letter sent by him offered to make a single payment of £500 in final settlement. None of the correspondence was marked 'without prejudice' and nothing was paid. In June 2003 the claimant issued proceedings claiming the sum of £15,583 together with statutory interest and alleged that the 2001 correspondence had acknowledged the debt. The defendant argued that the letters had been sent on a without prejudice basis and that they were therefore inadmissible, and his arguments were accepted by the Court of Appeal. The House of Lords reversed the Court of Appeal, and although the law lords were unanimous in the result reached, they differed in their reasoning. Lord Hoffmann's judgment provides a useful analysis of the problems caused by the approach taken by the Court of Appeal:

> 'They looked only at encouraging the debtor to be open with his creditor without fear of what he said being used against him. But it takes two to negotiate and there is also a public policy in encouraging the creditor not to initiate legal proceedings. The acknowledgment rule plays an important part in furthering this policy because it means that a creditor, negotiating on the basis that his debt has been acknowledged, can proceed with the negotiations and give time to pay without being distracted by the sound of time's winged chariot behind him. It is also unfair

96 *Ofulue v Bossert* [2009] UKHL 16, [2009] 1 AC 990.

97 *Fursdon v Clogg* (1842) 10 M & W 572.

98 *Archangel v Lambeth London Borough Council* [2000] All ER (D) 2077 (CA). See also the remarkable case of *Lambeth London Borough Council v Bigden* (2001) 33 HLR 43, [2000] EG 147 (CS), where a petition sent by squatters to the borough council asking it not to sell the property was found to be a sufficient acknowledgment of title, as it acknowledged that the council had a right to sell.

99 *Jayne v Hughes* (1854) 10 ExCh 430.

100 [2006] UKHL 37, [2006] 1 WLR 2066.

that a debtor who does not dispute his indebtedness should be able to ask for time and use that indulgence to rely on the statute.'[101]

6.23 In reconciling the potential for conflict between the without prejudice rule and the admissibility of acknowledgments, a number of different approaches were adopted by the law lords. Lord Hoffmann stated that he would have held that the without prejudice rule 'does not apply at all to the use of a statement as an acknowledgment'.[102] However, the speech of Lord Brown enjoyed majority support and focused instead on whether the letters sent by the defendant's agent fell within the ambit of the without prejudice rule at all. He held that the without prejudice rule has no application to apparently open communications which were designed only to discuss the repayment of an admitted liability rather than to negotiate and compromise a disputed liability. The critical question which he asked was whether 'it is clear from the surrounding circumstances that the parties were seeking to compromise the action'.[103] In *Bradford & Bingley v Rashid*, no 'statements or offers' were made with a view to settling a dispute, and in the words of Lord Brown, 'since the debt was admitted, there *was* no dispute … Mr Rashid was simply asking for a concession; he was not giving one'.[104]

6.24 The admissibility of without prejudice communications containing an acknowledgment, in this case of the claimant's title, came before the House of Lords again in *Ofulue v Bossert*.[105] The claimants in this case were the registered owners of a property and the defendant was in occupation from 1981, with the consent of the then tenants. In 1987 the claimants brought possession proceedings against the defendant, which were met with a counterclaim seeking the grant of a 14-year lease based on certain improvements they had carried out and representations which had allegedly been made by the claimants.[106] In January 1992 the defendant by a letter marked 'without prejudice' offered to buy the property. The claimants rejected that offer but failed to pursue the possession proceedings, which were stayed and ultimately dismissed in 2002 for want of prosecution. In 2003 the claimants issued new possession proceedings in which they sought to

101 [2006] UKHL 37, [2006] 1 WLR 2066 at para 3; to similar effect are the comments of Lord Brown at para 74.

102 Lord Hope would have held that a clear admission of a fact (in this case a debt), made without qualification rather than hypothetically, could never gain the benefit of the without prejudice rule if it did not form part of the offer to compromise, relying on Scottish cases such as *Watson-Towers Ltd v McPhail* (1986) SLT 617. This approach was not accepted by the other law lords.

103 Per Lord Griffiths in *Rush & Tompkins Ltd v Greater London Council* [1989] AC 1280 at 1299.

104 [2006] UKHL 37, [2006] 1 WLR 2066 at para 73. As was stated by Lord Mance at para 83, the defendant's offer of payment of a smaller sum in purported discharge of a larger admitted indebtedness would have fallen foul of the rule in *Foakes v Beer* (1884) 9 App Cas 605 in any event, and it certainly did not evidence any dispute as to the existence or amount of the debt, such as if the defendant had alleged, for example, that his house had been sold at an undervalue in 1991 and the correspondence was directed towards resolving that issue.

105 [2009] UKHL 16, [2009] 1 AC 990.

106 An acknowledgment of the claimants' title to the land which was contained in the defendant's defence and counterclaim in the first set of proceedings was held not to constitute a continuing acknowledgment of title: see Lord Hope at paras 80–84.

argue that the 1992 letter was admissible and fell outside the without prejudice rule and that it contained an acknowledgment of their title. They relied on two reasons in support of their argument that the letter should be admissible in evidence: first, they argued that title to the property was not an issue that was in dispute between the parties in 1992; and secondly, that the rule had no application in this case as the fact in question was at that time an agreed fact.

6.25 The House of Lords held that the defendant had properly asserted a claim of without prejudice privilege over the letter and that it was not admissible in the new proceedings. Although, if viewed from a certain perspective, the letter in *Ofulue* was not related to the claim for possession at that time being pursued, it was held that the offer of a compromise did contain within it an implied admission that the defendant's defence to the claim for possession was unsustainable.[107] The approach taken by the House of Lords is clear from the following comments of Lord Hope:

> 'But where the letters are not headed "without prejudice" unnecessarily or meaninglessly … the court should be very slow to lift the umbrella unless the case for doing so is absolutely plain.'[108]

The point was also made that the letter should be admissible in the new proceedings as the public policy reasons supporting the without prejudice rule did not apply to prevent the use of the letter other than in the proceedings in which it was created. This argument was rejected, although it was not clear from Lord Neuberger's comments whether he was stating a generally applicable principle or merely reaching his decision on the facts of this case.[109]

6.26 The court also gave guidance as to the general approach to be adopted for statements made in the course of without prejudice negotiations. The leading speech in the House of Lords was that of Lord Neuberger, who followed the statement of the law as set out in the 'invaluable judgment'[110] of Robert Walker LJ in *Unilever Plc v The Procter & Gamble Co.*[111] In that case, after considering a number of authorities, Robert Walker LJ said that the cases he had been considering:

> '[M]ake clear that the without prejudice rule is founded partly in public policy and partly in the agreement of the parties. They show that the protection of admissions against interest is the most important practical effect of the rule. But to dissect out identifiable admissions and withhold protection from the rest of without prejudice communications (except for a special reason) would not only create huge practical difficulties but would be contrary to the underlying objective of giving protection to the parties … to speak freely about all issues in the litigation … Parties cannot

107 [2009] UKHL 16, [2009] 1 AC 990 at paras 10 and 11, per Lord Hope.
108 [2009] UKHL 16, [2009] 1 AC 990 at para 2.
109 [2009] UKHL 16, [2009] 1 AC 990 at para 87.
110 Per Lord Neuberger at para 89 of his judgment.
111 [2000] 1 WLR 2436. The law lords also followed *Cutts v Head* [1984] Ch 290 and *Rush & Tomkins Ltd v Greater London Council* [1989] AC 1280.

> speak freely at a without prejudice meeting if they must constantly monitor every sentence, with lawyers … sitting at their shoulders as minders.'[112]

In adopting this approach, the House of Lords chose not to follow the comments expressed by Lord Hoffmann in the Court of Appeal in *Muller v Linsley & Mortimer*[113] to the effect that 'the public policy aspect of the rule is not … concerned with the admissibility of statements which are relevant otherwise than as admissions, ie independently of the truth of the facts alleged to have been admitted'.[114] These views were expanded upon by Lord Hoffmann in *Bradford & Bingley Plc v Rashid*,[115] although they did not find favour in that court either.[116]

PART PAYMENT

What constitutes a part payment?

6.27 Part payment is a particular type of acknowledgment: by paying money to a creditor, a debtor acknowledges that a debt is due and owing. Problems arising from part payments of debts have given rise to few reported judgments. The word 'payment' has been broadly interpreted such that delivery of goods to a creditor[117] or his agent,[118] and permitting the creditor to live rent free in premises belonging to the debtor,[119] have all been held to be sufficient. By virtue of s 29(6) of the LA 1980, a payment of interest in whole or in part is treated as payment in respect of the principal debt. A payment by compulsion of law, such as payment of part of a debt by a sheriff out of the proceeds of an execution levied under a judgment, is a valid part payment.[120] Other than in cases of involuntary payment, what must be shown is that the part payment constitutes an admission that the balance of the debt remains due. Thus, if a debtor makes clear that a payment is being made in respect of a part of a debt which is admitted to be due, this will not extend the limitation period in respect of the contested part of the debt.[121] Where a defendant makes a payment to repay part of a debt which is subsequently held to be ultra vires and void *ab initio*, the claimant cannot retrospectively appropriate the payment to another valid debt.[122] A payment made in respect of any debt

112 [2000] 1 WLR 2436 at 2448–2449, as quoted by Lord Neuberger at para 89 of his judgment.
113 [1996] PNLR 74.
114 [1996] PNLR 74 at 79.
115 [2006] 1 WLR 2066 at paras 16–18.
116 See the comments of Lord Walker at paras 41–42; Lord Hope at para 35; Lord Brown at para 67; and Lord Mance at para 93. In *Ofulue v Bossert* [2009] 1 AC 990, Lord Neuberger at para 95 stated that, '[d]espite … the intellectual attraction of the distinction which he draws, I am inclined to think that it is a distinction which is too subtle to apply in practice'.
117 *Moore v Strong* (1835) 1 Bing NC 441 at 442; *Hooper v Stephens* (1835) 4 Ad & El 71; *Hart v Nash* (1835) 2 CrM & R 337; *Collinson v Margesson* (1858) 27 LJ Ex 305.
118 *Pearce v Selby* (1842) 6 Jur 896.
119 *Re Wilson, Ex p Wilson v Trustee of Deed of Arrangement* [1937] Ch 675.
120 *Brew v Brew* [1899] 2 IR 163; *Bradford & Bingley Plc v Cutler* [2008] EWCA Civ 74.
121 *Surrendra Overseas Ltd v Sri Lanka Government* [1977] 1 WLR 565.
122 *Kleinwort Benson Ltd v South Tyneside Metropolitan BC* [1994] 4 All ER 972.

or other liquidated pecuniary claim binds all persons liable in respect of it.[123] The effect of this proposition is not limited to co-debtors; in *UCB Corporate Services Ltd v Kohli*,[124] it was held that a payment by a principal debtor binds a surety.

Position in cases of multiple debts

6.28 An acknowledgment or part payment must be referable to a particular debt or debts and if the document is not clear on its face then extrinsic evidence may be admissible to assist in its construction.[125] If the liabilities and payments are carried in order of date into a single account then the true nature of the debtor's liability is a single undivided debt for the amount of the balance. In *Re Footman Bower & Co Ltd*,[126] where this occurred (and where none of the debts were statute barred at the date of the payment), it was held that each payment was 'in respect of' the entire balance and that time started to run afresh from the date of each payment on the balance outstanding. If there are separate debts and the debtor makes a payment to the creditor, the debtor is able to choose to appropriate the payment towards a particular debt or debts. If he does not make an election then the creditor may appropriate the debt towards a particular debt.[127] If neither party appropriates the payment to any particular debt or debts, then if some or all of the debts are not statute barred, it was held in *Nash v Hodgson*[128] that the non-statute barred debts should be paid before the statute barred debts.

Payment by debtor or his agent to creditor or his agent

6.29 Section 30(2) of the LA 1980 provides that a part payment *may* be made by the agent of the person by whom it is required to be made and that it *shall* be made to the person or the agent of the person in respect of whose claim payment is being made. As with an acknowledgment, the payment must be made towards a liquidated debt and not in respect of a liability to pay unliquidated damages or compensation.[129] In *Bradford & Bingley Plc v Cutler*,[130] payments made to the claimant bank by the Benefits Agency from monies deducted from the defendant's social welfare entitlements (by operation of law) were found to have been payments made by his agent. In *Good Challenger Navegante SA v Metalexportimport SA*,[131] payments made by a company under common ownership with the debtor were accepted as being made by the debtor's agent, even though no formal arrangement was ever proven in evidence. In that case the

123 LA 1980, s 31(7).
124 [2004] EWHC 1126 (Ch), [2004] 2 All ER (Comm) 422.
125 See para 6.04.
126 [1961] Ch 443.
127 *Mills v Fowkes* (1839) 5 Bing (NC) 455.
128 (1855) 6 De GM & G 474.
129 See para 6.10.
130 [2008] EWCA Civ 74.
131 [2003] EWHC 10 (Comm), [2003] 1 Lloyd's Rep 471 (affd [2003] EWCA Civ 1668, [2004] 1 Lloyd's Rep 67); see also *Scott v Synge* (1891) 27 LR Ir 560.

court accepted that a payment made at the request of the debtor was a payment made by its agent. In *UCB Corporate Services Ltd v Kohli*,[132] it was held that a bank which sold a property as mortgagee in possession and then credited the mortgagor's account did not do so as agent of the debtor, and the payment had no effect on the limitation period. Instead it was an example of the mortgagee's obligation to account to the mortgagor for any monies received by it arising out of the sale of the mortgagor's property.[133]

Sufficiency of payment

6.30 The requirement that a payment actually be made has in certain cases been relaxed, such as in *Maber v Maber*,[134] where a son, after returning from a period abroad, offered to repay a debt to his father and put his hand into his pocket as if to produce the money. The father stopped him and indicated that he would make a gift of the payment to his son's wife and indorsed the son's promissory note to that effect. A majority of the Court of Exchequer Chamber held that this 'deemed' payment was sufficient to constitute a payment of the debt for limitation purposes. A more general rule can also apply, which is that where the hand to pay and the hand to receive are one and the same, time does not run.[135] However, in *Re Finnegan's Estate*,[136] the fact that a mortgagee of land was himself the owner of an undivided portion of the mortgaged land did not, prior to 1926, give rise to such constructive payment of interest as to prevent time from running in favour of the owner of the remaining portion.

132 [2004] EWHC 1126 (Ch), [2004] 2 All ER (Comm) 422.

133 Similarly, rents received by a mortgagee in possession are not payments in respect of the mortgage debt: *Cockburn v Edwards* (1881) 18 Ch D 449. The position is otherwise if the net rents are paid by a receiver appointed by the mortgagee to manage the property, who in most cases will be agent of the mortgagor.

134 (1867) LR 2 ExCh 153.

135 *Hodgson v Salt* [1936] 1 All ER 95 at 98; *Burrell v Earl Egremont* (1844) 7 Beav 205; *Topham v Booth* (1887) 35 Ch D 607; *Re Hawes, Re Burchell, Burchell v Hawes* (1892) 62 LJ Ch 463.

136 [1906] 1 IR 360.

CHAPTER 7

Fraud, Concealment and Mistake

INTRODUCTION

7.01 The equitable principle that a statute should not be used as an instrument of fraud has long been relied upon by the courts of equity as a reason to disapply the statutory limitation period.[1] The principles developed by the courts of equity were codified for the first time by s 26 of the Limitation Act 1939 and are now contained in s 32 of the Limitation Act 1980 ('LA 1980'). Section 32(1) of the LA 1980 provides that, subject to limited exceptions,[2] where a period of limitation is prescribed by the Act and either:

(a) the action is based upon the fraud of the defendant,

(b) any fact relevant to the claimant's right of action has been deliberately concealed from him by the defendant, or

(c) the action is for relief from the consequences of a mistake,

the period of limitation shall not begin to run until the claimant has discovered the fraud, concealment or mistake (as the case may be) or could with reasonable diligence have discovered it. References in this subsection to the defendant include references to the defendant's agent and to any person through whom the defendant claims and his agent. Section 32(2) adds that, for the purposes of subsection (1), 'deliberate commission of a breach of duty in circumstances where it is unlikely to be discovered for some time amounts to deliberate concealment of the facts involved in that breach of duty'.

1 See *Lawrance v Lord Norreys* (1890) 15 App Cas 210 and Lightwood, *The Time Limit for Actions* (London: Butterworth & Co, 1909) at 297: '[d]elay, it was said in *Alden v Gregory* (1764) 2 Eden 280, will never purge a fraud'.

2 Excluded are: (i) actions against a *bona fide* purchaser of property for valuable consideration without notice: s 32(3), discussed in para 7.23; (ii) actions under the Fatal Accidents Act 1976: s 12(3); and (iii) the ten-year long-stop for claims under the Consumer Protection Act 1987: ss 11A(3) and 32(4A).

GENERAL PRINCIPLES APPLICABLE IN CASES OF FRAUD, DELIBERATE CONCEALMENT AND MISTAKE

The limitation period 'shall not begin to run'

7.02 A question of some controversy and importance is whether a deliberate concealment which occurs some time after the cause of action has accrued (and not been concealed) has any effect under section 32(1)(b). In *Tito v Waddell (No 2)*,[3] Megarry J commented that a subsequent concealment of a cause of action will not lead to an extension to the limitation period. However, this *obiter dictum* was not followed by the House of Lords, by a majority, in *Sheldon v Outhwaite*,[4] where Lord Nicholls held (with some reluctance) that the limitation period started to run afresh if it was deliberately concealed at a later time and that the period of time which had passed prior to the concealment occurring is set at naught. This decision has been the subject of some academic criticism,[5] but on balance the approach of the House of Lords has much to recommend it if the claimant had not become aware of the wrong prior to the defendant's later acts of concealment. If, however, the claimant has knowledge of a fact which he subsequently forgets about, which the defendant later takes steps to conceal, the Court of Appeal in *Ezekiel v Lehrer*[6] held that the claimant will be treated as having had knowledge of the fact at all times, with the consequence that s 32(1)(b) will have no role to play. The potentially broad effect of this is evident from the approach taken by Peter Smith J in *Bocardo SA v Star Energy UK Onshore Ltd*,[7] who noted that knowledge in this context includes knowledge of facts that would have been discovered with reasonable diligence, and that if there is constructive knowledge, a subsequent concealment does not give rise to an extension to the limitation period.

Fraud of the defendant or his agent, or any person through whom he claims

7.03 Section 32(1) provides that the deliberate concealment may be that of either the defendant or his agent or any person through whom the defendant claims or his agent. This provision has been widely interpreted and is not confined to a person who represents a principal in relations with third parties.[8] For example, in *Applegate v Moss*,[9] it was held that the reference to an agent included an independent contractor, and that, for limitation purposes, a delinquent builder was the 'agent' of the defendant developer who had sold a property to the claim-

3 [1977] Ch 106 at 245.
4 [1996] 1 AC 102.
5 McGee (1995) 111 LQR 562.
6 [2002] EWCA Civ 16; see also *Mellor v Partridge* [2013] EWCA Civ 477.
7 [2008] EWHC 1756 (Ch), [2009] 1 All ER 517 at para 122. The findings on limitation were not challenged on appeal: see [2011] 1 AC 380.
8 *Eddis v Chichester Constable* [1969] 2 Ch 345.
9 [1971] 1 QB 406.

ant. In *GL Baker Ltd v Medway Building and Supplies Ltd*,[10] the auditor of a company who was permitted to receive money on its behalf in fraudulent breach of trust made payments to the defendant, an innocent third party who did not give full value for the payments. The claimant's action against the defendant was brought more than six years after the payments had been made. In response to a limitation defence, it argued that the cause of action had been concealed by the auditor, and that it was through his fraud that they had their claim to the money. The arguments of the claimant were accepted, with Danckwerts J finding that the auditor's concealment of the payments affected the defendant's ability to rely on a limitation defence.[11]

Fraud, concealment and mistake must be specifically pleaded

7.04 Where fraud, deliberate concealment or mistake is relied upon as postponing the limitation period, it must be sufficiently alleged in the pleading to bring the case within the appropriate statutory provision.[12] In an action where the expiry of the limitation period bars the remedy but not the substantive right, a plea of deliberate concealment can be advanced in a reply to defence,[13] as may a plea that time only ran from the date of discovery of the fraud of the defendant.[14] However, where the title is barred as well as the remedy, it is suggested in *Halsbury's Laws* that the plea must be contained in the particulars of claim as it is part of the cause of action.[15] While many of the cases cited in support of these propositions are of some antiquity, it is submitted that they are sound in principle and continue to have effect, as CPR 15.8 has retained the ability of a claimant to file a reply to defence. The particulars of claim must contain precise and full allegations of the facts and circumstances of the fraud or deliberate concealment (or mistake) alleged to have occurred.[16] As was stated by Millett LJ in *Armitage v Nurse*:[17]

> 'If the facts pleaded are consistent with innocence, it is not open to the court to find fraud unless an allegation of fraud or dishonesty is expressly made. Thus an allegation that a Defendant "knew or ought to have known" is not a clear and unequivocal allegation of actual knowledge and will not, without more, support a finding of fraud.'

This statement of principle was recently followed in *Seaton v Seddon*[18] by Roth J who rejected an argument that the difference in wording between the old RSC Ord 18, r 12 and the new CPR 16.4(1) and PD 16, para 8(2) had the effect that a

10 [1958] 1 WLR 1216.
11 The aspects of his judgment which deal with an allegation of fraudulent breach of trust are discussed in Ch 17.
12 *Halsbury's Laws of England* (5th edn, LexisNexis 2008), vol 68, para 948.
13 *Gibbs v Guild* (1881) 8 QBD 296
14 *Lynn v Bamber* [1930] 2 KB 72.
15 *Halsbury's Laws of England* (5th edn, LexisNexis 2008), vol 68, para 948.
16 *Lawrance v Lord Norreys* (1890) 15 App Cas 210 (HL).
17 [1998] Ch 241 at 256–257.
18 [2012] EWHC 735 Ch, [2013] 1 All ER 29.

claimant alleging fraud no longer had to furnish full particulars of the facts alleged to constitute the fraud. In so finding, he noted that the continued application of the old rules about furnishing full particulars of an allegation of fraud had been upheld by the House of Lords in *Three Rivers DC v Bank of England (No 3)*[19] as remaining relevant under the CPR.

Burden of proof and meaning of 'reasonable diligence'

7.05 The important question of who bears the burden of proof on the issue of whether reasonable diligence was exercised was addressed in *Paragon Finance Plc v DB Thakarar & Co (a firm)*,[20] where it was held that the claimant bears the burden of proof. In his judgment in *Paragon Finance*, Millett LJ stated as follows:

> '[T]he question is not whether the claimants should have discovered the fraud sooner; but whether they could with reasonable diligence have done so. The burden of proof is on them. They must establish that they could not have discovered the fraud without exceptional measures which they could not reasonably have been expected to take.[21] In this context the length of the applicable period of limitation is irrelevant. In the course of argument May LJ observed that reasonable diligence must be measured against some standard, but that the six year limitation period did not provide the relevant standard. He suggested that the test was how a person carrying on a business of the relevant kind would act if he had adequate but not unlimited staff and resources and were motivated by a reasonable but not excessive sense of urgency. I respectfully agree.'[22]

In his judgment in the Court of Appeal in *Law Society v Sephton & Co*,[23] Neuberger LJ (as he then was) approved of the 'authoritative guidance' contained in the judgment of Millett LJ in *Paragon Finance Plc v DB Thakarar & Co (a firm)*[24] and stated that there must be an assumption that the claimant desires to discover whether or not there has been a fraud. Not making any such assumption would rob the effect of the word 'could' of much of its significance, noting also that reasonable diligence carries with it 'the notion of a desire to know, and, indeed, to investigate'.

Exercise of reasonable diligence to discover the fraud or mistake

7.06 It will be a question of fact and degree whether a claimant could have discovered the fraud, concealment or mistake with the exercise of reasonable diligence. In *Deutsche Morgan Grenfell Group Plc v IRC*,[25] the House of Lords

19 [2001] UKHL 16, [2001] 2 All ER 513.
20 [1999] 1 All ER 400.
21 [2005] QB 1013 at para 116.
22 [1999] 1 All ER 400 at 418.
23 [2004] EWCA Civ 1627, [2005] QB 1013 at para 110.
24 [1999] 1 All ER 400.
25 [2006] UKHL 49, [2007] 1 AC 558.

held that a revenue payment made under a provision which was struck down by the European Court of Justice had been made due to a mistake on the part of the claimant. This mistake (that the sums were due) was only 'discovered' when the judgment was delivered and was not something that could have been discovered sooner with the exercise of reasonable diligence.[26] In litigation which followed *Deutsche Morgan Grenfell*, it was held by the Northern Ireland Court of Appeal in *Mallusk Cold Storage Ltd v Department of Finance and Personnel*[27] that the failure by the claimant to pursue litigation at an earlier stage, the outcome of which was uncertain, did not amount to a failure to use reasonable diligence in discovering that an assessment was mistaken. The client of a solicitor is not expected to hire a second firm of solicitors to check on the work of a first, but is entitled to assume that the work has been competently done. However, at a certain point the negligence will be so gross as to be obvious to a non lawyer, in which case a claimant will not get the benefit of s 32(1).

Lack of diligence by the claimant's agent

7.07 A lack of diligence on the part of the claimant's agent in discovering the fraud, concealment or mistake has been held to justify the normal running of time in some cases,[28] but this rule is not universal and depends on the facts of the case.[29] In *Peco Arts Inc v Hazlitt Gallery Ltd*,[30] it was held that the negligence of the claimant's agent in failing to notice that a painting was a cheap reproduction and not an original was not to be attributed to the claimant. Webster J noted that the final clause in s 32(1) states that 'references in this subsection to the defendant includes references to the defendant's agent'; by application of the doctrine *expressio unius, exclusio alterius*, an inquiry into whether the claimant had been diligent precluded an inquiry into whether his agent had been diligent.

Relationship between s 32(1) and sections extinguishing title and rights of action upon the expiration of the limitation period

7.08 If a party is able to rely on s 32(1)(a), (b) or (c) then the limitation period does not 'begin to run' and consequently does not 'expire' such as would lead to a claimant's title to a chattel[31] or title to land[32] being extinguished. However, the ten-year long-stop for actions under Pt 1 of the Consumer Protection Act 1987,[33] which runs from the date the product was supplied by a producer or importer

26 [2006] UKHL 49, [2007] 1 AC 558 at para 31.
27 [2006] NICA 50.
28 *Gray v TP Bennett & Son* (1987) 43 BLR 63.
29 *William Hill Organisation Ltd v Bernard Sunley & Sons Ltd* (1982) 22 BLR 1 (CA); *Lewisham Borough Council v Leslie & Co Ltd* (1978) 12 BLR 22. In the latter case, Lord Denning MR noted at 28 that '[t]he architects and supervisors may even have turned a blind eye to the defects … there are still people about who have an "itching palm", as Shakespeare described it'.
30 [1983] 1 WLR 1315 at 1326, per Webster J.
31 LA 1980, s 3(2); *Eddis v Chichester Constable* [1969] 2 Ch 345.
32 LA 1980, s 17.
33 LA 1980, s 11A(3).

to another person,[34] may not be extended even in the case of fraud or deliberate concealment.[35] Section 32(5) of the LA 1980 expressly provides that if s 32(1)(b) applies then neither s 14A (three-year date of knowledge extension) nor s 14B (overriding 15-year time limit) shall apply. The difficult relationship between ss 14A and 32(5) was considered by the Court of Appeal in *Williams v Lishman, Sidwell, Campbell and Price Ltd*,[36] where the claimants brought proceedings in relation to negligent pension advice. They argued that because the first loss they suffered (a £38,000 transfer penalty) was concealed from them, this meant they could rely on s 32(1)(b) even though they later discovered a second head of loss (that it was not capital guaranteed) which they claimed was subject to s 14A of the LA 1980. The court held that the first loss was no longer 'relevant to their cause of action' once they found out about the second loss, but the comments of Rix LJ[37] are of interest in discussing a number of other variants on the facts that were before the court.

ACTIONS BASED ON FRAUD

7.09 Section 32(1)(a) of the LA 1980 refers to a right of action which is 'based upon the fraud of the defendant'. The phrase has led to difficulty in relation to causes of action which can arise either with or without fraudulent intent, such as conversion. In *Beaman v ARTS Ltd*,[38] the claimant left goods with the defendant for storage in 1935 and moved to Turkey. World War II commenced and, believing the claimant could not be traced, the defendant gave away the goods. After the war ended, the claimant demanded the return of her goods and, in response to a limitation defence, argued that her action was based on fraud and that there had been a fraudulent concealment of the defendant's wrong.[39] Denning J held there had been no fraud as the defendants had acted honestly. The Court of Appeal affirmed this decision, but for a different reason, namely that the phrase 'based upon the fraud' requires that fraud is an essential element of the claimant's action. This requirement was not satisfied in this case as conversion may occur without any fraud.[40] Instead, the section applies only to actions in deceit and other actions where the pleading would be defective without an allegation of fraud, such as fraudulent misrepresentation.[41] It has been held not to cover claims based solely on the unconscionable behaviour of a defendant.[42] In

34 Consumer Protection Act 1987, s 4(2).

35 LA 1980, s 32(4A). The extension of time that arises where an action seeks relief from the consequences of mistake within the meaning of s 32(1)(c) is unlikely to arise in this context.

36 [2010] EWCA Civ 418, [2010] PNLR 25.

37 [2010] EWCA Civ 418, [2010] PNLR 25 at paras 40–52.

38 [1949] 1 KB 550.

39 The fraudulent concealment aspect is discussed in para 7.15.

40 In the words of Lord Greene MR at 558, 'the word 'fraudulent' in connexion with conversion, however important it may be in a criminal matter is, in the civil action of conversion, so far as regards the cause of action, nothing more than an abusive epithet'.

41 *Regent Leisuretime Ltd v NatWest Finance Ltd* [2003] EWCA Civ 391 at para 100.

42 *Chagos Islanders v Attorney General* [2004] EWCA Civ 997; *The Times*, 21 September 2004.

Director of the Assets Recovery Agency v Szepietowski,[43] the provision was held not to apply in favour of a third party such as the Assets Recovery Agency which was not the party defrauded. In addition, the Court of Appeal noted that the allegation of 'mortgage fraud' which gave rise to the claim encompassed a number of causes of action where fraud was not a constituent element and as such fell outside the statutory provision.[44]

Knowledge of fraud requires knowledge of intention

7.10 In *Barnstaple Boat Co Ltd v Jones*,[45] the claimant brought proceedings in deceit alleging, *inter alia*, that a scheme whereby monies were advanced to a company to purchase a boat on the defendant's behalf had been an elaborate fiction. The company subsequently ended up in insolvent liquidation and the managing director was sued personally. While it was accepted by the Court of Appeal that it was 'blindingly obvious' that the company had dishonestly obtained the money in 1998, this was not sufficient knowledge on the claimant's part for the purpose of the LA 1980.[46] It stated that such an argument:

> '[F]ails to distinguish between dishonest acts of conversion or dishonestly interfering with such contract as there was between [the company and the claimant], where fraud is not a necessary allegation in pleading the case, and, the tort of deceit, where it is.'[47]

As the claimant did not know that the representations were untrue to the knowledge of the representor until discovery was obtained of the company's papers in the other proceedings in 2005, its claim was not statute barred as it had no knowledge of the fraud until that date.[48]

ACTIONS DELIBERATELY CONCEALED BY THE DEFENDANT

Concealment of 'any fact relevant to the claimant's right of action'

7.11 The phrase 'any fact relevant to the claimant's right of action' has been held to limit the effect of the section to situations where the concealed fact is a fact without which the claimant's case could not be pleaded rather than being a fact which would improve his prospect of success at trial, which is sometimes

43 [2007] EWCA Civ 766, *Times Law Reports,* 21 August 2007, [2008] Lloyd's Rep FC 10.
44 [2007] EWCA Civ 766 at para 46.
45 [2007] EWCA Civ 727, [2008] 1 All ER 1124.
46 As this was an application to strike out the claim, the Court of Appeal was content to say that the claimant had made out a strongly arguable case that reasonable diligence had been used to obtain the documents.
47 [2007] EWCA Civ 727, [2008] 1 All ER 1124 at para 33.
48 See also *Goose v Wilson Sandford & Co (a firm)* [1999] All ER (D) 57.

referred to as the 'statement of claim test'.[49] As was stated by Buxton LJ in *AIC Ltd v ITS Testing Services (UK) Ltd (The Kriti Palm)*, '[t]he court therefore has to look for the gist of the cause of action that is asserted, to see if that was available to the claimant without knowledge of the concealed material'.[50] In *Williams v Lishman, Sidwell, Campbell & Price*,[51] a first item of loss flowing from negligent advice was concealed but a second item of loss flowing from the same advice was not. In those circumstances, the Court of Appeal held that from the date the claimant discovered (or ought reasonably to have discovered) that he suffered the second loss, the suffering of the first loss was no longer a fact relevant to his cause of action as he knew enough to plead a case in negligence.[52] In commenting on this issue in *Ford & Warren v Warring-Davies*,[53] Coulson J held that it was unnecessary for a claimant to know why a defendant has breached the contract and that this is not a fact relevant to the cause of action, noting that '[i]t is the breach itself that gives rise to the cause of action, not the explanation for it'.[54]

Wording in s 26 of the Limitation Act 1939 and s 32(1)(b) of the LA 1980

7.12 The predecessor to s 32(1)(b) of the LA 1980 was s 26 of the Limitation Act 1939, which spoke of 'fraudulent concealment'. However, as was noted by Megarry J in *Tito v Waddell (No 2)*[55] as follows:

> '[T]he word "fraud" is here used in a sense which embraces conduct or inactivity which falls far short of fraud at common law ... Indeed, on the authorities, it can be said that in the ordinary use of language not only does "fraud" not mean "fraud" but also "concealed" does not mean "concealed," since any unconscionable failure to reveal is enough'.[56]

While the amended language in s 32(1)(b) of the LA 1980 is different from its predecessor, it was not intended to change the existing law 'but to bring the statute more obviously into line with the interpretation which the courts had put upon it'.[57] Section 32(2) of the LA 1980 adds that 'deliberate commission of a breach of duty in circumstances in which it is unlikely to be discovered for some

49 See *Johnson v Chief Constable of Surrey*, unreported, 19 October 1992 (CA) and *C v Mirror Group Newspapers* [1997] 1 WLR 131 (CA).

50 [2006] EWCA Civ 1601, [2007] 1 All ER (Comm) 667 at para 453. See also the comments of Rix LJ in *AIC Ltd v ITS Testing Services* at para 317.

51 [2010] EWCA Civ 418, [2010] PNLR 25.

52 See [2010] EWCA Civ 418 at paras 41–46 for a discussion of some interesting issues that might arise in cases involving variations on the facts in that case.

53 [2012] EWHC 3523 (QB).

54 [2012] EWHC 3523 (QB) at para 54. He sagely added that 'there are many cases of negligence and breach of contract where, even at the end of a trial, no one knows precisely why the Defendant acted in the way that he did": *ibid.*

55 [1977] Ch 106.

56 [1977] Ch 106 at 245.

57 *Clerk and Lindsell on Torts* (20th edn, London: Sweet & Maxwell, 2010) at para 32-24, referring to the Law Reform Committee's Twenty-First Report, Cmnd 6923 (1977), Pt II; see in particular paras 2.22–2.25.

time amounts to a deliberate concealment', which codifies the approach adopted by Lord Denning MR in *King v Victor Parsons & Co*,[58] quoted below. In his speech in *Cave v Robinson Jarvis & Rolf*,[59] Lord Millett expressed reservations as to whether the pre-LA 1980 case law remained relevant in interpreting the wording of the current provision. However, he said it was still possible to have regard to the prior case law to explain why parliament had used the wording contained in s 32(2), and in so doing narrowed the words used in the subsection to limit its effect to codifying the prior case law rather than giving the words their full ordinary meaning.

The test to be applied in cases of deliberate concealment

7.13 The precise ambit of what constitutes 'deliberate concealment' is not entirely clear, but Lord Evershed MR's discussion of the phrase 'fraudulent concealment' in his judgment in *Kitchen v Royal Air Force Association*[60] is widely quoted and is as follows:

> 'But it is now clear that the word fraud in the Limitation Act 1939 is by no means limited to common law fraud or deceit. Equally, it is clear, having regard to the decision in *Beaman v ARTS Ltd*[61] that no degree of moral turpitude is necessary to establish fraud within the section. What is covered by equitable fraud is a matter which Lord Hardwicke did not attempt to define 200 years ago, and I certainly shall not attempt to do so now, but it is, I think, clear that the phrase covers conduct which, having regard to some special relationship between the two parties concerned is an unconscionable thing for the one to do towards the other.'[62]

7.14 A second judgment which is often quoted is that of Lord Denning MR in *King v Victor Parsons & Co*,[63] which makes no reference to the need to establish a special relationship between the parties. In his judgment, he stated as follows:

> 'In order to show that he concealed the right of action by fraud, it is not necessary to show that he took active steps to conceal his wrongdoing or breach of contract. It is sufficient that he *knowingly* committed and did not tell the owner anything about it. He did the wrong or committed the breach secretly. By saying nothing he kept it secret. He conceals the right of action. He conceals it by fraud as those words have been interpreted in the cases. To this word "knowingly" there must be added "recklessly".'[64]

As against this, Lord Denning MR added:

> 'If however the defendant was quite unaware that he was committing a wrong or a breach of contract it would be different. So if by an honest blunder he unwittingly

58 [1973] 1 WLR 29.
59 [2003] 1 AC 384 at paras 19 and 23; see also the comments of Lord Scott at paras 43–45.
60 [1958] 1 WLR 563.
61 [1949] 1 KB 550.
62 [1958] 1 WLR 563 at 572–573.
63 [1973] 1 WLR 29.
64 [1973] 1 WLR 29 at 33–34.

> commits a wrong … or a breach of contract … then he could avail himself of the Statute of Limitations.'[65]

7.15 A further approach is evident in *Beaman v ARTS Ltd*,[66] where the Court of Appeal held that the defendant had fraudulently concealed its conversion of the claimant's goods, despite the trial judge's finding that there had been no dishonesty.[67] As stated by Lord Greene MR:

> 'A wrongdoer who "chooses his opportunity so wisely and acts so warily that he can safely calculate on not being found out for many a long day", cannot claim the advantage of the limitation period.'[68]

7.16 The different formulations of the test for deliberate concealment were the subject of consideration by the House of Lords in *Cave v Robinson Jarvis & Rolf*,[69] where it was argued that there was an inconsistency between *Beaman v ARTS Ltd*[70] and *King v Victor Parsons & Co.*[71] Lord Millett sought to reconcile the two decisions on grounds that what was at issue in the former case was an intentional tort which the claimant was unlikely to find out about for a long time, whereas the latter case involved a claim in negligence where different principles apply. This judicial gloss was required following the judgment of the Court of Appeal in *Brocklesby v Armitage & Guest (Note)*,[72] which held that a professional defendant would fall foul of s 32(2) if he had deliberately carried out the act alleged to constitute the negligence and had failed to disclose it to the defendant, if the wrong was unlikely to be discovered for some time. Lord Millett was receptive to arguments that this 'subvert[ed] the whole purpose of the Limitation Acts'[73] as it meant that a professional defendant would not gain the benefit of a limitation defence at all unless he was not negligent. He continued, summarising the test which should be applied in future in the following terms:

> 'In my opinion, s 32 deprives a defendant of a limitation defence in two situations: (i) where he takes active steps to conceal his own breach of duty after he has become aware of it; and (ii) where he is guilty of deliberate wrongdoing and conceals or fails to disclose it in circumstances where it is unlikely to be discovered for some time. But it does not deprive a defendant of a limitation defence where he is charged with negligence if, being unaware of his error or that he has failed to take proper care, there has been nothing for him to disclose.'[74]

While this attempt to rationalise the case law is useful, it may be asked whether Lord Millett's formulation of the test to be applied may operate unduly favour-

65 [1973] 1 WLR 29 at 34.
66 [1949] 1 KB 550 (CA). The facts of this case are set out above at para 7.09.
67 The Court of Appeal did, however, find that there had been some moral turpitude in the defendant's actions.
68 [1949] 1 KB 550 at 570.
69 [2003] 1 AC 384 at 394, per Lord Millett.
70 [1949] 1 KB 550.
71 [1973] 1 WLR 29.
72 [2002] 1 WLR 598.
73 [2002] UKHL 18, [2003] 1 AC 384 at para 15.
74 [2002] UKHL 18, [2003] 1 AC 384 at para 25.

ably towards professional defendants who negligently cause loss and do not disclose their negligence. The second speech delivered in *Cave v Robinson Jarvis & Rolf*[75] was that of Lord Scott, which envisages a wider role for s 32(2), which he notes focuses less on the concealed facts and more on the manner of the commission of the breach of duty. He said that the subsection applies where the defendant 'knew he was committing a breach of duty',[76] which, in the circumstances, is a breach the defendant was unlikely to discover for some time. This formulation includes both acts and omissions which occur deliberately in breach of duty. This formulation is more in keeping with the language actually used in the subsection and less likely to protect undeserving defendants, although neither version is obviously correct.

7.17 The decision in *Cave v Robinson Jarvis & Rolf*[77] was applied in *Giles v Rhind*,[78] where a liquidator applied to set aside various transactions entered into by the defendant under s 423 of the Insolvency Act 1986 and sought to rely on s 32(1)(b) to overcome a limitation defence. The Court of Appeal held that the reference in s 32(2) to the deliberate commission of an actionable wrong included not just a breach of duty (whether contractual, tortious or fiduciary) owed to the claimant but also entering into a transaction to defraud his creditors contrary to statute. The differences in approach between the speeches of Lord Millett and Lord Scott were the subject of some comment in *Williams v Fanshaw Porter & Hazelhurst (a firm)*.[79] In this case, a trainee solicitor acting for the claimant had consented to an order letting a party to the claimant's proceedings out of the case and a subsequent application to re-join him to the proceedings was unsuccessful. He was embarrassed by his mistake and did not tell the claimant, but the Court of Appeal held that he had deliberately concealed facts relevant to the cause of action against his firm because of his conscious decision not to inform the claimant and that his motive was irrelevant. Mance LJ noted that a solicitor owes a duty to keep his client informed about the general conduct of a matter he is handling and that a conscious decision had been made not to disclose facts relevant to the claimant's cause of action such that s 32(1)(b) was clearly applicable. His judgment proceeded to consider whether deliberate concealment of facts known to give rise to a cause of action is necessary, or whether a failure to disclose relevant facts, such as on account of laziness, would suffice; however, as a resolution of these issues was not necessary for his decision, he preferred to offer no views as to which he considered the correct approach to take.[80] The same issues arose again, but did not require a definitive ruling, in *Mortgage Express v Abensons Solicitors*,[81] where HH Judge David Cooke held that a distinction may exist between concealment arising in the context of an actual conflict of interest (where intention may not be required) and preferring the interests of one client

75 [2003] 1 AC 384. Technically, the speech of Lord Scott enjoyed the support of one more member of the House of Lords than did that of Lord Millett.
76 [2003] 1 AC 384 at para 60.
77 [2003] 1 AC 384.
78 [2008] EWCA Civ 118, [2009] Ch 191.
79 [2004] EWCA Civ 157, [2004] 1 WLR 3185.
80 See [2004] EWCA Civ 157, [2004] 1 WLR 3185 at paras 35–39.
81 [2012] EWHC 1000 (Ch), [2012] 2 EGLR 83.

over another (where deliberate conduct may be required) such that the application of s 32(2) operates differently in each case.

Concealment of identity of defendant

7.18 There is a lack of clarity in the case law as to whether a defendant who conceals his identity is guilty of fraudulent concealment of the cause of action. In *RB Policies at Lloyd's v Butler,*[82] a motor vehicle was stolen in 1940 by a person or persons unknown. The insured recovered the value of the vehicle from his insurers and transferred title to the vehicle to them. In 1947 the vehicle, now in the hands of a third party who had purchased it for value, was located and the insurance company sought its return. Its claim was held to be statute barred, with Streatfeild J finding that the cause of action had not been concealed by fraud, as it 'was only too obvious the moment when the owner missed his motor car'.[83] While this authority has long been relied upon and quoted in the textbooks, it is suggested that it no longer represents the law and may not have accurately stated the law when decided, albeit that it is correct on its facts. First, the facts satisfied Lord Greene MR's fraudulent concealment test in *Beaman v ARTS Ltd*[84] of the wise and wary thief, now embodied in s 32(2) of the LA 1980. Secondly, the approach takes no account of the specific protection afforded to an innocent purchaser for value without notice, which was contained in s 26 of the Limitation Act 1939 and has been retained in s 32(3) of the LA 1980. Although the clause is quoted in full in the headnote for the case report, the text of the judgment is to all intents and purposes *per incuriam* the innocent purchaser defence: Streatfeild J should have found that fraudulent concealment was established but that the innocent purchaser response was open to the defendant. As a sub-element of the first point, while a cause of action will accrue even if a claimant is ignorant of the facts constituting his cause of action,[85] knowledge of the name of the wrongdoer is a constituent element of the cause of action as in the words of Rix LJ in *Cressey v E Timm & Son Ltd*, 'one cannot sue "the driver of the other car", or even "my employer": a name has to be provided'[86]. For example, in *Photinopoulos v Photinopoulos*,[87] it was held by the Alberta Court of Appeal that an assault carried out by masked men had been planned so as to conceal the identities of the perpetrators, and as such the action was concealed by fraud within the meaning of their equivalent section. By contrast, if a defendant (whose identity is known) conceals his whereabouts or assets, this will not constitute the concealment of a fact relevant to the claimant's cause of action.[88]

82 [1950] 1 KB 76.
83 [1950] 1 KB 76 at 80.
84 [1949] 1 KB 550 (CA). The facts of this case are set out above at para 7.09.
85 *Cartledge v E Jopling & Sons Ltd* [1963] AC 758.
86 [2005] EWCA Civ 763, [2005] 1 WLR 3926 (CA) at para 35; see also *Taylor v McConville* [2009] NIQB 22, [2010] NIJB 31.
87 (1988) 54 DLR (4th) 372, (1988) CanLII 165 (AB CA); see also *Jonker v Davydov* (1995) CanLII 9033 (AB QB).
88 See the comments of Lord Lloyd in *Lowsley v Forbes* [1999] 1 AC 329 at 343.

Concealment and sexual abuse of minors

7.19 The Canadian courts have used the 'fraudulent concealment' provisions in their limitation legislation to deal with cases of incest and sexual abuse brought many years after they might ordinarily have been statute barred.[89] In *KM v HM*,[90] the Supreme Court of Canada applied a reasonable discoverability test to a case of sexual assault and incest, which it held constituted a breach of fiduciary duty on the part of the abuser. In addition, it commented that a plea of fraudulent concealment can be raised in incest cases, as the abuse tends to take place in a climate of secrecy and as the victim's silence will often be obtained through various insidious means by a trusted family member who conditions the victim to conceal the wrong from him/herself. As the Canadian case law on the limitation of actions imposes a discoverability test as a general rusle,[91] it has not proven necessary to develop the principles of concealment in the context of sexual abuse. Equally, in light of the decision in *A v Hoare,*[92] which held that an action claiming damages for trespass to the person (ie including sexual assault) is a personal injuries action and thus subject to s 33 of the LA 1980, it has not proven necessary for the courts in England to consider the Canadian case law in this area.

ACTIONS SEEKING RELIEF FROM THE CONSEQUENCES OF MISTAKE

Mistake must form part of the cause of action

7.20 Section 32(1)(c) of the LA 1980 uses the phrase 'action ... for relief from the consequences of mistake' in describing the class of action which may benefit from an extension of time on grounds of mistake. This phrase was considered in *Phillips-Higgins v Harper*,[93] where the claimant had been underpaid sums due to her under a contract, which due to a mistake on her part she had not noticed (though her employer, the defendant, had). She sought to rely on the predecessor to s 32(1)(c) but was unsuccessful as it was held that the provision is limited to cases where mistake forms part of the cause of action, but does not extend to cases where the claimant was mistaken as to, or ignorant of, his rights. In his judgment at first instance in *Phillips-Higgins*, not challenged on appeal, Pearson J stated as follows:

> 'What, then, is the meaning of provision (c)? The right of action is for relief from the consequences of a mistake. It seems to me that this wording is carefully chosen to indicate a class of actions where a mistake has been made which has had certain consequences and the plaintiff seeks to be relieved from those consequences. Familiar examples are, first, money paid in consequence of a mistake: in such a

89 See generally, Grace and Vella, *Civil Liability for Sexual Abuse and Violence in Canada* (Toronto: Butterworths, 2000).
90 (1992) 96 DLR (4th) 289.
91 *City of Kamloops v Nielsen* [1984] 2 SCR 2; *Central Trust Co v Rafuse* [1986] 2 SCR 147.
92 [2008] UKHL 6, [2008] 1 AC 844.
93 [1954] 1 QB 411.

case the mistake is made, in consequence of the mistake the money is paid, and the action is to recover that money back. Secondly, there may be a contract entered into in consequence of a mistake, and the action is to obtain the rescission or, in some cases, the rectification of such a contract. Thirdly, there may be an account settled in consequence of mistakes; if the mistakes are sufficiently serious there can be a reopening of the account.'[94]

7.21 In his speech in the Supreme Court decision in *Test Claimants in the FII Group Litigation v Revenue and Customs Comrs,*[95] Lord Walker noted that he and Lord Hoffmann had expressed doubts concerning the correctness of *Phillips-Higgins* in *Deutsche Morgan Grenfell Group Plc v IRC*,[96] as had several academic commentators,[97] but stated as follows:

> 'Having considered the matter with the benefit of much fuller argument than in *DMG*, I have reached the clear conclusion that *Phillips-Higgins v Harper* [1954] 1 QB 411 was rightly decided ... [D]eparture from Pearson J's relatively narrow interpretation would bring a real risk ... that "the scope of [s 32(1)(c)] might be expanded dangerously close to the basic rule of common law limitation that ignorance of the existence of a cause of action does not prevent time from running. It would be difficult to find any principled stopping-place for the expansion.'[98]

The decision in *Phillips-Higgins v Harper*[99] should now be regarded as settled law. It should also be noted that s 32(1)(c) makes no provision for cases where there has been a concealment of a right of action by mistake.

Judicial pronouncements and the discovery of mistakes of law

7.22 In *Kleinwort Benson Ltd v Lincoln City Council,*[100] it was held by the House of Lords that an action to recover sums paid under a mistake of law fell within s 32(1)(c) of the LA 1980 even where the payment had been made under a settled understanding of the law which was subsequently departed from by judicial decision. While it was argued that the word 'discovered' could not be applied to a situation where reliance on a settled understanding of the law (ie non-recoverability of monies paid by reason of a mistake of law), especially as a mistake of law of this type might lie undiscovered for many years,[101] it was held that the wording of the section was clear and that any change to the rule was a matter for

94 [1954] 1 QB 411 at 418.

95 [2012] UKSC 19, [2012] 2 AC 337.

96 [2006] UKHL 49, [2007] 1 AC 558 at paras 22, 91 and 147.

97 Such as Edelman, 'Limitation Periods and the Theory of Unjust Enrichment' (2005) 68 MLR 848; however, he noted that the case note of Burrows, 'Restitution in Respect of Mistakenly Paid Tax' (2005) 121 LQR 540 was generally supportive of the decision.

98 [2012] UKSC 19, [2012] 2 AC 337 at paras 62–63.

99 [1954] 1 QB 411.

100 [1999] 2 AC 349. This judgment extended the scope of *In re Diplock* [1948] Ch 465, which had held that an action for monies paid under a mistake of fact came within the statutory provision: see Lord Goff at 388.

101 [1999] 2 AC 349 at 389, per Lord Goff: 'the effect of s 32(1)(c) is that the cause of action in a case such as the present may be extended for an indefinite period of time'.

parliament. These principles were applied in *Deutsche Morgan Grenfell Group Plc v IRC*,[102] where the House of Lords held that a revenue payment made under a provision which was struck down by the European Court of Justice had been made due to a mistake on the part of the claimant. This mistake (that the sums were due) was only 'discovered' when the judgment was delivered, and was thus recoverable outside the ordinary limitation period.

DEFENCE FOR INNOCENT PURCHASER OF PROPERTY WITHOUT NOTICE

7.23 Section 32(3) of the LA 1980 provides that the section may not be relied upon to extend the limitation period for an action to recover any property, recover the value of the property,[103] set aside any transaction affecting or enforce any charge against any property, where the property has been purchased for valuable consideration by an innocent third party after the fraud, concealment or mistaken transaction occurred. A purchaser is an innocent party in the case of the fraud or the concealment of a fact, as the case may be, if he neither knew nor had reason to believe that the fraud or concealment had taken place.[104] The knowledge of an agent of the defendant may be attributed to the defendant.[105] In the case of a mistake, he comes within the subsection if he did not at the time of the purchase know or have reason to believe that a mistake had been made.[106] Difficulty arises in cases where the 'innocent' defendant or his agent deliberately refrained from making inquiries, the results of which he might not care to know, and in several such cases the courts have held that this precludes him from relying on his lack of knowledge.[107] There are also dicta to the effect that the fact that a defendant ought to know, but does not know, of circumstances which would give rise to a right of action for the claimant, is not sufficient to establish concealment by fraud.[108] Ultimately, it is a question of fact and degree and the courts retain a significant discretion in applying s 32(3).

102 [2006] UKHL 49, [2007] 1 AC 558.

103 The subsection codifies the broad interpretation given to the Limitation Act 1939, s 26 by Lord Denning MR in *Eddis v Chichester Constable* [1969] 2 Ch 345.

104 LA 1980, s 32(4)(a).

105 *Eddis v Chichester Constable* [1969] 2 Ch 345.

106 LA 1980, s 32(4)(b).

107 *Westminster City Council v Croyalgrange Ltd* [1986] 1 WLR 674 (HL) and *Mallon v Allon* [1964] 1 QB 385 at 394.

108 *King v Victor Parsons & Co* [1973] 1 All ER 206 at 212, per Megaw LJ.

PART III

Contract, Unjust Enrichment and Tort

CHAPTER 8

Contract

INTRODUCTION

8.01 The Limitation Act 1980 ('LA 1980') provides that a limitation period of six years applies to an action for breach of a simple contract[1] and that a 12-year limitation period applies to an action for breach of a contract under seal.[2] The limitation period runs from the date of accrual of the cause of action, which in the case of both simple contracts and contracts under seal is the date on which the breach of contract occurs. Time runs from the date of breach even where the claimant has not suffered any loss at that time or if he does not know of the breach (absent fraud, concealment or mistake).[3] Most importantly, if the damages claimed by a claimant consist of or include damages for personal injuries, the action is governed by ss 11–14 and 33 of the LA 1980 and not s 5.[4] While an extended limitation period was introduced for non-personal injuries negligence actions by the Latent Damage Act 1986, this does not cover actions for breach of contract.[5] No limitation period applies if equitable relief (such as an order for specific performance or an injunction) is claimed, as opposed to a claim for damages,[6] but in such cases the equitable defences of acquiescence and *laches* may be raised.[7] The limitation period for an action for breach of contract will be extended in cases of disability;[8] acknowledgment or part payment;[9] and fraud, deliberate concealment or mistake.[10]

1 LA 1980, s 5. An action on a foreign judgment is treated as an action on a contract debt: see *Grant v Easton* (1883) 13 QBD 302; *Berliner Industriebank Aktiengesellschaft v Jost* [1971] 2 All ER 1513. The Contracts (Rights of Third Parties) Act 1999, s 7(3) applies the LA 1980 ss 5 and 8 (as appropriate) to a claim brought by any party in reliance on the rights afforded by the 1999 Act.

2 LA 1980, s 8. A contract under seal is a type of 'specialty' and the requirements for entering into a contract under seal are discussed in Ch 20.

3 *Lynn v Bamber* [1930] 2 KB 72.

4 LA 1980, s 11(1); see Ch 13.

5 LA 1980, s 14A(1); see Ch 12.

6 LA 1980, s 36(1)

7 LA 1980, s 36(2); see Ch 18.

8 LA 1980, s 28; see Ch 5.

9 LA 1980, ss 29–31; see Ch 6.

10 LA 1980, s 32; see Ch 7.

CLASSIFICATION OF CAUSES OF ACTION

Concurrent liability in contract and tort

8.02 If the same set of facts gives rise to a cause of action in contract and in tort,[11] a claimant may choose to pursue whichever claim gives him the most advantageous limitation period.[12] In cases brought against professional advisers, this rule will have the result that an action in tort may present the more attractive limitation period to a claimant, as the limitation period in tort only runs from the date when the claimant first suffers loss or damage, which may be after the date when the breach of contract occurred.[13]

Contract and personal injuries

8.03 If an action for breach of contract 'consists of *or includes*' a claim for damages for personal injuries then the entire action is treated as a personal injuries action[14] and is subject to a three-year limitation period.[15] This unusual feature of the limitation code is most likely to arise in cases primarily focusing on financial loss where a secondary claim for personal injuries is advanced, for example in defective premises or solicitor's negligence cases where the claimant advances a claim for damages for distress, anxiety or depression. A claimant may apply to amend his pleadings to delete the claim for damages for personal injuries, but the courts will not in all cases allow such an amendment to be made.[16]

ACCRUAL OF THE CAUSE OF ACTION FOR BREACH OF CONTRACT

The cause of action for breach of contract: general principles

8.04 There is no statutory definition for the expression 'cause of action'. The classic definition of a cause of action is that of Lord Esher MR in *Read v Brown*:[17]

> '[E]very fact which it would be necessary for the claimant to prove, if traversed, in order to support his right to the judgment of the court. It does not comprise every piece of evidence which is necessary to prove each fact, but every fact which is necessary to be proved.'[18]

11 See eg *Midland Bank Trust Co Ltd v Hett, Stubbs & Kemp* [1977] Ch 384 (solicitors); *London Congregational Union Inc v Harriss & Harriss* [1988] 1 All ER 15 (architects); and *Pirelli General Cable Works Ltd v Oscar Faber & Partners* [1983] AC 1 (engineers).
12 *Henderson v Merrett Syndicates Ltd* [1995] 2 AC 145.
13 See *Law Society v Sephton & Co* [2006] 2 AC 543.
14 LA 1980, s 11(1).
15 LA 1980, s 11(4), subject to extension on date of knowledge grounds under ss 11–14 or the potential to disapply the limitation period under s 33: see further, Ch 13.
16 See *Azaz v Denton* [2009] EWHC 1759 (QB), discussed in para 13.04.
17 (1888) 22 QBD 128.
18 (1888) 22 QBD 128 at 131.

In an action for breach of contract the cause of action is the breach, as a right of action accrues as soon as there has been a breach of contract, notwithstanding that no damage (or only nominal damage) has been suffered at that time.[19] There must also be in existence a competent claimant and competent defendant in order for the limitation period to run: the special rules relating to unadministered intestate estates[20] and defendants having diplomatic immunity[21] were considered earlier in the book. The fact that a defendant cannot be traced is not an impediment to the running of time[22] and nor are a number of procedural bars to the bringing of proceedings.[23] It is a question of fact in each case as to whether, or when, a breach occurred and the case law concerning different types of breach of contract is discussed below.

Anticipatory, repudiatory, successive and continuing breaches

8.05 If, prior to the date fixed for performance of a contractual obligation, a party to a contract demonstrates a clear and unequivocal intention not to perform their obligations,[24] the contract is breached and the other party may sue for breach of contract without waiting for the date of performance to arrive.[25] But if the contract is not discharged, either because the breach is not sufficiently fundamental or because the innocent party does not accept the repudiation, each breach will give rise to a separate cause of action.[26] A covenant may be breached on multiple occasions, such as an obligation to pay monthly instalments of interest[27] or rent,[28] each of which gives rise to a separate cause of action. Some covenants, such as a covenant to repair,[29] may give rise to a continuing breach. In the case of either a series of breaches or a continuing breach, a defendant will have a limitation defence for the discrete breaches and the portion of the continuing breach which occurred more than six (or 12) years prior to the bringing of the proceedings.

19 See *Gibbs v Guild* (1881) 8 QBD 296 at 302.

20 See *Burdick v Garrick* (1870) LR 5 Ch App 233 at 241; the position is different if there is an executor named in the will: see *Meyappa Chetty v Supramanian Chetty* [1916] 1 AC 603 at 608; see the discussion in paras 1.20 and 19.05.

21 *Musurus Bey v Gadban* [1894] 2 QB 352, discussed in para 1.20.

22 *RB Policies at Lloyd's v Butler* [1950] 1 KB 76, discussed in para 7.16.

23 See para 1.22.

24 The necessary clear intention can be established by showing either an express representation (see *Hochster v De La Tour* (1853) 2 El & Bl 678; 118 ER 922) or that the promisor had put himself in a position where he could no longer perform the promise (see *Synge v Synge* [1894] 1 QB 466).

25 *Hochster v De La Tour* (1853) 2 El & Bl 678 at 691, 118 ER 922 at 927.

26 *Amott v Holden* (1852) 18 QB 593; 118 ER 224; *Hochster v De La Tour* (1853) 2 El & Bl 678 at 691, 118 ER 922 at 927; *Eaglehill Ltd v J Needham (Builders) Ltd* [1973] AC 992.

27 Bowyer v Woodman (1867) LR 3 Eq 313. Technically, a right of action to recover arrears of interest in respect of monies charged on land is governed by the LA 1980, s 20.

28 *Archbold v Scully* (1861) 9 HLC 360, see the LA 1980, s 19.

29 *Spoor v Green* (1874) LR 9 Ex 99 at 111.

Continuing obligations and failure to perform a contractual obligation

8.06 If the breach of contract involves a failure to perform a contractual obligation, the claimant's cause of action will accrue on the date when the obligation should have been performed.[30] An exception exists in the case of parties who remain in a contractual relationship. In *Midland Bank Trust Co Ltd v Hett, Stubbs and Kemp*,[31] it was held that time will not start to run in such a case until the date when the relevant obligation became impossible to perform. In *Bell v Peter Browne & Co*,[32] it was stated by Nicholls LJ that a request by a claimant that the defendant remedy a breach will not cause the six-year limitation period to run afresh, and that a remediable breach of contract is just as much of a breach as an irremediable breach. While this would appear to be in conflict with *Midland Bank Trust Co Ltd v Hett, Stubbs and Kemp*, the solicitors in the latter case had continued to act for the claimant after the breach of contract whereas the solicitors in *Bell v Peter Browne & Co* had ceased to act for the claimant more than six years before the proceedings were issued.

8.07 In *Green v Eadie*,[33] a firm of solicitors failed to investigate title properly in relation to a conveyance leading to a mapping discrepancy. The claimant issued proceedings claiming damages for breach of contract (and negligence) more than six years after the contract for sale was signed but less than six years after completion, in circumstances where the parties appear to have accepted that the claimant could have rescinded the contract prior to completion because of the discrepancy. The claim was found to be statute barred as, even if the defendant owed the claimant a continuing contractual duty to remedy their breach, the failure to remedy the breach did not give rise to a new cause of action on each day it remained unremedied. The decision in *Green* relied on *Bell v Peter Browne & Co*,[34] but an important factor in *Bell* was that the court rejected the claimant's suggestion that it should recognise an 'implied and presumably gratuitous'[35] duty to revisit earlier and completed work and be vigilant to correct mistakes. By contrast, the decision in *Green v Eadie* hollows out a solicitor's obligation to advise his client in relation to her right to rescind a contract prior to completion (which could apparently have been done without difficulty), even if this is part of the duties undertaken in return for the professional fees charged. As the 'continuing to act' factor separating *Midland Bank Trust Co Ltd v Hett, Stubbs and Kemp*[36] and *Bell v Peter Browne & Co*[37] was not determinative in *Green v Eadie*, this leaves only the misfeasance/non-feasance distinction separating the two lines of authority, which does not appear to have been the basis for the decision. While

30 *Bell v Peter Browne & Co* [1990] 2 QB 495.
31 [1979] Ch 384.
32 [1990] 2 QB 495 at 500–501.
33 [2011] EWHC B24 (Ch), [2012] Ch 363; see also *Vai Industries (UK) Ltd v Bostock & Bramley* [2003] EWCA Civ 1069.
34 [1990] 2 QB 495.
35 [1990] 2 QB 495 at 512, per Mustill LJ.
36 [1979] Ch 384.
37 [1990] 2 QB 495.

further reconciliation of the two lines of authorities may be anticipated, in all cases it is important to focus on the precise breach and loss alleged as including a statute barred claim can prove fatal to the overall action.

Claims arising out of the sale of goods

8.08 Unless the date for payment is specified in the contract,[38] a seller may maintain an action for the price of goods from the date when the property in the goods has passed to the buyer.[39] The passing of property is governed by the intention of the parties,[40] with s 18 of the Sale of Goods Act 1979 ('SOGA 1979') setting out five rules for ascertaining the intention of the parties which apply 'unless a different intention appears'. The most straightforward of these states that where there is an unconditional contract for the sale of specific goods in a deliverable state, the property in the goods passes when the contract is made.[41] Viewed from a limitation perspective, this provision is in slight conflict with s 28 of the SOGA 1979, which states that, unless otherwise agreed, there is an implied term that the obligation to pay arises at the same time as the obligation to deliver the goods.[42] If a period of credit is allowed, a breach of contract only occurs if payment is not made when the term of credit expires.[43] A buyer's right of action for breach of the implied term as to title accrues at the time of the sale, and in the case of an agreement to sell, at the time when the property is to pass.[44] If the goods are defective, time starts to run against the vendor from the time the goods were received and not when the defect becomes apparent. Thus in *Lynn v Bamber*,[45] the purchaser of young plum trees who only found out years later that the wrong species had been supplied was held to be statute barred in his claim against the vendor.

Claims for works done and materials, or for services rendered

8.09 In the absence of an express provision, the obligation to pay arises when the work as a whole is completed.[46] If the parties agree that payment should be made by instalments, or that a period of credit should be extended after the work has been completed, the contract is breached if payment is not made when the instalment falls due or the term of credit expires.[47] In construction contracts, it

38 SOGA 1979, s 49(2).
39 SOGA 1979, s 49(1).
40 SOGA 1979, s 17.
41 SOGA 1979, s 18, r 1.
42 SOGA 1979, s 28. The rules about delivery are set out in s 29 of the Act.
43 *Helps v Winterbottom* (1831) 2 B & Ad 431, 109 ER 1203.
44 SOGA 1979, s 12(1). This section also deals with the implied terms about quiet possession and the transfer of the property free from incumbrance.
45 [1930] 2 KB 72; fraud and fraudulent concealment were pleaded but were not made out on the facts.
46 *Coburn v Colledge* [1897] 1 QB 702; *Emery v Day* (1843) 1 CM&R 245, 149 ER 1071. The special rules governing a solicitor's action to recover fees from his own client are discussed below in para 8.21.
47 *Helps v Winterbottom* (1831) 2 B & Ad 431, 109 ER 1203.

is frequently provided that a third party (such as an architect) will issue interim payment certificates for work done followed by a final certificate at the end of the contract. The right of action in respect of the work included in an interim certificate accrues when the certificate is (or ought to be) issued rather than when the work is done.[48] However, a claim on a final certificate gives rise to a new cause of action as this contains the certifying party's definitive view of the value of the work.[49] In general the cause of action for defective work will arise at the time when the works as a whole are, or ought to have been, completed.[50] If the claimant also has a concurrent cause of action in tort, this will in many cases afford him a more generous limitation period, as time will only run from when damage is suffered[51] or could reasonably have been observed or ascertained.[52] In the case of a failure to complete on time, the cause of action will arise at the date when the works ought to have been completed.[53]

8.10 The principles outlined in the previous paragraph are well illustrated by the facts of *Smales v Lea*,[54] a case where a surveyor carried out work for an insured in relation to an insurance claim, with the remedial works being completed by late 1998. The contract of insurance provided for payment of surveyors' fees and the surveyor furnished his account to the insurers in 2001. The insurers thought his account too high and in 2006 made their final offer of payment in part. In 2008 the claimant issued proceedings against his client and argued that time only ran from 2006 as he was obliged to recover as much as possible from the insurers prior to looking to them for payment. The Court of Appeal held that his claim was statute barred and that it would be rare that a contract to provide professional services would be found to be an 'entire agreement'[55] where the professional could only sue for his fees where every item of work had been completed. It also rejected an argument that time only ran from when the insurers had made an offer in respect of part of his fees and held that time had run from a short time after the works were completed, at the latest from 1999. As this rendered the action long statute barred, the court did not have to go further and ask whether his fees fell due in tranches as work was carried out between 1996 and 1998 or only at their overall conclusion. The answer to this issue, in any particular case, will depend on whether the claimant could have sued for his fees at that time and on whether the work done can readily be broken down into discrete items of work, each giving rise to a separate right to payment.

48 *Henry Boot Construction Ltd v Alstom Combined Cycles Ltd* [2005] EWCA Civ 814, [2005] 3 All ER 932.

49 *Henry Boot Construction Ltd v Alstom Combined Cycles Ltd* [2005] EWCA Civ 814, [2005] 3 All ER 932; but cf *Birse Construction Ltd v McCormick (UK) Ltd* [2004] EWHC 3053 (TCC), (2004) 99 Con LR 181, affd [2005] EWCA Civ 940, [2005] BLR 523, where the cause of action was held to have accrued when the work was done.

50 *Bellway (South East) Ltd v Holley* (1984) 28 BLR 139; *Chelmsford District Council v Evers* (1984) 25 BLR 99.

51 *Pirelli General Cable Works Ltd v Oscar Faber & Partners* [1983] AC 1.

52 LA 1980, s 14(A); see further Ch 12.

53 *Kitney v Jones Lang Wootton* (1988) 20 EG 88.

54 [2011] EWCA Civ 1325, (2012) 140 Con LR 70; see also the solicitor's fees case *Phillips & Co (a firm) v Bath Housing Co-Operative Ltd* [2012] EWCA Civ 1591.

55 *Hoenig v Isaacs* [1952] 2 All ER 176.

Contracts of loan

8.11 If monies are loaned, it is a matter of construction of the contract to determine the date from which the limitation period will run. If a time for repayment is stipulated, time will run from that date. For example, in *Reeves v Butcher*,[56] a loan was made to the defendant for a two-year period, subject to a provision granting the right to reclaim the principal sum if an instalment of interest became overdue by 21 days. It was held that the right of action for the return of the principal sum ran from the date interest was overdue by 21 days rather than the end of the two-year period. Prior to the passing of the LA 1980, a rule of some antiquity[57] held that if no time for repayment was specified or if the loan was expressed to be repayable 'on demand', time ran from the moment the loan was made, which had unforeseen consequences for informal loans (especially involving family members) and led to much case law on the issue of whether the making of a demand was in fact a condition precedent to a right of action accruing.[58] The purpose of the rule may have been to allow creditors to bring proceedings without serving a formal demand for payment first,[59] but it has now been replaced by s 6 of the LA 1980. This section applies where the loan agreement does not provide for payment on a specific date and where the obligation to repay is not dependent on a demand being made.[60] In such a case, time only runs from the date of demand.[61] The final clause in s 6(2) provides that the section shall not apply where the debtor enters into 'any collateral obligation to pay the amount of the debt ... (as, for example, by delivering a promissory note as security for the debt) on terms which would exclude the application of this provision to the contract of loan if they applied directly to repayment of the debt'. This clause was successfully invoked in *Boot v Boot*,[62] where the Court of Appeal held that in such circumstances the time for repayment of the loan ran from the date it was made and not the date of demand. Once the right to recover the principal is statute barred, any claim for payment of interest on the principal is also irrecoverable, even if it fell due within the previous six years, as the interest is accessory to the principal.[63]

Loans secured by a mortgage or charge over real or personal property

8.12 If a loan agreement is secured by a mortgage or charge over real or personal property, the limitation period is the 12-year period contained in s 20(1) of the LA 1980 and not the six-year period contained in s 5. Time runs from the date

56 [1891] 2 QB 509.

57 It was regarded as settled law in *Norton v Ellam* (1837) 2 M&W 461; 150 ER 839.

58 See *Re Brown's Estate* [1893] 2 Ch 300 and *Lloyd's Bank v Margolis* [1954] 1 WLR 644.

59 McGee, *Limitation Periods*, 5th edn (London: Sweet & Maxwell, 2006), para 10.014.

60 LA 1980, s 6(2).

61 LA 1980, s 6(3); see *Re Westminster Property Management Ltd (No 4); Boyden v Stern* [2002] EWHC 520 (Ch), [2004] BCC 599.

62 [1996] 2 FCR 713, (1996) 73 P & CR 137.

63 *Hollis v Palmer* (1836) 2 Bing (NC) 713, 132 ER 275; *Elder v Northcott* [1930] 2 Ch 422.

on which the right to receive the money accrued.[64] This section and the related sections on other contractual rights relating to land, such as the limitation period for an action to recover rent,[65] are considered further in Chapter 15.

Trading accounts and bank accounts

8.13 In the case of trading accounts, one must again ascertain whether the account is payable as soon as an amount is outstanding on it, or only when a demand is made. It would appear that in the absence of the parties having addressed their minds to when the account is payable, a demand is not a precondition to the account being due and time runs from the date that a sum became outstanding on the account.[66] The rules on acknowledgment and part payment are particularly important in these circumstances.[67] In *Re Footman Bower & Co Ltd*,[68] a case where none of the debts were statute barred at the date of the payment, it was held that each payment towards an account was 'in respect of' the entire balance and that time started to run afresh from the date of each payment on the entire balance outstanding.

8.14 The position at common law in respect of monies held in a bank account is that, unless the contrary is agreed, a demand by the customer is a condition precedent to payment.[69] Accordingly, time runs from the date of demand[70] and not the date on which monies were lodged, even if the monies have lain dormant in the bank account for many years. If the relationship of banker and customer is terminated before a demand is made, the money thereupon becomes repayable.[71] If unauthorised debits are made from a customer's account, it was held in *National Bank of Commerce v National Westminster Bank*[72] that time starts to run from the date on which the customer demands repayment of the monies in his account.

8.15 An overdraft is simply a loan by the banker to the customer. In *Parr's Banking Co v Yates*,[73] it was held that a demand was not a condition precedent to the bank bringing an action and that time ran against the bank in respect of each advance from the time when it was made. However, the correctness of this decision has been challenged and it may not still represent the law,[74] and in addition

64 LA 1980, s 20(1).
65 LA 1980, s 19: six-year limitation period.
66 *Lloyd's Bank v Margolis* [1954] 1 WLR 644.
67 See Ch 6 and in particular para 6.28.
68 [1961] Ch 443.
69 *Atkinson v Bradford Third Equitable Building Society* (1890) 25 QBD 377 (deposit accounts); *N Joachimson v Swiss Bank Corporation* [1921] 3 KB 110 (current accounts).
70 Repeated demands do not start time running afresh: *Bank of Baroda v Mahomed* [1999] Lloyd's Rep Bank 14.
71 *Re Russian Commercial and Industrial Bank* [1955] Ch 148.
72 [1990] 2 Lloyd's Rep 514.
73 [1898] 2 QB 460.
74 Hapgood, *Paget's Law of Banking* (13th edn, London: Butterworths, 2007) at 155, doubts whether *Parr's Banking* continues to represent the law.

one must have regard to the standard terms and conditions of the bank in question which will usually supersede the default common law rules.

Bills of exchange

8.16 If a bill of exchange is payable on demand or on maturity, time ordinarily runs from the date of making or accepting the instrument,[75] or its maturity,[76] as applicable, and no demand is necessary. Where a bill is payable at sight, time begins to run from the date of its presentment.[77] In *Eaglehill Ltd v J Needham (Builders) Ltd*,[78] the House of Lords held that the date of accrual of a cause of action based on the dishonouring of a bill of exchange was the date when the notice of dishonour was received, and that it was irrelevant that the dishonour was inevitable in advance of that date.

Contracts of guarantee

8.17 The issue of when a guarantee becomes enforceable depends on the construction of the contract of guarantee. For example, in a case where the guarantee was for the safety of the money advanced, it was held that time only ran from the date when the security was shown to be unsafe.[79] If there is no express provision requiring a demand, the guarantor's liability will arise at the same time as that of the principal debtor.[80] If the guarantee is of an existing debt, this will mean that the cause of action on the guarantee will accrue as soon as it is given.[81] If a principal sum is guaranteed together with interest, this can have the result that the creditor's claim will be statute barred in respect of the principal but not in respect of interest payments which fell due within the previous six years.[82] It was held by Chitty J in *Re Brown's Estate*[83] that as a guarantee involves a promise to pay a collateral sum rather than a present debt, a guarantee payable 'on demand' is treated differently to a loan payable on demand, and the making of a demand in such a case is a condition precedent to a liability arising. This can lead to a guarantee remaining valid for many years, as in *Bradford Old Bank v Sutcliffe*,[84] where a demand made 21 years after a guarantee had been entered into was found to be valid.

75 *Norton v Ellam* (1837) 2 M & W 461.
76 *Wittersheim v Lady Carlisle* (1791) 1 H Bl 631, 126 ER 360.
77 *Holmes v Kerrison* (1810) 2 Taunt 323; *In re Compania de la Electricidad* [1980] Ch 146.
78 [1973] AC 992.
79 *Sheers v Thimbleby & Son* (1897) 76 LT 709.
80 *Parr's Banking Co v Yates* [1898] 2 QB 460.
81 *Birks v Tripett* (1666) 1 Wms Saund 28; 85 ER 32.
82 *Parr's Banking Co v Yates* [1898] 2 QB 460.
83 [1893] 2 Ch 300.
84 [1918] 2 KB 833; see also *Esso Petroleum Co Ltd v Alstonbridge Properties Ltd* [1975] 1 WLR 1474.

Claims by a surety against a co-surety or against the principal debtor

8.18 Where more than one person guarantees the payment of the same debt, an equity arises such that if one of them pays more than his due proportion of the debt, he is entitled to a contribution from his co-guarantors.[85] The normal rule is that each guarantor will pay the same amount, which was held to apply in *Hampton v Minns*[86] even in a situation where the two shareholders who guaranteed a company's debt held different percentages of the shares in the company. It would appear that declaratory orders can be sought prior to the excess payments being made,[87] but that a money claim can only be brought after the payments in excess of the surety's obligations are made.[88] A guarantor is also entitled to an indemnity from the principal debtor on whose behalf the guarantee monies were paid. The same limitation rules apply in this case and time will only run from the date when monies are paid.[89] In *Coneys v Morris*,[90] a guarantor was refused an indemnity from the principal debtor in circumstances where payment had been made to the creditor of a statute barred debt.

Contracts of indemnity

8.19 By contrast with a guarantor, a person who provides an indemnity is liable as principal. Although the wording of the contract will govern, this makes it less likely that service of a demand will be found to be a condition precedent to a liability arising. An action relating to a contract of indemnity is not a 'contribution action'[91] and is instead subject to its own rules on limitation because the parties are not liable 'in respect of the same damage' in the sense of having both contributed to the loss that occurred. The issue which has troubled the courts in this area is whether time runs from the date a liability is incurred or the date it is ascertained or paid. In *Bosma v Larsen*,[92] charterers under a charterparty agreed to indemnify the owners of the vessel against 'all consequences or liabilities' arising out of certain events. The owners incurred liabilities to a third party which they discharged. In proceedings against the charterers, it was held by McNair J that the cause of action on the indemnity accrued when the liability was incurred rather than when it was ascertained. This decision was distinguished in *Telfair*

85 Such a claim is not a claim for contribution within the meaning of the Civil Liability (Contribution) Act 1978 or the LA 1980, s 10.

86 [2002] 1 All ER (Comm) 481.

87 Wolmerhausen v Gullick [1893] 2 Ch 514.

88 *Davies v Humphreys* (1840) 6 M & W 153; *Stimpson v Smyth* [1999] 1 Ch 340; *Roche v Wymes* [2008] IEHC 141.

89 *Davies v Humphreys* (1840) 6 M & W 153.

90 [1922] 1 IR 81. However, see also *Wolmerhausen v Gullick* [1893] 2 Ch 514; *Alexander v Vane* (1836) 1 M & W 511; and *Argo Caribbean Group Ltd v Lewis* [1976] 2 Lloyd's Rep 289 (CA) on this point.

91 Within the meaning of the Civil Liability (Contribution) Act 1978; LA 1980, s 10.

92 [1966] 1 Lloyd's Rep 22; this decision was not followed in *County and District Properties Ltd v C Jenner & Son Ltd* [1976] 2 Lloyd's Rep 728.

Shipping Corporation v Inersea Carriers SA (The Caroline P),[93] where Neill J carefully analysed the authorities. He noted the distinction between 'indemnities against liability', where the cause of action will come into existence when the liability is incurred (which may include a contingent liability), and 'general indemnities', where the cause of action will come into existence where the liability is ascertained.[94] While the wording of an express indemnity will always be crucial, he stated that the express indemnity in *Bosma v Larsen* had been held to be an indemnity against liability,[95] whereas he held that an implied indemnity will prima facie be a general indemnity.

Contracts of insurance

8.20 A contract of insurance is an express contract of indemnity and the applicable limitation rules to contracts of insurance contain the same nuances and complexities to those discussed in the previous paragraph.[96] The date of accrual of a cause of action by an insured against his insurance company will be governed by the terms of the contract. For a policy of liability insurance, it was held by the House of Lords in *Bradley v Eagle Star Insurance Co*[97] that the insured person cannot sue for an indemnity from the insurers 'unless and until the existence and amount of his liability to a third party has been established by action, arbitration or agreement'.[98] However, if the insurer repudiates prior to the liability being ascertained, and this repudiation is accepted, time will run from this date. By contrast, as occurred in *Lefevre v White*,[99] if the insured does not accept the repudiation (in like manner as an anticipatory breach need not be accepted) the contract remains open for performance and time will only run from the date when liability is established and ascertained. For marine policies,[100] critical illness policies,[101] life policies,[102] and property policies,[103] in the absence of contractual terms governing the matter,[104] the limitation period begins to run

93 [1985] 1 WLR 553.

94 See further the detailed analysis in *Halsbury's Laws of England*, Financial Services and Institutions (5th edn, LexisNexis 2008) vol 48, paras 1183–1186.

95 By contrast, he noted that the express indemnity in *R & H Green & Silley Weir Ltd v British Rlys Board* [1985] 1 All ER 237 was held to be a general indemnity. Neill J also expressed criticism of the classification of the indemnity in *Bosma v Larsen* and its failure to deal with the phrase 'all consequences': see [1985] 1 WLR 553 at 556–557.

96 See Oughton, Lowry and Merkin, *Limitation of Actions* (London: LLP Reference Publishing, 1998) at 193–208 for a detailed discussion of the case law.

97 [1989] AC 957. The phrase 'indemnity policy of insurance' has the same meaning: see *William McIlroy Swindon Ltd v Quinn Insurance Ltd* [2011] EWCA Civ 825, [2012] 1 All ER (Comm) 241.

98 [1989] AC 957 at 966, per Lord Brandon.

99 [1990] 1 Lloyd's Rep 569.

100 See *Chandris v Argo Insurance Co* [1963] 2 Lloyd's Rep 65.

101 *Virk v Gan Life Holdings* (1999) 52 BMLR 207, [2000] Lloyd's Rep IR 159.

102 *London & Midland Bank v Mitchell* [1899] 2 Ch 161.

103 *Callaghan v Dominion Insurance Co Ltd* [1997] 2 Lloyd's Rep 541.

104 In *Virk v Gan Life Holdings* (1999) 52 BMLR 207, [2000] Lloyd's Rep IR 159, time was found not to run for a further 30 days after the insured event occurred on account of the wording of the policy in this case.

as soon as the insured event occurs, even though no claim has been made. This general rule was applied in the case of a fidelity insurance policy in *Universities Superannuation Scheme Ltd v Royal Insurance*,[105] where Langley J held that an insured's cause of action against its insurance company accrued as soon as a dishonest employee misappropriated money, even though the loss was not immediately discovered, with the effect that a claim brought within six years of the employer finding out about the misappropriation was statute barred. For resinsurance, the cause of action accrues when the liability is ascertained by agreement, award or judgment and is not postponed until the rendering of an account.[106] If an insured's rights against his insurer are transferred to the injured party to whom the liability was incurred, upon his insolvency, under the Third Parties (Rights Against Insurers) Act 1930,[107] the injured party does not gain any extension to the limitation period that applied to any right of action the insured had against his insurers.[108]

Solicitors' costs

8.21 In relation to miscellaneous work done by a solicitor, time begins to run from the completion of the whole of each piece of work.[109] For work done by a solicitor acting for a client in litigation, the limitation period only begins to run from the date when the proceedings conclude or the date when the solicitor's retainer is terminated.[110] If there is an appeal from the judgment and the solicitor continues to act for the client, time does not begin to run against the solicitor until the appeal is decided.[111] Costs incurred subsequent to the judgment (or appeal) do not extend the limitation period for earlier items.[112] While a solicitor cannot sue a client for costs until the expiration of one month after delivery of a signed bill,[113] the limitation period will run against the solicitor from the date of completion of the work and not from the delivery of the bill.[114] In *Phillips & Co (a firm) v Bath Housing Co-Operative Ltd*,[115] it was held by the Court of Appeal that a solicitor's claim for costs, billed but not yet fixed by assessment or agreement, can be the subject of an acknowledgment or part payment,[116] such as occurred in that case, with the result that time ran afresh from the date of the acknowledgment.[117]

105 [2000] 1 All ER (Comm) 266.
106 *Halvanon Insurance Co Ltd v Cia de Seguros do Estado de Sao Paulo* [1995] LRLR 303 (CA).
107 See now the Third Parties (Rights Against Insurers) Act 2010, s 12(4), which has not yet been commenced at the date of writing.
108 *Firma C-Trade SA v Newcastle Protection and Indemnity Association, The Fanti* [1991] 2 AC 1.
109 *Beck v Pierce* (1889) 23 QBD 316 at 323.
110 *Martindale v Falkner* (1846) 2 CB 706; *Whitehead v Lord* (1852) 7 Ex Ch 691.
111 *Harris v Quine* (1869) LR 4 QB 653.
112 *Rothery v Munnings* (1830) 1 B&Ad 15; but see *Re Romer and Haslam* [1893] 2 QB 286; *Baile v Baile* (1872) LR 13 Eq 497.
113 Solicitors Act 1974, s 69. Leave to issue proceedings within the period of one month can be obtained in exceptional circumstances set out in s 69(1).
114 *Coburn v Colledge* [1897] 1 QB 702; see further para 1.22.
115 [2012] EWCA Civ 1591.
116 LA 1980, s 29(5).
117 See further Ch 6.

CHAPTER 9

Unjust Enrichment

9.01 A claim in unjust enrichment will arise where a claimant can establish that the defendant has been enriched at his expense by reason of an unjust factor which the courts recognise as giving rise to an obligation to compensate him.[1] Examples of such unjust factors include mistake, compulsion, duress and undue influence. This area of law is now generally referred to as the law of 'restitution'or 'unjust enrichment',[2] although the cause of action is still often pleaded as an action for money had and received or for payment on a *quantum meruit* or *quantum valebat*.[3] The limitation provisions that govern actions in restitution or unjust enrichment are to be found in the shadows of the Limitation Act 1980 ('LA 1980') and have been accurately stated in Goff and Jones to be 'in a poor state .... a ragged patchwork of rules'.[4] As the drafters of the Limitation Act 1939 and the LA 1980 did not have the law of unjust enrichment to the forefront of their minds when drafting the two statutes, the limitation rules governing actions in this area have developed in an *ad hoc* manner. One major consequence of this is that an unjust enrichment claim which can be shoehorned into the classification for limitation purposes of being an action based on fraud or seeking relief from the consequences of mistake will gain a more favourable limitation treatment than if it is based on an allegation of failure of consideration, absence of basis, duress or illegality.[5] Just as different torts are governed by

1 Goff and Jones, *The Law of Unjust Enrichment* (8th edn, London: Sweet & Maxwell, 2011) ('Goff and Jones') at para 1-18. The approach of Birks, *Unjust Enrichment* (2nd edn, Oxford: Oxford University Press, 2005), asks whether there is an 'absence of basis' rather than an 'unjust factor': see *Deutsche Morgan Grenfell Group Plc v IRC* [2006] UKHL 55, [2007] 1 AC 558 at para 21, per Lord Hoffmann and paras 150–158, per Lord Walker; *Test Claimants in FII Group Litigation v Revenue* [2012] UKSC 19, [2012] 2 AC 337 at para 162, per Lord Sumption.

2 See generally Burrows, *A Restatement of the English Law of Unjust Enrichment* (Oxford: Oxford University Press, 2012); Goff and Jones, *The Law of Unjust Enrichment* (8th edn, London: Sweet & Maxwell, 2011); Burrows, *The Law of Restitution* (3rd edn, Oxford: Oxford University Press, 2010); Birks, *Unjust Enrichment* (2nd edn, Oxford: Oxford University Press, 2005); McLean, 'Limitation of Actions in Restitution' (1989) CLJ 472; Edelman, 'Limitation and Unjust Enrichment' (2005) 68 MLR 848.

3 Goff and Jones, para 1–002.

4 Goff and Jones, para 33–02.

5 See, for example, the decision of the Supreme Court in *Test Claimants in FII Group Litigation v Revenue* [2012] UKSC 19, [2012] 2 AC 337, discussed in para 9.07, below.

different limitation periods, so too the different 'unjust factors' have their own separate limitation rules.

9.02 Notwithstanding the imperfections in the limitation framework for unjust enrichment claims, an attempt can be made to make the process of ascertaining the applicable limitation period more manageable. While there may be exceptions which do not fit neatly into the questions listed below, the following four-part test should be of assistance in ascertaining the limitation period that applies to an action seeking restitution for unjust enrichment:

1 First, one must ask whether the action is governed by the LA 1980 or whether it falls outside[6] the Act and is instead governed by the equitable defences of *laches* and acquiescence.

2 Secondly, if the action is governed by the LA 1980, one must determine whether the unjust factor giving rise to the claim is subject to the six-year limitation period for 'an action founded on simple contract', which has been given an expansive interpretation in *In re Diplock; Diplock v Wintle*[7] and *Kleinwort Benson Ltd v South Tyneside Metropolitan BC*,[8] or whether it is governed by a different statutory limitation period.

3 Thirdly, one must then ascertain when the cause of action accrued to the claimant, ie the date from which the limitation period runs.

4 Fourthly, one must determine whether any reason exists to extend or postpone the limitation period, such as disability,[9] part payment and acknowledgment,[10] fraud,[11] deliberate concealment[12] or mistake.[13] Detailed discussion of each of the foregoing is contained in their respective chapters in the book, apart from acknowledgment (including part payment) and mistake, as the former raises particular issues in unjust enrichment claims and as the latter is of significant importance in ascertaining the limitation period in many unjust enrichment claims.

WHETHER STATUTORY LIMITATION RULES OR EQUITABLE PRINCIPLES APPLY

9.03 In most unjust enrichment cases, the parties will find that the LA 1980 will contain the applicable limitation period for the action. However, this will

6 Section 21(1)(a) (fraudulent breach of trust) and (b) (trust property retained by trustee) are both treated as being 'outside' the LA 1980 for these purposes as no limitation period is prescribed by statute and the equity time limits apply.

7 [1948] Ch 465, affd sub nom *Ministry of Health v Simpson* [1951] AC 251.

8 [1994] 4 All ER 972; see further West, 'Section 5 of the Limitation Act 1980 and Restitutionary Claims for Money Had and Received' (2011) CJQ 367.

9 LA 1980, s 28; see Ch 5.

10 LA 1980, ss 29–31; see Ch 6.

11 LA 1980, s 32(1)(a); see Ch 7.

12 LA 1980, s 32(1)(b); see Ch 7.

13 LA 1980, s 32(1)(c); see Ch 7.

not always be the case, and the equitable principles of *laches* and acquiescence will instead apply if the claimant is a beneficiary who alleges a breach of trust of a type expressly excluded from the LA 1980 (ie if it relates to a fraud or fraudulent breach of trust,[14] or if the claimant is seeking to recover trust property or its proceeds from a trustee[15]) or if the claimant is seeking equitable relief,[16] except insofar as the courts would have applied a common law limitation period by analogy prior to the passing of the Limitation Act 1939.[17] This last question asks whether the cause of action fell within the 'exclusive equitable jurisdiction' or the 'concurrent equitable jurisdiction' of the courts of equity prior to the fusion of the courts of common law and equity in the nineteenth century. Examples within the former category are applications for injunctions or specific performance and claims of breach of the fiduciary duty of loyalty or fidelity (or claims for the imposition of a constructive trust by reason of that breach), which had no analogy at common law. An example of the latter is a claim for damages for negligence against a trustee, which has a direct analogy with a common law claim for damages for negligence or breach of contract.

WHETHER ACTION GOVERNED BY CONTRACT LIMITATION PERIOD OR AN ALTERNATIVE STATUTORY LIMITATION PERIOD

9.04 As stated somewhat obliquely at the start of this chapter, neither the LA 1980 nor its predecessor, the LA 1939, make reference to 'unjust enrichment', 'restitution' or the cause of action for 'money had and received' in their text. However, the Limitation Act 1623 imposed a six-year limitation period on all claims in *assumpsit*,[18] which included both express and implied promises. Although no longer part of the legal lexicon, the definition of *assumpsit* would appear to cover all common law claims in relation to what would now be described as unjust enrichment.[19] In the Court of Appeal in *In re Diplock; Diplock v Wintle*,[20] Lord Greene MR stated that the phrase 'action founded on simple contract' contained in s 2(1)(a) of the LA 1939, 'must be taken to cover actions for money had and received ... The assumption must, we think, be made, though the words used cannot be regarded as felicitous'.[21] More recently, the House of Lords in *Deutsche Morgan Grenfell Group Plc v IRC*[22] held that a restitutionary claim for the repayment of tax (which had been found not to be due) came within

14 Section 21(1)(a).
15 Section 21(1)(b).
16 Section 36(1).
17 Section 36(1).
18 Limitation Act 1623, s 3.
19 Goff and Jones, at para 33–04.
20 [1948] Ch 465.
21 [1948] Ch 465 at 514; to similar effect are the comments of Hobhouse J in *Kleinwort Benson Ltd v Sandwell BC* [1994] 4 All ER 890 at 942–943.
22 [2006] UKHL 49, [2007] 1 AC 558.

s 5 of the LA 1980.[23] Thus, in simple terms, the starting point for identifying the limitation period for a claim in unjust enrichment is that the six-year limitation period for an action founded on contract applies, unless displaced by a different statutory limitation period. Regard must therefore be had to the following, which are the main alternative statutory limitation periods:

1 the six-year limitation period for an action to recover any sum recoverable by virtue of any enactment: s 9 of the LA 1980;[24]

2 the two-year limitation period for a claim for contribution: s 10 of the LA 1980;[25]

3 the 12-year limitation period for a claim by a beneficiary to the personal estate of a deceased person: s 22(1) of the LA 1980;[26]

4 the six-year limitation period for a claim by a beneficiary to recover trust property transferred to a third party in breach of trust: s 21(3) of the LA 1980;[27] and

5 the two-year limitation period for a claim in respect of salvage: s 224 of the Merchant Shipping Act 1995.[28]

ACCRUAL OF THE CAUSE OF ACTION FOR UNJUST ENRICHMENT CLAIMS

9.05 The cause of action in unjust enrichment accrues on the date when the enrichment is received or the date of the 'unjust' factor (such as a total failure of consideration), whichever is later.[29] Thus, in *Maskell v Horner*,[30] a stallholder paid unlawful market dues under duress of goods for 12 years. In his action to recover the monies paid, it was held that his cause of action in respect of each payment accrued when it was made, the duress being operative at the same time, with the consequence that he recovered only the dues paid in the six years prior to the proceedings being brought.[31] In *Guardian Ocean Cargoes Ltd v Banco do*

23 The House of Lords also held that the action involved a claim for a refund of monies paid by mistake and came within s 32(1)(c); the six-year limitation period therefore only ran from the date the tax provision was struck down: see further para 9.06, below.
24 See Ch 21; this would include claims based on the Law Reform (Frustrated Contracts) Act 1943.
25 See Ch 25; but see also *Hampton v Minns* [2002] 1 WLR 1, where the contribution claim governed by equitable principles and the LA 1980, s 9.
26 See Ch 19.
27 See Chs 17–18; for a discussion of the difference between the LA 1980, ss 21(3) and 22(a), see *Davies v Sharples* [2006] EWHC 362 (Ch), [2006] WTLR 839.
28 See para 22.05.
29 Burrows, *The Law of Restitution* (2nd edn, London: Butterworths, 2002) at 546; McLean, 'Limitation of Actions in Restitution'(1989) CLJ 472 at 476; *Kleinwort Benson Ltd v South Tyneside Metropolitan BC* [1994] 4 All ER 972 at 978.
30 [1915] 3 KB 106.
31 In commenting on the area, it is stated in Goff and Jones at para 33-39 that the absence of any extension or postponement of the limitation period after the claimant became free from pressure 'is a matter for regret'.

Brasil,[32] the Court of Appeal held that the cause of action for the restitution of money paid in respect of a contract which did not materialise, accrued when the contractual negotiations failed. Despite the much criticised[33] decision in *Freeman v Jeffries*[34] being to the contrary, it is reasonably settled law that a cause of action to recover money paid by mistake is not dependent on a demand for repayment being made, and it was correctly held in *Baker v Courage & Co Ltd*[35] that the making of such a demand will not extend the limitation period.

ACTIONS SEEKING RELIEF FROM THE CONSEQUENCES OF MISTAKE

9.06 In cases where the 'unjust' factor which gives rise to the obligation to make restitution is a mistake, and the action is for 'relief from the consequences of mistake' within the meaning of s 32(1)(c) of the LA 1980,[36] the limitation period will run from when the claimant discovered the mistake or could, with reasonable diligence, have discovered it.[37] In *Kleinwort Benson Ltd v Lincoln City Council*,[38] it was held by the House of Lords that this provision applies even in the case of a payment made under a settled understanding of the law which was subsequently departed from by judicial decision. The 'mistake' in such a case is as to the applicable law (properly construed) and the 'relief from the consequences of mistake' is the demand for repayment of monies paid by reason of that mistake. This principle was then seamlessly applied in *Deutsche Morgan Grenfell Group Plc v IRC*,[39] where the House of Lords held that a revenue payment made under a provision which was later struck down by the European Court of Justice had been made due to a mistake on the part of the claimant. This mistake (that the sums were due) was only 'discovered' when the judgment was delivered, and thus the action was not statute barred as it had been commenced within six years of that date.

9.07 More recently, the Supreme Court in *Test Claimants in the FII Group Litigation v Revenue and Customs Comrs*[40] had to rule on a different issue arising in another action where the claimants sought the repayment of taxes paid under a statute which was subsequently found to be unlawful. The claimants' cause of action could either be described as a claim for relief from the consequences of mistake or as a claim for repayment of monies paid pursuant to an *ultra vires* demand (as recognised by the House of Lords in *Woolwich Equitable Building*

32 [1994] 2 Lloyd's Rep 152.
33 Oughton, Lowry and Merkin, *Limitation of Actions* (London: LLP Reference Publishing, 1998) at 226; Goff and Jones at para 33-39.
34 (1869) LR 4 Exch 189.
35 [1910] 1 KB 56 at 65; see also *Fuller v Happy Shopper Ltd* [2001] 2 Lloyd's Rep 49.
36 See paras 7.20–7.21.
37 See paras 7.05–7.07.
38 [1999] 2 AC 349. This judgment extended the scope of *In re Diplock; Diplock v Wintle* [1948] Ch 465, which had held that an action for monies paid under a mistake of fact came within the statutory provision: see the comments of Lord Goff at 388.
39 [2006] UKHL 49, [2007] 1 AC 558.
40 [2012] UKSC 19, [2012] 2 AC 337.

Society v Inland Revenue Cmmrs[41]). The Supreme Court held that the claimants were entitled to frame their action as a claim for relief from the consequences of mistake so as to gain the benefit of the more generous limitation period contained in s 32(1)(c) of the LA 1980.[42] The lucid and erudite, though *obiter*, comments of Lord Walker in *FII Group Litigation* on the correctness of the narrow interpretation given to what is now s 32(1)(c) in *Phillips-Higgins v Harper*[43] are worthy of comment at this point. In that case, the claimant (though not the defendant) had made a mistake as to her entitlements under a contract. Her subsequent claim for damages representing the monies she had mistakenly not sought earlier was held not to constitute an action seeking relief from the consequences of mistake. In his judgment at first instance in *Phillips-Higgins*, not challenged on appeal, Pearson J stated as follows:

> 'What, then, is the meaning of provision (c)? The right of action is for relief from the consequences of a mistake. It seems to me that this wording is carefully chosen to indicate a class of actions where a mistake has been made which has had certain consequences and the plaintiff seeks to be relieved from those consequences. Familiar examples are, first, money paid in consequence of a mistake: in such a case the mistake is made, in consequence of the mistake the money is paid, and the action is to recover that money back. Secondly, there may be a contract entered into in consequence of a mistake, and the action is to obtain the rescission or, in some cases, the rectification of such a contract. Thirdly, there may be an account settled in consequence of mistakes; if the mistakes are sufficiently serious there can be a reopening of the account.'[44]

Lord Walker noted that he and Lord Hoffmann had expressed doubts concerning the correctness of *Phillips-Higgins* in *Deutsche Morgan Grenfell Group plc v IRC*,[45] as had several academic commentators,[46] but stated as follows:

> 'Having considered the matter with the benefit of much fuller argument than in *DMG*, I have reached the clear conclusion that *Phillips-Higgins v Harper* [1954] 1 QB 411 was rightly decided ... [D]eparture from Pearson J's relatively narrow interpretation would bring a real risk ... that "the scope of [section 32(1)(c)] might be expanded dangerously close to the basic rule of common law limitation that ignorance of the existence of a cause of action does not prevent time from running." It would be difficult to find any principled stopping-place for the expansion.'[47]

41 [1993] AC 70.

42 A further issue before the court was whether two statutory provisions which sought to preclude reliance on s 32(1)(c) in tax refund cases breached EU law: this was found not to be *acte clair* and was the subject of a reference to the European Court of Justice.

43 [1954] 1 QB 411.

44 [1954] 1 QB 411 at 418.

45 [2006] UKHL 49, [2007] 1 AC 558 at paras 22, 91 and 147.

46 Such as Edelman, 'Limitation Periods and the Theory of Unjust Enrichment' (2005) 68 MLR 848; however, he noted that the case note of Burrows, 'Restitution in Respect of Mistakenly Paid Tax' (2005) 121 LQR 540 was generally supportive of the decision.

47 [2012] UKSC 19, [2012] 2 AC 337 at paras 62–63.

ACKNOWLEDGMENT AND PART PAYMENT

9.08 The provisions in the LA 1980 on acknowledgment and part payment have been held to apply to cases where restitutionary relief is sought, but care should be taken given the wide range of causes of action which come within this rubric. In *Amantilla Ltd v Telefusion Ltd*,[48] it was held by Judge John Davies QC that a claim by a builder for a reasonable sum on a *quantum meruit* for works carried out was a claim for a 'liquidated pecuniary claim' within the meaning of s 29(5) of the LA 1980 as he found it to be sufficiently certain to be capable of ascertainment rather than amounting to a claim for damages to be assessed. However, counsel for the defendant in *Amantilla* conceded that there was a contract between the parties and the judge expressly relied on this fact in reaching his decision.[49] More recently, it was held by the Court of Appeal in *Phillips & Co v Bath Housing Co-operative Ltd*[50] that a solicitor's bill, even though not yet fixed by assessment or otherwise, was a liquidated pecuniary claim which could be, and was found to have been, acknowledged by the defendant. In *FJ Chalke Ltd v HMRC*,[51] it was held that a statutory claim to recover overpaid VAT and a common law claim to recover compound interest on the user value of the money were separate claims. Thus, repayment of the principal did not amount to a part payment towards the overall sum (ie including the interest) claimed. However, at first instance Henderson J commented that the claim for interest was capable of acknowledgment under s 29(5) as it was 'more akin to the *quantum meruit* claim in *Amantilla* than to a claim for damages in tort or contract'.[52]

48 (1987) Con LR 139.

49 See Oughton, Lowry and Merkin, *Limitation of Actions* (London: LLP Reference Publishing, 1998) at 226–227.

50 [2012] EWCA Civ 1591, [2012] All ER (D) 92 (Dec); to similar effect is *Byatt v Nash* [2002] All ER (D) 254 (Jun).

51 [2009] EWHC 952 (Ch), [2009] STC 2027, affd [2010] EWCA Civ 313, [2010] STC 1642.

52 [2009] EWHC 952 (Ch), [2009] STC 2027 at para 157; see also *Kleinwort Benson Ltd v South Tyneside Metropolitan Borough Council* [1994] 4 All ER 972.

CHAPTER 10

Actions in Tort: General Principles

INTRODUCTION

10.01 This Chapter discusses the general principles applicable to all actions in tort,[1] in particular issues relating to the accrual of a cause of action in tort. The starting point for a discussion of the tort limitation period is that s 2 of the Limitation Act 1980 ('LA 1980') provides that an action founded on tort shall not be brought after the expiration of six years from the date on which the cause of action accrued. Unfortunately, this section now provides only the starting point for an individual seeking to ascertain the limitation provision governing a claim in tort as a large number of other provisions, discussed in greater detail in the chapters identified below, interact with or replace s 2 as follows:

(a) **Personal injuries actions**

These are subject to a limitation period of three years from the date of accrual of the cause of action or the claimant's date of knowledge, if later, which may be disapplied if it is equitable to allow the action to proceed.[2]

(b) **Defamation and malicious falsehood actions**

A one-year limitation period applies to actions for defamation, slander of title and other malicious falsehood, which may be disapplied if it is equitable to allow the action to proceed.[3]

(c) **Actions relating to the conversion of a chattel**

The six-year limitation period in s 2 applies to a conversion claim, but other sections also apply that extinguish title to the chattel upon the expiry of the limitation period subject to exceptions in the case of theft and under the Proceeds of Crime Act 2002.[4]

1 For limitation purposes, 'tort' should be read as including actions against the State for breach of European Union law (*R v Secretary of State for Transport, Ex p Factortame (No 7)* [2001] 1 WLR 942), which are discussed in Ch 26, and actions for breach of intellectual property law (see *Sevcon Ltd v Lucas Ltd* [1986] 1 WLR 462), which are discussed in Ch 31.
2 LA 1980, ss 11, 12–14 and 33: see Ch 13.
3 LA 1980, ss 4A and 32A: see Ch 14.
4 LA 1980, ss 3, 4, 27A and 27B: see Chs 15 and 30.

(d) Actions under Pt 1 of the Consumer Protection Act 1987

A three-year limitation period applies to defective products claims brought under Pt 1 of the Consumer Protection Act 1987.[5] This may be extended on date of knowledge grounds but is subject to a ten-year long-stop provision.[6]

(e) Actions governed by the Latent Damage Act 1986

The LDA 1986 governs all claims in negligence other than those claiming damages for personal injuries, even those not involving latent damage. It applies a limitation period of the longer of six years from the accrual of a right of action or three years from the claimant's date of knowledge.[7] It also imposes an overriding time limit of 15 years within which a non-personal injuries negligence action must be brought.[8]

(f) Actions based on fraud

Section 2 applies to an action based on fraud (ie a claim in deceit) but the six-year limitation period only starts to run from the date on which the fraud was discovered or could with reasonable diligence have been discovered.[9]

(g) Actions governed by the carriage statutes

An action governed by one of the international conventions or European Regulations on the carriage of people, luggage and goods falls outside the scope of the LA 1980 and regard must be had to the time limit contained in the applicable Convention or Regulation. Particular care should be taken as these time limits are often quite short, most notably the two-year limitation period for personal injuries claims contained in the Montreal Convention and the Athens Convention, respectively.[10]

For all tort actions regard should be had to the provisions of the LA 1980 dealing with disability,[11] deliberate concealment[12] and cross-border mediations,[13] but it should be noted that acknowledgment and part payment play no role in tort claims.[14]

ACCRUAL OF THE CAUSE OF ACTION

What is a cause of action?

10.02 The limitation period for an action in tort starts to run upon the accrual of the cause of action. There is no statutory definition of the expression 'cause of

5 LA 1980, s 11A: see Ch 11.
6 LA 1980, s 11A(3).
7 LA 1980, s 14A: see Ch 12.
8 LA 1980, s 14B.
9 LA 1980, s 32(1)(a): see Ch 7.
10 See Ch 22.
11 LA 1980, s 28: see Ch 5.
12 LA 1980, s 32(1)(b): see Ch 7.
13 LA 1980, s 33A: see para 23.16.
14 See para 6.10.

action' and one has to look to the case law for a definition. The classic definition is that provided by Lord Esher MR in *Read v Brown*,[15] as follows:

> '[E]very fact which it would be necessary for the [claimant] to prove, if traversed, in order to support his right to the judgment of the court. It does not comprise every piece of evidence which is necessary to prove each fact, but every fact which is necessary to be proved.'[16]

Torts actionable per se, torts requiring proof of damage and continuing wrongs

10.03 In examining issues relating to 'damage' and 'accrual', it is worth grouping the different types of torts into three categories by reference to the temporal aspect of the accrual of a cause of action in each case:

(i) torts actionable per se, namely actions in trespass (such as false imprisonment,[17] intentional assault[18] and trespass to land[19]) and actions in defamation[20]: the cause of action accrues upon the commission of the wrong;

(ii) torts requiring proof of damage, historically derived from actions on the case (such as negligence,[21] nuisance[22] or misfeasance in public office[23]): the cause of action accrues upon the claimant suffering damage;[24] and

(iii) continuing torts, which may fall into either category above, such as a continuing trespass to land[25] or continuing breach of statutory duty[26]: a fresh cause of action accrues every day, but the right of action is restricted to that part of the wrong committed in the past six years.[27]

15 (1888) 22 QBD 128; see also *Letang v Cooper* [1965] 1 QB 232 at 242.
16 (1888) 22 QBD 128 at 131.
17 *Coventry v Apsley* (1691) 2 Salk 420.
18 *Cole v Turner* (1704) 6 Mod 149.
19 *League Against Cruel Sports Ltd v Scott* [1986] 1 QB 240.
20 Libels and some forms of slander are actionable per se but other forms of slander require proof of special damage: see *Clerk and Lindsell on Torts* (20th edn, London: Sweet & Maxwell, 2010) at para 23.53 and *Grappelli v Derek Block (Holdings) Ltd* [1981] 1 WLR 822.
21 *Pirelli General Cable Works Ltd v Oscar Faber & Partners Ltd* [1983] 2 AC 1.
22 *St Helen's Smelting Co v Tipping* (1865) 11 HLC 642; *Sedley-Denfield v O'Callaghan* [1940] AC 880 at 896. *Clerk & Lindsell on Torts* (20th edn, London: Sweet & Maxwell, 2010) at paras 20.26–20.27 note that nuisances involving damage to property require proof of damage, whereas a nuisance involving an encroachment or interference with enjoyment of property is presumed to cause damage.
23 *Watkins v Secretary of State for the Home Department* [2006] UKHL 17, [2006] 2 AC 395.
24 All damages must then be claimed in one set of proceedings: see para 10.05.
25 *Clarke v The Midland Great Western Railway Co* [1895] 2 IR 294; *Whitwham v Westminster Brymbo Coal and Coke Company* [1896] 2 Ch 538; and *Konskier v B Goodman Ltd* [1928] 1 KB 421.
26 *Phonographic Performance Ltd v Department of Trade and Industry* [2004] 1 WLR 2893.
27 Special mention should also be made of the difficult case of *Darley Main Colliery Co v Mitchell* (1886) 11 App Cas 127, where damage to land caused by mining underneath was held to give rise to a new cause of action *de die et diem* rather than from the date of the first damage being suffered, explained by Lord Hoffmann in *Homburg Houtimport BV v Agrosin Private Ltd* [2003] UKHL 12, [2004] 1 AC 715 at para 91 as being a case where the acts complained of were not wrongful in themselves.

Concurrent liability in contract and tort

10.04 The same set of facts may give rise to a cause of action in both contract and tort. In *Henderson v Merrett Syndicates Ltd*,[28] it was held by the House of Lords that a claimant is entitled to pursue whichever cause of action will give him the most advantageous limitation period. For example, if a defendant commits a breach of contract, which is also a breach of his duty of care to the claimant, who only suffers damage some time later, the tort limitation period will start to run from the date the damage is suffered. Importantly, s 14A(4) of the LA 1980, which governs an action claiming damages for negligence not involving personal injuries, does not apply to an action for breach of contract.[29]

The two loss problem (the 'single action rule')

10.05 It is a long established rule at common law that if a claimant has suffered actionable damage as a result of a defendant's breach of duty, in a case where damage is the gist of the action (such as in negligence), he can and must claim damages in a single action for all the damage that he has suffered or will suffer in consequence of that breach of duty.[30] As was stated by Lord Pearce in *Cartledge v E Jopling & Sons Ltd*:[31]

> 'In 1701 in the case of *Fitter v Veal* or *Fetter v Beale* or *Ferrer v Beale*[32] the [claimant] after recovering damages for assault and battery discovered that his injuries were more serious than had been supposed. He sought to bring a second action for the fresh damage. It was held, however, that he had but one cause of action which had been extinguished by the judgment in the former case. That principle has never since been doubted. It has been applied daily in countless actions for damages for personal injuries. In each case the judge assesses the damages once and for all, with the knowledge that the [claimant] can get no further damages for the possible traumatic consequences, such as arthritis or epilepsy, which may occur in the years to come.'[33]

Lord Reid commented that once a claimant suffered personal injury beyond what can be regarded as negligible, even when that injury is unknown to and could not be discovered by the sufferer, any further injury arising from the same act at a later date does not give rise to a further cause of action.[34] Time runs from the first damage being suffered, and a claimant cannot defeat a defence under the LA 1980 by claiming only in respect of damage which occurred within the limitation period if he has suffered damage from the same wrongful act outside

28 [1995] 2 AC 145.
29 See Ch 12.
30 *Rothwell v Chemical & Insulating Co Ltd* [2007] UKHL 39, [2008] 1 AC 281 at para 13, per Lord Hoffmann.
31 [1963] AC 758.
32 (1701) 12 Mod 543; 1 Salk 11; 1 Ld Raym. 692.
33 [1963] AC 758 at 780.
34 [1963] AC 758 at 771.

that period.[35] Care must be taken to ascertain when the cause of action accrued.[36] However, separate actions may be maintained in respect of damage to person and damage to property arising out of the same act or omission[37] or if the breach is a continuing tort for which a cause of action accrues from day to day.[38]

10.06 The scope and practical effect of the single action rule is best understood by analysing two recent decisions that fell close to the dividing line: *Green v Eadie*[39] and *St Anselm Development Company Ltd v Slaughter and May (a firm)*.[40] In *Green v Eadie*, the court had to determine whether the failure by the claimant's solicitors to notice a mapping discrepancy prior to a contract being signed gave rise to a different loss to their subsequent failure to notice the same discrepancy between exchange of contracts and completion (during which time the contract could still have been rescinded). In *St Anselm Development Company Ltd v Slaughter and May*, negligent advice was given by the defendant firm in March 1999 in relation to the granting of a lease and the question was whether this gave rise to a single cause of action when it was relied upon in June 1999 or whether it gave rise to a second cause of action when it was relied upon on a second occasion in November 1999. A further issue was whether time ran for all purposes from the date of the negligent advice, which was relied upon immediately in negotiations, or only from when defective leases were signed. In *Green v Eadie*, it was held by Mark Cawson QC sitting as a deputy High Court judge that the limitation period ran from the earlier date, as he was not persuaded to impose an ongoing duty to review the file *de novo* immediately prior to completion. He also held that the entry into the flawed transaction constituted sufficient damage by reason of the aggravation of rescinding and the possibility that the deposit would be irrecoverable. By contract, in *St Anselm Development Company Ltd*, it was held by David Richards J that the entry into each lease gave rise to a separate loss and a separate cause of action, primarily because the instruction to the solicitor was to advise in relation to each lease, rather than to give a single piece of advice in relation to all leases. Distinctions are drawn in both cases that are slender and care should be taken in drafting particulars of claim where this issue arises given the elusive contours of this rule.

What damage is actionable?

10.07 The question of what 'damage' can give rise to a claim for damages in negligence is of importance in determining when a cause of action accrues, and thus the date from which a limitation period will start to run. Newly developing heads of loss, such as the 'loss of a chance' of recovery by reason of medical negligence, may require some care in assessing when, or if, damage occurred.[41]

35 *Knapp v Ecclesiastical Insurance Group Plc* [1998] PNLR 172.
36 See *Darley Main Colliery Co v Mitchell* (1886) 11 App Cas 127.
37 *Brunsden v Humphrey* (1884) 14 QBD 141.
38 *Clarkson v Modern Foundries* [1957] 1 WLR 1210; *Cartwright v GKN Sankey Ltd* [1972] 2 Lloyd's Rep 242.
39 [2011] EWHC B24 (Ch), [2012] Ch 363.
40 [2013] EWHC 125 (Ch).
41 See *Gregg v Scott* [2005] UKHL 2, [2005] 2 AC 176.

In personal injuries cases where the sole injury is psychiatric (with no physical injuries), a claimant must tread with some care, as if he merely suffers distress and anxiety following the incident and is not diagnosed as having suffered a recognised psychiatric condition, these injuries are not such as constitute a recoverable head of damage in the tort of negligence.[42]

10.08 The question of what constitutes 'personal injuries' has come to the fore recently in a number of cases involving persons who have been exposed to asbestos dust. In *Rothwell v Chemical & Insulating Co Ltd*,[43] the House of Lords had to consider whether a claimant who had developed pleural plaques[44] as a result of exposure to asbestos dust had suffered a personal injury for which he could claim damages in tort. The presence of pleural plaques proved that a person's lungs had been penetrated by asbestos fibres and that they had an increased chance of developing an asbestos-related disease. However, the presence of pleural plaques was held not, of itself, to constitute an injury as it did not, of itself, shorten life expectancy.[45] This being the case, the claimant had no cause of action unless and until he developed an actual illness. Ultimately, the question of whether a claimant has suffered an actionable personal injury yields a somewhat impressionistic response, albeit one where the threshold is low. In *Cartledge v E Jopling & Sons Ltd*,[46] Lord Evershed asked whether the claimant had suffered 'real damage as distinct from purely minimal damage'.[47] Lord Pearce added the following:

> 'Evidence that those [physical] changes are not felt by him and may never be felt tells in favour of the damage coming within the principle of *de minimis non curat lex*. On the other hand, evidence that in unusual exertion or at the onslaught of disease he may suffer from his hidden impairment tells in favour of the damage being substantial.'[48]

10.09 One of the main battlefields at the boundaries of tort law in the past 40 years relates to the recoverability of damages in relation to defective buildings (and other products). In this area, an initial distinction should be drawn between non-dangerous defects, which under English law can only give rise to a claim for breach of contract,[49] and dangerous defects in a building that cause damage to a person or to other property, which constitute sufficient damage to sue in the tort of negligence. While recovery was allowed by the House of

42 *McLoughlin v O'Brian* [1983] 1 AC 410; *Hatton v Sutherland* [2002] 2 All ER 1.

43 [2007] UKHL 39, [2008] 1 AC 281; see Leczykiewicz, 'Plural plaques, the concept of damage and liability for psychiatric injury' (2008) 124 LQR 548.

44 Pleural plaques are fibrous thickening of the pleural membrane which surrounds the lungs.

45 See the comments of Lord Hope at [2008] 1 AC 281 at para 49.

46 [1963] AC 758.

47 [1963] AC 758 at 773–774.

48 [1963] AC 758 at 779. In discussing this passage in *Rothwell v Chemical & Insulating Co Ltd* [2008] 1 AC 281 at para 67, Lord Scott noted that a risk, produced by a negligent act or omission, of an adverse condition arising at some time in the future does not constitute damage sufficient to complete a tortious cause of action, relying on *Law Society v Sephton & Co* [2006] 2 AC 543 (discussed in para 10.14).

49 See *Simaan General Contracting v Pilkington Glass (No 2)* [1988] QB 758.

Lords for non-dangerous defects in *Junior Books Ltd v Veitchi Co Ltd*,[50] the courts have subsequently retreated from this position.[51] If what are believed to be non-dangerous defects (such as cracking) are present (and even visible) at a certain date, the cause of action is not complete and the limitation clock will only start to run when recoverable damage, such as personal injury, is suffered.[52] An exception was suggested in *Anns v Merton London Borough Council*,[53] namely that damages could be awarded in respect of the cost of remedying defects which give rise to a 'present or imminent danger to the health or safety of persons occupying it'.[54] However, the House of Lords subsequently held that if defects are discovered before they cause damage or personal injury, the cost of repair is pure economic loss which is not recoverable in the absence of *Hedley Byrne* liability.[55] If the defective building or product damages *a different* product or neighbouring building, this damage is a recoverable head of loss.[56] A possible gloss on these rules may exist in the case of 'complex structures', where one component of a product damages other parts of a complex structure, which loss may be recoverable.[57]

Date of accrual: general principles and personal injuries cases

10.10 No definition is provided in the LA 1980 of when a cause of action 'accrues' for torts actionable upon proof of damage. It is far from self-evident that this should be interpreted to allow a cause of action to accrue before a claimant became, or could by exercising reasonable diligence have become, aware that he had suffered loss. The United States Supreme Court,[58] the Supreme

50 [1983] AC 520. While *Pirelli General Cable Works Ltd v Oscar Faber & Partners Ltd* [1983] 2 AC 1 and *Junior Books Ltd v Veitchi Co Ltd* [1983] AC 520 were treated as cases involving damage to property when they were decided, they are probably now best analysed as pure economic loss cases: see *Murphy v Brentwood DC* [1991] 1 AC 398; McKendrick, '*Pirelli* Re-Examined' (1991) 11 *Legal Studies* 326.

51 See *D & F Estates Ltd v Church Commissioners of England* [1989] 1 AC 177 and *Murphy v Brentwood DC* [1991] 1 AC 398. Recovery is allowed for non-dangerous defects in Australia (*Bryan v Maloney* (1995) 182 CLR 609) and New Zealand (*Invercargill City Council v Hamlin* [1994] 3 NZLR 513, [1996] AC 624) as pure economic loss.

52 *Nitrigin Eireann Teoranta v Inco Alloys Ltd* [1992] 1 All ER 854.

53 *Anns v Merton London Borough Council* [1978] AC 728.

54 *Anns v Merton London Borough Council* [1978] AC 728 at 760, per Lord Wilberforce. The same position has been adopted by the Supreme Court of Canada in *Winnipeg Condominium Corporation (No 36) v Bird Construction Co Ltd* (1995) 121 DLR (4th) 193.

55 *Murphy v Brentwood DC* [1991] 1 AC 398.

56 *Muirhead v Industrial Tank Specialities Ltd* [1988] QB 507.

57 *D & F Estates Ltd v Church Commissioners of England* [1989] 1 AC 177 at 207; but see also *Bellefield Computer Services Ltd v E Turner & Sons Ltd* (2000) BLR 97 (CA), noted in Duncan Wallace, '*Donoghue v Stevenson* and "Complex Structures": *Anns* Revisited?' (2000) 116 LQR 530.

58 *Urie v Thompson* (1949) 337 US 163; *United States v Kubrick* (1979) 444 US 111. Lord Pearce in *Cartledge v E Jopling & Sons Ltd* [1963] AC 758 at 781 referred to the former judgment, but chose not to follow it.

Court of Canada,[59] the Court of Appeal of New Zealand[60] and the Privy Council on appeal from New Zealand,[61] though not the High Court of Australia[62] or the Supreme Court of Ireland,[63] have all held that a cause of action in negligence only accrues from the date a claimant ought reasonably to have discovered that he had suffered loss or damage. However, the law in England has been settled since the decision of the House of Lords in *Cartledge v E Jopling & Sons Ltd*,[64] where it was held that a cause of action in negligence accrues when 'personal injury beyond what can be regarded as negligible'[65] is suffered, even if the claimant was not aware of having suffered the damage. The claimants in *Cartledge* developed the lung disease pneumoconiosis after inhaling silica dust at their place of work over many years. Although the damage to the claimants' lungs was progressive and the symptoms only became apparent some years after it had occurred,[66] the House of Lords held that their claims were statute barred. The logic underpinning this judgment is as follows: if it was necessary for s 26 of the Limitation Act 1939[67] to provide that fraudulent concealment will delay the running of the limitation period until the concealed facts were discoverable, by implication, in all other cases time must start to run even if the damage was not discoverable by a person exercising reasonable diligence. The law lords expressed disquiet at their decision, with Lord Reid stating that it was 'unreasonable and unjustifiable'.[68]

59 *City of Kamloops v Nielsen* (1984) 10 DLR (4th) 641; *Central Trust Co v Rafuse* [1986] 2 SCR 147; *Winnipeg Condominium Corporation No 36 v Bird Construction Co* (1995) 121 DLR (4th) 193.

60 *Invercargill City Council v Hamlin* [1994] 3 NZLR 513; *S v G* [1995] 3 NZLR 681 and *GD Searle & Co v Gunn* [1996] 2 NZLR 129; however, in *Murray v Morel & Co Ltd* [2007] NZSC 27, [2007] 3 NZLR 721, the court refused to extend it to money claims.

61 *Invercargill City Council v Hamlin* [1996] AC 264: the Privy Council in its judgment in *Invercargill* held that the law in New Zealand was different to that applied by the House of Lords in England.

62 *Hawkins v Clayton* (1988) 164 CLR 539; *Wardley Australia Ltd v State of Western Australia* (1992) 175 CLR 514.

63 *Tuohy v Courtney* [1994] 3 IR 1.

64 [1963] AC 758. This was applied to property damage cases in *Pirelli General Cable Works v Faber* [1983] 2 AC 1 and remains good law in England: see *Law Society v Sephton & Co* [2006] 2 AC 543.

65 [1963] AC 758 at 772, per Lord Reid. The words used by Lord Evershed, at 774, refer to the date when the claimant had suffered 'real damage as distinct from purely minimal damage'; Lord Pearce, at 779, held that what was actionable damage was a question of degree and referred to the principle of *de minimis non curat lex*.

66 The medical evidence was that if x-rays of their lungs had been carried out more than six years prior to the writs issuing, these would have shown that they had suffered the damage already.

67 See now the LA 1980, s 32(1)(b), discussed in Ch 7.

68 [1963] AC 758 at 772. A claim that the equivalent section in the Irish Statute of Limitations 1957, which had been interpreted in like manner to *Cartledge*, breached the Constitution of Ireland 1937 by failing to vindicate the claimant's personal rights was rejected by the Irish Supreme Court in *Tuohy v Courtney* [1994] 3 IR 1.

Date of accrual in property damage cases

10.11 In *Pirelli General Cable Works Ltd v Oscar Faber & Partners*,[69] it was held that the date of accrual of the cause of action in property damage cases is governed by the same principles that apply to personal injuries cases. The claimant in *Pirelli* engaged the defendant firm of engineers to advise on the design of an addition to their factory premises and in 1969 the building works, including the construction of a 160-foot-high chimney, were completed. Unsuitable materials were used in the construction of the chimney leading to cracking at the top of the chimney which occurred not later than April 1970. It was held that the claimant could not with reasonable diligence have discovered the cracking before October 1972; the damage was actually discovered in November 1977. A writ was issued in October 1978 which the House of Lords held was statute barred as the cause of action had accrued in April 1970. The speeches of the law lords noted that the legal issues were analogous to those determined in *Cartledge v E Jopling & Sons Ltd*[70] and that, first, time ran from the date on which damage was suffered regardless of whether the claimant knew about the damage, and secondly, that reform of the law was a matter for parliament.[71] Reforming legislation was thereafter enacted in the form of the Latent Damage Act 1986, which is discussed in Chapter 12.

Defects vs damage and properties 'doomed from the start'

10.12 The speech of Lord Fraser in *Pirelli General Cable Works Ltd v Oscar Faber & Partners*[72] contains an interesting and important discussion of the distinction between *damage* being suffered to the claimant's property and a latent *defect* in the foundations of a building. He stated as follows:

> 'Unless the defect is very gross, it may never lead to any damage at all to the building. It would be analogous to a predisposition or natural weakness in the human body which may never develop into disease or injury. The claimant's cause of action will not accrue until damage occurs, which will commonly consist of cracks coming into existence as a result of the defect even though the cracks or the defect may be undiscovered and undiscoverable. There may perhaps be cases where the defect is so gross that the building is doomed from the start, and where the owner's cause of action will accrue as soon as it is built, but it seems unlikely that such a defect would not be discovered within the limitation period. Such cases, if they exist, would be exceptional.'[73]

It is not immediately apparent how this doctrine can be reconciled with the general approach to what constitutes damage in the tort of negligence, the

69 [1983] 2 AC 1. In *Abbott v Will Gannon & Smith Ltd* [2005] EWCA Civ 198, (2005) 103 ConLR 92, the Court of Appeal confirmed that *Pirelli* remained good law.
70 [1963] AC 758.
71 [1983] 2 AC 1 at 19, per Lord Scarman.
72 [1983] 2 AC 1.
73 [1983] 2 AC 1 at 16.

irrecoverability of the cost of repair prior to damage being suffered and to decisions such as *Rothwell v Chemical & Insulating Co Ltd.*[74] In *Ketteman v Hansel Properties Ltd*,[75] Lord Keith of Kinkel stated that a building should not be considered 'doomed from the start' for limitation purposes merely because it had a latent defect which must inevitably result in some damage at a later stage. The *obiter* comments of Lord Fraser espousing a sub-category of damage that is actionable today for losses that may occur tomorrow should perhaps best be treated as a proposition which complicates matters more than it assists and which may not still have a role to play in the law of tort.

Date of accrual in economic loss cases

10.13 The cases discussed in the previous section were all pleaded as 'property damage' cases although, somewhat confusingly, several could be also described in the taxonomy of tort law as being 'pure economic loss' cases.[76] The cases which are discussed in this section of the chapter are all 'pure economic loss' cases properly described, where liability is based on the principles set out in *Hedley Byrne Ltd v Heller & Partners Ltd.*[77] This class of liability covers cases where solicitors, accountants, valuers, advisers and businessmen assume responsibilities towards third parties which lead the courts to impose liability if they are negligent in carrying out those duties and cause that other person financial loss. There are a large number of reported cases on limitation issues arising in this area but the two most important are the decisions of the House of Lords in *Nykredit Mortgage Bank Plc v Edward Erdman Group Ltd (No 2)*[78] and *Law Society v Sephton & Co*,[79] which have attempted to clarify when negligence causing a 'risk' of an adverse future event will be held to have caused a present loss. Unfortunately, other than a general leaning towards the courts finding that solicitors and financial advisors generally by their negligence cause an immediate loss if a claimant enters into a transaction and receives a flawed asset or damaged bundle of rights or incurs greater risks than were necessary,[80] the terminology is not used consistently and the area continues to cause difficulty in borderline cases.[81]

74 [2007] UKHL 39, [2008] 1 AC 281.

75 [1987] AC 189 at 205. See also *Jones v Stroud District Council* [1986] 1 WLR 1141 (CA), which gave a restrictive interpretation to the scope of this doctrine.

76 See *Invercargill City Council v Hamlin* [1994] 3 NZLR 513, [1996] AC 264; however, in English law they continue to be treated as cases involving property damage: see *Abbott v Will Gannon & Smith Ltd* [2005] EWCA Civ 198, (1995) 103 ConLR 92.

77 [1964] AC 465.

78 [1997] 1 WLR 1627.

79 [2006] UKHL 22, [2006] 2 AC 543.

80 See, for example, *Axa Insurance Ltd v Akther & Darby* [2009] EWCA Civ 1166, [2010] 1 WLR 1662 and *Lane v Cullens Solicitors* [2011] EWCA Civ 547, [2012] QB 693.

81 For criticism of the current state of the law, see *Axa Insurance Ltd v Akther & Darby* [2009] EWCA Civ 1166, [2010] 1 WLR 1662 at para 28, per Arden LJ; see also the comments of Fennelly J in the Irish Supreme Court in *Gallagher v ACC Bank Plc* [2012] IESC 35, [2012] PNLR 29, (SC (Ire)).

Negligence leading to a purely contingent liability

10.14 In *Law Society v Sephton & Co*,[82] the defendant accountants certified that a fraudulent solicitor's accounts complied with the Solicitors' Accounts Rules for each of the years 1989 to 1995. During that period, the errant solicitor misappropriated the sum of £750,000, which only came to light in May 1996. The first claim for compensation made on the Solicitors' Compensation Fund by a former client was lodged in July 1996 and compensation payments were subsequently made by the Law Society. Four days before six years had expired from the date of the first claim on the fund, the Law Society sued the negligent accountants. A defence was raised that the claim was statute barred, on grounds that the loss had arisen on the date the accounts were certified in each year.[83] The House of Lords held that the negligence of the defendant had initially caused only a purely contingent loss which only led to a real loss when a claim was made on the fund,[84] and accordingly the claim was not statute barred. As was stated by Lord Hoffmann:

> 'A contingent liability is not as such damage until the contingency occurs. The existence of a contingent liability may depress the value of other property … or it may mean that a party to a bilateral transaction has received less than he should have done, or is worse off than if he had not entered into the transaction … But, standing alone as in this case, the contingency is not damage.'[85]

10.15 Neuberger LJ, in his judgment in the Court of Appeal in *Law Society v Sephton & Co*,[86] stated that the English law was different to that applied by the High Court of Australia in *Wardley Australia Ltd v State of Western Australia*.[87] However, Lord Hoffmann expressed himself in 'complete agreement' with that case,[88] where it had been held that a misrepresentation that led to the claimant agreeing to indemnify a bank in respect of loans made to a third party only caused the claimant to suffer a contingent loss at that time. Based on that finding, the High Court of Australia held that the cause of action was only complete and actual loss was only suffered when the indemnity was relied upon.[89] The same result (ie risk of future liability not present damage) was reached in *Sephton & Co*, whereas in *Forster v Outred & Co*[90] a contingent loss that was secured by a mortgage on the claimant's property was held to have caused an immediate loss for limitation purposes. The important distinction to be noted is between an unsecured and a secured contingent liability, as the latter is treated as immediately depressing the value of the claimant's property. This has been referred to

82 [2006] UKHL 22, [2006] 2 AC 543.

83 This argument was accepted by Michael Briggs QC, sitting as a deputy High Court judge: [2004] EWHC 544 (Ch), reversed on appeal: [2005] QB 1013.

84 The fact that the claims were enforceable only in public law was held not to affect this fact.

85 [2006] UKHL 22, [2006] 1 AC 543 at para 30.

86 [2005] QB 1013.

87 (1992) 175 CLR 514.

88 [2006] UKHL 22, [2006] 1 AC 543 at para 18.

89 See also *Gordon v JB Wheatley & Co* [2000] Lloyd's Rep PN 605 (CA), which the House of Lords in *Law Society v Sephton & Co* suggested had been wrongly decided.

90 [1982] 1 WLR 86.

as the 'damaged asset rule'. However, as Arden LJ noted in *Axa Insurance Ltd v Akther & Darby*,[91] an unsecured liability would still in general be capable of quantification, leaving an arbitrary dividing line for cases involving 'pure contingencies' and a distinction between a diminution in the value of a person's assets and the value of their net worth, which was stated to be 'difficult to rationalise'. A further possible restriction on the principle contained in *Sephton & Co*, taken from the speech of Lord Mance[92] in that case, is that the legal position of the Law Society was unchanged until a claim was received on the compensation fund, whereas in nearly all other cases the legal position of the claimant is changed at the time of the negligent act, generally when they act upon advice received.[93] A final attempt to pinpoint the scope of the applicability of the principle in *Sephton*, this time taken from the judgment of Longmore LJ in *Axa Insurance Ltd v Akther & Darby*,[94] is to limit it to cases where the liability is in the nature of a 'liability against indemnity' as that phrase has been interpreted in cases such as *Bradley v Eagle Star Insurance Co*.[95] This is an interesting point, which would treat the Law Society's rights as analogous to those seeking to recoup from a principal debtor monies paid in discharge of their guaranteed debt, albeit it is not a point that appears to have been relied upon in *Law Society v Sephton & Co*.

Claims against valuers and the 'benefits and burdens' test

10.16 The limitation principles governing claims by lending institutions[96] against valuers must be considered at this point, as what can be viewed as a different approach is taken in these cases. The complicating factor which differentiates these from other types of case is that where a bank receives negligent advice from a valuer as to the value of security being provided for a loan, the value of the property may still provide adequate security for the loan at the outset and for a lengthy time thereafter, before falling in value at a later point leading to losses being suffered. In *Nykredit Mortgage Bank Plc v Edward Erdman Group Ltd (No 2)*[97] the claimant loaned £4.4345 million in March 1990 to a third party to purchase property which had been negligently overvalued by £1.434 million by the defendant. It was subsequently held that the property had been worth slightly

91 [2009] EWCA Civ 1166, [2010] 1 WLR 1662 at para 15.

92 See the discussion in *Axa Insurance Ltd v Akther & Darby* [2009] EWCA Civ 1166, [2010] 1 WLR 1662 at paras 15 and 29.

93 A further exception to the application of the pure contingency rule is where negligent advice is given in relation to the entry into a transaction, where the 'bundle of rights' (or 'package of rights') the claimant received is less than he should have received, or where the burdens or obligations are greater than they should have been. This provides a second reason why it could be argued that the claimant in *Forster v Outred & Co* [1982] 1 WLR 86 suffered immediate loss: see *Axa Insurance*, cited above, at paras 31 and 57.

94 [2009] EWCA Civ 1166, [2010] 1 WLR 1662 at para 81.

95 [1989] AC 957; see the discussion of insurance cases in para 8.20.

96 Where the valuer acts for the property owner or intended purchaser, the limitation issues referred to in this paragraph will not arise: a negligent valuation of the property will in general cause an immediate loss upon the transaction being entered into, even if the transaction remains profitable due to an increase in property prices.

97 [1997] 1 WLR 1627.

less than the loan monies advanced for the purchase. The borrower defaulted and the property was later sold at a significant loss. In deciding on when the cause of action accrued,[98] the House of Lords was faced with three options: first, the date the monies were advanced; secondly, the date the borrower defaulted; or thirdly, the date the security was realised. It held that, as there were both benefits and burdens to the transaction, during the period when the benefits exceeded the burdens (ie while the security exceeded the loan) the claimant had suffered no loss. It was only when the loan exceeded the value of the security that loss was suffered; as this occurred on the date the loan was advanced, the claimant had suffered damage from the outset. The decision in *Nykredit* followed the earlier decision of the Court of Appeal in *First National Commercial Bank Plc v Humberts (a firm)*,[99] where it was held that the loss had been suffered *after* the loan monies had been advanced, as the security was sufficient (albeit less than had been represented) to secure repayment of the entirety of the loan on that date and had only subsequently fallen in value such that a deficiency arose. In his speech in *Law Society v Sephton & Co*,[100] Lord Hoffmann stated that *Nykredit* decides that:

> '[I]n a transaction in which there are benefits (covenant for repayment and security) as well as burdens (payment of the loan) and the measure of damages is the extent to which the lender is worse off than he would have been if he had not entered into the transaction, the lender suffers loss and damage only when it is possible to say that he is on balance worse off. It does not discuss a purely contingent liability.'[101]

It is unclear whether this test applies only to lenders or whether it might also apply, for example, to investors in a business. A logical limit on the doctrine is that the 'benefit' to the bank in *Nykredit* was capped at repayment of the principal, whereas in other cases the incorrect valuation will mean that the client overpays for an asset at the outset. If the claimant in *Forster v Outred & Co*,[102] who guaranteed her son's debt, had received a payment from him for going surety, there would have been benefits to her in entering into the transaction. Would one then have had to examine when her son's business started to become loss making in assessing when the burdens outweighed the benefits? Equally, could a court not assess the actuarial risk of loss to a bank if its security covers 50% of the value of the monies advanced instead of 90%? The approach of Lord Walker in *Law Society v Sephton & Co*[103] was to ask whether the negligence left the claimant (in a 'benefits and burdens' test) 'financially worse off' as opposed to 'worse off' (ie having suffered detriment). Although the approach in *Nykredit* has been largely subsumed within the 'package of rights' test referred to in the next paragraph, it is submitted that there is a tension between the two approaches.

98 Although the issue before the court asked when the cause of action accrued so that the court could fix the date from which interest ran, Lord Hoffmann made clear that the same principles would apply for limitation purposes: see [1997] 1 WLR 1627 at 1638.
99 [1995] 2 All ER 673.
100 [2006] UKHL 22, [2006] 2 AC 543.
101 [2006] UKHL 22, [2006] 2 AC 543 at para 20.
102 [1982] 1 WLR 86.
103 [2006] UKHL 22, [2006] 2 AC 543 at para 43.

Negligence leading to an immediate loss

10.17 In any particular case it may prove difficult to ascertain whether a party has suffered either a purely contingent liability or an actual present loss,[104] in particular if a contract contains benefits and burdens and a party only later realises that the burdens outweighed the benefits.[105] Where a party enters into a transaction (such as the purchase of an interest in land) as a result of negligent advice and obtains less than what he expected to obtain, the cause of action accrues when he enters into the transaction.[106] Where negligent tax advice is given by an accountant, the loss will in general be suffered when it is acted upon and the loss becomes inevitable,[107] even where a claimant subsequently disputes the Revenue's appraisal of the transaction: in such a case a finding of loss is not dependent on a decision of a tax tribunal.[108] In *DW Moore & Co Ltd v Ferrier*,[109] the defendant solicitor was negligent in drafting a non-compete clause in 1971, which was ineffective to prevent a former director from competing with the company when he left in 1980. It was held by the Court of Appeal that damage had been suffered in 1971 when the claimant had received a worthless covenant rather than a valuable chose in action. As time had started running against the defendant in 1971, the cause of action was statute barred by 1980 and the fact that the breach was a continuing breach did not affect this fact.

10.18 In *Forster v Outred & Co*,[110] the claimant signed a mortgage in 1973 by which she charged her farm to secure money which her son was borrowing. In 1975 she was called upon to discharge her son's indebtedness. In 1980 she issued a writ against the solicitors who had advised her in 1973 in which she alleged negligence by them in the advice which they had given her, as she had understood that the security she was offering was only in respect of a bridging loan. She argued that she was only subject to a contingent liability prior to 1975, when a demand was made. The Court of Appeal did not accept this argument and held that her action was statute barred. Upholding the correctness of this decision in *Law Society v Sephton & Co*,[111] Lord Hoffmann commented that detriment was suffered when the mortgage was signed, as by that act her freehold became encumbered even though the amount of the liability which she suffered was contingent at that time. In his speech in the same case, having discussed the bank valuer case *First National Commercial Bank Plc v Humberts*,[112] Lord

104 See *Knapp v Ecclesiastical Insurance Group Plc* [1998] PNLR 172, where it was held that a defendant who had caused a claimant to enter into a voidable contract caused him actual loss at that time, even though the contract was only avoided at a later date.

105 See *Axa Insurance Ltd v Akther & Darby* [2009] EWCA Civ 1166, [2010] 1 WLR 1662.

106 *Green v Eadie* [2011] EWHC B24 (Ch), [2012] Ch 363: here it was held that loss was suffered from when the contract for sale was signed and prior to completion occurring.

107 *Pegasus Management Holdings SCA v Ernst & Young* [2010] EWCA Civ 181, [2010] 3 All ER 297.

108 *Integral Memory Plc v Haines Watts* [2012] EWHC 342 (Ch).

109 [1988] 1 WLR 267.

110 [1982] 1 WLR 86.

111 [2006] UKHL 22, [2006] 1 AC 543 at paras 11–19.

112 [1995] 2 All ER 673.

Walker analysed the common features in cases where a client had, through the negligence of his professional adviser, ended up with a package of rights less valuable than he was entitled to expect, such as a mortgage securing a guarantee having more onerous terms than explained,[113] a reinsurance policy voidable for misrepresentation or non-disclosure,[114] or a deed which failed to protect his beneficial interest in the proceeds of sale of a property.[115] He commented:

> 'In all these cases the claimant has as a result of professional negligence suffered a diminution (sometimes immediately quantifiable, often not yet quantifiable) in the value of an existing asset of his, or has been disappointed (as against what he was entitled to expect) in an asset which he acquires, whether it is a house, a business arrangement, an insurance policy, or a claim for damages.'[116]

10.19 The claimant in *Axa Insurance Ltd v Akther & Darby*[117] sued a large number of defendant solicitors in relation to the provision of 'ATE' ('after the event') legal costs insurance. It alleged that the defendants had been negligent in vetting applications for ATE cover by stating the actions had a greater than 50% chance of success when they had not, and secondly, in their subsequent conduct in failing to reassess the chances of success prior to trial which should have led to cover being withdrawn. The claimant argued that it suffered loss when the actions were unsuccessful and that the outcome was a contingency which had to occur prior to loss being suffered. The Court of Appeal, by a majority, held that the 'package of rights' that the claimant had obtained at the outset was less valuable than it should have been and that loss was suffered when the ATE contracts were incepted. This was held to be different to a case where subsequent fluctuations in the value of the asset affected the question of whether loss had been suffered, as can arise in situations governed by *Nykredit,* where one must look to the benefits and burdens involved. In relation to the conduct breaches, the loss was held to have occurred when the defendant failed to notify the claimant of the decrease in the chance of success. In his concurring judgment, Longmore LJ succinctly stated that the defendants were alleged to be negligent in failing to inform the claimant that the actions had a less than 51% chance of success. By failing to communicate this fact, '[t]he loss to insurers was therefore in the natural order of things bound to occur'[118] and was not a contingency.

113 *Forster v Outred & Co* [1982] 1 WLR 86.

114 *Iron Trade Mutual Insurance Co Ltd v JK Buckenham Ltd* [1990] 1 All ER 808.

115 *Bell v Peter Browne & Co* [1990] 2 QB 495.

116 [2006] UKHL 22, [2006] 1 AC 543 at para 48. Although expressed differently by the Court of Appeal, the wording used by Flaux J in the High Court in *Axa Insurance*, quoted at [2009] EWCA Civ 1166, [2010] 1 WLR 1662 at para 7, expresses the principle well: 'When the professional's duty is to procure that a transaction has a particular characteristic or feature and the professional breaches that duty, the cause of action accrues on entering the flawed transaction'.

117 [2009] EWCA Civ 1166, [2010] 1 WLR 1662; see also *Arrowhead Capital Finance Ltd (in liquidation) v KPMG LLP* [2012] EWHC 1801 (Comm), where allegedly negligent advice in relation to a due diligence strategy for the recovery of input tax gave rise to a loss at the outset and not when the claimant discovered that the strategy had proven ineffective.

118 [2009] EWCA Civ 1166, [2010] 1 WLR 1662 at para 82.

10.20 Issues concerning alleged contingent losses arose again in *Pegasus Management Holdings SCA v Ernst & Young*,[119] where the claimant was given negligent tax advice which led him to invest £90 million in a company in April 1998. The invested funds then had to be invested in qualifying transactions over three years, which started in April 2000, to avail of certain capital gains tax reliefs. It was only discovered in October 2002 that the manner in which the investment had been structured created a liability to corporation tax which could have been avoided if the assets of the company, rather than the company, had been purchased in April 1998. A claim form seeking damages for negligence was issued in November 2005. The Court of Appeal held that the claimant did not receive what he should have received from the transaction, ie the advice and the contractual arrangements, which caused him loss as soon as he relied on the negligent advice in April 1998 and which was incapable of being cured subsequently. Rimer LJ categorised the types of cases in this area as falling into (i) no transaction cases; (ii) wrong transaction cases; and (iii) other cases. However, it is hard to see how this provides a useful method of approaching matters as, for example, *Nykredit* and *Forster v Outred & Co* were both classified as 'no transaction' cases but fall on different sides of the line. In *Lane v Cullens Solicitors*,[120] the claimant was the personal representative of a deceased who alleged that the defendants failed to warn him not to make any distributions from the assets of the estate after he was notified by a third party that she had a claim against the estate. He paid out the sum of £40,000 prior to the third party's proprietary estoppel claim succeeding and then issued proceedings more than six years after the payments were made but less than six years after the third party's claim against the estate was successful. The Court of Appeal held that his claim was statute barred as he had suffered actual loss from when he altered his position to his detriment and made the payments. Similarly, in a number of cases where proceedings were brought against solicitors who failed to protect the interests of their client or made conveyancing or mapping mistakes, such as *Nouri v Marvi*,[121] *Bowling & Co Solicitors v Edehomo*[122] and *Green v Eadie*,[123] measurable loss was held to have occurred when a contract for sale was signed or the property was accepted as security and that the cause of action accrued prior to registration of the sale, or in the case of *Green v Eadie*, prior to completion of the sale.

Recent foreign decisions and conclusion on contingent loss cases

10.21 The New Zealand Supreme Court in *Davys Burton v Thom*[124] and the Irish Supreme Court in *Gallagher v ACC Bank Plc*[125] have both recently had

119 [2010] EWCA Civ 181, [2010] 3 All ER 297; see also *Shore v Sedgwick Financial Services Ltd* [2008] EWCA Civ 863, [2008] PNLR 37, a case concerning negligent pension advice where advice leading to the claimant investing in a riskier pension scheme was held to have caused him loss when it was acted upon.

120 [2011] EWCA Civ 547, [2012] QB 693.

121 [2010] EWCA Civ 1107, [2010] 3 EGLR 79.

122 [2011] EWHC 393 (Ch), [2011] 1 WLR 2217.

123 [2011] EWHC B24 (Ch), [2012] Ch 363.

124 [2008] NZSC 65, [2009] 1 NZLR 437.

125 [2012] IESC 35.

cause to consider *Law Society v Sephton & Co* and *Nykredit Mortgage Bank Plc v Edward Erdman Group Ltd (No 2)*. In *Davys Burton*, the claimant entered into a separation agreement in 1990 which, due to flaws in its drafting, failed to contract out of the matrimonial property legislation. He issued proceedings in 2002 and claimed that the initial mistake only caused a contingent loss which developed into proper loss when the family court held in 1999 that the agreement was ineffective. While he succeeded on this point before the High Court, the Supreme Court held that he had suffered an immediate loss, namely the cost of remedying the defective agreement and the fact that the bundle of rights he obtained was defective. The decision is clearly correct and noteworthy for the evident disfavour displayed by the court towards the 'unsecured guarantee' and 'guarantee secured by a mortgage' distinction relied upon in *Sephton*, but is otherwise consistent with the English case law. The judgments[126] delivered by the Supreme Court in *Gallagher v ACC Bank Plc* demonstrate the importance of focusing closely on the facts where contingent losses are involved, as the court reversed the judgment of Charleton J in the High Court on his findings of fact,[127] while also adding some comments on the law. Mr Gallagher received bad advice from the defendant as a result of which he borrowed money from it to invest in its poorly structured product, whose excessive administrative charges and interest costs levied on the borrowed money left him with a very high risk of losing money. He argued that because there was a small chance that the monies invested on his behalf would have earned sufficient profits to leave him in a net positive position, one had to wait for the investment bond to mature before knowing whether the 'benefits' of the product had outweighed its 'burdens' and this argument was accepted by Charleton J. This decision was reversed on appeal, with Fennelly J delivering an erudite judgment containing a detailed analysis of the English case law,[128] which concluded with him ruefully approving of comments recently expressed by Lewis J that, '[u]nfortunately this concentration of judicial firepower does not give easy answers for the first instance judge'.[129] He noted the preponderance of cases where a risk which later eventuated was held to constitute a present loss, commenting that 'recent cases exhibit little concern for the striking of a just balance between the rights of plaintiffs and defendants'[130] and speculated that the passing of the Latent Damage Act 1986 may have influenced judicial thinking as to what is required to constitute actionable loss. A discussion of the recent New Zealand and Irish cases to have considered *Nykredit* and *Sephton* is an appropriate place to conclude this analysis with a brief comment that further refinement of the principles relating to contingent loss and the accrual of a cause of action should be expected.

126 Fennelly J delivered the main judgment of a unanimous court; O'Donnell J delivered a concurring judgment.

127 [2011] IEHC 367.

128 See in particular [2012] IESC 35 at paras 82–88 and 107 for well-reasoned criticism of *Shore v Sedgwick Financial Services Ltd* [2008] EWCA Civ 863, [2008] PNLR 37, to the effect that the claimant had received full market value when his pension was transferred and that it would not have been possible for him to show loss at that time.

129 *Pegasus Management Holdings SCA v Ernst & Young* [2008] EWHC 2720 (Ch), [2009] PNLR 209 at para 56.

130 [2012] IESC 35 at para 94.

Accrual of cause of action in relation to proceedings struck out for want of prosecution

10.22 In *Hatton v Chafes*,[131] the defendant firm of solicitors instituted proceedings on behalf of the claimant in 1987, in which he claimed damages from his former accountants. Those proceedings were struck out for want of prosecution in 1999. In 2000 he brought proceedings against the defendants for negligence in relation to the proceedings which had been struck out. The defendant raised a limitation defence and the Court of Appeal had to consider when he had first suffered damage. It held that he had certainly suffered damage from the time he had 'no arguable defence' to the application to dismiss the 1987 proceedings for want of prosecution, which was held to have been inevitable from 1994. As the proceedings had only been brought over six years after his claim would certainly have been struck out, the Court of Appeal noted that it was not necessary to decide whether a test of 'more probable than not' or 'had reduced his chances of success' should be applied in more borderline cases.[132]

Failing to act and ongoing obligations to remedy a problem

10.23 In cases where a solicitor's negligence consists of a failure to do something, the cause of action will not accrue until the last date on which it could properly have been done. In *Midland Bank v Hett, Stubbs & Kemp (a firm)*,[133] the defendants failed to register an interest in land and it was held that the cause of action only accrued on the date when it became too late to register the interest. This can be stated more accurately in the following terms: there was a continuing breach of duty by the defendants which led to a fresh cause of action accruing each day they failed to perform their obligations, but no loss of any significance was suffered until it was too late to register the land. This case was distinguished in *Bell v Peter Browne & Co*,[134] where it was held that the defendant solicitors did not remain under a continuing obligation to remedy their default after their retainer had been terminated. A limitation defence succeeded in *Green v Eadie*,[135] where an initial mapping error by the claimant's solicitors caused her loss when she entered into a contract for sale (outside the limitation period) as well as causing her to fail to rescind the contract during the limitation period and prior to completion. The finding that the claimant had suffered loss on a date prior to the contract becoming irrevocable (ie while rescission was still possible) is close to the borderline and the reference to 'more than trivial loss'[136] and the 'practical inconvenience' of exercising a right to rescind sets the bar very low for the running of time; reference to 'wasted costs' would seem to refer to costs that the

131 [2003] EWCA Civ 341, [2007] Lloyd's Rep PN 15.

132 [2003] EWCA Civ 341, [2007] Lloyd's Rep PN 15 at para 64; see also *Khan v Falvey* [2002] EWCA Civ 400, [2002] Lloyd's Rep PN 369; *Jessup v Wetherell* [2006] EWHC 2582 (QB); and *Berney v Saul t/a Thomas Saul & Co* [2013] EWCA Civ 640.

133 [1979] Ch 384.

134 [1990] 2 QB 495; see also *Nouri v Marvi* [2009] EWHC 2725 (Ch).

135 [2011] EWHC B24 (Ch), [2012] Ch 363.

136 [2011] EWHC B24 (Ch), [2012] Ch 363 at para 57.

solicitors would have charged her for their services, although it is arguable that no fee would have been recoverable by them in the circumstances. The judgment and outcome in this case endorses the approach adopted in *Bell v Peter Browne & Co*,[137] which values a certain limitation period running from the date of an initial act or omission over allowing an extended limitation period which would end up penalising a professional who remained in an ongoing relationship with a client.

Solicitors' duties owed to third parties

10.24 If a solicitor is negligent in acting for a client (whether in his advice or his drafting) in relation to a will, or fails to prepare a will at all, when does the cause of action accrue? In *Bacon v Howard Kennedy (a firm)*,[138] it was held that the cause of action only accrues to the beneficiaries upon the death of the testator, although McGee[139] has noted the difficulties in distinguishing this case from *Forster v Outred & Co.*[140] In *Daniels v Thomson*,[141] it was held a cause of action relating to negligent tax advice given to a person to minimise the liability to tax which the personal representatives to his estate would face upon his death only accrued upon his death. In cases where the negligence of the solicitor leads to litigation in which a will (or transfer) is challenged, the date on which loss is in fact suffered by a beneficiary may occur at a later date. In the Irish case of *Darby v Shanley practising as Oliver Shanley & Co*,[142] it was held by Irvine J that the loss in such circumstances only occurs when the litigation concludes, as it is only at this date that one can say with certainty that loss has in fact been suffered. This decision may go too far although its application of the principles discussed in this chapter to a case where the claimant is a beneficiary and not the recipient of advice is of interest given the absence of many decided cases to have considered the types of issues that arose in *Bacon v Howard Kennedy (a firm)*.

137 [1990] 2 QB 495.
138 [1999] PNLR 1.
139 McGee, *Limitation Periods* (6th edn, London: Sweet & Maxwell, 2010) at para 5.034.
140 [1982] 1 WLR 86.
141 [2004] EWCA Civ 307, [2007] Lloyd's Rep PN 16. This finding is technically *obiter dictum* as the case failed on a pleading point.
142 [2009] IEHC 459.

CHAPTER 11

The Consumer Protection Act 1987

INTRODUCTION

11.01 Part 1 of the Consumer Protection Act 1987 ('CPA 1987') transposes the Product Liability Directive[1] into English law. The Directive and the CPA 1987 supplement the common law cause of action for negligence by providing an additional remedy for personal injuries or property damage caused by a defective product.[2] Section 11A of the Limitation Act 1980 ('LA 1980'), as inserted,[3] contains[4] the limitation provisions for an action under Pt 1 of the CPA 1987 and provides that a three-year limitation period applies to both personal injuries and property damage claims under the Act. This three-year limitation period is subject to extension on grounds of date of knowledge,[5] disability,[6] fraud or concealment[7] and the discretion to disapply the limitation period contained in s 33 of the LA 1980.[8]

11.02 Where the claim is in respect of the death of a deceased person under s 1 of the Law Reform (Miscellaneous Provisions) Act 1934, the three years run from the date of death and the relevant person's date of knowledge is that of the personal representative.[9] However, in all cases it is subject to a ten-year long-stop that extinguishes any liability under the Act upon its expiry.[10]

1 Council Directive 85/374/EEC of 25 July 1985 on the approximation of the laws, regulations and administrative provisions of the Member States concerning liability for defective products.
2 'Product' is defined in s 1(2)(c) of the Act as meaning 'any goods or electricity and [excluding suppliers of raw materials and component parts] includes a product which is comprised in another product, whether by virtue of being a component part or raw material or otherwise'.
3 CPA 1987, s 6(6); Sch 1.
4 LA 1980, s 11A(1) and (2).
5 LA 1980, s 14(1A).
6 LA 1980, s 28(7).
7 LA 1980, s 32(4A).
8 LA 1980, s 33.
9 LA 1980, s 11A(5); see further subs (6) for a definition of personal representative for this section and subs (7) which states that if there is more than one personal representative the earliest date of knowledge governs.
10 LA 1980, s 11A(3).

11.03 Two aspects of the CPA 1987 are particularly noteworthy. First, the extension to the limitation period on date of knowledge grounds applies to both personal injuries and property damage actions.[11] Secondly, the Act contains a long-stop provision, inserted as s 11A(3) in the LA 1980, which extinguishes any right of action ten years from the date the product was supplied to another person by the producer, by any person holding himself out as the producer or by the importer,[12] regardless of whether (or when) any right of action under the Act had accrued. This will, in some personal injuries cases, have the result of imposing a shorter limitation period for claims relying on the CPA 1987 to that which will apply to a common law claim in the tort of negligence arising on the same facts.

DEFENDANTS TO CLAIMS UNDER THE CPA 1987

11.04 The parties liable under the CPA 1987 for damage caused by a defective product are the producer of the defective product,[13] any party holding himself out as the producer,[14] and, if the product was imported from outside the EU, the party who imported it into the EU in the course of his business.[15] If a supplier of the product is asked to identify the manufacturer or other person potentially liable under s 2(2) and fails to do so within a reasonable time, he is made liable for the damage.[16]

ACCRUAL OF THE CAUSE OF ACTION

11.05 A cause of action under the Act accrues when a person suffers damage by reason of a defect in a product.[17] Damage is defined as meaning 'death or personal injury or any loss of or damage to any property (including land)',[18] but excludes damage to the product itself.[19] The CPA 1987 provides that personal injury 'includes any disease and any other impairment of a person's physical or mental condition'[20] and that damage to property 'shall be regarded as having occurred at the earliest time at which a person with an interest in the property had knowledge of the material facts about the loss or damage'.[21]

11 LA 1980, s 11A(4).
12 CPA 1987, s 4.
13 CPA 1987, s 2(2)(a). The producer is defined in s 1(2) as the person who manufactured the product, who won or abstracted a substance which is not manufactured or, if the type of products does not fall within the foregoing categories, the person who carried out the industrial process which gave the product its essential characteristics.
14 CPA 1987, s 2(2)(b).
15 CPA 1987, s 2(2)(c).
16 CPA 1987, s 2(3).
17 CPA 1987, s 2(1).
18 CPA 1987, s 5(1).
19 CPA 1987, s 5(2).
20 CPA 1987, s 45(1).
21 CPA 1987, s 5(5); the balance of s 5 defines 'knowledge' in this context as including some, but not all, of the elements that constitute a person's date of knowledge (discussed below), rendering the test in s 5(5) somewhat otiose.

DATE OF KNOWLEDGE

11.06 Section 14(1A) of the LA 1980 contains the date of knowledge provisions for claims brought under Pt 1 of the CPA 1987. It contains slightly different wording to that used in s 14(1), but this is unlikely to lead to a different result on the facts of any particular case. It states that a person's date of knowledge for a claim for personal injuries or death caused by a defective product brought under Pt 1 of the CPA 1987 is the date on which the claimant first had knowledge of the following facts:

(a) such facts about the damage caused by the defect as would lead a reasonable person who had suffered such damage[22] to consider it sufficiently serious to justify his instituting proceedings for damages against a defendant who did not dispute liability and was able to satisfy a judgment;

(b) that the damage was wholly or partly attributable to the facts and circumstances alleged to constitute the defect; and

(c) the identity of the defendant.

The subsection continues by stating that in determining the date on which a person first had such knowledge, that person's knowledge of whether particular facts or circumstances would or would not, as a matter of law, constitute a defect, or whether he had a right of action by virtue of Pt 1 of the CPA 1987, shall be disregarded. It concludes by adding that, in a case relating to loss of or damage to property, time for the purpose of the date of knowledge test runs from the date of knowledge of the plaintiff or, if earlier, of any person in whom his cause of action was previously vested. This proviso appears to apply to the same circumstance as is catered for by s 3 of the Latent Damage Act 1986. Given the paucity of case law on the CPA 1987, readers are referred to the personal injuries date of knowledge case law for guidance on the interpretation of s 14(1A).[23]

DISABILITY, DELIBERATE CONCEALMENT AND S 33 OF THE LA 1980

11.07 Section 6(6) of the CPA 1987 provides that Sch 1 of the Act shall amend the LA 1980 in the manner set out therein, which includes amendments to the provisions on disability,[24] deliberate concealment[25] and disapplication of the personal injuries limitation period.[26] In the case of all three inserted provisions, it is stated that they may not be used to override the ten-year long-stop contained in s 11A(3) of the LA 1980 for claims under Pt 1 of the CPA 1987. In the case of

22 Section 5(4) provides that no damages shall be awarded in respect of damage to property if the amount of any award would be less than £275. It is not made clear whether financial loss below this threshold could still constitute damage for the purpose of s 14(1A)(a), although this is presumably not the case.

23 See Ch 13.

24 LA 1980, s 28(7).

25 LA 1980, s 32(4A).

26 LA 1980, s 33 as amended.

s 28(7), it provides that a person under a disability shall have three years from when they cease to be under a disability or die to bring proceedings under the Act. In the case of s 33 of the LA 1980, the amended provision confirms that the discretion to disapply the limitation period does not apply to property damage claims.

LONG-STOP EXTINGUISHING LIABILITY AFTER TEN YEARS

11.08 Section 11A(3) of the LA 1980 imposes a ten-year long-stop on claims for damages brought pursuant to Pt I of the CPA 1987. Time runs from 'the relevant time', as defined in s 4 of the CPA 1987, namely the date that the producer, the person holding himself out as a producer or the importer of the product into the EU supplied the product to another.[27] In all other cases, 'the relevant time' is the time when the product was last supplied by a person to whom s 2(2) of the CPA 1987 does apply in relation to the product.[28] The long-stop operates regardless of whether (or when) a right of action had accrued by that date. The phrase 'the relevant time' is used in the English legislation in place of the phrase 'first put into circulation' in the Directive, which was considered by the European Court of Justice in *O'Byrne v Sanofi Pasteur MSD Ltd.*[29] The ECJ held that a product was put into circulation when it was taken out of the manufacturing process operated by the producer and entered a marketing process in the form in which it was offered to the public in order to be used or consumed. The marketing process might or might not be done by a subsidiary of the manufacturer, and this was not the determining factor. When the proceedings returned to the English courts following this decision by the ECJ, the claimant sought liberty to substitute the producer for the party originally named as defendant, a subsidiary company which was only a distributor of the product. The application was brought under CPR 19.5(3)(a) based on an alleged mistake on the part of the claimant's solicitor. The case proceeded under the name *O'Byrne v Aventis Pasteur SA* and the Court of Appeal allowed the substitution,[30] but the House of Lords held[31] that a second reference to the European Court of Justice was necessary for guidance on the meaning of the phrase 'instituted proceedings against the producer'. The European Court of Justice held that it was not permissible to add the producer as an additional defendant in proceedings after the expiration of the ten-year long-stop period, even if they had not been joined by reason of a mistake. The ECJ added a proviso though and stated that the substitution should be allowed if the putting into circulation of the product by the subsidiary was

27 CPA 1987, s 4(2)(a).
28 CPA 1987, s 4(2)(b).
29 (Case C-127/04) [2006] 1 WLR 1606.
30 [2007] EWCA Civ 939, [2008] 1 WLR 1188; see also *Horne-Roberts v SmithKline Beecham* [2001] EWCA Civ 2006, [2002] 1 WLR 1662.
31 [2008] UKHL 34, [2008] 4 All ER 881.

determined by the producer.[32] It stated that it was for the national court to rule on whether the case came within this test. When the proceedings resumed before the United Kingdom Supreme Court, it held that the substitution should not be allowed as the putting into circulation by the subsidiary had not been determined by the producer.[33]

32 (C-358/08) [2010] 1 WLR 1375. In his speech in the House of Lords decision that followed this reference, Lord Rodger noted that this proviso probably only overlaps with a situation where a supplier comes within the definition of a producer in art 3(1) of the Directive: see [2010] UKSC 23, [2010] 1 WLR 1412 at para 35.

33 [2010] UKSC 23, [2010] 1 WLR 1412.

CHAPTER 12

The Latent Damage Act 1986

INTRODUCTION

12.01 The law on limitation has always struggled to deal with situations where a claimant suffers damage that is latent, by which is meant damage[1] of which he is unaware. To a lesser extent, it has struggled to deal with situations where a claimant knows he has suffered an injury but is ignorant of either the identity of the wrongdoer[2] or the causality between their actions and the injury suffered. In the area of personal injuries, claimants who had developed slowly accruing and progressive lung diseases, where the first injury had been suffered long before they had reason to believe they had been injured, found their claims to be statute barred in *Cartledge v E Jopling & Sons Ltd*.[3] This result was reached despite Lord Reid lamenting the fact that it was 'unreasonable and unjustifiable in principle that a cause of action should be held to accrue before it is possible to discover any injury'[4] while finding that he was unable to reach a different result as this would have rendered the discoverability test applicable in cases of fraud and concealment otiose. The Limitation Act 1963 was enacted to remedy this problem, which has been retained with modifications in s 11 of the Limitation Act 1980 ('LA 1980').[5] This is now settled law, but it is worth noting in passing that the United States Supreme Court in *Urie v Thomson*,[6] the Supreme Court of Canada in *City of Kamloops v Nielsen*[7] and the New Zealand Court of Appeal in

1 In tort law in England, a somewhat artificial distinction is drawn between a defect which has not yet caused 'damage' and the 'damage' which it subsequently causes, with defects that render a product less valuable or leave a risk of causing injury held to only be actionable within the law of contract: see *Murphy v Brentwood DC* [1991] 1 AC 398 at 475, per Lord Bridge.
2 See *RB Policies at Lloyds v Butler* [1950] 1 KB 76.
3 [1963] AC 758.
4 [1963] AC 758 at 771.
5 Significantly, the LA 1980, ss 33 and 4A also give the court the power to disapply the limitation period in personal injuries actions and defamation actions, respectively.
6 (1949) 337 US 163; *United States v Kubrick* (1979) 444 US 111.
7 (1984) 10 DLR (4th) 641; *Central Trust Co v Rafuse* [1986] 2 SCR 147; *Winnipeg Condominium Corporation No 36 v Bird Construction Co* (1995) 121 DLR (4th) 193.

Invercargill City Council v Hamlin[8] (affirmed on appeal by the Privy Council[9]), though not the High Court of Australia in *Hawkins v Clayton*,[10] have all held that a cause of action in negligence only accrues from the date a plaintiff ought reasonably to have discovered that he had suffered the loss or damage.

12.02 While the state of the law as it applied to personal injuries actions was clarified in *Cartledge v E Jopling & Sons Ltd*,[11] which was thereafter reversed by statute, the law remained uncertain in the area of non-personal injuries cases, in particular property damage and pure economic loss cases in tort.[12] This was no doubt due in large part to the fact that the contours of the underlying cause of action in negligence and recoverability of damages were themselves the subject of much debate.[13] However, in *Pirelli General Cable Works Ltd v Oscar Faber & Partners Ltd*,[14] the House of Lords confirmed that the lacuna in the legislation remained unremedied for non-personal injuries actions and that the cause of action could become statute barred prior to the claimant becoming aware that he had suffered any damage. This was because it held that the cause of action in defective buildings cases accrues when, but not before, physical damage occurs, but that it will accrue whether or not its existence or potential existence is, or could reasonably have been, known to the claimant. This outcome was thought to work an injustice on many wronged parties which, in turn, led to the Twenty-Fourth Report of the Law Reform Committee[15] and the passing of the Latent Damage Act 1986 ('LDA 1986').

OVERVIEW OF THE PROVISIONS OF THE LDA 1986

12.03 The LDA 1986 inserted ss 14A and 14B (the main provisions), 28A (disability) and 32(5) (concealment) into the LA 1980. In addition, s 3 of the Act creates a right of action for successive owners of a property in respect of latent damage to the property. It only applies to non-personal injuries actions claiming damages in the tort of negligence.[16] In cases where s 14A applies, the general tort limitation period contained in s 2 does not apply,[17] instead s 14A(4) provides that the limitation period is six years[18] from the date of accrual of the cause of action

8 [1994] 3 NZLR 513; *S v G* [1995] 3 NZLR 681 and *GD Searle & Co v Gunn* [1996] 2 NZLR 129; however, in *Murray v Morel & Co Ltd* [2007] NZSC 27, [2007] 3 NZLR 721, the court refused to extend it to money claims.

9 [1996] AC 264: the Privy Council held that the law in New Zealand was different to that applied by the House of Lords in England.

10 (1988) 164 CLR 539; *Wardley Australia Ltd v State of Western Australia* (1992) 175 CLR 514.

11 [1963] AC 758.

12 See *Sparham-Souter v Town and Country Developments (Essex) Ltd* [1976] QB 858.

13 See *Anns v Merton LBC* [1978] AC 728; *Murphy v Brentwood DC* [1991] 1 AC 398.

14 [1983] 2 AC 1.

15 Cmnd 9390.

16 LA 1980, s 14A(1); see para 12.04.

17 LA 1980, s 14A(2).

18 LA 1980, s 14A(4)(a).

or three years[19] from the 'starting date', as further defined in the section,[20] if that period expires later. The 'starting date' for the running of time under s 14A is the date the claimant had knowledge of the following: that he had suffered damage,[21] the identity of the defendant[22] (and, if relevant, the facts relevant to vicarious liability[23]) and knowledge that the damage is attributable to the acts alleged to constitute the negligence.[24] The LDA 1986 also introduced an overriding time limit of 15 years for non-personal injuries actions claiming damages for negligence, which runs from the date of the act (or last of a series of acts) alleged to constitute the negligence or cause of the damage.[25] It is important to note that the overriding time limit has application beyond cases where s 14A is invoked.

CAUSES OF ACTION FALLING WITHIN THE LDA 1986

12.04 Section 14A(1) is reasonably clear on its face in stating that it only applies to claims for damages for negligence, particularly if read in conjunction with s 14A(2) which states that the tort limitation period contained in s 2 shall not apply if the LDA 1986 provisions apply. For this reason the decision at first instance of Kenneth Rokison QC in *Iron Trade Mutual Insurance Co Ltd v JK Buckenham Ltd*,[26] which held that s 14A does not apply to a claim based on an express or implied term in a contract imposing a duty to take care and which was followed by the Court of Appeal in *Société Commerciale de Réassurance v ERAS (International) Ltd*,[27] is clearly correct. Section s 14A has also been held not to apply to actions claiming damages for misrepresentation contrary to s 2 of the Misrepresentation Act 1967[28] or damages for breach of the Defective Premises Act 1972.[29] Thus, in *Robinson v PE Jones (Contractors) Ltd*,[30] where it was held by the Court of Appeal that the agreement between the parties by its terms precluded the existence of a concurrent duty of care in tort, there were no means by which the claimant could invoke s 14A so as to extend time for an action arising out of what appears to have been accepted by all parties to have been latent damage. Similarly, s 14A would appear not to apply to an action claiming restitution for unjust enrichment or claiming damages for any other tort such as nuisance. This leads to the undesirable consequence that the limitation period for an action pleaded as a claim in the tort of negligence can differ greatly, and without any reason, from that applicable to a claim for breach of contract or money due under an enactment (such as the Misrepresentation Act 1967).

19 LA 1980, s 14A(4)(b).
20 LA 1980, s 14A(5).
21 LA 1980, s 14A(6)(a).
22 LA 1980, s 14A(8)(b).
23 LA 1980, s 14A(8)(c).
24 LA 1980, s 14A(8)(a).
25 LA 1980, s 14B(1); see para 12.12.
26 [1990] 1 All ER 808.
27 [1992] 2 All ER 82.
28 *Laws v Lloyds* [2003] EWCA Civ 1887, [2003] All ER (D) 392 (Dec).
29 *Payne v John Setchell Ltd* (2002) BLR 489.
30 [2011] EWCA Civ 9, [2012] QB 44.

THE 'STARTING DATE' IN THE LDA 1986

12.05 The phrase 'date of knowledge' is not used in s 14A and instead it refers to a claimant's 'starting date'[31] being the date when he had 'knowledge required for bringing an action',[32] a somewhat circular phrase that is further defined in s 14A(6)–(10). Although the nomenclature differentiates the section from the personal injuries discoverability provisions in ss 11 and 14, there are similarities between both sets of provisions and personal injuries limitation judgments have been relied upon in many of the decisions to have considered s 14A. A summary of the elements of the knowledge required for bringing an action is as follows:

(a) knowledge of the material facts about the damage;[33]

(b) knowledge that the damage was attributable in whole or in part to the act or omission which is alleged to constitute negligence,[34] but failure to appreciate the legal consequences of the acts or omissions is not relevant in determining the starting date;[35]

(c) knowledge of the identity of the defendant;[36] and

(d) if the negligent act was that of a third party, knowledge of the identity of that person and the additional facts supporting the bringing of an action against the defendant.[37]

BURDEN OF PROOF

12.06 A claimant who seeks to rely on the extended limitation period in s 14A bears the burden of proving that he first had knowledge of the material facts referred to in s 14A within three years prior to the action being brought.[38]

DEGREE OF KNOWLEDGE REQUIRED AND 'CONSTRUCTIVE KNOWLEDGE'

12.07 The phrase 'constructive knowledge' is not used in s 14A but it provides a useful heading for the facts and knowledge that are attributed to a claimant by s 14A(10). Knowledge attributed to the claimant includes knowledge he might reasonably be expected to acquire, (i) from facts observable or ascertainable by him, and (ii) from facts ascertainable by him with the help of appropriate expert

31 LA 1980, s 14A(4)(b) and (5).
32 LA 1980, s 14A(5).
33 LA 1980, s 14A(6)(a).
34 LA 1980, s 14A(8)(a).
35 LA 1980, s 14A(9).
36 LA 1980, s 14A(8)(b).
37 LA 1980, s 14A(8)(c).
38 *Haward v Fawcetts (a firm)* [2006] UKHL 9, [2006] 1 WLR 682 at para 106, per Lord Mance; see further para 2.21 for a more detailed discussion of the burden of proof.

advice which it is reasonable for him to seek, but not (iii) facts ascertainable only with the help of expert advice so long as he has taken all reasonable steps to obtain (and, where appropriate, to act on) that advice. In addition to this statutory statement of what a person is deemed to know, the case law has examined in some detail the level of knowledge required for time to start to run. A particularly lucid discussion of the level of certainty required is contained in *Haward v Fawcetts (a firm)*,[39] where Lord Nicholls stated as follows:

> 'Thus, as to the degree of certainty required, Lord Donaldson of Lymington MR gave valuable guidance in *Halford v Brookes* [1991] 1 WLR 428 at 443. He noted that knowledge does not mean knowing for certain and beyond possibility of contradiction. It means knowing with sufficient confidence to justify embarking on the preliminaries to the issue of a writ, such as submitting a claim to the proposed defendant, taking advice, and collecting evidence: "Suspicion, particularly if it is vague and unsupported, will indeed not be enough, but reasonable belief will normally suffice." In other words, the claimant must know enough for it to be reasonable to begin to investigate further.'[40]

It remains to be seen whether the approach adopted by the Supreme Court in *AB v Ministry of Defence*[41] to the degree of knowledge required for s 14(1)(b) will be applied unaltered to s 14A. Although one distinguishing factor is that a claimant is unable to disapply the limitation period in s 14A, it is likely that the interpretation given to the personal injuries provisions will influence the approach to s 14A. However, the question of whether facts were observable or ascertainable by a claimant will in all cases be fact specific, whichever formulation of general principle is adopted.

12.08 Given the broad interpretation that has been given to 'knowledge' in the decisions on s 14A, and the fact that the failure to appreciate that known facts constitute negligence at common law is irrelevant,[42] the amplification of the claimant's actual and deemed knowledge by s 14A(10) has played less of a role in the case law.[43] A fairly typical example of knowledge which is observable or ascertainable by a claimant is the content of documents, even legal documents whose precise effect might not be understood. Thus, in *Webster v Cooper & Burnett (a firm)*,[44] the Court of Appeal held that the claimant was fixed with knowledge of the fact that an 'all sums due mortgage' had been entered into by her as she signed the document. This finding was reached despite the claimant alleging she had not read the document at the time and had instead relied on advice from the defendants. Whether it is reasonable to seek expert advice is a fact-specific question; for

39 [2006] UKHL 9, [2006] 1 WLR 682.
40 [2006] UKHL 9, [2006] 1 WLR 682 at para 9.
41 [2012] UKSC 9, [2013] 1 AC 78.
42 See para 12.12.
43 See also *Finance for Mortgages Ltd v Farley & Co (a firm)* [1998] PNLR 145; *Oakes v Hopcroft* (2000) 56 BMLR 136; *Graham v Entec Europe Ltd* [2003] EWCA Civ 1177; *Gravgaard v Aldridge & Brownlee (a firm)* [2004] EWCA Civ 1529; and *Harris Springs Ltd v Howes* [2007] EWHC 3271 (TCC), [2008] BLR 229.
44 [1999] All ER (D) 1086; see also *Chandra v Booke North (a firm)* [2013] EWHC 417 (QB) for a case where knowledge of the content of documents was not attributed to the claimants.

example, in *The Mortgage Corp v Lambert & Co*,[45] the claimants were held by the Court of Appeal not to have come under an obligation to question the advice received by it from the defendant valuers from the date a borrower defaulted and proceedings were brought, but only from when it was reasonable for it to have sought a retrospective valuation. In *Harris Springs Ltd v Howes*,[46] the defendant structural engineer was engaged by the claimant's architect for a construction project. He designed the foundations in early 1994, and the extension was completed that November. The widening of an expansion joint between the floor slab of the extension and a wall was noted in August 1995; the defendant carried out an inspection and suggested that the contractors carry out certain further investigations into its cause and monitoring. Thereafter, the claimant noticed a crack in the floor slab in October 2003 and brought proceedings in July 2006, claiming that the defendant had negligently designed the foundations. HH Judge Raynor QC held that the claim was not statute barred: not even the defendant regarded the movement noticed in 1995 as significant and the claimant was able to obtain subsidence insurance cover despite this issue. It was also held that it would not have been reasonable for the claimant to have sought expert engineering advice from anyone other than the defendant prior to the cracking of the floor slab. In *St Anselm Development Company Ltd v Slaughter and May (a firm)*,[47] the defendants gave negligent advice to the claimant in March 1999 in relation to the drafting of two leases, following which the claimant entered into new leases not containing an indemnity clause for ground rent payments made by it to the head landlord. It was held by David Richard J that, there being no concealment alleged and both the defendants and the tenant having explained why the ground rent payments had ceased in late 1999, the claimant had knowledge of sufficient facts to give it reasonable cause to start asking questions about the advice received even though, at that time, it still did not know that the absence of the indemnity clause was not required by statute as had been its understanding at the outset.

KNOWLEDGE OF THE MATERIAL FACTS ABOUT THE DAMAGE: S 14A(6)(A) AND (7)

12.09 In considering whether a claimant has knowledge of the 'material facts about the damage',[48] regard must be had to s 14A(7), which adds that this must be such 'as would lead a reasonable person who had suffered such damage to consider it sufficiently serious to justify his instituting proceedings for damages against a defendant who did not dispute liability and was able to satisfy a judgment'. There is an element of unpredictability about what level of financial loss would cause a reasonable person to commence litigation: the decision of Judge Bowsher QC in *Horbury v Craig Hall & Rutley*,[49] which held that time ran from

45 [2000] All ER (D) 524; see also *Finance for Mortgages Ltd v Farley & Company (A Firm)* [1998] PNLR 145 and *Rehman v Jones Lang Lasalle Ltd* [2013] EWHC 1339 (QB).

46 [2007] EWHC 3271 (TCC), (2008) BLR 229.

47 [2013] EWHC 125 (Ch).

48 LA 1980, s 14A(6)(a).

49 (1991) 7 PN 206.

the point when a cost of £132 to repair a chimney had been known about, would have been harsh even in 1991. In *Eagle v Redlime Ltd*,[50] the claimant engaged the defendant to lay a concrete foundation on which a building was erected. He noticed subsidence, cracking in the walls and the need for repairs to the plasterwork, which the defendant denied were signs of defects, and obtained an engineer's report confirming that significant defects with the foundations were causing the damage and that it was far more serious than he thought. Eder J held that he had sufficient knowledge 'to justify embarking on the preliminaries to the issue of a writ'[51] from prior to receipt of the expert report and that his claim was statute barred. In *3M United Kingdom Plc v Linklaters & Paines*,[52] the defendants were negligent in 1989 in failing to appreciate that their advice to the claimant to assign a lease to a related company would lead to a break clause becoming inoperative. An in-house solicitor for the claimant became aware of this fact in August 1995 but, in response to a limitation defence, the claimant sought to argue that it only had knowledge of damage within the meaning of s 14A(7) from September 1995, when the landlord found out that it was no longer bound by the break clause. The Court of Appeal rejected this argument and held that the claimant had knowledge of the material facts about the damage (the loss of the break clause, not the breakdown in negotiations) from the earlier date. It proceeded to find that it was not appropriate to allow the claimant time to 'wait and see' if the landlord noticed the difficulty, as it was inevitable that it was going to cause problems. Despite the claimant believing there was a chance that the problem could be rectified by executing a re-assignment, this was held not to affect the outcome as it would have led to further legal costs being incurred, which was itself a recoverable head of loss. In commenting on s 14A(7), Moore-Bick LJ noted as follows: 'In a commercial context damage does not have to be very substantial to satisfy those requirements in view of the limited cost of issuing proceedings'.[53] While *Horbury* and *3M* have set the level for qualifying damage in s 14A at a low level, it still remains unclear what monetary threshold applies. Given the effect of the single action rule,[54] the fact that not all legal or witness costs are recoverable even if a party is successful and the stresses involved in successful litigation, it is submitted that there is room for arguing that a higher (and inflation-adjusted) monetary threshold to that found sufficient in *Horbury* should apply.

KNOWLEDGE THAT THE DAMAGE IS ATTRIBUTABLE TO THE WRONGFUL ACTS: S 14A(8)(A)

12.10 This provision has a direct analogy in s 14(1)(b) and has been the focus of much of the reported litigation concerning s 14A. In *Hallam-Eames v Merrett*

50 [2011] EWHC 838 (QB), (2011) 136 Con LR 137.
51 *Haward v Fawcetts (a firm)* [2006] UKHL 9, [2006] 1 WLR 682 at para 9, per Lord Nicholls.
52 [2006] EWCA Civ 530, [2006] All ER (D) 37 (May).
53 [2006] EWCA Civ 530, [2006] All ER (D) 37 (May) at para 33.
54 This rule limits a claimant to one action in respect of all damage suffered by reason of the negligence of a defendant: see *Hamlin v Edwin Evans* [1996] 2 EGLR 106; *Williams v Lishman, Sidwell, Campbell & Price* [2010] EWCA Civ 418, [2010] PNLR 25; and paras 10.05–10.06.

Syndicates Ltd,[55] it was held by Hoffmann LJ that the act or omission of which the claimant must have knowledge must be one which is causally relevant for the purposes of an allegation of negligence. He therefore held that knowledge that certain contracts which were reinsured by Lloyd's Names showed increasing renewal premia over successive years did not set time running. Instead what was required was knowledge of facts that would make it reasonable for them to instruct an expert to advise them that no reasonable underwriter would have underwritten the risks. In *Haward v Fawcetts (a firm)*,[56] the House of Lords gave what remains the most important decision in the area. The claimant in this case retained the defendants as his advisers for investments made from 1994 onwards in a business which failed, where he knew all of his money had been lost by December 1998. His evidence was that he believed that the business had failed due to a variety of economic factors and that he only began to question the advice he had been given in the middle of 1999. He issued proceedings in December 2001. The defendants alleged that any loss suffered more than six years prior to the action being brought was statute barred and, in response, the claimant sought to rely on s 14A. The House of Lords noted that the business had made large losses over a number of years and required several cash injections. In circumstances where the facts were not terribly complicated and did not require an expert report to explain issues of technical complexity, the House of Lords held that the claimant had sufficient knowledge long before December 1998 to commence the preliminaries required to bring proceedings. Lord Nicholls stated that 'it is not necessary for the claimant to have knowledge sufficient to enable his legal advisers to draft a fully and comprehensively particularised statement of claim'.[57] He followed the approach adopted by the Court of Appeal in *Nash v Eli Lilly & Co*,[58] which held that 'attributable' means 'a real possibility, and not a fanciful one, a possible cause of the damage as opposed to a probable one'.[59] However, as was stated by Lord Scott and Lord Mance in *Haward v Fawcetts*,[60] the claimant must still know the factual essence of what is subsequently alleged as negligence in the claim.

12.11 The decision in *Haward v Fawcetts* has been applied in a number of more recent decisions.[61] In *Chandra v Brooke North (a firm)*,[62] the claimants alleged that the defendants had been negligent in advising them about advice given to them in the course of negotiations with a bank and building contractors between 1999 and May 2003. When their business failed they defended the proceedings brought against them by the bank and issued proceedings against the

55 [1996] 7 Med LR 122, [2001] Lloyd's Rep PN 178.

56 [2006] UKHL 9, [2006] 1 WLR 682. See also *Brown v Bird and Lovibond (a firm)* [2002] EWHC 719 (QB) and *Shore v Sedgwick Financial Services Ltd* [2007] EWHC 2509 (Admin), [2007] All ER (D) 132 (Nov).

57 [2006] UKHL 9, [2006] 1 WLR 682 at para 10.

58 [1993] 1 WLR 782.

59 [1993] 1 WLR 782 at 797–798.

60 [2006] UKHL 9, [2006] 1 WLR 682, per Lord Scott at para 49 and Lord Mance at para 113.

61 In addition to the cases referred to above, see also *Renwick v Brooke* [2011] EWHC 874 (TCC) and *Youlton v Charles Russell (a firm)* [2010] EWHC 1032 (Ch).

62 [2013] EWHC 417 (QB).

defendants in May 2009 (six years after the last loan agreement) and, following review of the decision of David Richards J in the bank proceedings delivered in January 2010, sought to add extra allegations against the defendants. It was held that the latter allegations were not statute barred as they only gained knowledge of the facts that constituted the negligence from the date of the judgment as prior to that date they thought their losses had been caused by the stubborn behaviour of the bank and not their solicitor's negligence. *Hunt v Optima Cambridge Ltd*[63] is another case involving defective building work, where one of the claimants (Mrs Wyatt) was aware of smells, leaks and noise problems in her flat but not of the underlying problems causing these issues. It was held that she did not have knowledge of the defects in the roof of her apartment block, nor the foul drainage issues, nor the defects in constructing the floors from when she was aware of the minor issues, but only from when she received the content of an expert report. In *Integral Memory v Haines Watts*,[64] it was held that the claimant had sufficient knowledge that it had received negligent tax advice from the defendant from when the Revenue made demands for payment of tax, even though these demands were fully contested, as it knew all of the facts that constituted the allegation of negligence from that date with sufficient confidence to justify engaging in the preliminaries to the issue of a writ.

KNOWLEDGE THAT ACTS OR OMISSIONS DID NOT, AS A MATTER OF LAW, INVOLVE NEGLIGENCE IS NOT RELEVANT: S 14A(9)

12.12 Section 14A(9) provides that knowledge that an act or omission did or did not, as a matter of law, involve negligence is irrelevant for the purpose of determining the 'starting date'. This provision echoes the equivalent clause in s 14(1) which relates to a claimant's date of knowledge in a personal injuries action. It is largely unobjectionable when applied to personal injuries and property damage cases; however, in the context of non-personal injuries negligence claims, it may provide an unwarranted defence to legal advisers (and other advisers whose advice has legal consequences unforeseen by them) not afforded to architects, engineers and financial advisers.[65] In this regard, Lord Nicholls in *Haward v Fawcetts (a firm)*[66] stated that a distinction must be drawn between knowledge that something had gone wrong or advice was flawed, which is relevant, and knowledge that the conduct was negligent in legal terms, which is not. Further, it only applies where a claimant knew the 'facts' but not their 'legal consequences'. In the speech of Lord Scott in *Haward*, a further point of distinction was noted, namely that in the case of defective legal

63 [2013] EWHC 681 (TCC).

64 [2012] EWHC 341 (Ch); see to similar effect *Boycott v Perrins Guy Williams* [2011] All ER (D) 113 (Oct).

65 See *Haward v Fawcetts (a firm)* [2006] UKHL 9, [2006] 1 WLR 682 at para 15 and O'Sullivan, 'Limitation, latent damage and solicitors' negligence' (2004) 20 PN 218.

66 [2006] UKHL 9, [2006] 1 WLR 682 at para 13; see also *Dobbie v Medway Health Authority* [1994] 1 WLR 1234 and *Hallam-Eames v Merrett Syndicates Ltd* [1996] 7 Med LR 122, [2001] Lloyd's Rep PN 178.

advice, although the legal defects in the advice are irrelevant, if the claimant did not realise that he had suffered loss by the acts or omissions giving rise to the claim then the claimant will lack the knowledge required for the 'starting date' by s 14A(6).[67]

KNOWLEDGE OF IDENTITY OF THE DEFENDANT OR FACTS CONNECTING DEFENDANT TO ACTS OR OMISSIONS OF THIRD PARTY: S 14A(8)(B) AND (C)

12.13 Section 14A(7)(b) and (c) deal with cases where a claimant does not know the identity of the wrongdoer or the facts that render the defendant vicariously liable for the wrongdoer. These subsections do not appear to have led to any reported decisions so regard should be had to the case law on the related provisions in s 14 that apply to personal injuries actions.[68]

OVERRIDING 15-YEAR TIME LIMIT

12.14 Section 14B of the LA 1980 at first blush appears to introduce a 15-year long-stop for claimants who might otherwise not be subject to any limitation period for their claims by reason of the provisions of s 14A. However, upon closer inspection it is clear that s 14B instead introduces a 15-year time limit for all non-personal injuries actions in negligence regardless of whether s 14A is invoked.[69] Noteworthy also is that time runs from the date (or, if there are more than one, the last of the dates) of the negligent acts which caused the damage,[70] ie it does not run from the date the damage was suffered. It will bar the right of action notwithstanding that the claimant's cause of action has not yet accrued or his 'starting date' as referred to in s 14A(4)(b) has not yet occurred.[71] Section 14B states that it bars the claimant's right of action once the 15-year period expires and in *Financial Services Compensation Scheme v Larnell*,[72] it was held that it does not operate in like manner to the long-stop provision for defective products cases under the Consumer Protection Act 1987, which extinguishes the cause of action upon its expiry.[73] Instead, a defence that arises pursuant to s 14B must be specifically pleaded and relied upon.

67 See [2006] UKHL 9, [2006] 1 WLR 682 at paras 60–61 and his discussion of whether *HF Pension Trustees Ltd v Ellison* [1999] Lloyd's Rep PN 489 was correctly decided.
68 See further paras 13.29–13.30.
69 But see also the comments in *Financial Services Compensation Scheme v Larnell* [2005] EWCA Civ 1408, [2006] QB 808 on this point.
70 LA 1980, s 14B(1).
71 LA 1980, s 14B(2)(a) and (b).
72 [2005] EWCA Civ 1408, [2006] QB 808.
73 LA 1980, s 11A(3).

RIGHT OF ACTION AFFORDED TO SUCCESSIVE PURCHASERS OF A PROPERTY

12.15 Section 3(1) of the LDA 1986 provides a cause of action to the purchaser[74] of a property where a cause of action in negligence has accrued to the vendor (or his predecessor in title) in respect of damage to the property and the purchaser is not aware of the material facts[75] concerning the damage at the time of the purchase. This statutory cause of action is treated as having accrued on the date as the original cause of action accrued to the person who then held an interest in the property.[76] It is dependent on that particular cause of action having originally accrued to the vendor (or his predecessor in title), which was fatal to the claimant's case in *Broster v Galliard Docklands Ltd*,[77] in circumstances where that party had a different cause of action open to it at the time. The general provisions on disability[78] do not apply to this statutory cause of action.[79] Section 3 of the LDA 1986 binds the Crown, but does not extend liability further than the extent to which the Crown is made liable in tort by the Crown Proceedings Act 1947.[80]

DISABILITY

12.16 The general provisions on disability are discussed in Chapter 5.[81] Section 3(3) of the LDA 1986 states that the general provisions on disability in s 28 of the LA 1980 do not apply to a claim brought by a party who purchases a property after a cause of action had already accrued in respect of the property. Section 28A of the LA 1980 instead applies to such a claim although, misleadingly, this section of the Act is described as applying to all claims coming within s 28 and the true effect of the section is a little unclear. The effect of s 28A is that the inquiry into whether the claimant was under a disability should focus on his condition on the date when he both had the knowledge referred to in s 14A and a sufficient interest in the property to bring an action in respect of the damage.

DELIBERATE CONCEALMENT

12.17 Section 32(5) of the LA 1980[82] provides that neither s 14A nor 14B apply to an action where the provisions on deliberate concealment contained in

74 The LDA 1986, s 3(4) excludes from the ambit of the act persons who acquire an interest in the damaged property or in whom the original cause of action vests by operation of law or by virtue of an order vesting company property in a liquidator.

75 The phrase 'material facts' is defined in the LDA 1986, s 3(5) and (6) in like manner to the definition contained in the LA 1980, s 14A.

76 LDA 1986, s 3(2)(b). The cause of action is deemed to that of breach of duty at common law: s 3(2)(a).

77 [2011] EWHC 1722 (TCC), (2011) 137 Con LR 26.

78 LA 1980, s 28.

79 LDA 1986, s 3(3); the LA 1980, s 28A applies instead: see para 12.14.

80 LDA 1986, s 3(7).

81 LA 1980, s 28.

82 As inserted by the LDA 1986, s 2.

s 32(1)(b) apply. Accordingly, the limitation period in such a case will be the six-year tort limitation period[83] which runs from when the claimant knew or could with reasonable diligence have discovered the concealed facts. Importantly, this is not subject to the overriding time limit contained in s 14B. Somewhat incongruously, a claim based on fraud is subject to the 15-year overriding time limit. In *Williams v Lishman, Sidwell, Campbell & Price*,[84] the claimants alleged that they suffered financial loss following the receipt of negligent pension advice in 1997. They issued proceedings in October 2006 and argued that they only knew or had constructive knowledge of their cause of action (within the meaning of s 14A) and only knew or could reasonably have discovered certain facts relevant to their cause of action (within the meaning of s 32(1)(b)), namely that they had to pay a £38,000 penalty for transferring their funds, shortly before they brought the proceedings. The court also held that, as the claimants had pleaded one cause of action but several heads of damage,[85] once their cause of action had accrued based on facts within their knowledge from not later than early 2003,[86] the facts which were deliberately concealed relating to other losses were no longer facts 'relevant to their cause of action', as that phrase has been interpreted,[87] and thus s 32(1)(b) ceased to be of effect from that date. While this was sufficient to dispose of the appeal, the Court of Appeal had evident difficulty in deciding whether s 14A had any role to play once s 32(1)(b) was relied upon, and the consideration of a number of hypothetical situations by Rix LJ makes clear that the issues may give rise to difficulty again in the future.[88]

83 LA 1980, s 2.
84 [2010] EWCA Civ 418, [2010] PNLR 25; see also the discussion of the case in para 7.08.
85 See [2010] EWCA Civ 418, [2010] PNLR 25 at para 46.
86 The court held that they had sufficient knowledge to commence inquiries, including knowledge attributed to them by s 14A(10) that they should have acquired with expert advice.
87 See *AIC Ltd v ITS Testing Services (UK) Ltd (The Kriti Palm)* [2006] EWCA Civ 1601, [2007] 1 All ER (Comm) 667.
88 [2010] EWCA Civ 418 at paras 48–52, per Rix LJ.

CHAPTER 13

Personal Injuries Actions

INTRODUCTION

13.01 The phrase 'personal injuries action' used in this chapter refers to an action where damages are claimed in respect of 'negligence, nuisance or breach of duty'[1] causing personal injuries or death, within the meaning of s 11(1) of the Limitation Act 1980 ('LA 1980'). Personal injuries actions are one of only three types of action where the limitation period may be disapplied if it is equitable to allow the action to proceed,[2] the others being defamation actions[3] and claims against a public authority under the Human Rights Act 1998.[4] Whether a personal injuries action is pleaded as an action in tort, contract or breach of statutory duty, for limitation purposes it is treated as a tort action, albeit governed by the personal injuries limitation framework and not s 2 of the LA 1980,[5] and regard should be had to the discussion in Chapter 10 of the principles relating to the accrual of a cause of action for actions founded on tort.[6] The following are the limitation periods for the different types of personal injuries actions considered in this chapter:

1 Section 11(4) of the LA 1980 provides that the limitation period for a personal injuries action is three years from –

   (a) the date on which the cause of action accrued, or

   (b) the date of knowledge (if later) of the person injured.

2 Section 11(5) contains the limitation period for causes of action surviving for the benefit of the estate under s 1(1) of the Law Reform (Miscellaneous Provisions) Act 1934 ('LRMPA 1934'),[7] which is three years from –

1 The question of whether an action claiming damages for trespass to the person is a personal injuries action is discussed in paras 13.06–13.08. Section 11(1A) provides that the section does not apply to an action for damages brought under the Protection from Harassment Act 1997, s 3.
2 LA 1980, s 33, discussed in para 13.32 et seq.
3 LA 1980, ss 32A, discussed in Ch 14.
4 Human Rights Act 1998, s 7(5), discussed in Ch 28.
5 LA 1980, s 11(2); see para 13.05.
6 See Ch 10; see also para 13.03.
7 Section 11(5) only applies where the injured person dies before the expiration of the limitation period in s 11(4); an application to disapply the limitation period under s 33 may still be brought: see para 13.42.

(a) the date of death, or

(b) the date of the personal representative's date of knowledge,

whichever is the later.

3 Section 12(2) contains the limitation period for an action under the Fatal Accidents Act 1976 ('FAA 1976'),[8] which is three years from –

(a) the date of death, or

(b) the date of knowledge of the person for whose benefit the action is brought,

whichever is the later.

4 Section 33 of the LA 1980 gives the court a discretion to disapply the limitation period for a personal injuries action, including an action brought under the LRMPA 1934 or the FAA 1976, if it is equitable to allow the action to proceed.

The above limitation provisions do not apply to any action for which a period of limitation period is prescribed by any other enactment,[9] in particular to a personal injuries action governed by one of the international carriage conventions[10] such as the Athens Convention (passenger sea travel)[11] or the Warsaw or Montreal Conventions (air travel),[12] or a claim by a defendant claiming contribution from a co-defendant in a personal injuries action.[13] Significantly, a claimant in any of the foregoing excluded classes of action cannot seek to rely on s 33 of the LA 1980 to disapply the limitation period if his claim is governed by a different enactment.

PERSONAL INJURIES ACTIONS AND ACCRUAL OF THE CAUSE OF ACTION IN NEGLIGENCE

Damages 'in respect of personal injuries'

13.02 The expression 'personal injuries' is defined in s 38(1) of the LA 1980 as including 'any disease and any impairment of a person's physical or mental condition'. While 'disease' connotes a condition susceptible to medical diagnosis, 'impairment' has a less precise meaning. In *Walkin v South Manchester HA*,[14]

8 LA 1980, s 12(1) states that an action shall not be brought under the FAA 1976 if the injured person's cause of action was statute barred at the date of his death; however, an application to disapply the limitation period under s 33 may still be brought: see para 13.42.

9 LA 1980, s 39.

10 See Ch 22.

11 See *Higham v Stena Sealink Ltd* [1996] 1 WLR 1107 (CA).

12 See *Sidhu v British Airways Plc* [1997] AC 430 (HL).

13 See Ch 24.

14 [1995] 4 All ER 132. As it is treated as a claim for personal injuries and not pure economic loss, s 33 may be invoked: see *Godfrey v Gloucestershire Royal Infirmary NHS Trust* [2003] EWHC 549 (QB); see also *Rees v Darlington Memorial Hospital NHS Trust* [2003] UKHL 52, [2004] 1 AC 309 which has restricted the recoverability of damages in such cases.

a case in which the claimant sought damages for an unwanted pregnancy and the birth of a healthy child following a negligently performed sterilisation, it was held that the pain and suffering of childbirth was an injury and that the unwanted conception was an 'impairment' and that accordingly time ran from the date of the unwanted conception. In *Adams v Bracknell Forest BC*,[15] it was held that damage caused by a failure to diagnose and treat dyslexia so as to ameliorate the condition was a form of personal injury. While a body of case law supports this finding,[16] such a claim is very close to a claim for economic loss. In *Ackbar v Green*,[17] a claim against insurance brokers for damages for negligently failing to arrange passenger liability insurance was held not to be a claim in respect of personal injuries. This is consistent with the principle that negligence leading to the loss of a claim for damages does not give rise to a claim 'in respect of personal injuries'.[18] By contrast, it was held by the Court of Appeal in *Howe v David Brown Tractors (Retail) Ltd*[19] that the damages claimed by the claimant firm for loss of profits arising out of personal injuries suffered by a member of the firm were claimed 'in respect of personal injuries'. In *Yearworth v North Bristol NHS Trust*,[20] it was held that a claim relating to damage caused to semen which was in storage pending IVF treatment was not a personal injuries action.

Accrual of a cause of action in negligence claiming damages for personal injuries

13.03 The question of when a cause of action in tort accrues is discussed at greater length in Chapter 10. This concept is not defined by statute and an understanding of the term must be sought in the case law. The leading case in a personal injuries context remains *Cartledge v E Jopling & Sons Ltd*,[21] a case where the claimants developed the lung disease pneumoconiosis after inhaling silica dust at their place of work over many years. Although the damage to the claimants' lungs was progressive and the symptoms only became apparent some years after it had occurred,[22] the House of Lords held that their claims were statute barred. This conclusion was reached in circumstances where it was held that a cause of action in negligence accrues when, in the words of Lord Reid, 'personal injury beyond what can be regarded as negligible'[23] is suffered, even if the claimant was not aware of having suffered the damage. The other speeches in *Cartledge* use slightly different forms of words, asking when the claimant had suffered 'real damage as distinct from purely minimal damage'[24] and elsewhere stating that what was actionable damage was a question of degree and relying on

15 [2004] UKHL 29, [2005] 1 AC 76.
16 See *Phelps v Hillingdon LBC* [2001] 2 AC 619.
17 [1975] QB 582.
18 *Lefevre v White* [1990] 1 Lloyd's Rep 569.
19 [1991] 4 All ER 30; see also *Norman v Ali, The Times*, 25 February 2000.
20 [2009] EWCA Civ 37, [2010] QB 1.
21 [1963] AC 758.
22 The medical evidence was that if x-rays of their lungs had been carried out more than six years prior to the writs issuing, these would have shown they had suffered the damage already.
23 [1963] AC 758 at 772, per Lord Reid.
24 [1963] AC 758 at 774, per Lord Evershed.

the principle *de minimis non curat lex.*[25] The decision in *Cartledge v E Jopling & Sons Ltd* was thought to be unfair to claimants and has been largely superseded by ss 11 and 33 of the LA 1980, neither provision having had an equivalent in the Limitation Act 1939.

Damages that 'consist of or include' damages for personal injuries

13.04 The wording used in s 11(1) has the effect that the inclusion of a personal injuries element, however slight, means that the three-year limitation period applies to the entire action and not the six-year limitation period contained in s 2 of the LA 1980 for torts generally: either damages are claimed in respect of personal injuries, or they are not. For example, in *Bennett v Greenland Houchen & Co,*[26] a solicitor's negligence action which included a claim for damages for stress and depression fell within s 11, with the result that it was held to be statute barred. In a number of cases, a claimant who has been met with a limitation defence which would not arise if the six-year limitation period applied has sought to amend his pleadings to delete reference to a claim for personal injuries. In *Pounds v Eckford Rands (a firm),*[27] a claimant was granted leave to amend in a case where the bulk of her claim was for economic loss in a solicitor's negligence action. By contrast, in *Azaz v Denton,*[28] the claimant persevered with a claim for personal injuries, as well as separate causes of action which would otherwise be subject to longer limitation periods, with the result that the entire action was found to be statute barred.

Whether the duty exists by virtue of a contract or otherwise

13.05 It is not open to a claimant to rely on the six-year limitation period applicable to an action for breach of contract if the reality is that it is an action for negligence claiming damages for personal injuries. Section 11(1) of the LA 1980 provides that the personal injuries limitation period applies 'whether the duty exists by virtue of a contract or of a provision made by or under a statute or independently of any contract or any such provision'.

Personal injuries actions and damages claims for trespass to the person

13.06 The majority of actions claiming damages for personal injuries are framed as cases in negligence. However, personal injuries may also be suffered as a result of a trespass to the person (ie battery). In those cases, it can be argued

25 [1963] AC 758 at 779, per Lord Pearce.

26 [1998] PNLR 458; to similar effect is *Oates v Harte Reade & Co* [1999] 1 FLR 1221.

27 [2003] Lloyd's Rep PN 195.

28 [2009] EWHC 1759 (QB); see also *Oates v Harte Reade & Co* [1999] 1 FLR 1221, where leave to amend was refused, and *Shade v Compton Partnership (a firm)* [2000] Lloyd's Rep PN 81, where some criticism of the approach in *Oakes* is evident.

that the six-year limitation period contained in s 2 of the LA 1980 should apply rather than the three-year limitation period which applies to claims in negligence, nuisance and breach of duty. Until 1993, although there were some divergent decisions,[29] the law in England was to the effect that the phrase 'breach of duty' used in s 11(1) included intentional torts, such as trespass to the person, false imprisonment and malicious prosecution.[30] This proposition was rejected in *Stubbings v Webb*,[31] where the House of Lords refused to give the phrase 'breach of duty' this extended definition, with the rationale for the decision being contained in the following passage from the speech of Lord Griffiths:

> 'The phrase lying in juxtaposition with negligence and nuisance carries with it the implication of a breach of duty of care not to cause personal injury, rather than an obligation not to infringe any legal right of another person. If I invite a lady to my house one would naturally think of a duty to take care that the house is safe but would one really be thinking of a duty not to rape her?'[32]

13.07 Despite the assured tone of Lord Griffiths' speech, when the issue next came before the House of Lords in *A v Hoare*,[33] it overruled *Stubbings v Webb*.[34] Having examined the legislative history of the provisions in question, Lord Hoffmann continued as follows:

> 'But there could be no moral or other ground for denying to a victim of intentional injury the more favourable limitation treatment introduced by the 1975 Act for victims of injuries caused by negligence. The inference I would draw is that in using the same form of words in the 1975 Act, Parliament must have intended them to bear the meaning which they had been given in the uniform line of authority in England and Australia to which I have referred.'[35]

Accordingly, he concluded that all actions claiming damages for personal injuries against a defendant, whether based on a claim of battery or one of negligence, are subject to the same limitation period and, as relevant, also benefit from the same reasons to extend or disapply the limitation period.[36]

13.08 Lord Hoffmann noted that the decision of the House of Lords ended an anomaly in the law which arose where a third party (typically, though not

29 See *Fowler v Lanning* [1959] 1 QB 426.

30 *Letang v Cooper* [1965] 1 QB 232 (CA); *Long v Hepworth* [1968] 1 WLR 1299; as well as the decision of a strong Court of Appeal in *Stubbings v Webb* [1992] QB 197.

31 [1993] AC 498; see McGee, 'Trespass and Limitation' (1993) 109 LQR 356, where it is described as an 'unnecessary and regrettable' decision, and Rogers, 'Limitation and Intentional Torts' (1993) 143 NLJ 258. The claimant subsequently argued unsuccessfully that English law violated the European Convention on Human Rights in *Stubbings v United Kingdom* (1996) 23 EHRR 213.

32 [1993] AC 498 at 508.

33 [2008] UKHL 6, [2008] 1 AC 844, following the decision of the High Court of Australia in *Stingel v Clark* [2006] HCA 37, (2006) 288 ALR 229.

34 [1993] AC 498.

35 [2008] UKHL 6, [2008] 1 AC 844 at para 14.

36 Namely, the date of knowledge extension and the court's power under s 33 to disapply the limitation period.

always, an employer) was alleged to have caused or permitted the sexual abuse of the claimant to have occurred. In such a case, although any claim against the perpetrator was subject to a non-extendable six-year limitation period, the claim in negligence against the party who was not the perpetrator could gain the benefit of an extension of time if the claimant's date of knowledge came after the date of the abuse. The 'most remarkable example of the anomaly'[37] came before the courts in *S v W (child abuse: damages)*,[38] where the claimant sued her father and mother for sexual abuse by the father. The proceedings were issued nearly ten years after the last act of abuse and the claim against her father was dismissed as being statute barred. However, the court allowed the claim against her mother to proceed on account of an extension of time available only in negligence cases. Sir Ralph Gibson commented that the result was 'illogical and surprising'.[39]

DISCOVERABILITY AND THE DATE OF KNOWLEDGE

Introduction

13.09 Parliament intervened to ameliorate the position of claimants following the decision of the House of Lords in *Cartledge v E Jopling & Sons Ltd*[40] by introducing a 'date of knowledge' test. The wording used in the Limitation Act 1963 was widely criticised[41] and was replaced by the Limitation Act 1975, whose wording has been retained in the LA 1980. Section 11(4) of the LA 1980 provides that the limitation period for a personal injuries action is three years from the date of accrual of the cause of action, or from the person's 'date of knowledge' (if later). The reference to the person's[42] 'date of knowledge' asks when that person first had knowledge of the following facts, as set out in s 14(1) of the LA 1980:

> '(a) that the injury in question was significant; and
>
> (b) that the injury was attributable in whole or in part to the act or omission which is alleged to constitute negligence, nuisance or breach of duty; and
>
> (c) the identity of the defendant; and
>
> (d) if it is alleged that the act or omission was that of a person other than the defendant, the identity of that person and the additional facts supporting the bringing of an action against the defendant;
>
> and knowledge that any acts or omissions did or did not as a matter of law, involve negligence, nuisance or breach of duty is irrelevant.'

37 [2008] 1 AC 844 at para 23, per Lord Hoffmann.
38 [1995] 1 FLR 862.
39 [1995] 1 FLR 862 at 867.
40 [1963] AC 758.
41 Lord Reid in *Central Asbestos Co Ltd v Dodd* [1973] AC 518 at 529 commented that the 1963 Act had 'a strong claim to the distinction of being the worst drafted Act on the statute book'.
42 In most cases the person here referred will be the claimant, but in cases surviving for the benefit of the estate it will be the personal representative (s 11(5)(b)) and in cases brought under the Fatal Accidents Act 1976 it will be the dependants (s 12(2)(b)).

13.10 The knowledge possessed by the person whose date of knowledge is being considered includes 'constructive knowledge' that is attributed to him by s 14(3), which provides as follows:

> 'For the purposes of this section, a person's knowledge includes knowledge which he might reasonably have been expected to acquire:
>
> (a) from facts observable or ascertainable by him; or
>
> (b) from facts ascertainable by him with the help of medical or other appropriate expert advice which it is reasonable for him to seek;
>
> but a person shall not be fixed under this subsection with knowledge of a fact ascertainable only with the help of expert advice so long as he has taken all reasonable steps to obtain (and, where appropriate, to act on) that advice.'

13.11 A number of significant decisions of the Supreme Court (*AB v Ministry for Defence*[43]) and House of Lords (*Adams v Bracknell Forest Borough Council*[44] and *A v Hoare*[45]) in the last decade have narrowed the scope of s 14 significantly. This has occurred in circumstances where the courts have shifted the focus of the personal injuries limitation provisions to the discretion to disapply the limitation period in s 33 (see in particular *Horton v Sadler*[46] and *A v Hoare*[47]).[48] Notwithstanding the downgrading in importance of the date of knowledge provisions relative to the s 33 discretion, they continue to be of core importance to an understanding of this area.

Knowledge of the claimant and knowledge of his parents

13.12 The 'person' whose state of knowledge is examined in ascertaining the date of knowledge is the claimant himself,[49] except for actions brought following the death of the injured party, which are discussed in the next paragraph. In *O'Driscoll v Dudley Health Authority*,[50] knowledge possessed by the claimant's parents was imputed to the claimant where there was a free flow of information between them, but not knowledge of facts which they had failed to investigate. However, Poole J acknowledged that the facts of the case were unusual as the claimant was profoundly physically handicapped and more might be expected of a less injured claimant. In *Whiston v London Strategic Health Authority*,[51] the claimant suffered from cerebral palsy as a result of brain damage caused by oxygen deficiency at his birth in 1974, but despite his physical complaints he

43 [2012] UKSC 9, [2013] 1 AC 78: this case dealt with the meaning of 'knowledge'.
44 [2004] UKHL 29, [2005] 1 AC 76: this case concerned s 14(3).
45 [2008] UKHL 6, [2008] 1 AC 844: this case concerned, *inter alia*, s 14(2).
46 [2006] UKHL 27, [2007] 1 AC 307.
47 [2008] UKHL 6, [2008] 1 AC 844.
48 Section 33 is discussed in para 13.32 et seq.
49 LA 1980, s 11(4)(b).
50 [1997] 7 Med LR 408.
51 [2010] EWCA Civ 195, [2010] 1 WLR 1582.

was an intelligent and well-educated individual. He brought proceedings in 2006 claiming damages for negligence during his birth. The trial judge held that he did not have actual knowledge of the elements of his case against the defendant until 2005. In assessing the state of his knowledge, the Court of Appeal held that he could reasonably have been expected to question his mother about his birth when his health had deteriorated in early adulthood and so had acquired constructive knowledge of the relevant facts no later than 1998. However, the knowledge of his parents was not imputed to him: instead the court had regard to what his parents knew and what questions he should reasonably have asked of them.

Actions for the benefit of the estate of a deceased person and actions under the Fatal Accidents Act 1976 and the relevant date of knowledge

13.13 Where an injured person dies prior to the limitation period for his personal injuries action having expired, a cause of action survives for the benefit of his estate under s 1(1) of the Law Reform (Miscellaneous Provisions) Act 1934. The limitation period for this action is contained in s 11(5) of the LA 1980 and it is three years from his date of death or three years from his personal representative's date of knowledge, whichever is later. Section 11(6) gives an extended definition to 'personal representative' and s 11(7) provides that if there is more than one personal representative and they have different dates of knowledge, time runs from the earliest of those dates of knowledge. Section 12(2) provides the limitation period for an action under the Fatal Accidents Act 1976 of either (a) three years from the date of death, or (b) three years from the date of knowledge of the person for whose benefit the action is brought, whichever is the later. Section 13(1) provides that where there is more than one person for whose benefit an action under the FAA 1976 is brought, s 12(2)(b) shall be applied separately to each of them. If the action would be outside the time limit contained in s 12(2) for some, but not all, of the persons for whose benefit it is brought, the court shall direct that any person whose claim would be statute barred shall be excluded from those for whom the action is brought. However, s 12(3) further provides that a direction to exclude such a person shall not be made if that person can establish that the action would not be defeated by a defence of limitation, whether by reason of an agreement not to plead the statute, a disability on the part of the deceased person which extends the limitation period, or otherwise.

Definition of 'expert'

13.14 The LA 1980 does not define who is an 'expert' for the purposes of s 14. While it will normally be clear whether someone is acting in the capacity of an 'expert', it has been held in a series of cases that a solicitor is not an expert for these purposes but is instead the client's agent. This has the effect that knowledge the solicitor might reasonably be expected to acquire is attributed to the claimant, even if he failed to acquire that knowledge. Thus, in *Henderson v Temple Pier*,[52]

52 [1998] 1 WLR 1540.

a solicitor was found not to be an expert for the purpose of making inquiries to ascertain the owner of a ship, as this simply required a search in the appropriate register. However, one must look at precisely what task was being undertaken by the solicitor and there remains a possibility that a solicitor could be found to be an expert for certain purposes.

Suspicions, beliefs and knowledge: AB v Ministry for Defence

13.15 'Knowledge' is the touchstone for the assessment of a claimant's date of knowledge, but the word itself has an open-textured meaning. There are levels of what can broadly be described as 'knowledge of facts' ranging from suspicion, intuitive belief or irrational belief on the one hand, to knowledge that a certain state of affairs exists which has been verified or confirmed beyond a reasonable doubt on the other. The meaning of the crucial word 'knowledge' was recently exhaustively considered by the Supreme Court in *AB v Ministry of Defence*,[53] in litigation relating to the exposure of army servicemen to radiation in the 1950s. The test claimants whose cases were before the court (apart from one whose injuries were recent) all had variants of the same limitation problem. Well-publicised efforts to secure compensation for them based on their subjective beliefs that exposure to radiation in the 1950s had caused them ill health had been ongoing since the 1980s. Apart from funding issues, litigation had not been brought earlier as they still lacked expert evidence to prove that their injuries were caused by (ie attributable to[54]) the actions of the defendant. Apart from holding out a forlorn hope that the Supreme Court would change the common law rules on causation, or that some further helpful evidence would be discovered, their actions were all bound to fail on a causation point. This was clearly a hard case and the Supreme Court held, by a four to three majority, that the 'subjective belief'[55] or 'reasonable belief'[56] of a claimant that his injuries were attributable to the actions or omissions of the defendant equated to 'knowledge' within the meaning of s 14(1). As the claimants had such a belief, their claims were all found to be statute barred, except for those where the injuries suffered were recent. The court approved of the approach of Lord Donaldson MR in *Halford v Brookes*[57] to the effect that a belief would amount to knowledge for the purposes of s 14 if it was held 'with sufficient confidence to justify embarking on the preliminaries to the issue of a writ, such as submitting a claim to the proposed defendant, taking legal and other advice and collecting evidence'.[58] As subsidiary findings, the Supreme Court held that a person can have a reasonable belief in a state of facts even if unable to prove those facts and, in fact, even if those facts do not exist. Secondly, the court

53 [2012] UKSC 9, [2013] 1 AC 78.
54 Within the meaning of the LA 1980, s 14(1)(b).
55 The phrase 'subjective belief' was used in the dissenting judgment of Lord Phillips but its use was criticised in the judgment of Lord Wilson; however, as the facts show that the belief was not objectively justified (based on current scientific knowledge) it would appear appropriate to refer to subjective belief on the part of the claimants.
56 Lord Wilson, at para 11, also used the phrase 'reasoned belief'.
57 [1991] 1 WLR 428.
58 [1991] 1 WLR 428 at 443.

held that it is logically not possible for a claimant's date of knowledge to come after the date on which proceedings are brought.

13.16 An unusually strongly worded dissent was delivered by Lord Phillips, which noted that both the majority and the minority endorsed the decision of the House of Lords in *Haward v Fawcetts*[59] as correctly stating the law and carefully examined the context of each of the judgments from which quotations were relied upon in the majority judgments. There is merit in the comments of Lady Hale, who also dissented, noting that:

> '[If] "knowledge of the facts" is to be interpreted as firm belief in a state of affairs, it surely must have that meaning for each of the circumstances in which it is employed. Therefore ... the claimant need only have a *belief* in the identity of the defendant ...'[60]

She added that 'the word knowledge ... is in no sense a natural synonym for belief'.[61] The decision of the majority may betray a level of dissatisfaction with a set of proceedings which had little to no chance of success and which were likely to cost the taxpayer a lot of money.[62] By raising the fact that a person's date of knowledge is unconnected to when they have sufficient evidence to prove their case, the majority did not have regard to the fact that the claimants not only lacked evidence, they lacked facts that were necessary to establish their case. A note of frustration is evident from the statement of Lord Brown that the minority approach would lead to a situation where 'the more hopeless the claim, the likelier it is that the claimant will be in a position to defeat the Limitation Act defence'.[63] Notwithstanding the foregoing, *AB v Ministry of Defence* now represents the law and is likely to lead to a further narrowing of the classes of person who may gain the benefit of s 14 and increase the focus on the s 33 discretion to disapply the limitation period where it is equitable to allow the action to proceed. Its application to the context of non-personal injuries negligence claims in s 14A of the LA 1980 is also likely to lead to claimants finding it more difficult to rely upon that section.

Constructive knowledge of facts observable or ascertainable and from advice it was 'reasonable for him to seek'

13.17 The purpose of s 14(3) clearly encourages a claimant to make inquiries and to seek expert advice. In the latter regard, it has been noted that, '[i]f he does not, time runs against him. If he does, he is not prejudiced by being deemed to know all that the expert should have discovered but did not, or discovered

59 [2006] UKHL 9, [2006] 1 WLR 682.

60 [2012] UKSC 9, [2013] 1 AC 78 at para 187.

61 [2012] UKSC 9, [2013] 1 AC 78 at para 188.

62 The judgment of Lord Phillips, at paras 90 and 106, noted that there were 1,011 claimants and that their legal costs, if successful, were estimated at £17.5 million.

63 [2012] UKSC 9, [2013] 1 AC 78 at para 72.

but failed to tell him'.[64] Facts may be ascertainable through various avenues, for example, through newspaper and television reports, through questioning a family member about injuries suffered at birth,[65] through making inquiries about the owner of a property,[66] or through an official report on the accident.[67] In *Adams v Bracknell Forest Borough Council*,[68] the House of Lords examined the issue of when it was reasonable for a claimant to seek expert advice. Lord Hoffmann stated as follows:

> 'Section 14(3) requires one to assume that a person who is aware that he has suffered a personal injury, serious enough to be something about which he would go and see a solicitor if he knew he had a claim, will bc sufficiently curious about the causes of the injury to seek whatever expert advice is appropriate.'[69]

The speech of Lord Hoffmann in *Adams*, which enjoyed the support of a majority of the law lords, favours a strongly objective approach to the question of what advice it was reasonable for the claimant to seek. He departed from the mainly subjective test which had been suggested by Lord Reid in *Smith v Central Asbestos Co Ltd*,[70] commenting that 'the Court of Appeal in *Forbes v Wandsworth HA*[71] was right in saying that the introduction of the discretion under section 33 had altered the balance'.[72] The mainly objective test asks what knowledge someone in the situation of the claimant (in that case an adult who knows he is illiterate) could reasonably be expected to acquire and asked whether the claimant's dyslexia (which he alleged had remained untreated due to the negligence of the defendant) inhibited him in seeking advice. Personal characteristics such as shyness and embarrassment, which would not be expected to have inhibited others with a like disability, should be left out of the equation. On the facts of the case, the House of Lords held unanimously that the claimant should have sought expert advice in relation to his dyslexia at an earlier stage and that he was fixed with constructive knowledge of what such a report would have revealed.[73] While Lord Phillips noted that it would be rare when a case turned on the true construction of that subsection,[74] Baroness Hale preferred a more subjective test and Lord Walker posited a middle ground between the two positions. While the subsequent decisions have largely applied a strictly objective approach,[75] there remains some uncertainty on precisely how to approach the question of what

64 *Clerk and Lindsell on Torts* (20th edn, London: Sweet & Maxwell, 2010) at para 33.52.
65 *Whiston v London Strategic Health Authority* [2010] EWCA Civ 195, [2010] 1 WLR 1582.
66 *Cressey v E Timm & Son* [2005] EWCA Civ 763, [2005] 1 WLR 3926 at para 36.
67 *Leadbitter v Hodge Finance Ltd* [1982] 2 All ER 167.
68 [2004] UKHL 29, [2005] 1 AC 76.
69 [2004] UKHL 29, [2005] 1 AC 76 at para 47.
70 [1973] AC 518 at 530, followed in *Nash v Eli Lilly & Co* [1993] 1 WLR 782 (CA).
71 [1997] QB 402.
72 [2004] UKHL 29, [2005] 1 AC 76 at para 45.
73 See also *Smith v Hampshire County Council* [2007] EWCA Civ 246.
74 [2004] UKHL 29, [2005] 1 AC 76 at para 57.
75 *AB v Nugent Care* [2009] EWCA Civ 827, [2010] 1 WLR 516.

expert advice it was reasonable for the claimant to seek,[76] and some refinement of the principles is to be expected in future case law.

13.18 In *Forbes v Wandsworth HA*,[77] it was held by the Court of Appeal that if a claimant fails to obtain expert advice, the question is not whether the claimant acted unreasonably in not obtaining expert advice, but whether it was *reasonable for him* to seek such advice. Thus, even if legitimate reasons exist as to why advice was not sought (eg impecuniosity), the claimant will be fixed with knowledge that such advice would have revealed. If a claimant received erroneous advice from his employer (falling short of fraudulent concealment), this may mean that it was reasonable for him not to obtain expert advice.[78] In cases where it was reasonable for the claimant to seek expert advice, it has been held that he is entitled to some time to recover from what has happened before seeking expert advice as to possible claims. For example, in *Forbes v Wandsworth HA*,[79] it was stated that a period of 12 to 18 months would have been allowed as a reasonable period prior to the claimant obtaining expert advice after which it was reasonable for him to seek advice, although the precise length of time to be allowed will depend on the facts of the case.

Knowledge that the injury was significant: s 14(1)(a) and (2)

13.19 The first element of a person's date of knowledge requires that he knows that he suffered a significant injury.[80] The requirement that a claimant must know that he had suffered an 'injury' has occasionally arisen as a discrete issue in medical negligence and defective medication cases. In *Nash v Eli Lilly & Co*,[81] a number of claimants brought proceedings arising out of side-effects suffered as a result of taking the drug Opren. The Court of Appeal accepted as valid a distinction between an expected, or accepted, side-effect and an injurious and unacceptable consequence of taking a drug and held that it was only when a claimant suffered 'an effect completely outside that of an acceptable side effect [that it could] reasonably be said that the patient was aware of a significant injury'.[82] However, in *Dobbie v Medway Health Authority*,[83] a case concerning an unnecessary mastectomy, the Court of Appeal held that the claimant knew of her injury from the outset (ie that her breast had been removed) and the fact that she did not know that it was unnecessary was irrelevant to s 14(1)(a) as, in the words of Steyn LJ, '[t]he contextual meaning of 'injury' in s 14(1) is a personal injury

76 In *Whiston v London Strategic Health Authority* [2010] EWCA Civ 195, [2010] 1 WLR 1582, the comments of Lord Hoffmann quoted above were treated as *obiter dictum* and in *Khairule v North West Strategic Health Authority* [2008] EWHC 1537 (QB) at para 60 they were distinguished as having less force in cases where a person had suffered from a condition from birth.

77 [1997] QB 402.

78 *Smith v Central Asbestos Co Ltd* [1972] 1 QB 244.

79 [1997] QB 402 at 414, per Stuart-Smith LJ.

80 LA 1980, s 14(1)(a).

81 [1993] 1 WLR 782.

82 [1993] 1 WLR 782 at 791, per Purchas LJ.

83 [1994] 1 WLR 1234.

without any further gloss other than by the express definition of "significant" in s 14(2).'[84] However, in commenting on *Dobbie v Medway* in *Hallam-Eames v Merrett Syndicates Ltd*,[85] Hoffmann LJ observed as follows:

> 'If one asks on common sense principles what Mrs Dobbie was complaining about, the answer is that the surgeon had removed a healthy breast. It would in our view be a seriously incomplete statement of her case to say that it was simply that the surgeon had removed her breast.'[86]

The approach of the court in *Nash v Eli Lilly & Co*[87] was followed in *James v East Dorset Health Authority*,[88] where a claimant who suffered post-operative symptoms which worsened progressively was held not to have knowledge that he had suffered an 'injury' until he became aware that this should not have occurred, even though he was painfully aware of those symptoms. Although there are clearly conflicting authorities at Court of Appeal level on the point discussed in this paragraph, it is submitted that the approach in *Nash v Eli Lilly & Co*[89] has much to recommend it and that, in the words of Sedley LJ in *James v East Dorset Health Authority*,[90] s 14(1)(a) is not designed 'to place at a disadvantage those who do not assume the worst when there is nothing to alert them to it'.[91]

13.20 Section 14(2) states that an injury is to be considered significant if the person whose date of knowledge is in question 'would reasonably have considered it sufficiently serious to justify his instituting proceedings for damages against a defendant who did not dispute liability and was able to satisfy a judgment'. The wording of this section requires the court to decide how that claimant would have behaved if acting reasonably. Although *Adams v Bracknell Forest Borough Council,*[92] discussed above,[93] was a decision on the interpretation of s 14(3), its preference for a more objective test was applied to s 14(1)(a) by the Court of Appeal in *McCoubrey v Ministry for Defence*.[94] The claimant in *McCoubrey* was exposed to a thunderflash while on a training exercise and immediately noticed some hearing symptoms. He was reviewed by an ENT specialist in 1994 who confirmed he had suffered some hearing loss, but the damage did not worsen and did not affect his work duties until 2001 (temporarily) and 2004 (on a permanent basis), at which point he issued proceedings. His claim was found to be clearly statute barred by the Court of Appeal, which held that s 14(1)(a) must be determined by reference to the seriousness of the injury and not by reference to its effect on the claimant's private life or career and that the

84 [1994] 1 WLR 1234 at 1248. This decision was followed by the Irish Supreme Court in *Gough v Neary* [2003] 3 IR 92.
85 [1996] 7 Med LR 122.
86 [1996] 7 Med LR 122 at 126.
87 [1993] 1 WLR 782.
88 (1999) 59 BMLR 196.
89 [1993] 1 WLR 782.
90 (1999) 59 BMLR 196.
91 (1999) 59 BMLR 196 at 201.
92 [2004] UKHL 29, [2005] 1 AC 76.
93 See para 13.17.
94 [2007] EWCA Civ 17, [2007] 1 WLR 1544.

test under s 14(2) whether a claimant ought to appreciate that his injury was serious was a substantially objective test.

13.21 One of the five conjoined appeals in *A v Hoare*[95] was an appeal from *Young v Catholic Care (Diocese of Leeds)*.[96] The claimant in this action alleged that he had been subjected to physical and sexual assaults while residing in care homes between 1974 and 1977 and issued proceedings claiming damages in 2003. The Court of Appeal held that he had knowledge that he had suffered a significant injury for a period of in excess of three years prior to the proceedings being brought, and this decision was affirmed on appeal in *A v Hoare*, with Lord Hoffmann stating as follows:

> 'The material to which that test applies is generally "subjective" in the sense that it is applied to what the claimant knows of his injury rather than the injury as it actually was ... But the test itself is an entirely impersonal standard: not whether the claimant himself would have considered the injury sufficiently serious to justify proceedings but whether he would "reasonably" have done so. You ask what the claimant knew about the injury he had suffered, you add any knowledge about the injury which may be imputed to him under section 14(3) and you then ask whether a reasonable person with that knowledge would have considered the injury sufficiently serious to justify his instituting proceedings for damages against a defendant who did not dispute liability and was able to satisfy a judgment.'[97]

13.22 In *KR v Bryn Alyn Community Holdings Ltd*,[98] the Court of Appeal held that victims of child sexual abuse may regard such conduct by persons in authority as normal and that the court must examine 'whether such an already damaged child would reasonably turn his mind to litigation as a solution to his problems'.[99] Lord Hoffmann held that this was the wrong test and overruled *KR v Bryn Alyn* in relation to this aspect of the decision. Thus, an argument that the fact of the abuse (or memories of it) were repressed or were normalised by the abuser are matters to be considered only within the context of s 33(3)(a) of the LA 1980, which looks to the 'reasons ... for the delay' in an application to disapply the limitation period.[100]

13.23 An assessment of whether an injury was 'significant' leads to the imposition of a low threshold against which the knowledge required by s 14(1)(a) is to be judged, as the definition of 'significant' in s 14(2) deviates from the ordinary meaning of the word. Accordingly, it has been stated that knowledge of an injury

95 [2008] UKHL 6, [2008] 1 AC 844.

96 The Court of Appeal judgment is reported *sub nom Young v South Tyneside MBC* [2006] EWCA Civ 1534, [2007] QB 932.

97 [2008] UKHL 6, [2008] 1 AC 844 at para 34, per Lord Hoffmann. Similarly, Lord Carswell, at para 68, stated that the court should not 'import the circumstances, character or intelligence of the claimant into the determination of reasonableness under section 14(2). It is irrelevant whether the claimant is intelligent or unintelligent or whether his personal characteristics or his circumstances may influence his decision not to sue at that time.'

98 [2003] EWCA Civ 85, [2003] QB 1441.

99 [2003] EWCA Civ 85, [2003] QB 1441 at para 42, per Auld LJ.

100 See para 13.36 et seq.

which is more than *de minimis*,[101] or in the words of Bingham LJ in *Dobbie v Medway Health Authority*,[102] anything worse than an injury the claimant 'could reasonably have accepted ... as a fact of life or not worth bothering about', will set time running under s 14(1)(a). The test has an exclusive focus on the quantum of damages that the injury might attract at trial and factors such as wanting to avoid conflict where the claimant's job is insecure[103] or where the claimant does not want to be seen as sponging[104] would not appear to be relevant.[105] In a situation where a claimant was expecting side-effects from drugs, or a period of time to recover from an operation, and only later realised that something was amiss, there may be a significant dispute as to when he had knowledge that the injury was significant. Similarly, in cases where exposure to noise leads to hearing loss, the appreciation that hearing loss may have been suffered may occur over time. Thus, in *Furniss v Firth Brown Tools*,[106] the Court of Appeal held that a claimant who noted minor inconvenience and an insignificant injury to his hearing did not have knowledge of a significant injury until he was diagnosed with hearing loss, although a second factor was that it had been suggested to him that his difficulties were caused by a build-up of wax in his ear. By reason of the 'single action rule',[107] once a claimant has knowledge of a 'significant injury' (even if relatively minor) then time runs against all injuries, even if more serious, arising out of the same breach of duty.[108]

Knowledge that the injury was attributable to the act or omission constituting the breach of duty: s 14(1)(b)

13.24 The attribution element of the date of knowledge test, contained in s 14(1)(b), has led to some difficulties of interpretation. The first reason for this is that it is sometimes difficult to pinpoint when vague dissatisfaction matures into suspicions of negligence and ultimately into conviction of fault. The second reason is the tension which exists between s 14(1)(b) and the clause at the end of s 14(1) which states that knowledge that an act or omission did not, as a matter of law, involve negligence is not relevant to ascertaining a claimant's date of knowledge.[109] A summary of what the law requires in order for knowledge of

101 Oughton, Lowry and Merkin, *Limitation of Actions* (London: LLP Reference Publishing, 1998) at 288.
102 [1994] 4 All ER 450.
103 *McCafferty v Metropolitan Police District Receiver* [1977] 1 WLR 1073.
104 *Buck v English Electric Co Ltd* [1978] 1 All ER 271.
105 See *Young v South Tyneside MBC* [2006] EWCA Civ 1534, [2007] QB 932 at para 86, per Buxton LJ.
106 [2008] EWCA Civ 182.
107 See para 10.05.
108 See *Miller v London Electrical Manufacturing Co Ltd* [1976] 2 Lloyd's Rep 284 (CA) and *Brooks v J & P Coates (UK) Ltd* [1984] 1 All ER 702.
109 The proviso to s 14(1) is discussed in para 13.31.

attributability to be established, which has since been widely relied upon,[110] was attempted by Brooke LJ in *Spargo v North Essex Health Authority*,[111] where he stated as follows:

> '(1) The knowledge required to satisfy s 14(1)(b) is a broad knowledge of the essence of the causally relevant act or omission to which the injury is attributable;
>
> (2) "Attributable" in this context means "capable of being attributed to", in the sense of being a real possibility;
>
> (3) A claimant has the requisite knowledge when she knows enough to make it reasonable for her to begin to investigate whether or not she has a case against the defendant. Another way of putting this is to say that she will have such knowledge if she so firmly believes that her condition is capable of being attributed to an act or omission which she can identify (in broad terms) that she goes to a solicitor to seek advice about making a claim for compensation;
>
> (4) On the other hand, she will not have the requisite knowledge if she thinks she knows the acts or omissions she should investigate but in fact is barking up the wrong tree: or if her knowledge of what the defendant did or did not do is so vague or general that she cannot fairly be expected to know what she should investigate; or if her state of mind is such that she thinks her condition is capable of being attributed to the act or omission alleged to constitute negligence, but she is not sure about this, and would need to check with an expert before she could be properly said to know that it was.'[112]

13.25 The judgment of Hoffman LJ in *Hallam-Eames v Merrett Syndicates Ltd*[113] contains a number of very helpful statements of principle for what is required for a claimant to have knowledge of attribution within the meaning of s 14(1)(b), including the following:

> 'It is this idea of causal relevance which various judges of this court have tried to express by saying the claimant must know "the essence of the act or omission to which the injury is attributable" (Purchas LJ in *Nash v Eli Lilly & Co* [1993] 1 WLR 782, at 799) or "the essential thrust of the case" (Sir Thomas Bingham MR in *Dobbie v Medway HA* [1994] 1 WLR 1234) or that one should "… look at the way the claimant puts his case, distill what he is complaining about and ask whether he had in broad terms knowledge of the facts on which that complaint is based" (Hoffmann LJ in *Broadley v Guy Clapham & Co* [1994] 4 All ER 439).'[114]
>
> 'The claimant does not need to know that he has a cause of action or that the defendant's acts can be characterised in law as negligent or as falling short of some

110 See for example, the references in *AB v Ministry for Defence* [2012] UKSC 9, [2013] 1 AC 78 at para 48, per Lord Walker ('well known survey'), para 79, per Lord Brown, and para 119, per Lord Phillips ('treated as definitive'), although it is noted that it does not deal with constructive knowledge: *ibid*.

111 [1997] 8 Med LR 125.

112 [1997] 8 Med LR 125 at 129.

113 [1996] 7 Med LR 122. The judgment considered the analogous attribution provision in s 14A(8)(a) but nothing turns on the point.

114 [2001] Lloyd's Rep PN 178 at 181.

standard of professional or other behaviour ... He must have known the facts which can fairly be described as constituting the negligence of which he complains. It may be that knowledge of such facts will also serve to bring home to him the fact that the defendant has been negligent or at fault. But that in itself is not a reason for saying that he need not have known them.'[115]

13.26 The interpretation to be given to s 14(1)(b) was reviewed in *AB v Ministry of Defence*[116] and the effect of this decision is discussed above.[117] The judgments in *AB v Ministry of Defence* all expressed approval of the decision of the House of Lords in *Haward v Fawcetts,*[118] where Lord Brown noted that knowledge that the injuries are attributable to the acts or omissions requires that the claimant knows 'the substance of what ultimately comes to be pleaded as his case in negligence'[119].

13.27 It may be worthwhile now to turn to the manner in which the different formulations of the test for s 14(1)(b) has been applied by the courts. In *AB v Ministry of Defence,*[120] the Supreme Court held that the claimants all had knowledge, in the sense of a reasonable belief, that their injuries were attributable to the actions of the defendant for in excess of three years prior to the action being brought. The judgment of Lord Wilson (the main judgment for the majority) analysed the position of the nine claimants whose appeals were before the court and had particular regard to their knowledge of, and in some cases participation in, the activities of the British Nuclear Tests Veterans Association (BNTVA). This association had been founded in 1983 with the aim of attempting to secure compensation for its members. Several of the veterans had applied for army disability pensions and asserted that nuclear exposure was the cause of their injuries; several had made statements to the press or their doctors in which they had blamed the Ministry of Defence for their ailments, and one had written a book about his experiences. For all of these reasons, even though a sufficient expert report to prove causation was lacking, their claims were found to be statute barred. The claimant in *Harrison v Isle of Wight NHS Primary Care Trust*[121] issued a claim form in March 2012 claiming damages in respect of an operation performed on her in October 2005. The claimant engaged a firm of solicitors in 2006, but based on the reports then in her possession was told by counsel in February 2009 that she had no claim worth pursuing. She received a further medical opinion in March 2009 which revealed a different injury to that she was aware of previously and issued proceedings within three years of receipt of that opinion. Judge McKenna, sitting as a High Court judge, held that her claim was not statute barred as she had been 'barking up the wrong tree'[122] when advised prior to March 2009 as to her precise injury and what had caused that injury.

115 [2001] Lloyd's Rep PN 178 at 181.
116 [2012] UKSC 9, [2013] 1 AC 78.
117 See para 13.15.
118 [2006] UKHL 9, [2006] 1 WLR 682.
119 [2006] UKHL 9, [2006] 1 WLR 682 at para 90.
120 [2012] UKSC 9, [2013] 1 AC 78.
121 [2013] EWHC 442 (QB).
122 [2013] EWHC 442 (QB) at para 49.

13.28 While the prior case law will now have to be read in the light of *AB v Ministry of Defence*,[123] some earlier examples of the application of the test in some of the older cases may be helpful. In *Driscoll-Varley v Parkside Health Authority*,[124] the claimant thought that an injury to her leg had been caused by a surgeon's negligence. She later discovered that the real cause was not the operation but the removal of the leg from traction during subsequent treatment and was held not to have knowledge of attribution from that earlier date. In *Spargo v North Essex District Health Authority*,[125] the claimant had been mistakenly diagnosed with brain damage and had been confined to a psychiatric hospital for six years. Having consulted a solicitor, she first obtained an unfavourable medical opinion. Subsequently, she received a favourable second opinion and commenced proceedings, claiming that she had suffered injury as a result of having been given the wrong treatment and that, had she been properly treated, she would have been cured. The judge held that her date of knowledge arose only when she received an expert opinion definitely linking her injuries with the misdiagnosis and that the claim was therefore made within the three years before the commencement of proceedings. The Court of Appeal reversed the judge's decision, finding that the claimant had known about her injury many years previously, about the causally relevant omission and about the link between the two. A final example, which 'might have been devised as an examination question on limitation'[126] is *Sniezek v Bundy (Letchworth) Ltd.*[127] The claimant experienced a sensation of burning on his lips and throat and formed the firm view that this was the result of exposure to polymer at his workplace. He stopped work because of this in 1988 and sought legal and medical advice. He was seen by a number of experts, all of whom could find nothing wrong with him. One indeed concluded that his symptoms were psychosomatic. Ultimately, in 1994 a senior ENT Registrar advised that his symptoms might well be attributable to exposure to polymer. The trial judge took that as the date on which he acquired knowledge for the purpose of s 14. The Court of Appeal did not agree, holding that the claimant's firm belief in the face of expert advice to the contrary constituted knowledge for the purpose of the section. These older decisions illustrate the point that, notwithstanding the recent disagreement at the highest level as to the precise form of words that is used in describing the level of knowledge necessary to satisfy s 14(1)(b), time may run from a point when inquiries remain ongoing and a claimant is not entitled to wait until he has firm proof to support an assertion that his injuries are attributable to the acts or omissions of the defendant.

123 [2012] UKSC 9, [2013] 1 AC 78.

124 [1991] 2 Med LR 346. This was described as 'a rather marginal example of barking up the wrong tree' by Lord Walker in *AB v Ministry for Defence* [2012] UKSC 9, [2013] 1 AC 78 at para 38.

125 [1997] 8 Med LR 125. See also *Rowbottom v Royal Masonic Hospital* [2002] EWCA Civ 87, (2002) 65 BMLR 103 where it was held that it was not until the claimant received an expert's second report that she could properly be said to have known it was the defendant's omission which caused injury.

126 *AB v Ministry of Defence* [2012] UKSC 9, [2013] 1 AC 78 at para 120, per Lord Phillips.

127 [2000] PIQR P213.

Identity of defendant who committed the wrong: s 14(1)(c)

13.29 In some cases, a claimant may not know the identity of the party who caused him to suffer his injuries. The classic example is a claimant who is injured in a hit-and-run incident, which formed the background to *Taylor v McConville*,[128] where Gillen J in the Northern Irish High Court held, somewhat generously, that it was reasonable for the claimant's solicitor not to rely on newspaper reports naming the suspected driver and instead to await a response to formal inquiries to the police. The leading authority in the area has long been *Simpson v Norwest Holst Southern Ltd*,[129] where the claimant suffered injuries in an accident at work but did not know the name of his employer as his wage slips named it as the 'Norwest Holst Group'. Pre-action correspondence asking his employer's insurers to clarify the name of his employer was ignored and he ultimately brought proceedings against the wrong company within the group. The Court of Appeal held that time only started to run from when he should reasonably have discovered the identity of his employer, which was after they had pointed out his mistake to him. This was followed in *Cressey v E Timm & Son*,[130] where the claimant suffered an accident at work and sued the company named on his wage slips. It transpired that a sister company was his employer. When this entity was sued (out of time), it raised a limitation defence and argued that the claimant knew the 'identity' of his employer at all times and that he should have issued proceedings and, if he made a genuine mistake about their 'name', he could have applied to correct their title in the proceedings.[131] The Court of Appeal rejected the limitation defence, with Rix LJ commenting that in most straightforward situations the identity of a defendant will be known to or ascertainable by a victim at the time of the accident. However, he added that, 'One cannot sue "the driver of the other car", or even "my employer": a name has to be provided. Moreover, artificial persons, such as companies, can hardly even be described, save by their name.'[132] Where the identity of the employer is uncertain, as in *Simpson*, where the legal entity owning a property is unclear (as discussed in *Cressey*), or where the identity of an employer is wrongly stated to the claimant, as in *Cressey*, while the date of knowledge may be postponed, Rix LJ added that, '[i]n general I do not believe that it can be postponed for long: only as long as it reasonably takes to make and complete the appropriate enquiries'.[133]

Knowledge of facts which support a claim against the defendant for act or omission of third party: s 14(1)(d)

13.30 This provision deals with cases where the claimant alleges that the defendant is vicariously liable for the acts of its servant or agent. In such cases, the limitation clock will not start to run under the LA 1980 until the person

128 [2009] NIQB 22, [2010] NIJB 31.
129 [1980] 1 WLR 968; see also *Leadbitter v Hodge Finance Ltd* [1982] 2 All ER 167.
130 [2005] EWCA Civ 763, [2005] 1 WLR 3926.
131 An application could then have been brought under CPR 17.4(3) or CPR 19.5.
132 [2005] EWCA Civ 763, [2005] 1 WLR 3926 at para 35.
133 [2005] EWCA Civ 763, [2005] 1 WLR 3926 at para 28.

whose date of knowledge is relevant knows (or ought to know) the identity of the employer, the nature of the employment relationship with the third party and other circumstances which support the bringing of an action against the employer. The claimant will still have the alternative of suing the original tortfeasor and s 14(1)(d) does not operate so as to postpone the running of time in respect of that action.

Knowledge that acts or omissions did not, as a matter of law, involve negligence is irrelevant: s 14(1)

13.31 The proviso to s 14(1) provides that knowledge of legal consequences of facts is irrelevant. Thus, the fact that the claimant in *Farmer v National Coal Board*[134] was given incorrect legal advice that his claim had no chance of success did not prevent time running against his cause of action. Commenting on the equivalent clause in s 14A, Lord Nicholls in *Haward v Fawcetts (a firm)*[135] stated that a distinction must be drawn between knowledge that something had gone wrong or advice was flawed, which is relevant, and knowledge that the conduct was negligent in legal terms, which is not. Although ignorance of the law, or the legal consequences of the facts, is irrelevant to a party's date of knowledge under s 14, it is a factor relevant to the exercise of the discretion to disapply the limitation period in s 33, being relevant to the factors listed in s 33(3)(a) and (e).[136]

SECTION 33 AND THE POWER TO DISAPPLY THE LIMITATION PERIOD

Introduction – the statutory provisions

13.32 Section 33 of the LA 1980 gives the court the power to direct that the limitation period for a personal injuries action contained in s 11 (personal injuries actions), 11A[137] (personal injuries actions under Pt 1 of the Consumer Protection Act 1987) or 12 (Fatal Accidents Act 1976 actions) shall not apply to an action or to any specified cause of action to which the action relates. However, s 33 cannot be relied upon to disapply the ten-year long-stop in s 11A(3) for claims under the Consumer Protection Act 1987[138] or to claims where the applicable time limit is contained in one of the international carriage statutes.[139] Although the wording in s 33(2) concerning the latter exclusion is not entirely clear, it has been consist-

134 *The Times*, 27 April 1985 (CA).

135 [2006] UKHL 9, [2006] 1 WLR 682 at para 13; see also *Dobbie v Medway Health Authority* [1994] 1 WLR 1234 and *Hallam-Eames v Merrett Syndicates Ltd* [1996] 7 Med LR 122, [2001] Lloyd's Rep PN 178.

136 *Coad v Cornwall and Isles of Scilly HA* [1997] 1 WLR 189.

137 Section 33(1A) excludes actions under Pt 1 of the 1987 Act that relate only to property damage from the scope of s 33.

138 LA 1980, s 33(1A).

139 LA 1980, s 33(2). The Carriage Statutes are discussed in Ch 22.

ently held in cases such as *Higham v Stena Sealink Ltd*[140] and *Sidhu v British Airways Plc*[141] that s 33 may not be invoked if the governing limitation period is prescribed by another enactment.[142] The court has an unfettered discretion[143] in a s 33 application and the test is whether it appears to the court that it would be equitable to allow the action to proceed.[144] The claimant bears the burden of proof on an application under s 33 but the courts have cautioned against embellishing the language of the section with references to the burden being 'heavy' or 'light'.[145] The court is required to have regard to the degree to which the effect of s 11, 11A or 12 would prejudice the claimant or any person whom he represents and the degree to which a direction under s 33 would prejudice the defendant. Section 33(3) then states that, in considering an application under the section, 'the court shall have regard to all the circumstances of the case and in particular to' what have been described as 'a curious hotchpotch'[146] of matters:

(a) the length of, and the reasons for, the delay on the part of the claimant;

(b) the extent to which, having regard to the delay, the evidence adduced or likely to be adduced by the claimant or the defendant is likely to be less cogent than if the action had been brought within the time allowed;

(c) the conduct of the defendant after the cause of action arose, including the extent (if any) to which he responded to requests reasonably made by the claimant for information or inspection for the purpose of ascertaining facts which were or might be relevant to the claimant's cause of action against the defendant;

(d) the duration of any disability of the claimant arising after the date of the accrual of the cause of action;

(e) the extent to which the claimant acted promptly and reasonably once he knew whether or not the act or omission of the defendant, to which the injury was attributable, might be capable at that time of giving rise to an action for damages; and

(f) the steps, if any, taken by the claimant to obtain medical, legal or other expert advice and the nature of any such advice he may have received.

The modern approach of the courts to s 33 and the balance of prejudice

13.33 The modern approach of the courts to s 33 is contained in the decision of the House of Lords in *Horton v Sadler*[147] and the Court of Appeal in *Cain v*

140 [1996] 3 All ER 660 (CA): Athens Convention, art 16.
141 [1997] AC 430 (HL): Warsaw Convention, art 29.
142 LA 1980, s 39.
143 *Horton v Sadler* [2006] UKHL 27, [2007] 1 AC 307.
144 LA 1980, s 33(1).
145 *Sayers v Lord Chelwood* [2012] EWCA Civ 1715, [2013] 2 All ER 232.
146 *Thompson v Brown* [1981] 1 WLR 744 at 751, per Lord Diplock.
147 [2006] UKHL 27, [2007] 1 AC 307.

Francis[148] and *AB v Nugent Care Society.*[149] In *Horton v Sadler*, the House of Lords departed from its earlier decision in *Walkley v Precision Forgings Ltd,*[150] which precluded a claimant who issued proceedings within the limitation period (which did not proceed to trial) from relying on s 33 in a second set of proceedings in respect of the same wrong brought after the expiration of the limitation period. The House of Lords held that the section conferred a wide and unfettered discretion which could not be limited by a rule of this nature.[151] Lord Hoffmann noted that although the Twentieth Report of the Law Reform Committee[152] intended the discretion now contained in s 33 to apply only in exceptional cases, the section had been drafted in general terms and provided an unfettered discretion. He continued, stating that:

> '[T]he practice of the courts has been regularly to exercise the discretion in favour of the claimant in all cases in which the defendant cannot show that he has been prejudiced by the delay. No matter how negligent the claimant's solicitors may have been in the simple task of keeping a diary, the plea of limitation which the statute confers upon the defendant is, in the absence of forensic prejudice, described as a windfall of which he can properly be deprived.'[153]

13.34 The issue of the s 33 discretion received brief discussion in *A v Hoare,*[154] where Lord Brown noted that the main finding in the case – that battery (ie sexual assault) claims were personal injuries actions – would lead to many applications to disapply the limitation period being brought in future for such claims. Given the long lapses of time which frequently occur prior to actions relating to sexual abuse being brought, he cautioned that the discretion would not always be exercised in favour of the action being allowed to proceed if a fair trial was impossible after a long delay. The question of whether a fair trial would be possible is dealt with in para 13.37, below.

The balance of prejudice

13.35 The most important factor in a s 33 application is the extent to which the statute bar causes prejudice to the claimant (or the estate or dependants, as appropriate) and the extent to which the exercise of the s 33 discretion in favour of the claimant would prejudice the defendant. The starting point is the question of whether the claimant has a strong case with an entitlement to a significant award of damages, or whether by contrast his case is weak and his injuries modest. In *AB v Nugent Care Society*,[155] the Court of Appeal approved of the approach of the

148 [2008] EWCA Civ 1451, [2009] QB 754.
149 [2009] EWCA Civ 827, [2010] 1 WLR 516.
150 [1979] 1 WLR 606, HL.
151 See further *Aktas v Adepta; Dixie v British Polythene Industries Ltd* [2010] EWCA Civ 1170, [2011] QB 894, where *Horton* was applied.
152 Cmnd 5630.
153 [2006] UKHL 27, [2007] 1 AC 307 at para 44.
154 [2008] UKHL 6, [2008] 1 AC 844 at paras 84–89.
155 [2009] EWCA Civ 827, [2010] 1 WLR 516.

trial judge[156] which took into account the strength of the claimant's case and the seriousness of the allegations as relevant factors, as well as whether the claimant was impecunious, as the costs of any claim successfully defended which cannot be recovered from a claimant constitute a form of prejudice to the defendant. Similarly, in *AB v Ministry for Defence*,[157] the weaknesses in the claimant's cases were fatal to the Supreme Court's exercise of the s 33 discretion. In *Cain v Francis*,[158] the Court of Appeal held that the loss of a limitation defence was not a matter which a court could consider as 'prejudice' within the meaning of s 33(1)(b). Sir Andrew Morritt C based that finding on the wording of the subsection,[159] making it an absolute rule, and both he and Smith LJ stated that the 'prejudice to the defendant' to be considered was 'if the passage of time has significantly diminished his opportunity to defend himself (on liability and/or quantum)'.[160] It remains to be seen whether the absolute rule expressed by Sir Andrew Morritt C will find favour if the issue comes before the Supreme Court. The question of whether a claimant for whom the limitation period is not disapplied will suffer any prejudice if he has a strong negligence claim against his solicitor was also considered in *Horton v Sadler*.[161] While Lord Bingham expressed agreement[162] with the statement of Lord Diplock in *Thompson v Brown*[163] that a claimant would still suffer some prejudice in those circumstances, Lord Hoffmann preferred simply to state that there are 'arguments on both sides'[164] in response to the defendant's challenge to that approach.

Discussion of the six factors listed in s 33(3)

Length of and reasons for the delay: s 33(3)(a)

13.36 The 'delay' referred to in subsection (a) relates primarily to delay after the expiration of the limitation period,[165] although delay from the date of accrual of the cause of action will be relevant if that affects the defendant's insurance cover[166] or the insurer's interests.[167] A delay of days or weeks[168] would weigh in favour of the exercise of the discretion, whereas a delay of five or six years[169] will give rise to a rebuttable presumption of prejudice. The reasons for the delay are relevant and in *Coad v Cornwall HA*[170] the court accepted a genuinely held but

156 [2009] EWHC 481 (QB), Irwin J.
157 [2012] UKSC 9, [2013] 1 AC 78: the facts of this case are discussed in para 13.15.
158 [2008] EWCA Civ 1451, [2009] QB 754; not following comments of Lord Diplock in *Thompson v Brown* [1981] 1 WLR 744 and not following the Court of Appeal in *Hartley v Birmingham City District Council* [1992] 1 WLR 968.
159 [2008] EWCA Civ 1451, [2009] QB 754 at para 80.
160 [2008] EWCA Civ 1451, [2009] QB 754 at para 69, per Smith LJ.
161 [2006] UKHL 27, [2007] 1 AC 307.
162 [2006] UKHL 27, [2007] 1 AC 307 at para 32.
163 [1981] 1 WLR 744 at 750–752.
164 [2006] UKHL 27, [2007] 1 AC 307 at para 49.
165 *Thompson v Brown* [1981] 1 WLR 744 at 751.
166 *Smith v Leicestershire Health Authority* (1996) 36 BMLR 23.
167 *McDonnell v Walker* [2009] EWCA Civ 1257, [2010] PIQR P5.
168 *Firman v Ellis* [1978] QB 886; *Hartley v Birmingham City District Council* [1992] 1 WLR 968.
169 *Buck v English Electric Co Ltd* [1977] 1 WLR 806.
170 [1997] 1 WLR 189; see also *Halford v Brookes* [1991] 1 WLR 428.

unreasonable belief, and the fact that the claimant did not appreciate his legal rights, as relevant considerations. In *A v Hoare*,[171] the claimant was the subject of a violent assault and attempted rape in 1988 but did not sue the defendant at the time as he had no money. It was held that her decision not to sue him at the time and only to sue him in 2004 after he won £7 million on the National Lottery provided a good reason for the delay and the court disapplied the limitation period for the proceedings. Other cases to have considered subs (a) have taken into account the fact that a claimant initially thought his injuries were minor,[172] that he did not want to be thought of as 'sponging' on his employers[173] or that he did not want to sue a surgeon who was still providing treatment.[174] While delay on the part of the claimant personally is more important than delay on the part of his legal advisers, the claimant still bears some responsibility for the delay of his solicitors.[175] Inhibitions falling short of legal disability, such as those that are experienced by many victims of sexual abuse, are properly considered under this heading.[176] In *Mutua v Foreign and Commonwealth Office*,[177] the claimants brought proceedings in 2009 in relation to allegations of serious assaults (torture, rape, castration and severe beatings) they alleged had been perpetrated while they were detained by the colonial administration in Kenya at various times between 1954 and 1959. The very lengthy passage of time was held to be excused in large part due to the fact that the claimants were uneducated farmers living in remote rural areas of Kenya, as any collective gatherings of members of the proscribed organisation of which they were members were banned until 2003, and as it was only when historians and human rights bodies investigated the incidents thoroughly from the mid-2000s that they became aware in a real sense that they had a case worth pursuing which was supported by evidence. A period of delay following a diagnosis of noise-induced hearing loss in 2002, and leisurely progress thereafter until proceedings were brought in September 2009 were factors which led to the Court of Appeal refusing to disapply the limitation period in *Sayers v Lord Chelwood,*[178] in a claim brought by the defendant's former gardener. The lack of explanation for the passage of time coupled with prejudice to the defendant in the form of the death of a witness, the dimming memory of the elderly defendant and the loss of insurance documents were all important factors that led to the application being refused.

Extent to which evidence will be less cogent: s 33(3)(b)

13.37 In light of the decisions of the Court of Appeal in *Cain v Francis*[179] and *AB v Nugent Care Society*,[180] this factor is now crucial and is the main element

171 [2008] UKHL 6, [2008] 1 AC 844 (see in particular para 88, per Lord Brown) and [2008] EWHC 1573 (QB).
172 *McCafferty v Metropolitan Police District Receiver* [1977] 1 WLR 806.
173 *Buck v English Electric Co Ltd* [1977] 1 WLR 806.
174 *Driscoll-Varley v Parkside HA* [1991] 2 Med LR 346.
175 *Horton v Sadler* [2006] UKHL 27, [2007] 1 AC 307 at para 53, per Lord Carswell.
176 *AB v Nugent Care Society* [2009] EWCA Civ 827, [2010] 1 WLR 516.
177 [2012] EWHC 2678 (QB), [2012] All ER (D) 48 (Oct).
178 [2012] EWCA Civ 1715, [2013] 2 All ER 232.
179 [2008] EWCA Civ 1451, [2009] QB 754.
180 [2009] EWCA Civ 827, [2010] 1 WLR 516.

considered in assessing prejudice to the claimant and the defendant. Under this heading the court examines whether a fair trial is possible, which will depend on when a complaint or notification was first made, what witnesses are available to give evidence, what relevant documents have been lost since the events under review, or by contrast whether a complaint is made out of the blue. This will depend on the precise issues to be tried in each case and, if the cogency of the evidence has diminished over time, this factor will weigh against the discretion to disapply being exercised. In *Mutua v Foreign and Commonwealth Office*,[181] it was held that, despite the fact that many of the witnesses to the events had died in the very lengthy period that had elapsed prior to the proceedings being brought, there was detailed documentary evidence still in existence and some witnesses, and the evidence remained sufficiently cogent for a fair trial to be possible. The assessment of this factor in *AB v Nugent Care Society*[182] is considered below.

The conduct of defendant in response to claim: s 33(3)(c)

13.38 This factor looks not to the conduct of the defendant that caused the accident but instead to his subsequent conduct, in particular his forensic tactics, such as facilitating an inspection of the accident locus and pre-trial co-operation and responses to requests for information. While a defendant is not obliged to volunteer information, if his conduct, or that of his solicitors or insurers, hinders or delays the claimant in progressing his claim, this factor will weigh in favour of the exercise of the s 33 discretion.[183]

The duration of any disability of claimant after cause of action accrued: s 33(3)(d)

13.39 The word 'disability' is defined in s 38(1) of the LA 1980 and is discussed in Chapter 5. This subsection overcomes the problem that a supervening disability does not stop time running under s 28. While a mental or physical incapacity not amounting to a 'disability' properly so called falls outside this subsection, in *Yates v Thakeham Tiles Ltd*[184] it was held that it is still a factor which can be taken account of within s 33.

The extent to which claimant acted promptly and reasonably once he knew the act or omission of the defendant might be capable of giving rise to an action: s 33(3)(e)

13.40 This factor overlaps with subsection (a), except that it might also encompass an inquiry into whether the claimant notified the defendant in good time that a claim was being contemplated so that reasonable investigations and preservation of records and evidence could be undertaken.

181 [2012] EWHC 2678 (QB), [2012] All ER (D) 48 (Oct).
182 [2009] EWCA Civ 827, [2010] 1 WLR 516.
183 See *Halford v Brookes* [1991] 1 WLR 428 and *Thomson v Brown* [1981] 1 WLR 744.
184 [1995] PIQR P135 (CA); see also *Thomas v Plaistow* [1997] PIQR P540 (CA).

The steps taken by the claimant to obtain medical, legal and other expert advice and the nature of the advice received: s 33(3)(f)

13.41 Advice as to the legal consequences of an act or omission is not relevant to an assessment of a claimant's date of knowledge,[185] but it is a factor relevant to the exercise of the s 33 discretion. In light of the decision of the Supreme Court in *AB v Ministry for Defence*,[186] the fact that expert advice on liability or causation was not available will not preclude a claimant having knowledge of the facts that constitute his date of knowledge if he firmly believed that the defendant's acts or omissions caused his injuries. However, s 33(3)(f) allows a claimant to point to the fact that expert advice advised against issuing proceedings at an earlier point in time in support of an application under s 33.

Section 33 and actions where the injured person is deceased

13.42 If a claimant dies after his cause of action for personal injuries has become statute barred then, viewed narrowly, there is no claim to survive for the benefit of his estate within the meaning of s 1(1) of the Law Reform (Miscellaneous Provisions) Act 1934. However, s 33(1), (4) and (5), when read together, make clear that it is open to his personal representative to ask the court to disapply the limitation period for the bringing of such a claim. Section 33(1), (2), (4)–(6), when read together, make clear that an application may be made under s 33 to disapply the limitation period for an action brought on behalf of the dependants of a deceased under the Fatal Accidents Act 1976. In both situations, s 33(4) and (5) apply, the first of which provides specifically that 'the court shall have regard in particular to the length of, and the reasons for, the delay on the part of the deceased'. Section 33(5) provides that where the relevant date of knowledge in relation to the limitation period for an action is that of a person other than the claimant, s 33(3) 'shall have effect with appropriate modifications' as if references to the claimant included references to any person whose date of knowledge is or was relevant in determining a time limit.

Section 33 and sexual abuse cases

13.43 As discussed above,[187] the House of Lords in *A v Hoare*[188] held that an action claiming damages for trespass to the person (ie battery) was to be treated as a 'personal injuries action' within the meaning of s 11(1) of the LA 1980. This has had the consequence that claimants seeking damages for sexual abuse may now seek to disapply the limitation period for their proceedings. Although the appeals before the House of Lords in *A v Hoare* were not from decisions of the lower courts on the exercise of the s 33 discretion – the issue had not arisen for

185 LA 1980, s 14(1).
186 [2012] UKSC 9, [2013] 1 AC 78.
187 See paras 13.06–13.08.
188 [2008] UKHL 6, [2008] 1 AC 844.

consideration in the lower courts as *Stubbings v Webb*[189] was binding upon them, with the exercise of the discretion being remitted for consideration in light of the decision on appeal[190] – the speeches of the law lords offer guidance on how the section should be applied in sexual abuse damages claims.[191] While the length of, and reasons for, any periods of delay is always relevant to the exercise of the s 33 discretion,[192] the court took judicial notice of the fact that the effect of sexual abuse may operate as a form of disability that inhibits a claimant from bringing proceedings.[193] While appropriate expert evidence should be adduced in relation to the psychological effects of the abuse, the approach mandated by *A v Hoare* focuses on the cogency of the evidence and the question of whether a fair trial remains possible.[194] In this regard, Baroness Hale noted that it is in investigating this issue that the respective prejudices to the claimant and defendant in a s 33 application can be contrasted, and that:

> '[T]he injustice to a claimant who may be deprived of his claim, perhaps as a result of the very injuries which gave rise to it, can be balanced against the injustice to a defendant who may be called upon to defend himself a long time after the event when important evidence may no longer be obtainable.'[195]

Lord Brown added some comments specifically relevant to the exercise of the s 33 discretion in a case like *A* where suddenly, after many years, the prospective defendant becomes rich. He suggested that 'it would be most unfortunate if people felt obliged (often at public expense) to bring proceedings for sexual abuse against indigent defendants simply with a view to their possible future enforcement'.[196] He also offered some general comments, which are worth quoting *in extenso*:

> 'Whether or not it will be possible for defendants to investigate these sufficiently for there to be a reasonable prospect of a fair trial will depend upon a number of factors, not least when the complaint was first made and with what effect. If a complaint has been made and recorded, and more obviously still if the accused has been convicted of the abuse complained of, that will be one thing; if, however, a complaint comes out of the blue with no apparent support for it (other perhaps than that the alleged abuser has been accused or even convicted of similar abuse in the past), that would be quite another thing. By no means everyone who brings a late claim for damages for sexual abuse, however genuine his complaint may in fact be, can reasonably expect the court to exercise the section 33 discretion in his favour. On the contrary, a fair trial (which must surely include a fair opportunity for the

189 [1993] AC 498.

190 See *A v Hoare* [2008] EWHC 1573 (QB), discussed below.

191 While certain aspects of the decision of the Court of Appeal in *KR v Bryn Alyn Community Ltd* [2003] EWCA Civ 85, [2003] QB 1441 were overruled in *A v Hoare*, other aspects of the judgment continue to be relied upon: see *AB v Nugent Care Society – Practice Note* [2009] EWCA Civ 827, [2010] 1 WLR 516.

192 LA 1980, s 33(3)(a).

193 LA 1980, s 33(3)(d). See also the comments of Haddon-Cave J in *EL v Children's Society* [2012] EWHC 365 (QB) at para 67 on the effects of child sexual abuse.

194 LA 1980, s 33(3)(b).

195 [2008] UKHL 6, [2008] 1 AC 844 at para 60.

196 [2008] UKHL 6, [2008] 1 AC 844 at para 88.

defendant to investigate the allegations – see section 33(3)(b)) is in many cases likely to be found quite simply impossible after a long delay.'[197]

13.44 The first case to consider the new approach was the remitted hearing in *A v Hoare*,[198] where the claimant sought damages arising out of a violent attempted rape and serious sexual assault perpetrated upon her by the defendant in 1988. The defendant was convicted following a contested criminal trial in 1988 but was not sued by the claimant in civil proceedings as he had no money at the time. He won £7 million on the National Lottery in May 2004 and proceedings were issued against him in December of that year. Coulson J exercised his discretion in favour of disapplying the limitation period, finding that the appalling nature of the attack and the cogency of the evidence on liability (though there was modest prejudice in relation to causation and assessment of her PTSD symptoms) weighed strongly in the claimant's favour, as well as the slightly more strained finding that by committing a crime that led to his imprisonment, the defendant had caused himself to be impecunious and thus not worth suing at the time.

13.45 The judgment of Irwin J in *AB v Nugent Care Society*[199] contains a thorough analysis of the factors relevant to the exercise of the s 33 discretion in child sexual and physical abuse cases. An appeal from his judgment was dismissed, with the Court of Appeal using the opportunity of the appeal to give general guidance on the approach to be adopted to s 33 applications in such cases in future.[200] The four[201] claimants in *Nugent Care Society* whose applications were before the court alleged that they had been the victims of sexual and physical abuse, of varying severity, on different occasions mainly in the late 1970s while residing at the same children's home. Irwin J looked carefully at the cogency of the evidence in each case, finding that the allegations of abuse, though not the detail of what had occurred, were established. He proceeded to look to the medical evidence and the effect the claimants said the abuse had on them generally and their ability to bring proceedings. He placed particular weight on the seriousness of the allegations in each case and whether the issues at trial would be lengthy or not, with this going to an assessment of whether allowing the claims to proceed to trial would be proportionate, and ultimately disapplied the limitation period for two of the four claimants. The Court of Appeal held that Irwin J had erred in finding that the allegations of abuse were established rather than focusing on whether the evidence relating to the allegations was cogent and whether a fair trial remained possible,[202] but affirmed his exercise of the s 33 discretion in each case. It also

197 [2008] UKHL 6, [2008] 1 AC 844 at para 86.

198 [2008] EWHC 1573 (QB).

199 [2009] EWHC 481 (QB). See also *EB v Haughton* [2011] EWHC 279 (QB), [2011] All ER (D) 200 (Feb); *EL v Children's Society* [2012] EWHC 365 (QB) and *RAR v GGC* [2012] EWHC 2338 (QB).

200 *AB v Nugent Care Society - Practice Note* [2009] EWCA Civ 827, [2010] 1 WLR 516.

201 A fifth appeal was also before the court, from the decision of HH Judge Main QC in *R v Wirral MBC*, unreported, 15 December 2008 (QBD) but the judgment at first instance is not available.

202 To similar effect, see *Raggett v Society of Jesus Trust of 1929 for Roman Catholic Purposes* [2010] EWCA Civ 1002.

offered useful assistance on two procedural aspects of general relevance: first, that the width of the discretion is such that an appellate court should not intervene with a trial judge's decision unless it is 'so plainly wrong that [it] exceeded the ambit within which reasonable disagreement is possible';[203] and secondly, that it thought that there are now likely to be many cases in which a judge will decide that oral evidence will be required in order to reach a fair decision on the s 33 application, given that the strength of the claimant's case will be relevant to the exercise of the discretion.[204]

203 [2009] EWCA Civ 827, [2010] 1 WLR 516 at para 13.
204 [2009] EWCA Civ 827, [2010] 1 WLR 516 at para 21.

CHAPTER 14

Defamation

INTRODUCTION

14.01 Section 4A of the Limitation Act 1980 ('LA 1980') provides that the limitation period for an action for libel, slander, slander of title, slander of goods or other malicious falsehood is one year from the date of accrual of the cause of action.[1] Section 32A gives the court a discretion to disapply the limitation period if it is equitable to allow the action to proceed: while this section is clearly similar to s 33 (which relates to personal injuries actions) the treatment of applications under these two sections has been quite different and the case law on s 33 should not be used interchangeably with that on s 32A.[2] The boundaries of the types of action governed by s 4A are not particularly clear, given the possible breadth of an action for malicious falsehood. In *Cornwall Gardens Pte Ltd v RO Garrard & Co Ltd*,[3] it was held by the Court of Appeal that as the facts giving rise to the claim constituted a fully pleaded cause of action for malicious falsehood, the claimant was not entitled to rely on a parallel plea of 'wrongful interference with rights' so as to gain the benefit of the six-year limitation period in s 2 of the LA 1980, even though this claim was properly advanced.

ACCRUAL OF THE CAUSE OF ACTION FOR LIBEL

14.02 As a libel is actionable per se, time runs from the date of publication.[4] It is irrelevant for limitation purposes whether the claimant was aware of the publication of the libel. If he only finds out about the defamation more than one year after publication, the limitation period will have expired and, absent deliberate concealment of a fact relevant to his cause of action, he will have to attempt to

1 The shortening of the limitation periods to one year by the Defamation Act 1996 does not apply to Scotland and it was commented by Hale LJ in *Steedman v British Broadcasting Corporation* [2001] EWCA 1534, [2002] EMLR 318 at para 31 that the three-year limitation period for libel in Scotland may give rise to a risk of forum shopping.

2 See *Brady v Norman* [2011] EWCA Civ 107, [2011] EMLR 314, discussed in para 14.06 below.

3 [2001] EWCA Civ 699.

4 *Grappelli v Derek Block (Holdings) Ltd* [1981] 1 WLR 822.

invoke s 32A in order to overcome a limitation defence.[5] If a book or newspaper is published and offered for sale, a fresh cause of action arises on each sale, notwithstanding that the limitation period has elapsed since the first publication. For example, in *Duke of Brunswick v Harmer*,[6] a claim was brought in 1848 to recover damages for a libel published in a newspaper in 1830. A defence of limitation was unsuccessful as the claimant was able to point to the sale of one copy of the newspaper just before the proceedings were brought. In *Loutchansky v Times Newspapers Ltd*,[7] it was held that an article which is accessible on the internet is republished on each occasion that a person accesses that article, and that no 'internet single publication'[8] or 'archive privilege' rule applies. Given the extensive volume of material which is archived and available for download on the internet, this has the effective result that no limitation period applies to an action for defamation concerning any material which is available on the internet,[9] which has led to calls for reform of the rule.[10]

ACCRUAL OF THE CAUSE OF ACTION FOR SLANDER

14.03 A slander is only actionable if it causes special damage, save in four circumstances where a slander is actionable per se and without proof of special damage, namely if the slander imputes:

1 a criminal offence punishable by imprisonment,

2 a contagious disease,

3 in the case of a woman, unchastity, or

4 if it is likely to damage the claimant's reputation in relation to any office, profession, calling, trade or business.[11]

In the case of a slander actionable per se, time runs from the date of the slander; for a slander actionable upon proof of special damage, time runs from when the special damage is sustained.[12]

5 *Edwards v Golding* [2007] EWCA Civ 416, [2007] All ER (D) 36 (Apr).

6 (1849) 14 QB 185.

7 [2001] EWCA Civ 1805, [2002] QB 783. The defendant was subsequently unsuccessful in its challenge to the English law before the European Court of Human Rights: see *Times Newspapers Ltd (Nos 1 and 2) v United Kingdom* (Apps 3002/03 and 23676/03) [2009] ECHR 451, [2009] EMLR 254.

8 See in particular, a discussion of some of the United States case law in *Loutchansky v Times Newspapers Ltd* [2001] EWCA Civ 1805, [2002] QB 783 at paras 64–65.

9 The material must still be accessed by somebody for time to run afresh and in *Zinda v Ark Academies (Schools)* [2011] EWHC 3394 (QB), it was confirmed that republication is not assumed if material remains accessible on the internet.

10 See the Ministry of Justice Consultation Paper on 'Defamation and the Internet: The Single Publication Rule' (CP-20/09) (September 2009), which follows the Law Commission's scoping study entitled 'Defamation and the Internet: A Preliminary Investigation' (December, 2002), both of which expressed misgivings about this rule.

11 *Clerk & Lindsell on Torts* (20th edn, London: Sweet & Maxwell, 2010) at para 22.53.

12 See *Saunders v Edwards* (1662) 1 Sid 95; *Littleboy (Littlebury) v Wright* (1662) 1 Sid 85.

PERSONS UNDER A DISABILITY

14.04 Section 28(4A) of the LA 1980 provides that if a claimant is under a disability when a cause of action for libel, slander, slander of title, slander of goods or other malicious falsehood accrues to him, the action may be brought at any time before the expiration of one year from the date when he ceases to be under a disability. Section 32A(3)(b) applies to any cause of action for defamation or malicious falsehood that accrues to a person under a disability who subsequently dies and whose personal representative is also under a disability. It provides that in such a case, an application may still be brought under s 32A notwithstanding the general rule in s 28(3) which prevents a 'further extension of time' being granted in such circumstances. It is unclear why special treatment is afforded to persons under a disability who are defamed over other causes of action open to them, but the provision is very unlikely to arise much in practice.

DISCRETION TO DISAPPLY THE LIMITATION PERIOD

14.05 Section 32A(1) provides the court with a discretion to direct that the limitation period shall not apply to an action, or part of an action, for defamation or malicious falsehood if it is equitable to allow the action to proceed having regard to the degree to which the operation of s 4A will cause prejudice to the claimant and the degree to which the direction to disapply the section would prejudice the defendant. Section 32A(2) sets out the factors that the court should consider in deciding on an application to disapply the limitation period. The subsection states that the court 'shall have regard to all the circumstances of the case and in particular to:

(a) the lengths of, and the reasons for, the delay on the part of the claimant;[13]

(b) where the reason or one of the reasons for the delay was that all or any of the facts relevant to the cause of action did not become known to the claimant until after the end of the period mentioned in section 4A –

  (i) the date on which any such facts did become known to him, and

  (ii) the extent to which he acted promptly and reasonably once he knew whether or not the facts in question might be capable of giving rise to an action; and

(c) the extent to which, having regard to the delay, relevant evidence is likely –

  (i) to be unavailable, or

  (ii) to be less cogent than if the action had been brought within the period mentioned in section 4A.'

13 Section 32A(3)(a) states that in an action for slander of title, slander of goods or other malicious falsehood brought by a personal representative, the references to 'the claimant' should be construed as including the deceased person to whom the cause of action accrued and any personal representatives of that person.

An application to disapply the limitation period should be made on notice to the defendant and in *Oyston v Blaker*[14] an order obtained on an ex parte basis was set aside on grounds that it was irregular. If the limitation period has expired, a claimant can issue a Pt 7 claim form, wait for a limitation defence to be pleaded and then apply for an order under s 32A. Alternatively, he can instead bring an application under s 32A by a Pt 8 claim form at the outset.[15] The reference to 'facts relevant' to a cause of action in s 32A(3)(b) was held in *C v Mirror Group Newspapers*[16] to relate only to facts which must be pleaded by the claimant in its statement of claim and not to relate to matters which would rebut a possible defence, in this case that a matter had not been referred to in court and thus that privilege did not attach to the defendant's newspaper article.

14.06 Although ss 32A and 33 of the LA 1980 give the court the power 'to do the same thing' and draw the attention of the court to similar[17] factors as being relevant to the exercise of a general discretion, the approach of the courts to applications relying on these two provisions is quite different. This issue arose directly in *Brady v Norman*,[18] a case in which the claimant issued proceedings in June 2009 in respect of a defamatory allegation (of forgery) which had been uttered in June 2006 that he claimed to have heard about for the first time in September 2008. In relation to the delay after finding out about the libel (the comments having been transcribed), he alleged that he lacked the necessary funds to obtain legal representation. He was refused an extension of time under s 32A, with Eady J holding that the loss of a limitation defence constituted prejudice to the defendant. He appealed to the Court of Appeal, arguing that the approach at first instance conflicted with the decision of the Court of Appeal in *Cain v Francis*[19] which focused on whether it was possible for a fair trial on the merits and whether the claimant would suffer financial prejudice if refused relief (which took into account any claim he may have against his own solicitor). Sir Antony May P gave the judgment of the Court of Appeal dismissing the appeal and, having discussed the considerations relevant to the exercise of the s 33 discretion, continued as follows:

> 'Considerations in defamation claims are likely to be different. The policy behind the much shorter limitation period is clear. The defamatory impact of libel or slander is likely to be transient and Parliament evidently intended that a claimant should assert and pursue his need for vindication speedily. As Hale LJ said in *Steedman*,[20] it is for claimants to make out a case for the disapplication of the normal rule and, in our judgment, the Master and the judge were fully entitled to hold that Mr Brady had not done so. The present case is far removed from a personal injury claim in which the defendant ought, if he is held liable, to pay damages. The delay is more than two years and, on one view, the explanation for

14 [1996] EMLR 125.

15 *Brady v Norman* [2010] EWHC 1215 (QB); this point was not referred to on appeal: [2011] EWCA Civ 107, [2011] EMLR 314.

16 [1996] 4 All ER 511.

17 The factors listed in s 32A(2) correspond with s 33(3)(a), (b) and (e).

18 [2011] EWCA Civ 107, [2011] EMLR 314.

19 [2008] EWCA Civ 1451, [2009] 1 QB 754.

20 *Steedman v British Broadcasting Corporation* [2001] EWCA 1534, [2002] EMLR 318.

the delay between September 2008 and June 2009 is not persuasive. It is not a case in which the prejudice to the defendant from the loss of the limitation defence is so fortuitous that it is balanced out of existence by prejudice to the claimant in losing a claim which the defendant ought in justice and fairness to meet. *Steedman v BBC* and *Cain v Francis* do not articulate different and conflicting principles. They represent differing manifestations of the application of the same principles to be derived from the different circumstances to which adjacent sections of the 1980 Act are applicable.'[21]

14.07 The decision of the Court of Appeal in *Steedman v British Broadcasting Corporation*[22] contains a useful exposition of the factors relevant to the exercise of the s 32A discretion. The claimants in this action were eight police officers who issued proceedings 15 months after the publication of an allegedly defamatory article which, although not naming them, they said identified them by reason of the high profile of the incident under discussion. The Court of Appeal noted the policy reasons that support a strict interpretation being given to s 32A and a number of first instance decisions[23] which stated that the limitation period should only be disapplied in exceptional circumstances.[24] The court in *Steedman* proceeded to examine the strength of the claimants' case; their failure to inform the defendant of their claim within the limitation period; the lack of an explanation for delays on their part; and their chances of suing their own solicitors as factors which leaned against the disapplication of the limitation period. It held that the prejudice to the defendant in not being able to rely on a limitation defence outweighed the prejudice to the claimants in not being able to pursue their defamation claim, as the latter was ameliorated by their ability to sue their solicitors.

14.08 Delay, and in particular the presence of tactical reasons for the delay, led to the refusal of an application to disapply the limitation period in *Adelson v Associated Newspapers Ltd.*[25] Eady J noted that the claimants had delayed for over a year after receipt of a defence before making this application, during which time an application to substitute parties (whom it was alleged may have suffered the damage to reputation) on grounds of mistake had been unsuccessfully pursued as far as the Court of Appeal.[26] The lack of vigour in proceeding, coupled with the fact that adding the co-claimants had more to do with tactics and recouping costs rather than genuinely attempting to protect reputations, led to the court refusing the applications. Delay and the weakness of the claim were the main factors that led to the claimant's applications being refused in *Zinda*

21 [2011] EWCA Civ 107, [2011] EMLR 314 at para 21.

22 [2001] EWCA 1534, [2002] EMLR 318.

23 *Hinks v Channel 4 Television Corp*, unreported, 3 March 2000, Morland J; *Clarkson v Gilbert*, unreported, 26 February 2001, Eady J.

24 Examples of where it might be equitable to extend time were if there had been a very small slippage of time, as in *Hartley v Birmingham District Council* [1992] 1 WLR 968 (a personal injuries action), or where there had been early notification but the claimant was awaiting the outcome of other investigations, as in *Khalil v Bennett* [2000] EMLR 996.

25 [2007] EWHC 3028 (QB); the same factors were present in *Hunter (t/a Connect Computers) v Rxworks.com Ltd* [2005] All ER (D) 162 (Jun).

26 [2007] EWCA Civ 701, [2007] 4 All ER 330.

v Ark Academies (Schools).[27] Eady J, in *Buckley v Dalziel*,[28] was clearly unimpressed by what he considered to be a 'relatively trivial' allegation of defamation arising out of an out-of-control boundary dispute concerning the pruning of some trees and bushes and refused to disapply the limitation period.

14.09 Cases in which the s 32A discretion was exercised in the claimant's favour include *Wood v Chief Constable of the West Midlands Police*,[29] where the application was made at the conclusion of the trial in which a witness said that he had not received a letter but had discussed its contents with another person. In those circumstances, the trial judge held that it would be equitable to extend the limitation period so as to allow the claimant to add a plea of slander. In *Maccaba v Litchenstein*,[30] an order was made disapplying the limitation period for an amendment to proceedings where the factual allegations would have been admissible at trial in any event in relation to the claimant's non-statute barred allegation of harassment and as several defamatory comments already formed part of his case against the defendant.

27 [2011] EWHC 3394 (QB).
28 [2007] EWHC 1025 (QB), [2007] 1 WLR 2933.
29 [2004] EWCA Civ 1638, [2005] EMLR 20.
30 [2003] All ER (D) 266 (Apr).

PART IV

Real and Personal Property

CHAPTER 15

Real Property

INTRODUCTION

15.01 The limitation provisions relating to real property are inextricably connected to the substantive rights at issue, as '[p]ossession is the root of unregistered title, such title is relative, and the owner is the person who has the best right to possess the land'.[1] The law on adverse possession has an unusual role in the law on limitation as it converts a tortious act (ie a continuing trespass) or breach of contract (failure to discharge a loan while remaining in possession of mortgaged land) into a legally recognised estate in land and something of value that can be sold or transferred. Although criminal law lies outside the scope of this book, the effect of s 144 of the Legal Aid, Sentencing and Punishment of Offenders Act 2012, which makes squatting in a residential building a criminal offence, is considered in this chapter as recent case law is to the effect that squatting which amounts to a criminal offence cannot constitute 'adverse possession' for limitation purposes.[2] Ownership of real property is sub-divided into ownership of different interests or estates in the property and this chapter considers the limitation provisions and principles that apply to the different interests and estates in land. The main rights of action considered are the rights of an owner in fee simple (or other party having a superior title) against a squatter, a mortgagee's rights against a mortgagor (and vice versa), and a landlord's rights against a tenant. For unregistered land, the Limitation Act 1980 ('LA 1980') gives legislative imprimatur to the equation of possession with ownership and provides that, at the expiration of the limitation period, title to that interest in land is extinguished.[3] The limitation provisions for registered land underwent a seismic overhaul with the passing of the Land Registration Act 2002 ('LRA 2002'). In cases where the LRA 2002 applies,[4] adverse possession of the land for the limitation period does not automatically extinguish the title of the registered landowner

1 Megarry and Wade, *Law of Real Property* (8th edn, London: Sweet & Maxwell, 2012) ('Megarry and Wade') at para 35-001; by contrast, at para 35-071, they note that 'the register is conclusive as to the ownership of that registered estate', hence its different treatment; see further *Parshall v Hackney* [2013] EWCA Civ 240.

2 See *Smith v Land Registry* [2009] EWHC 328 (Admin) and the discussion in paras 15.06–15.07.

3 LA 1980, s 17.

4 See para 15.44 et seq.

and instead an application must be made to the Land Registry for registration as owner of the registered estate.

OVERVIEW AND GENERAL PRINCIPLES

History of limitation periods for real property

15.02 The ability to acquire a possessory title by adverse possession is not a novel legal concept. In discussing the principles applicable in Roman law, Lord Hoffmann in *R v Oxfordshire County Council, Ex p Sunningwell Parish Council*[5] stated that, '[t]he ancient *Twelve Tables* called it *usucapio*, meaning literally taking by use'. Medieval English law imposed a limitation period by reference to various past events. The Statute of Merton 1235[6] fixed this date as the date of accession of Henry II (1154), and the Statute of Westminster I 1275[7] extended it to the accession of Richard I in 1189.[8] These provisions were not updated for two and a half centuries, 'so that there gradually ceased to be any effective system of limitation'.[9] It was only during the reign of Henry VIII that a fixed limitation period was introduced by the Limitation of Prescription Act 1540,[10] which was extended to ejectment actions (the modern equivalent is a trespass action) by the Limitation Act 1623.[11] The Real Property Limitation Act 1833[12] simplified the law and contains provisions which have been retained in modified form up to the present date, although the general limitation period was only reduced to 12 years by the Real Property Limitation Act 1874.[13] Thereafter, the law on adverse possession was only subject to minor further amendment by the Limitation Act 1939 and the LA 1980, before the further significant changes effected by the LRA 2002.

The purpose and effect of the limitation provisions for real property

15.03 The provisions in the LA 1980 which govern actions relating to real property differ in their purpose and effect from the sections dealing with other[14]

5 [2000] 1 AC 335 at 349. The modern law on adverse possession continues to make use of a number of Latin phrases, including '*animus possidendi*' (the intention to possess: see para 15.26) although the phrase '*nec vi, nec clam, nec precario*' (not by force, nor stealth, nor licence) should be treated with care: see para 15.06 and *Higgs v Leshel Maryas Investment Co Ltd* [2009] UKPC 47 at para 55.

6 20 Hen 3, c 4.

7 3 Edw 1, c 39.

8 *R v Oxfordshire County Council, Ex p Sunningwell Parish Council* [2000] 1 AC 335.

9 Megarry and Wade at para 35.003.

10 32 Hen 8, c 2. This Act only applied to the 'real actions' and provided a limitation period of 60, 50 or 30 years, depending on the cause of action: Jourdan and Radley-Gardner, *Adverse Possession* (2nd edn, London: Bloomsbury Professional, 2011) ('Jourdan and Radley-Gardner') at para 2-02.

11 21 Jac 1, c 16. This Act provided a limitation period of 20 years for ejectment actions.

12 3 & 4 Will 4, c 27.

13 37 & 38 Vic, c 57.

14 With the exception of actions in respect of the conversion of a chattel, for which s 3(2) provides that, subject to exceptions discussed in Ch 16, title to the chattel is extinguished six years after a right of action for conversion accrued.

causes of action in an important respect: the limitation rules that govern civil wrongs such as torts and breaches of contract bar the remedy and not the right; by contrast, at the expiration of the limitation period for any person to bring an action to recover land from a squatter, the title of that person to the land is extinguished.[15] Prior to 1833, the effect of the expiry of the limitation period was merely to bar a landowner's remedy and not his rights. Thus, a person whose right to recover land had been barred could, if he recovered possession, reassert his old title.[16] The Real Property Limitation Act 1833[17] was the first limitation act to provide that a landowner's title was extinguished if a squatter was in possession of the land for the limitation period. If he subsequently re-entered possession without permission, he was trespassing.[18] This rule gives legal effect to the principle applicable to unregistered land that '[p]ossession, *prima facie*, is a title good against everyone who cannot prove a better title'.[19] The position is different in cases where title is registered; the provisions of the LRA 2002 are considered at length below.[20]

Justifications for extinguishing title to land by adverse possession

15.04 There are many justifications for a system of law that extinguishes title to unregistered land following a (reasonably lengthy) period of adverse possession. A finite time limit for the recovery of possession of land encourages landowners to make productive use of their land and penalises those who abandon their lands; similarly, it encourages parties not to sleep on their rights: *vigilantibus non dormientibus, jura subveniunt*.[21] As was stated by the Government of the United Kingdom in its submissions to the European Court of Human Rights in *JA Pye (Oxford) Ltd v United Kingdom*:[22]

> '[I]f land and its ownership are out of kilter, the land may become unmarketable. Where the registered owner has disappeared, and cannot be traced, and a squatter takes possession, the doctrine of adverse possession "does at least ensure that in such cases land remains in commerce and is not rendered sterile". Where there have been dealings "off the register", such as where a farmer agrees to a land swap with a neighbour under a "gentleman's agreement" but does not register the change, "adverse possession fulfils a useful function" ... Because in case of mistake the innocent but mistaken squatter of land may have incurred expenditure. In such circumstances adverse possession can be justified on grounds of hardship, and there are parallels with the principles of proprietary estoppel ... Because it facilitates and cheapens investigation of title to land.'[23]

15 LA 1980, s 17.
16 *Doe d Burrough v Reade* (1807) 8 East 353.
17 (3 & 4 Will 4, c 27) s 34.
18 *Incorporated Society for Protestant Schools v Richards* (1841) 4 Ir Eq Rep 177.
19 *Kennan v Murphy* (1880) 8 LR Ir 285 at 293, per Pallas CB.
20 Para 15.44 et seq.
21 'The laws come to the aid of the watchful, not the sleeping'.
22 App No 44302/02, [2007] ECHR 5559, (2008) 46 EHRR 45.
23 (2008) 46 EHRR 45 at para 30, quoting from the Law Commission Consultative Document on Land Registration (Law Com 254, 1998); see also Megarry and Wade, para 35.001 and Dockray, 'Why do we need adverse possession?' (1985) Conv 272.

As registration has replaced possession as the main *indicia* of ownership for registered estates in land, the advantage of quieting title by adverse possession is greatly lessened for registered land.[24] For this reason the LRA 2002 disapplies the limitation provisions in the LA 1980 where the landowner's title is registered. Instead of adverse possession extinguishing his title at the expiry of the limitation period, it now merely gives the squatter a right to be registered as owner of the registered estate by adverse possession if either the application is unopposed or if he comes within one of three narrowly circumscribed conditions.

Human rights aspects: JA Pye (Oxford) Ltd v United Kingdom

15.05 Notwithstanding the legitimate reasons which underpin the current law, following the decision of the House of Lords in *JA Pye (Oxford) Ltd v Graham*,[25] a case was taken by the unsuccessful claimant to the European Court of Human Rights (the 'European Court') to challenge the law then in force in England and Wales. The applicant argued that the LA 1980 did not adequately protect its property rights. At first instance these arguments were accepted and the Fourth Chamber of the European Court, which delivered its judgment in *JA Pye (Oxford) Ltd v United Kingdom*[26] in November 2005, held that English law on adverse possession was in breach of art 1 of Protocol No 1 of the European Convention on Human Rights ('ECHR'). This judgment was appealed but left the law on adverse possession in a state of flux between 2005 and 2007.[27] The Grand Chamber of the European Court delivered its judgment on the appeal in August 2007[28] and reversed the decision of the Fourth Chamber. It held that the provisions in the LA 1980 on adverse possession fell within the margin of appreciation afforded to a State to regulate the control of use of land such that there was no breach of the Convention. Following the decision of the Grand Chamber of the European Court in *Pye*, in *Ofulue v Bossert*[29] the Court of Appeal held that any issue concerning the compatibility of the law on adverse possession with the ECHR could not be raised again in the absence of special circumstances, which were not established. The human rights issues relating to the limitation provisions for real property now appear to be settled.

The interaction between criminal law and adverse possession

15.06 There is an unresolved tension in the law on adverse possession concerning the impact on the squatter's position if he either enters into possession

24 Although a series of mistakes by the Land Registry led to the wrong party being registered as owner of a piece of land in *Parshall v Hackney* [2013] EWCA Civ 240, the Court of Appeal held that correcting and giving effect to the register rather than giving effect to a lengthy period of possession by one party was the appropriate response.

25 [2002] UKHL 30, [2003] 1 AC 419.

26 App No 44302/02, [2005] ECHR 921, (2005) 43 EHRR 3.

27 See *Beaulane Properties Ltd v Palmer* [2005] EWHC 817 (Ch), [2006] Ch 79.

28 App No 44302/02, [2007] ECHR 5559, (2008) 46 EHRR 45.

29 [2008] EWCA Civ 7, [2009] 1 Ch 1, affd without reference to this point: [2009] UKHL 16, [2009] 1 AC 990.

by means that breach the criminal law, possesses contrary to a statutory prohibition or where the possession exercised by him constitutes a crime. In *McPhail v Persons Unknown*,[30] it was stated by Lord Denning MR that if squatters entered forcibly and in breach of the criminal law,[31] and the landowner never acquiesced in their presence, they 'never gained possession'.[32] A different approach is evident from the judgment of Lord Scott giving the advice of the Privy Council in *Higgs v Leshel Maryas Investment Co Ltd*,[33] where he stated that non-peaceable possession is still adverse possession and that an aggrieved landowner's remedy is to bring court proceedings. Section 6 of the Criminal Law Act 1977 now criminalises the use or threat of violence to secure entry to premises where there is someone on the premises at the time who is opposed to the entry. As the landowner must be dispossessed by force or threats of violence for this provision to apply, he will know of the squatting from the outset and it seems inevitable that 12 years' inactivity thereafter would be characterised as acquiescence. Turning to acts of possession which breach a statutory prohibition, such as the use of fishing nets that breached statutory requirements in *Lord Advocate v Lord Lovat*,[34] this poses no impediment to a squatter's possession being recognised.

15.07 The principles discussed in the previous paragraph were developed upon in the decision at first instance in *R (Smith) v Land Registry (Peterborough)*,[35] where Judge Pelling QC held that possession exercised in breach of the criminal law[36] cannot count towards the statutory period of adverse possession required to extinguish title. This has assumed greater importance with the passing of s 144 of the Legal Aid, Sentencing and Punishment of Offenders Act 2012, which makes knowingly trespassing in a residential building where the party intends to live there for any period a criminal offence. The approach adopted by Judge Pelling QC in *R (Smith) v Land Registry (Peterborough)* gives full effect to an *ex turpi causa non oritur actio* objection to adverse possession, but it is noticeable that the Court of Appeal shied away from confronting this point directly on appeal,[37] leaving it for determination in a future case. However, the Land Registry now precludes reliance on possession that constituted an obstruction of the public highway[38] or a criminal offence[39] in applications to register title by adverse possession. This point should not be considered settled for the present, and one leading textbook notes that '[i]t is not clear that this approach is correct'.[40] While this may be correct by reference to the decided case law on adverse possession,

30 [1973] Ch 447.
31 Forcible Entry Acts 1381 to 1623; now repealed by the Criminal Law Act 1977.
32 [1973] Ch 447 at 455.
33 [2009] UKPC 47 at para 55.
34 (1880) 5 App Cas 273.
35 [2009] EWHC 328 (Admin), affd without reference to this point: [2010] EWCA Civ 200, [2011] QB 413.
36 Obstruction of the public highway contrary to s 137 of the Highways Act 1980.
37 [2010] EWCA Civ 200, [2011] QB 413.
38 *Land Registry Practice Guide 4 (Adverse possession of registered land)* (April 2013) at para 5.
39 See 'Squatting and Adverse Possession' (Oct 2012) 32 Land Registry *Landnet* 5.
40 Jourdan and Radley-Gardner at para 7-139; see further Cant, 'Property: Criminal Gains' (2012) 162 NLJ 1309, and Clarke and Pawlowski, 'Moving In, Moving Out: Will Judges Allow Adverse Possession Claims Based on an Offence?' (2013) 157 Sol Jo 10.

regard should also be had to the approach adopted by Moses J in *City of Gotha v Sotheby's*[41] in an analogous area, where he held that it would be contrary to public policy[42] to allow a defendant who derived title from a thief to rely on the expiry of a German limitation period in defence of a claim for delivery up of the stolen painting. While the comments in *City of Gotha* were *obiter*, there are obvious reasons why they might influence the approach to be taken in the area of adverse possession of real property.

Definition of land – exclusion of incorporeal hereditaments

15.08 The definition of 'land' in s 38(1) of the LA 1980 is non-exhaustive and 'includes corporeal hereditaments, tithes and rent-charges, and any legal or equitable estate or interest therein' but save as aforesaid it excludes any incorporeal hereditaments. 'Corporeal hereditaments' is not defined in the LA 1980 but is usually taken to include all physical land, including buildings or parts of buildings, structures, lakes, rivers, streams and foreshore, airspace above land, mines and minerals.[43] Incorporeal hereditaments are a type of property right which includes easements and *profits à prendre*. The provisions on the acquisition of easements by prescription are different to those governing adverse possession of interests in land and are not considered in this book.

ACTIONS TO RECOVER LAND

Definition of an action to recover land

15.09 The phrase 'action to recover land' is given a broad definition in s 38(7) of the LA 1980 and 'includes references to a right to enter possession of the land or, in the case of rentcharges and tithes, to distrain for arrears of rent or tithe, and references to the bringing of such an action shall include references to the making of such an entry or distress'. It includes a mortgagee's right to recover possession of land from a mortgagor and somewhat curiously a mortgagee's right of foreclosure,[44] both of which are considered below in the section on mortgages, charges and debts secured on land[45] as they have little in common with a claim by a dispossessed landowner to evict a squatter. The word 'action' is defined as including 'any proceeding in a court of law'.[46] In *JA Pye (Oxford) Ltd v Graham*,[47] it was held by Neuberger J that an application to the Land Registry under the Land Registration Act 1925 did not constitute the bringing of an action to recover

41 Unreported, 9 September 1998 (QBD); *The Times*, 8 October 1998.
42 The public policy point was raised under the Foreign Limitation Periods Act 1984, s 2 (2): see further para 3.05.
43 Law of Property Act 1925, s 205(1)(ix); Jourdan and Radley-Gardner at para 1-12.
44 LA 1980, s 20(4).
45 See para 15.39.
46 LA 1980, s 38(1).
47 [2000] Ch 676; Jourdan and Radley-Gardner at para 1-24 suggest that the reference of a dispute by the registrar to the adjudicator should be treated as the bringing of an action to recover land.

land; nor were proceedings to remove cautions against the claimants' title in relation to the disputed land. In *Markfield Investments Ltd v Evans*,[48] it was held that unsuccessful proceedings will have no effect on the running of time. In *Higgs v Leshel Maryas Investment Co Ltd*,[49] it was held by the Privy Council that an action which claimed an injunction restraining interference with surveying work and clearing of boundaries was held to constitute an action to recover land. Lord Scott pointed to the fact that the success of the proceedings required the recognition of the documentary title as the reason why this was the case.

Limitation period for an action to recover land

15.10 Section 15(1) of the LA 1980 provides that no action to recover land shall be brought after the expiration of 12 years[50] from the date on which the right of action accrued to the claimant, or, if the claimant claims through some other person, to that person. At the expiration of the limitation period, the title of that person to the land is extinguished.[51]

Accrual of the right of action to recover land

15.11 Schedule 1, Pt I of the LA 1980 contains a number of paragraphs which deem a right of action to recover land to have accrued in certain circumstances. The first of these, contained in para 1, is the most frequently invoked and provides that where a person has been in possession of land and has been dispossessed or discontinued his possession, the right of action to recover land shall be deemed to have accrued on the date of the 'dispossession or discontinuance'. The paragraphs that follow in Sch 1, Pt I deal with situations where a person in possession dies,[52] where the land was assured otherwise than by will to the 'squatter',[53] the position in relation to future interests,[54] and a number of situations involving tenancies.[55] These deeming provisions must all be read subject to Sch 1, Pt I, para 8, which provides that no right of action shall be treated as accruing unless the land is in the possession of some person in whose favour the period of limitation can run, which is described as where that person is in 'adverse possession'. The wording in para 8 is crucial to an understanding of the law on adverse possession and is discussed at length below.[56]

48 [2001] 1 WLR 1321.
49 [2009] UKPC 47.
50 An extended limitation period applies to actions by the Crown or any spiritual or eleemosynary corporation: see further paras 15.12 and 31.09.
51 LA 1980, s 17.
52 LA 1980, Sch 1, Pt I, para 2: the right accrues on his death.
53 LA 1980, Sch 1, Pt I, para 3: the right accrues on the date the assurance took effect.
54 LA 1980, Sch 1, Pt I, paras 4 and 9, discussed below in para 15.15.
55 LA 1980, Sch 1, Pt I, paras 5–7, discussed below in para 15.29 et seq.
56 See para 15.23 et seq.

Action by the Crown or any spiritual or eleemosynary corporation

15.12 Schedule 1, Pt II of the LA 1980 modifies the limitation periods in s 15 of the LA 1980 for actions to recover land where the Crown or a spiritual or eleemosynary corporation sole is the claimant. The main modification is that the limitation period for the Crown or a spiritual or eleemosynary corporation sole to recover land (other than foreshore) is 30 years from the date on which the right of action accrued to that person.[57] The second main modification is that a limitation period of 60 years applies to an action by the Crown to recover foreshore.[58] These and the other modifications that exist where the claimant in an action to recover land is the Crown or a spiritual or eleemosynary corporation sole are discussed later in the book.[59]

Action to recover foreshore

15.13 Foreshore is defined as 'the shore and bed of the sea and of any tidal water, below the line of the medium high tide between the spring tides and the neap tides'[60] and while it will usually be owned by the Crown, this will not always be the case. A limitation period of 60 years applies in the case of an action by the Crown to recover foreshore, which is considered in a later chapter,[61] but the 12-year limitation period contained in s 15(1) will apply if the owner of the foreshore is not the Crown. This relatively obscure area of law has been considered in two recent decisions. In *Roberts v Swangrove Estates Ltd*,[62] the Court of Appeal delivered an interesting judgment on the entitlement of the claimant to possess parts of the bed of the estuary of the River Severn and the adjoining foreshore, though it was able to rest its decision on the narrow point that the Crown may acquire title by adverse possession. In *Port of London Authority v Ashmore*,[63] the owner of an 84-foot long flat-bottomed barge claimed adverse possession of the 'footprint' of the Thames over which it had been moored for in excess of 12 years. This land was tidal riverbed which was exposed at low tide and was held to come within the definition of foreshore. It was held by Stephen Smith QC, sitting as a deputy High Court judge, that it was possible to acquire title to part of the bed of a tidal river or the foreshore through the occupation of a vessel which, at least for some of the time, floated above that part and did not always rest on it. Unfortunately, the Court of Appeal[64] was not satisfied that the agreed statement of facts provided a sufficient basis for deciding a point of law of such general importance and it allowed an appeal from this decision without commenting on the legal principles.

57 LA 1980, s 15(1) as modified by Sch 1, Pt II, para 10.
58 LA 1980, s 15(1) as modified by Sch 1, Pt II, para 11(1).
59 See paras 31.08–31.09.
60 LA 1980, Sch 1, Pt II, para 11(3).
61 Paras 31.08–31.09.
62 [2008] EWCA Civ 98, [2008] Ch 439.
63 [2009] EWHC 954 (Ch), [2009] 4 All ER 665.
64 *Port of London Authority v Ashmore* [2010] EWCA Civ 30, [2010] 1 All ER 1139.

Land subject to a right of way and public highways

15.14 The special status afforded to public highways is worthy of note at this point as it was recently the subject of thorough analysis by the Court of Appeal in *R (Smith) v Land Registry (Peterborough).*[65] The applicant in this case was a squatter who had parked his caravan and associated structures on a byway for more than 12 years. He applied to the Land Registry to be registered as proprietor of the council's registered estate in the land, which was a public highway maintainable at the public expense under the Highways Act 1980. His challenge to the decision of the Land Registry refusing his application was unsuccessful before the High Court, where Judge Pelling QC found that as his squatting constituted a criminal offence it could not ground a claim of adverse possession. His appeal was dismissed by the Court of Appeal on the different ground that as s 263 of the Highways Act 1980 expressly vests a highway maintainable at the public expense in the appropriate highway authority, it is not possible to acquire title to land while it remains a public highway. This rule is limited to highways maintained at the public expense and, as was stated by Mummery LJ in *R (Smith) v Land Registry*, 'the existence of a right of way over land, whether it is a private right of way or a public highway, does not necessarily prevent a person from claiming adverse possession of that land'.[66] Thus, in both *Seddon v Smith,*[67] where there was only a private right of way over land, and *JA Pye (Oxford) Ltd v Graham,*[68] where a large expanse of land included a public footpath, title to the land was extinguished by adverse possession.

Future interests

15.15 Schedule 1, Pt I, para 4 of the LA 1980 provides that the right of action to recover land where the estate or interest claimed is a future interest (such as an estate or interest in remainder or reversion) is deemed to have accrued on the date on which the estate or interest fell into possession.[69] Section 15(2) of the LA 1980 then provides that if a period of adverse possession began before the remainder fell into possession, the limitation period expires after the later of either:

(i) 12 years from the date the adverse possession commenced, or

(ii) six years from the date on which the future interest vested in possession.

Fee tails

15.16 An exception to the rule that the owner of a future interest has the longer of the 12-year limitation period or six years from when his interest fell

65 [2009] EWHC 328 (Admin); affd [2010] EWCA Civ 200, [2011] QB 413.
66 [2010] EWCA Civ 200, [2011] QB 413 at para 57.
67 (1877) 36 LT 168.
68 [2002] UKHL 30, [2003] 1 AC 419.
69 When read together with the reference to 'not being a term of years absolute' in the LA 1980 s 15(2)(b), it seems clear that neither provision dealing with future interests applies to leases for a term of years absolute.

into possession within which to bring proceedings exists in the case of fee tails. Section 15(3) of the LA 1980 provides that a reversioner or remainderman expectant upon an entail in possession is not entitled to the alternative six-year period if his interest could have been barred by the tenant in tail. An assurance taking effect after the right of action to recover possession accrued does not add to the period within which the person by whom the assurance was made could have brought such an action.[70] If a person is entitled to an interest in possession as well as a future interest in the same estate in land, and his interest in possession is barred under the Act, he may not bring an action in respect of the future interest unless, in the meantime, possession is recovered by a person entitled to an intermediate estate.[71] Section 27 applies in the case of a person taking possession of land by virtue of a defective disentailing assurance made by a person entitled in remainder to an entailed interest in land. It provides that a 12-year limitation period applies to an action against the person entering into possession under the defective assurance, which runs from the date the assurance should have operated as an effective bar.

Settled land and land held on trust

15.17 Section 18 of the LA 1980 governs settled land and land held on trust and provides that, subject to s 21(1) and (2),[72] the provisions of the Act shall apply to equitable interests in land as they apply to legal estates. The issues are best approached from three perspectives:

(i) Trustees

In general, a trustee cannot bar the title of a beneficiary: no limitation period applies to an action by a beneficiary against his trustee to recover trust property where the claim is based upon fraud or for the recovery of property converted by the trustee to his own use,[73] though a defence of *laches* or acquiescence may be raised.[74] If there is no fraud, such as where a trustee pays money to the wrong person by mistake, the limitation period is six years.[75]

(ii) Beneficiaries

If settled land or land held on trust is in the possession of one of several beneficiaries, no right of action to recover the land accrues and thus a claim by a trustee (or a beneficiary not in possession) will not become statute barred.[76] An exception exists in the case of a person solely or absolutely entitled to the land, in which case time runs against the trustee from the moment the beneficiary is in possession. But equally, under the principle in

70 LA 1980, s 15(4).
71 LA 1980, s 15(5).
72 See generally Ch 17.
73 LA 1980, s 21(1)(a) and (b).
74 LA 1980, s 36(2).
75 LA 1980, s 21(3).
76 LA 1980, Sch 1, Pt 1, para 9.

Saunders v Vautier,[77] the sole beneficiary is entitled to call upon the trustees to convey the legal estate to him. A vendor of land who lets a purchaser into possession after the contract is signed but prior to completion may be a bare trustee in such circumstances against whom time will run.[78]

(iii) Strangers

By way of modification of the generally applicable 12-year limitation period for an action to recover land, s 18(2)–(4) of the LA 1980 provides that where land held on trust is possessed adversely by a stranger, the stranger does not bar the trustee's title until the estates of all of the beneficiaries have been barred. A trustee may bring an action as claimant on behalf of any person entitled to a beneficial interest whose right of action has not been barred, notwithstanding that the right of action of the trustee has itself been barred, but when every such right of action is barred the right of action by the trustees shall be extinguished.[79]

Successive squatters

15.18 As possession is the most basic form of title, a squatter may transfer his possessory title to unregistered land, even if not yet sufficient to extinguish the title of the landowner, to a third party by sale, gift or devise and his period of possession will then form part of the title of the transferee.[80] In *Site Developments (Ferndown) Ltd v Cuthbury Ltd*,[81] it was held by Vos J, who adopted a proposition of law taken from Megarry and Wade,[82] that a squatter who dispossessed a previous squatter could, as against the registered owner, add the former period of occupation to his own, as time runs against the true owner from when adverse possession began. The same authors suggest that the position is different as between the first squatter and the second squatter, in which case the second squatter must occupy for the full limitation period to bar his possessory title as against him.[83] If the squatter abandons his possession and a second squatter enters into possession of the land, the latter squatter cannot make use of the former's period of possession, as Sch 1, Pt I, para 8(2) provides that when land ceases to be in adverse possession the right of action lapses.

Co-ownership

15.19 The old rule at common law was that the unity of possession among co-owners meant that if one co-owner occupied the whole of the land (or took

77 (1841) 4 Beav 115.
78 Megarry and Wade at para 35-040; *Bridges v Mees* [1957] Ch 457; the position may be otherwise if the purchase monies have not been paid: *Hyde v Pearce* [1982] 1 WLR 560.
79 LA 1980, s 18(3).
80 *Mount Carmel Investments Ltd v Peter Thurlow Ltd* [1988] 1 WLR 1078.
81 [2010] EWHC 10 (Ch), [2011] Ch 226.
82 Now contained in the 8th edn, 2012, at para 35-022.
83 Megarry and Wade, *ibid*; however, it would also be arguable that a dispossessed squatter retains no residual rights if he cedes possession prior to the expiration of the limitation period.

the whole of the rents or profits) this, by itself, did not constitute adverse possession.[84] This rule was abolished in 1833[85] after which time ran as between co-owners from the date one co-owner was in possession of more than his undivided share for his own benefit as against any co-owner not in possession.[86] This was then changed by the Law of Property Act 1925 so that the interests of co-owners take effect behind a statutory trust which, since the passing of the Trusts of Land and Appointment of Trustees Act 1996, is known as a 'trust of land'. The limitation rules are thus those that govern trusts,[87] the most important being that the trustee cannot bar a beneficiary's interest and that one beneficiary cannot bar another beneficiary's interest.[88]

Adverse possession and estates of deceased persons

15.20 Schedule 1, Pt I, para 2 of the LA 1980 provides that a right of action to recover land that had been in the possession of a deceased person shall be treated as having accrued on the date of his death. This deeming provision has been described as 'wholly illusory'[89] as it is subject to Sch 1, Pt I, para 8(1), which states that time only runs from when a person is in adverse possession of a property. More importantly, one must bear in mind the general limitation principle that time can only run, and a person can only be in adverse possession of a property, from a date when there was a claimant in existence who could bring proceedings and one who could be named as a defendant in those proceedings.[90] No special rules arise in the case of lands owned by a deceased person if either the period of squatting commenced while the deceased was still alive and continued after his death, or if an executor is appointed under his will, as the estate of a deceased person vests in an executor from the date of death of the deceased.[91] However, if the deceased dies intestate and a person takes adverse possession of estate land after that date, two features of intestacies should be noted: first, that persons entitled to a property on an intestacy take their interest jointly, and thus as trustees, and the rule contained in Sch 1, Pt I, para 9 applies, as discussed in the previous paragraph.[92] Secondly, s 26 of the LA 1980 provides that administration dates back to the date of death for limitation purposes as if there had been no interval between that time and the grant of letters of administration. This creates an exception to the rule that time does not run against an administrator of an estate until he is appointed.[93]

84 *Scott v Knox* (1841) 4 Ir Eq R 397 at 409.
85 Real Property Limitation Act 1833 (3 & 4 Will 4, c 27), s 12.
86 See the decisions of the Privy Council on Commonwealth statutes retaining the pre-LPA 1925 wording in *Paradise Beach and Transportation Co Ltd v Price-Robinson* [1968] AC 1072 (beneficiaries under a will) and *Wills v Wills* [2003] UKPC 84, (2003) 64 WIR 176 (spouses).
87 LA 1980, Sch 1, Pt I, para 9.
88 See further para 15.17 above.
89 Jourdan and Radley-Gardner at para 31-03.
90 See para 1.20.
91 *Woolley v Clark* (1822) 5 B & Ald 744.
92 See *Earnshaw v Hartley* [2000] Ch 155.
93 *Atkinson v Bradford Third Equitable Building Society* (1890) 25 QBD 377 at 383, per Lopes LJ.

Claims for rent, damages or mesne rates after the estate is extinguished

15.21 In *Re Jolly*,[94] it was held that once a claimant's estate is extinguished by adverse possession then all of his rights are extinguished under the statute, including the right to claim rent which had fallen due within the applicable limitation period for claiming rent. This was followed in *Mount Carmel Investments Ltd v Peter Thurlow Ltd*,[95] where the Court of Appeal held that if the limitation period has run its course then the dispossessed landowner also loses his right to seek damages for trespass, even if part of the trespass occurred during the period prior to his title becoming statute barred. These two decisions have been the subject of some criticism both academically[96] and by Nicholas Strauss QC sitting as a deputy High Court judge in *Beaulane Properties Ltd v Palmer*,[97] who noted that the statutory provision at issue in *Re Jolly* expressly precluded the claim and had not been retained in the LA 1980. He stated that he would have chosen not to follow the earlier case law if he had found that the claimant's estate was extinguished by adverse possession.[98] As against this, the rule is consistent with *Elder v Northcott*,[99] which holds that an action for interest becomes statute barred once the action for the principal sum is barred.

The dispossessed landowner's title

15.22 For issues of adverse possession to arise at all, a landowner must first prove his title. Schedule 1, Pt I, para 1 of the LA 1980 refers to a person who had been 'in possession' of the land bringing an action to 'recover' land. This will ordinarily be done by him calling evidence to show that he is the owner of the paper title to the land and it has been held that, in the absence of evidence to the contrary, the owner of the paper title to land is deemed to be in possession of the land.[100] It is not necessary for the owner of the paper title to show that he entered into possession of the property at any stage, as will be frequently the case where a mortgagee sues for possession.[101] In fact, it is not necessary to show that the 'landowner' has any paper title, as possession 'is a title good against everyone who cannot prove a better title'.[102] It is not a good defence to a claim for possession to show that some party other than the claimant is the true owner of the land as this is *jus tertii*; all that is relevant is whether the claimant's title is better than the defendant's title.

94 [1900] 2 Ch 616.
95 [1988] 1 WLR 1078.
96 See McGee, *Limitation Periods* (6th edn, London: Sweet & Maxwell, 2010) at para 13.071: 'as unfortunate as it is surprising'.
97 [2005] EWHC 817 (Ch), [2006] Ch 79.
98 [2005] EWHC 817 (Ch), [2006] Ch 79 at para 220.
99 [1930] 2 Ch 422.
100 *Powell v McFarlane* (1977) 38 P & CR 452 at 470.
101 *National Westminster Bank Plc v Ashe* [2008] EWCA Civ 55, [2008] 1 WLR 710.
102 *Kennan v Murphy* (1880) 8 LR Ir 285 at 293, per Pallas CB.

Dispossession of the landowner and squatter taking possession

15.23 The next issue which must arises under Sch 1, Pt I, para 1 is whether the landowner was either dispossessed or discontinued his possession of the land, following which some other person entered into possession.[103] While these requirements have in some cases been viewed as cumulative,[104] it has also been stated that 'an inquiry into whether there has been discontinuance or dispossession is unnecessary and unhelpful. If there has been continuous adverse possession then time will have run in favour of the squatter'.[105] Accordingly, the first matter a squatter must establish is that he has been in 'possession' of the property for the applicable limitation period. The question of what is required to establish possession of land is a question of fact and degree. As was stated by Lord O'Hagan in *The Lord Advocate v Lord Lovat*:[106]

> 'As to possession, it must be considered in every case with reference to the peculiar circumstances. The acts, implying possession in one case, may be wholly inadequate to prove it in another. The character and value of the property, the suitable and natural mode of using it, the course of conduct with the proprietor might reasonably be expected to follow with a due regard to his own interests – all these things, greatly varying as they must, under various conditions, are to be taken into account in determining the sufficiency of a possession.'[107]

A further useful statement of what constitutes 'possession', which has subsequently found favour in the House of Lords[108] is that of Slade J in *Powell v McFarlane*:[109]

> 'Factual possession signifies an appropriate degree of physical control. It must be a single and [exclusive][110] possession, though there can be a single possession exercised by several persons jointly. Thus an owner of land and a person intruding on that same land cannot both be in possession of the land at the same time. The question of what acts constitute a sufficient degree of exclusive physical control must depend on the circumstances, in particular the nature of the land and the manner in which land of that nature is commonly used or enjoyed.'[111]

The strongest evidence of possession is if the squatter can prove that he locked the gates to (or otherwise enclosed) the disputed plot[112] or built a permanent structure on the land for his own use.[113] Acts such as grazing cattle might of

103 LA 1980, Sch 1, Pt I, para 1.
104 See *Buckinghamshire County Council v Moran* [1990] Ch 623 at 635, 644–645.
105 Jourdan and Radley-Gardner at para 5-01.
106 (1880) 5 App Cas 273.
107 (1880) 5 App Cas 273 at 288.
108 Lord Browne-Wilkinson in *JA Pye (Oxford) Ltd v Graham* [2003] 1 AC 419 at 432 commented that the principles set out by Slade J 'cannot be improved upon'.
109 (1977) 38 P & CR 452.
110 Although 'conclusive' is used in the case report, the word 'exclusive' was stated by Simon Brown LJ in *Burns v Anthony*, unreported, 15 July 1997 (CA) to have been what was intended.
111 (1977) 38 P & CR 452 at 470.
112 *Buckinghamshire County Council v Moran* [1990] Ch 623.
113 *Laing v Moran* (1952) 2 DLR 468; *Kierford Ridge Pty Ltd v Ward* [2005] VSC 215.

themselves be equivocal (and thus insufficient) in proving that possession had been taken of the land as it is appropriate to infer the lesser rather than the greater entitlement,[114] but if in addition fences were repaired and hedges trimmed this is likely to be sufficient to establish possession.[115] Acts involving dumping or storage are generally held not to be sufficient to establish possession,[116] but the position may be otherwise if these acts were carried out on land following the determination of a tenancy.[117]

Possession without the consent of the landowner

15.24 In modern usage[118] the phrase 'adverse possession' means 'possession inconsistent with and in denial of the title of the true owner. Possession is not normally adverse if it is enjoyed by a lawful title or with the consent of the true owner'.[119] This means that time cannot run in favour of a person who is in possession of land with the continuing permission or consent of the landowner,[120] which in legal terms requires the court to determine whether the facts establish that there is permission to occupy as a licensee[121] or tenant (including tenant at will),[122] both of which are discussed in the next paragraph, or pursuant to a mortgage debenture.[123] A tacit consent by which a mortgagee merely allowed a mortgagor to remain in possession was held in *National Westminster Bank Plc v Ashe*[124] not to stop the limitation clock from running and similarly, in *JA Pye (Oxford) Ltd v Graham,*[125] it was held that it is not relevant that the squatter would have paid rent if this had been requested by the landowner. Acts and words relied on as indicating consent must be 'probative of and not merely consistent with

114 *Gallagher v Northern Ireland Housing Executive* [2009] NICA 50; *Powell v McFarlane* (1977) 38 P & CR 452.

115 *Wallis' Cayton Bay Holiday Camp Ltd v Shell-Mex and BP Ltd* [1975] QB 94; *JA Pye (Oxford) Ltd v Graham* [2002] UKHL 30, [2003] 1 AC 419.

116 *Treloar v Nute* [1976] 1 WLR 1295; see also *Pilford v Greenmanor Ltd* [2012] EWCA Civ 756, where storage coupled with car parking was found to be sufficient.

117 *Griffin v Bleithin* [1999] 2 ILRM 182.

118 Prior to the Real Property Limitation Act 1833, there existed a doctrine of 'non-adverse possession': see the judgment of Lord Upjohn in *Paradise Beach and Transportation Co Ltd v Price-Robinson* [1968] AC 1072 (PC) at 1082–1083.

119 *Ramnarace v Lutchman* [2001] UKPC 25, [2001] 1 WLR 1651 at para 10, per Lord Millett giving the advice of the Privy Council.

120 See *Powell v McFarlane* (1977) 38 P & CR 452 at 469; *BP Properties Ltd v Buckler* (1987) 55 P & CR 337 (unilateral licence).

121 *J Alston & Sons Ltd v BOCM Ltd* [2008] EWHC 3310 (Ch), [2009] 1 EGLR 93.

122 See *Ramnarace v Lutchman* [2001] UKPC 25, [2001] 1 WLR 1651; *Bellew v Bellew* [1982] IR 447 (SC of Ireland).

123 See *Bula Ltd v Crowley (No 3)* [2003] 1 ILRM 55 (HC of Ireland); affd [2003] 1 IR 396 (SC), where it was held that the possession exercised by a receiver over a company's property was not adverse to the mortgagee's rights, on account of the terms of the mortgage debentures and the tripartite relationship between the parties.

124 [2008] EWCA Civ 55, [2008] 1 WLR 710; see also *Morris v Tarrant* [1971] 2 QB 143.

125 [2002] UKHL 30, [2003] 1 AC 419.

the giving of permission'.[126] On the most unusual facts of *Parshall v Hackney*,[127] where the Land Registry registered two parties as owners of the same plot in error (before compounding their error by deleting the registration of the party entitled to registration), it was held by the Court of Appeal that the person in possession, who had erroneously been named as registered owner at all times, was not a squatter. This was because, in the words of Mummery LJ, '[t]he determination of the question of rectification is logically prior to the determination of the question of possessory title'[128] and until the register was rectified to remove her as registered proprietor of the disputed land, her possession was lawful and not adverse to anybody.

Licences and tenancies at will

15.25 Two particular forms of consensual possession merit separate discussion, as most situations where there is a dispute about whether the landowner has given consent or permission to occupy will involve a consideration of whether either a licence to occupy or a tenancy at will exists. A tenancy at will is the most informal type of leasehold interest, which arises whenever a tenant, with the consent of the owner, occupies land on the terms that either party may determine the tenancy at any time.[129] It can be created expressly[130] or by implication[131] and may be gratuitous or involve the payment of rent; if rent is paid, it is a matter of looking to the probable intention of the parties to determine whether a tenancy at will or oral periodic tenancy was created.[132] A licence is a permission to occupy which does not create an estate in land,[133] which similarly may be gratuitous or involve payment. For limitation purposes it is not a matter of great significance today whether a person is in possession of land as licensee or tenant at will, although under the Limitation Act 1939 it was very significant as a tenancy at will was deemed to have determined at the expiration of one year from its commencement,[134] whereas the LA 1980 has retained this deemed determination provision solely for the case of oral periodic tenancies.[135] The law on whether a licence (or tenancy at will) can arise by unilateral conduct and when it will arise by implication is in a state of some uncertainty at present.[136] In *BP Properties Ltd v Buckler*,[137] it was held that it is possible for a landowner to give a unilateral

126 Megarry and Wade, para 35-016, adopted as correctly stating the law by Arden LJ in *Zarb v Parry* [2011] EWCA Civ 1306, [2012] 2 All ER 320 at paras 26–28: 'mere acquiescence in another's use of one's land is not the same as the grant of permission'.

127 [2013] EWCA Civ 240.

128 [2013] EWCA Civ 240 at para 89.

129 Megarry and Wade at para 17-102.

130 *Manfield & Sons v Botchin* [1970] 2 QB 612.

131 *Javad v Aqil* [1991] 1 WLR 1007.

132 See *Banjo v Brent LBC* [2005] EWCA Civ 292, [2005] 1 WLR 2520.

133 Megarry and Wade at para 34-001.

134 Limitation Act 1939, s 9(1); *Cobb v Lane* [1952] 1 All ER 1199 (CA); *Bellew v Bellew* [1982] IR 447 (SC of Ireland).

135 See para 15.33.

136 See Jourdan and Radley-Gardner, Ch 35.

137 (1987) 55 P & CR 337.

licence to a person occupying his property which will prevent him from being treated as being in adverse possession of the property, and while this decision has been the subject of academic criticism,[138] it has since been approved by the Court of Appeal.[139] In *R (Beresford) v Sunderland City Council,*[140] it was stated by Lord Walker that the implication of a licence requires a communication, by words or overt and unequivocal conduct, that was intended to be understood and was understood to give permission. However, a number of subsequent decisions[141] have applied a less onerous test that asks whether an inference arises that permission was in fact given, which has been the subject of well-founded academic criticism.[142] The terms of, or circumstances giving rise to, the licence or tenancy at will will determine the requirements for (and date of) termination. For example, if a licence is implied during negotiations for the sale or lease of property, this licence will come to an end when one party decides not to proceed.[143]

Intention to possess and animus possidendi

15.26 Although the phrase 'adverse possession' is used in the LA 1980, Lord Browne-Wilkinson in *JA Pye (Oxford) Ltd v Graham*[144] commented that 'much confusion and complication would be avoided if the phrase were to be avoided as far as possible'. Instead he said that one should look to the wording in the LA 1980, as:

> 'The question is simply whether the defendant squatter has dispossessed the paper owner by going into ordinary possession of the land for the requisite period without the consent of the owner.'[145]

Although the Latinism *animus possidendi* is frequently used by the courts to describe the 'intention to possess' that the squatter must have, it does not appear to have a fixed meaning, as the necessary intention has variously been described, *inter alia*, as requiring an intention to possess permanently and absolutely rather than until the landowner requires the land for a stated future use,[146] and intention for the time being to possess land to the exclusion of all persons.[147] This latter-mentioned meaning was adopted by the House of Lords in *JA Pye (Oxford) Ltd v Graham*,[148] where Lord Hope went so far as to say that where the evidence establishes that the squatter has occupied the land and made full use of it in the

138 Wallace, 'Limitation, Prescription and Unsolicited Permission' [1994] Conv 196; Jourdan and Radley-Gardner at paras 35-09–35-11.

139 *Markfield Investments Ltd v Evans* [2001] 1 WLR 1321 at para 12, per Simon Brown LJ.

140 [2004] 1 AC 889.

141 See, for example, *Hicks v Chaplin* [2007] 1 EGLR 1; *J Alston & Sons Ltd v BOCM Ltd* [2008] EWHC 3310 (Ch), [2009] 1 EGLR 93.

142 Jourdan and Radley-Gardner at para 35-20 et seq.

143 *Sandhu v Farooqui* [2003] EWCA Civ 531, [2004] 1 P & CR 3.

144 [2002] UKHL 30, [2003] 1 AC 419.

145 [2002] UKHL 30, [2003] 1 AC 419 at 434.

146 *Leigh v Jack* (1879) 5 ExD 264.

147 *Buckinghamshire County Council v Moran* [1990] Ch 623.

148 [2002] UKHL 30, [2003] 1 AC 419.

way in which an owner would, 'in the normal case he will not have to adduce additional evidence to establish that he had the intention to possess'.[149] It is only if the acts of possession are equivocal and open to more than one interpretation that he would have to adduce evidence of intention, with Lord Hope adding that:

> 'The only intention which has to be demonstrated is an intention to occupy and use the land as one's own … The possession that is required for that purpose is possession "openly, peaceably and without any judicial interruption"[150] on a competing title for the requisite period.'[151]

Relevance of future uses

15.27 The relevance of possible future uses of the property by the landowner is an issue which has caused particular difficulties for the courts. In *Leigh v Jack*,[152] it was held that if a landowner had a future use for the lands in mind, but no current use, then possession by the squatter was not adverse to his title. This doctrine has more recently been disavowed, with Lord Browne-Wilkinson stating in *JA Pye (Oxford) Ltd v Graham*[153] that '[t]he suggestion that the sufficiency of the possession can depend on the intention not of the squatter but of the true owner is heretical and wrong'.[154] However, the knowledge of future uses can still be relevant and regard should be had to the comments of Slade LJ in *Buckinghamshire County Council v Moran*[155] to the effect that, where the land in dispute is not built on, and the squatter is aware that the owner has a purpose in mind for its use in the future:

> '[T]he court is likely to require very clear evidence before it can be satisfied that the squatter who claims possessory title has not only established factual possession of the land, but also the requisite intention to exclude the world at large … so far as is reasonably practicable and so far as the processes of law will allow.'[156]

This would appear to lead to a situation where an acceptance of the true owner's title during the limitation period (often manifested by a willingness to pay rent, if asked) is irrelevant,[157] whereas a willingness to allow the true owner to carry out the future uses which the squatter knows he has for the land is relevant to the issue of whether the squatter merely had an intention to possess the land temporarily and not absolutely.[158]

149 [2003] 1 AC 419 at 447.

150 The Latin maxim *nec vi, nec dam, nec precario* ('without force, without secrecy, without permission') is often used to similar effect; see further para 15.07 above.

151 [2003] 1 AC 419 at 446.

152 (1879) 5 Ex D 264. This approach was followed by Lord Denning MR in *Wallis's Cayton Bay Holiday Camp Ltd v Shell-Mex and BP Ltd* [1975] 1 QB 94.

153 [2002] UKHL 30, [2003] 1 AC 419 at para 45.

154 This statement of the law reflects the wording in Sch 1, Pt I, para 8(4).

155 [1990] Ch 623.

156 [1990] Ch 623 at 639–640; see further Jourdan and Radley-Gardner at paras 9-135–9-154.

157 *JA Pye (Oxford) Ltd v Graham* [2003] 1 AC 419.

158 See the comments of Lord Browne-Wilkinson in *JA Pye (Oxford) Ltd v Graham* [2003] 1 AC 419 at para 45 that it is 'a possible, if improbable inference, in some cases'.

Stopping of time and fresh accrual

15.28 Schedule 1, Pt I, para 8(2) provides that if, at any time before a right of action to recover unregistered[159] land becomes statute barred, the land ceases to be in adverse possession, the right of action shall no longer be treated as having accrued. The effect of this deeming provision is that if the landowner retakes possession or the squatter ceases being in possession prior to the expiration of the limitation period then the limitation clock is reset and time runs afresh if either that squatter or a different squatter commences adverse possession. In *Mount Carmel Investments Ltd v Peter Thurlow Ltd*,[160] it was held that the sending of a letter by the documentary owner to the person in adverse possession demanding the delivery of possession did not amount to a re-entry of the property. In relation to any acts done by or on behalf of the landowner, Slade J stated in *Powell v McFarlane* that, 'the slightest acts done by or on behalf of an owner in possession will be found to negative discontinuance of possession'.[161] In the Irish case of *Dunne v Iarnród Éireann*,[162] the defendant argued that, even if the claimant had entered into possession of its lands, its subsequent acts on its lands had stopped time (within the limitation period) such that he had less than 12 years in possession of the lands. Clarke J, having quoted Slade J's statement of the law with approval, stated as follows:

> 'It is, therefore, important to emphasise that minimal acts of possession by the owner of the paper title will be sufficient to establish that he was not, at least at the relevant time of those acts, dispossessed. The assessment of possession is not one in which the possession of the paper title owner and the person claiming adverse possession are judged on the same basis. An owner will be taken to continue in possession with even minimal acts. A dispossessor will need to establish possession akin to that which an owner making full but ordinary use of the property concerned, having regard to its characteristics, could be expected to make.'[163]

He held that the defendant landowner had satisfied the applicable 'low threshold' of proof in relation to it retaking possession of the property by carrying out extensive repairs to a railway station located on the lands and repairing the fencing around the lands following a complaint from a neighbouring landowner. While the station occupied only a small part of the lands, Clarke J held that as the lands were not divided in any way, it was not possible to say that the claimant had remained in possession of part of the lands. By contrast, in *Zarb v Parry*,[164] the dispossessed landowner removed a fence, cut down a tree, banged in fence posts and linked them with surveyor's tape, which he stated at the time constituted the 'taking possession by force'. It was held by the Court of Appeal that this did not at law amount to the retaking of possession in circumstances

159 An application for registration as owner of an estate in registered land may still be made if the squatter was dispossessed otherwise than pursuant to a judgment for possession within six months prior to the application: LRA 2002, Sch 6, para 1(2).

160 [1988] 1 WLR 1078.

161 (1977) 38 P & CR 452 at 472.

162 [2007] IEHC 314.

163 [2007] IEHC 314 at para 4.8.

164 [2011] EWCA Civ 1306, [2012] 1 WLR 1240.

where their boundary markers were removed that same day after the 'squatters' said they were going to call the police; as the Zarbs had not excluded them from possession and had abandoned their actions before completion; and as the steps taken by them were largely symbolic. Each case should be approached on its own facts; short social visits by those who left have been held in some cases not to have been sufficient to prevent the statute running against them, although the cases involving family arrangements reveal many different factual situations.[165]

LEASES

Actions for breach of covenant or to recover arrears of rent

15.29 An action for damages for breach of covenant is subject to a 12-year limitation period if the lease was made by deed[166] and a six-year limitation period if made as a simple contract.[167] A claim for an injunction or other equitable relief falls outside the LA 1980 but the equitable defences of *laches* and acquiescence may be raised.[168] However, even if the lease was executed as a deed, s 19 of the LA 1980 provides that no action shall be brought, or distress made, to recover arrears of rent, or damages in respect of arrears, after the expiration of six years from the date on which the arrears fell due. In *Romain v Scuba TV Ltd*,[169] it was held that the reference to an action to recover 'damages' includes an action against a guarantor in respect of a lessee's failure to pay the rent, which was thus subject to a six-year limitation period even if the guarantee was executed under seal. It was also held in *Romain*, following *In re J Brown's Estate; Brown v Brown*,[170] that if a guarantee stipulates that a demand is necessary before a liability on the guarantee falling due, the cause of action against the guarantor accrues following the unsatisfied demand on the guarantee rather than upon the failure by the tenant to pay the rent reserved by the lease.

Adverse possession of rentcharges and tithes

15.30 Rentcharges and tithes are two less frequently encountered interests comprised within the definition of 'land' in s 38(1) of the LA 1980. Section 38(1) defines 'rentcharge' as 'any annuity or periodical sum of money charged upon or payable out of land, except a rent service or interest on a mortgage on land' and a right of action to recover land is defined as including an action in respect of non-payment of the rentcharge.[171] The creation of new rentcharges was prohibited by the Rentcharges Act 1977. A 'tithe' has been described as 'the right of a rector

165 See *Peakin v Peakin* [1895] 2 IR 359; *Woodhouse v Hooney* [1915] 1 IR 296.
166 LA 1980, s 8.
167 LA 1980, s 5.
168 LA 1980, s 36(1); see Ch 18.
169 [1997] QB 887 (CA).
170 [1893] 2 Ch 300.
171 LA 1980, s 38(7).

to a tenth part of the produce of all the land in his parish'[172] although the right to tithes 'has been almost entirely dismantled by a series of statutes'.[173] Schedule 1, Pt I, para 8(3) of the LA 1980 provides that possession of land subject to a rentcharge by a person who does not pay the rentcharge is adverse possession of the rentcharge, which must be read in conjunction with s 38(8) which provides that the date of dispossession of a rentcharge is the date of the last receipt of payment. Accordingly, a 12-year limitation period under s 15 of the LA 1980 runs from the date of the last rentcharge payment; at the expiration of this period title to the rentcharge is extinguished.[174] By contrast, there is no provision deeming non-payment of a tithe to constitute dispossession of the tithe, as the entitlement to the tithe is instead governed by the Tithe Acts.[175]

Consequence of squatter extinguishing tenant's leasehold estate

15.31 During the term of a lease, the landlord's interest is an estate in reversion and the 12-year[176] limitation period will not start to run against him until the determination of the lease.[177] This will be the case even if the tenant stops paying rent for a lengthy period: at no stage during the term of the lease will he become a squatter.[178] As a corollary of the fact that the landlord's interest is not vested[179] in possession, if a squatter bars a tenant's leasehold estate this will have no effect on the landlord's title. The landlord will have 12 years to bring proceedings to recover possession from the squatter from the end of the term of the lease.

15.32 Although the expiration of the limitation period will extinguish a leasehold estate in unregistered land in favour of a squatter, the tenant will remain liable to perform his obligations under the lease.[180] A squatter who extinguishes a leasehold estate in unregistered land gains a precarious interest against all bar the tenant whose right he has extinguished. In *Tichborne v Weir*,[181] it was held that the limitation provisions do not effect a 'parliamentary conveyance' of an unregistered[182] leasehold estate in favour of the squatter, with the effect that, as he has no privity with the landlord, he will be unable to seek relief against forfeiture

172 Megarry and Wade at para 31-008.
173 Megarry and Wade at para 31-008.
174 LA 1980, s 17; *Sykes v Williams* [1933] Ch 285.
175 See Jourdan and Radley-Gardner at para 32-20.
176 LA 1980, s 15(1); the proviso to s 15(2)(b) makes clear that the shorter limitation period for actions to recover land from a squatter where a reversionary interest falls into possession does not apply where the lease was for a term of years absolute.
177 LA 1980, Sch 1, Pt I, para 4; *Fairweather v St Marylebone Property Co Ltd* [1963] AC 510 at 536, per Lord Denning.
178 *Doe d Davy v Oxenham* (1840) 7 M & W 131.
179 Even if a landlord's right to forfeit the lease for breach of covenant becomes exercisable, this is not treated as vesting his interest in possession unless the lease is actually forfeit.
180 *Fairweather v St Marylebone Property Co Ltd* [1963] AC 510.
181 (1892) 67 LT 735
182 The position is otherwise in the case of registered leasehold estates: see *Spectrum Investment Co v Holmes* [1981] 1 WLR 221 and *Central London Commercial Estates Ltd v Kato Kagaku Ltd* [1998] 4 All ER 948.

for breach of covenant.[183] The position will be otherwise if the landlord, by his conduct, is found to be estopped from denying that he has granted the squatter a new lease.[184] In the controversial decision of the House of Lords in *Fairweather v St Marylebone Property Co Ltd*,[185] it was held that it remained open to a tenant to surrender his leasehold interest to his landlord even after his title has been extinguished by adverse possession. The legal consequence of this finding was that the leasehold and fee simple interests then merged thus allowing the landlord to immediately seek to recover possession from the squatter. This decision has been subject to academic criticism[186] and was not followed by the Supreme Court of Ireland in *Perry v Woodfarm Homes Ltd.*[187] It remains to be seen whether it still represents the law as it relies on a very fine distinction between title (extinguished) and estate (capable of surrender), whereas the view was stated by Walsh J in *Perry v Woodfarm Homes Ltd*[188] that once the title of the tenant to the leasehold estate is extinguished, he has nothing left to surrender.

Deemed determination of oral periodic tenancies

15.33 An exception to the general rule that a tenant is never in adverse possession of the demised land even if he ceases paying rent exists in the case of tenancies from year to year or other period without a lease in writing.[189] For such tenancies, Sch 1, Pt I, para 5(1) of the LA 1980 provides that the lease is deemed to be determined at the expiration of the first year or other period and the right of action to recover the land is treated as having accrued on that date. Where any rent is subsequently received, the right of action is treated as having accrued on the date of the last receipt of rent.[190] For a lease to be 'in writing' it must create the leasehold estate and it is not sufficient if the writing evidences the existence of the lease.[191] This provision has the potential to operate unfairly if a landlord generously waives payment of rent,[192] especially when contrasted with the situation arising in connection with a person occupying as tenant at will or licencee, which have many of the same legal features of an oral tenancy,[193] where indefinite possession without payment of rent but with the consent of the landlord does not constitute adverse possession.

183 *Tickner v Buzzacott* [1965] Ch 426.
184 *Ashe v Hogan* [1920] 1 IR 159.
185 [1963] AC 510.
186 Wade, 'Landlord, Tenant and Squatter' (1962) 78 LQR 541; see further Jourdan and Radley-Gardner at para 24-76.
187 [1975] IR 104.
188 [1975] IR 104 at 119.
189 The Limitation Act 1939 contained a second similar exception in the case of tenancies at will, but this was not retained by the LA 1980.
190 LA 1980, para 5(2).
191 *Long v Tower Hamlets London Borough Council* [1998] Ch 197.
192 *Hayward v Chaloner* [1968] 1 QB 107; but see *Smith v Lawson* (1998) 75 P & CR 466 where an estoppel was held to arise precluding a denial that rent had not been paid.
193 See the discussion in paras 15.24–15.25 of cases such as *Bellew v Bellew* [1982] IR 447 (SC of Ireland); *Ramnarace v Lutchman* [2001] 1 WLR 1651 (PC); and *J Alston & Sons Ltd v BOCM Ltd* [2008] EWHC 3310 (Ch), [2009] 1 EGLR 93.

Landlord's right of action to forfeit and recover possession

15.34 A breach of condition which gives rise to a right on the part of the landlord to forfeit the lease and recover possession gives rise to a right of action which is deemed to accrue on the date of the breach of condition.[194] The landlord then has 12 years to bring an action seeking possession or to effect a re-entry, failing which the right of action will be extinguished.[195] In this regard, s 38(7) of the LA 1980 provides that the reference to 'bringing an action' in the Act includes the effecting of a re-entry. Each separate breach of condition giving rise to a right to forfeit must be looked at separately and the loss of the right to re-enter in respect of an earlier breach does not debar a landlord from relying upon a more recent breach.[196]

Effect of payment of rent to wrong person

15.35 In the ordinary case, if a tenant pays rent to the wrong person this will have no effect on the landlord's rights against him, and the mistaken payment is merely a waste of money that confers no benefit on the payor. However, an exception exists in the case of a tenant holding under a lease in writing where the rent reserved is not less than £10 per annum who pays the rent to a person wrongfully claiming to be entitled to the land in reversion immediately expectant upon the determination of the lease. In such a case, Sch 1, Pt I, para 6 of the LA 1980 provides that the landlord's right of action to recover the land shall be treated as having accrued on the date when the rent was first received by the wrongful recipient. Schedule 1, Pt I, para 6(2) adds that this provision shall not apply to any lease granted by the Crown.[197]

Encroachments by tenant on a neighbouring property

15.36 A principle of some antiquity[198] provides that a tenant who encroaches on property neighbouring the demised property is presumed to do so for the benefit of the landlord. The cases are divided as to whether the rule applies only where the lands are adjacent or also where the lands are at a distance.[199] The doctrine was recently applied in *Tower Hamlets London Borough Council v Barrett*,[200] where Neuberger LJ explained that the presumption is a rebuttable presumption of fact and that all conduct of the parties can be taken into account in deciding whether the presumption has been rebutted.[201]

194 LA 1980, Sch 1, Pt I, para 7(1).
195 LA 1980, ss 15 and 17.
196 *Barratt v Richardson* [1930] 1 KB 686.
197 See further paras 31.08–31.09.
198 *Bryan d Child v Winwood* (1808) 1 Taunt 208.
199 See *Kingsmill v Millard* (1855) 11 Exch 313 and *Lord Hastings v Saddler* (1898) 79 LT 355.
200 [2005] EWCA Civ 923, (2006) 1 P & CR 132.
201 See further the detailed discussion in Jourdan and Radley-Gardner, Ch 25.

Commonhold

15.37 The Commonhold and Leasehold Reform Act 2002 ('CLRA 2002') introduced a new form of ownership of land which contains elements of freehold and leasehold estates. It is designed as an alternative form of title to a leasehold estate for ownership of units in a block of flats. Section 19A[202] of the LA 1980 provides that an action in respect of a right or duty of a kind referred to in s 37(1) of the CLRA 2002 shall not be brought after the expiration of six years from the date on which the cause of action accrued.

MORTGAGES, CHARGES AND DEBTS SECURED ON LAND

Action by mortgagee to recover land from a third-party squatter

15.38 The paragraphs in this section discuss limitation issues arising in connection with various incidents of mortgages and charges and focus primarily on the relationship between the mortgagor and mortgagee *inter se*. The principles discussed earlier in this chapter may still come to the fore if the person in adverse possession of the property is a third party, perhaps even in a situation where the mortgagor continues to make payments under the mortgage. In *Munster & Leinster Bank v Croker*,[203] it was held that if a third party is in adverse possession of land prior to the date of the mortgage, and if that third party remains in occupation for the limitation period, the rights acquired by him will be valid against the mortgagee and not just the mortgagor. Similarly, in *Halpin v Cremin*,[204] it was held that where a third party entered into possession of a property which was subject to a floating charge which had not yet been converted into a fixed charge, he barred the title of the mortgagee by remaining in possession for in excess of 12 years. However, the more usual factual position, as was before the Court of Appeal in *Ludbrook v Ludbrook*,[205] is where the mortgage is granted before the adverse possession commences, in which case time will not run against the mortgagee by virtue of that adverse possession.

Mortgagee's rights to possession, foreclosure and sale

15.39 Section 15(1) of the LA 1980 contains the limitation period for an action to recover land, which is 12 years from the date on which the right of action accrued. This provision, directly or indirectly, governs actions for possession, foreclosure and sale, although time will be calculated differently depending on which right is asserted. This arises as:

(i) the phrase 'action to recover land' is stated by s 38(7) to include a right to enter into possession of the land;

202 As inserted by the CLRA 2002, s 68 and Sch 5, para 4.
203 [1940] IR 185.
204 [1954] 1 IR 19.
205 [1901] 2 KB 96 (CA); see also *Carroll v Manek* (1999) 79 P & CR 173.

(ii) s 20(4) states that a foreclosure action in respect of mortgaged land is also governed by s 15; and

(iii) the mortgagee's right to sell the mortgaged property (whether by court order or out of court) is an incident of his estate in the land: once the limitation period in s 15 expires, his estate is extinguished by s 17 and so too is his right to sell.

The right to possession will ordinarily accrue on the date of execution of the mortgage,[206] although this will in many cases be varied by the terms of the mortgage, but the right to foreclose will only arise when the date for legal redemption has passed.[207] In *Yorkshire Bank Finance Ltd v Mulhall*,[208] it was held that, as an equitable chargee has no right to possession without a court order, time does not run against him under s 15(1). The more usual situation that will arise is where a mortgagor in possession of property makes no payments to the mortgagee for in excess of 12 years. This occurred in *National Westminster Bank Plc v Ashe*,[209] where the mortgagors brought proceedings 12 years after the date of their last payment to the mortgagee seeking a declaration that the bank's security had been extinguished pursuant to s 17 of the LA 1980. The Court of Appeal made the declaration sought, finding that the mortgagors were in adverse possession of the property during that period and that the lack of objection to or tolerance of their possession did not amount to the bank granting implied permission for them to remain. Section 20(3) adds that the right to foreclose on the property shall not be treated as accruing so long as that property comprises any future interest or any life insurance policy which has not matured or been determined. The provisions in the LA 1980 dealing with acknowledgments and payments towards a debt are of particular relevance in ascertaining the applicable limitation period for the exercise of the rights discussed in this paragraph.[210]

Actions to recover money secured by a mortgage or charge on land or in relation to the proceeds of sale of the land

15.40 Section 20(1) of the LA 1980 provides that no action shall be brought to recover any principal sum of money secured by a mortgage or charge on property, or the proceeds of sale of the land, after the expiry of 12 years from the date on which the right to receive the money accrued. The mortgagor's right to any surplus on the sale of the property gives rise to a trust in respect of those monies under s 105 of the Law of Property Act 1925, or under general equitable princi-

206 *Four-Maids Ltd v Dudley Marshall Properties Ltd* [1957] Ch 317; *Fisher and Lightwood's Law of Mortgage* (13th edn, London: LexisNexis Butterworths, 2010) at para 26.43.
207 *Williams v Morgan* [1906] 1 Ch D 804; *Fisher and Lightwood's Law of Mortgage* (13th edn, London: LexisNexis Butterworths, 2010) at paras 26.38 and 32.4.
208 [2008] EWCA Civ 1156, [2009] 2 All ER (Comm) 164; see also *Ezekiel v Orakpo* [1997] 1 WLR 340 (CA).
209 [2008] EWCA Civ 55, [2008] 1 WLR 710.
210 See Ch 6.

ples if the LPA 1925 does not apply,[211] and time will not run against the person entitled to the surplus if the selling mortgagee is guilty of a fraudulent breach of trust[212] or retains the surplus or converts it to his own use.[213] Section 20(3) adds that the right to receive the principal sum shall not be treated as accruing so long as that property comprises any future interest or any life insurance policy which has not matured or been determined. Where a first mortgagee sells the mortgaged property, the second mortgagee is entitled to all his arrears of interest out of any surplus proceeds, unless his mortgage is barred.[214] The crucial date for the purposes of s 20(1) is the date on which the 'right to receive the money' accrued, which will generally be earlier than the date of accrual of a right of action to sue on the debt. In *Gotham v Doodes*,[215] it was held that, while a charging order made against the property of a bankrupt under s 313 of the Insolvency Act 1986 created a charge in respect of a principal sum of money within the meaning of s 20(1), the right to receive the money would not accrue until the property was sold. As this had not yet occurred, no limitation issue arose in relation to the enforcement of the charge. In *Yorkshire Bank Finance Ltd v Mulhall*,[216] the Court of Appeal expressed doubts about whether s 20 applies at all to the enforcement of charging orders made under the Charging Orders Act 1979 but ultimately held that time runs from the date of enforcement of the charging order.

Action for the redemption of land

15.41 Section 16 of the LA 1980 provides that where a mortgagee of land has been in possession of any of the mortgaged land for a period of 12 years, no action to redeem the land of which the mortgagee has been in possession shall be brought after that period by the mortgagor or any person claiming through him. At the expiration of the limitation period for a mortgagor to bring an action to redeem the land, his title to the land is extinguished.[217] When a second mortgagee's rights against the mortgagor are barred, he can no longer exercise his right to redeem the first mortgage, because by s 17 his interest will have been extinguished.[218] The receipt of rents and profits by a mortgagee while in possession has been held not to constitute a payment in respect of the mortgage debt and thus does not set time running afresh.[219] This is an anomalous provision which fails to have regard to the fact that a mortgagee in possession is not a squatter, but it represents settled law.

211 *Banner v Berridge* (1881) 18 Ch D 254; *Fisher and Lightwood's Law of Mortgage* (13th edn, London: LexisNexis Butterworths, 2010) at para 30.45.
212 LA 1980, s 21(1)(a).
213 LA 1980, s 21(1)(b).
214 *Young v Clarey* [1948] Ch 191; *Cotterell v Price* [1960] 1 WLR 1097.
215 [2006] EWCA Civ 1080, [2007] 1 All ER 527.
216 [2008] EWCA Civ 1156, [2009] 2 All ER (Comm) 164; see also *Ezekiel v Orakpo* [1997] 1 WLR 340 (CA).
217 LA 1980, s 17.
218 *Cotterell v Price* [1960] 1 WLR 1097.
219 LA 1980, s 29; *Harlock v Ashberry* (1882) 19 Ch D 539.

Shortfall claims

15.42 If a mortgagee sells the mortgaged property for less than the mortgage debt, there will be a shortfall on the debt secured by the mortgage which remains due and owing. The question of whether the sum remaining should thereafter be treated as an unsecured debt or a debt secured by a mortgage or charge over land is arguable either way as it is not expressly dealt with in the LA 1980. When the issue came before the House of Lords in *West Bromwich Building Society v Wilkinson*,[220] it held that the subsequent sale of the property did not affect the initial characterisation of the cause of action for limitation purposes, and that the 12-year limitation period applies to a shortfall action.[221] It also held that the limitation period for the shortfall claim runs from the date when the payment fell due and that it is unaffected by the sale.

Action to recover interest on a mortgage debt

15.43 Section 20(5) of the LA 1980 provides that no action shall be brought to recover arrears of interest payable in respect of any sum of money secured by a mortgage or charge on land, or payable in respect of proceeds of sale of the land, or to recover damages in respect of the arrears,[222] after the expiration of six years from the date on which the interest became due. However, an important exception was confirmed in *Holmes v Cowcher*,[223] namely that where the mortgagor seeks to redeem the mortgage, or seeks payment from the surplus proceeds of sale,[224] the limitation period of six years is inapplicable (as the mortgagee is not bringing an action to recover the interest) and the mortgagor must pay all arrears of interest. Section 20(6) provides that where a prior mortgagee or other incumbrancer has been in possession of the property charged, and an action is brought within one year of the discontinuance of such possession by the subsequent incumbrancer, he may recover by that action all arrears of interest which fell due during the period of possession by the prior incumbrancer. Section 20(7) provides that where the property subject to a mortgage or charge comprises any future interest or life insurance policy, and it is a term of the deed that arrears of interest shall be treated as part of the principal debt, interest shall not be deemed to become due before the right to receive the principal sum of money has accrued or is deemed to have accrued. Once the mortgagee's right to the principal is statute barred, so too is his claim for interest.[225]

220 [2005] UKHL 44, [2005] 4 All ER 97, following *Bristol & West Plc v Bartlett* [2002] EWCA Civ 1181, [2002] 4 All ER 544.
221 LA 1980, s 20(1)(a).
222 References to claims for 'damages in respect of such arrears' should be understood to refer to a claim against a guarantor in respect of the debt: see para 15.29.
223 [1970] 1 WLR 834; *In re Owen Lewis' Estate* [1903] 1 IR 398.
224 *Re Lloyd* [1903] 1 Ch 385; this rule applies whether the mortgagee or the mortgagor is in possession of the proceeds of sale.
225 *Elder v Northcott* [1930] 2 Ch 422.

REGISTERED LAND

Overview of limitation provisions for registered land

15.44 A person who is in adverse possession of a registered estate in land (excluding a registered charge[226]) is treated very differently to a person who is in adverse possession of an unregistered estate in land. For actions that are governed by the LRA 2002 and not the LA 1980, the qualifying period of adverse possession to found a claim to the land is only ten years, but the expiry of this period does not automatically extinguish the registered landowner's title. Instead, if the application is opposed, the squatter must satisfy one of three narrowly drafted conditions in order to be registered as owner of the estate by adverse possession.[227] However, if the application is unsuccessful, the registered landowner then comes under an obligation to institute possession proceedings to evict the squatter. If he fails to take steps to evict the squatter, who then remains in adverse possession for a further period of two years, the squatter may lodge a second application for registration as owner of the registered estate by adverse possession and is entitled to automatic registration on that occasion.

Disapplication of LA 1980 for registered estates in land by the LRA 2002

15.45 Section 96(1) of the LRA 2002 provides that the limitation period in s 15 (action for the recovery of land) shall not run against any person, other than a chargee,[228] in relation to an estate in land or rentcharge the title to which is registered. Section 96(2) provides that the limitation period in s 16 (action to redeem land) shall not run against any person in relation to an estate in land or rentcharge the title to which is registered. As the primary limitation periods are disapplied, so too is s 17, which extinguishes title on the expiry of the limitation period.[229] However, the registered landowner cannot take advantage of the fact that the LA 1980 is disapplied by pre-emptively instituting proceedings, as s 98(1) of the LRA 2002 provides that the squatter will have a full defence to any such action if he can show that on the day preceding the date on which the action was brought he was entitled to make an application for registration under Sch 6, para 1 and would have satisfied one of the conditions in para 5(4).[230] A defence under s 98 was established in *IAM Group Plc v Chowdrey*,[231] where the defendant had been in possession of the registered property since 1993 and the Court of Appeal held that he would have satisfied the test in Sch 6, para 5(4) if he had applied to the Land Registry for registration. Section 97 then provides that Schedule 6 of the

226 LRA 2002, s 96(1).
227 The conditions are set out in the LRA 2002, Sch 6, para 5: see para 15.49 below.
228 The LA 1980 continues to govern adverse possession claims against the proprietor of a registered charge.
229 LRA 2002, s 96(3).
230 If the squatter establishes a defence under this section, s 98(5)(a) then provides that the court must register the squatter as owner of the registered estate in land.
231 [2012] EWCA Civ 505, [2012] 2 P & CR 13 (CA).

LRA 2002, which makes provision for the registration of an adverse possessor of an estate in land or a rentcharge, has effect instead of the disapplied sections in the LA 1980. Although likely to be of diminishing relevance with the passage of time, the provisions of ss 15–17 of the LA 1980 continue to apply to an action that relies entirely on a period of adverse possession which occurred prior to the commencement of the LRA 2002 on 13 October 2003.[232] The LA 1980 will also continue to govern the following cases:

(i) where there is a registered freehold title but an unregistered lease; and

(ii) where, even if the freehold is registered, the person claiming possession is not the registered proprietor (eg a licensee, tenant or previous squatter).

Adverse possession under Sch 6 of the LRA 2002

15.46 Schedule 6, para 1(1) of the LRA 2002 provides that a person may apply to the registrar to be registered as the proprietor of a registered estate in land if he has been in adverse possession of that estate for the period of ten years prior[233] to the date of the application.[234] An application is made by lodging a Form ADV1 together with a statement of truth or statutory declaration containing the facts giving rise to the application and identifying the land at issue.[235] An extended period of adverse possession of 60 years is required in the case of Crown foreshore.[236] Schedule 6, para 11 provides that the phrase 'adverse possession' in the LRA 2002 shall have the same meaning as under s 15 of the LA 1980,[237] with two modifications.[238] The first is that a person who has wrongly received rent under a lease in writing where the rent is less than £10 per annum is not treated as being in adverse possession of the reversion.[239] The second is that a person is not regarded as being in adverse possession of an estate at any time when the estate is subject to a trust, unless the interest of each of the beneficiaries is vested in possession.[240] Schedule 6, para 8 provides that an application for registration

232 However, as is noted by Jourdan and Radley-Gardner in their Preface at v, '[i]t is surprising how many squatters, on searching their memories are able to say confidently that they took possession of the disputed land on or before 13 October 1991'.

233 An application may still be made if the squatter was dispossessed otherwise than pursuant to a judgment for possession within the period of six months prior to the application: Sch 6, para 1(2).

234 For a more detailed discussion of the requirements of an application and the types of proof required, see the Land Registration Rules 2003 (SI 2003/1417), rr 187–194G, Form ADV1, *Land Registry Practice Guide 4 (Adverse possession of registered land)* (updated April 2013) and Jourdan and Radley-Gardner, Ch 22.

235 LRR 2003, s 188.

236 LRA 2002, Sch 6, para 13(1); 'foreshore' is defined as 'the shore and bed of the sea and of any tidal water, below which the line of the medium high tide between the spring and neap tides'.

237 The status of an acknowledgment of title or deliberate concealment of dispossession and its effect on whether the squatter can still prove 'adverse possession' is left unclear in Sch 6: see further Jourdan and Radley-Gardner at paras 22-40–22-41.

238 The position concerning successive squatters is clarified in Sch 6, para 11(2).

239 LRA 2002, Sch 6, para 11(3)(b); this section reverses the statutory effect of the LA 1980, Sch 1, para 6.

240 LRA 2002, Sch 6, para 12.

as proprietor of a registered estate may not be made if the registered proprietor was either:

(a) an enemy or detained in enemy territory within the period of 12 months prior to the application;[241] or

(b) unable because of mental disability to make decisions about the issues of the kind to which such an application would give rise, or unable to communicate such decisions because of disability or impairment.[242]

This paragraph provides an absolute defence to registered landowners who lack mental capacity, though, oddly, there is no modification of the general rule where a minor is the registered landowner. In addition, to avoid a multiplicity of proceedings, Sch 6, para 1(3) provides that a person may not make an application for registration where he is a defendant to proceedings which involve an assertion of a right to possession of the land, or where judgment for possession of the land has been obtained against him in the previous two years. In *Swan Housing Association Ltd v Gill*,[243] the purpose behind para 1(3) was considered by Eady J, who held that it is designed to avoid possession proceedings being side-tracked while an application is made to the Land Registry. The appropriate course for the squatter to take in such circumstances is to counterclaim for reliefs under s 98 of the LRA 2002.[244]

Procedure for registration and unopposed applications

15.47 After an application is made to be registered as proprietor of a registered estate in land by adverse possession, Sch 6, para 2 provides that the registrar must notify the proprietor of the registered estate to which the application relates, the proprietor of any registered charge on the estate, where the estate is leasehold the proprietor of any superior interests, any person who is registered in accordance with r 194 of the Land Registry Rules 2003 ('LRR 2003') as a person to be notified,[245] and such other persons as the LRR 2003 may provide.[246] The notification must[247] give notice to its recipients that if they do not oppose the application then the applicant is entitled to be entered in the register as the new proprietor of the registered estate. This notice is accompanied by a Form NAP,

241 LRA 2002, Sch 6, para 8(1). The terms 'enemy' and 'detained in enemy territory' are defined by reference to the definitions contained in the Limitation (Enemies and War Prisoners) Act 1945.

242 LRA 2002, Sch 6, para 8(2). Paragraph 8(3) attempts to further define the phrase 'mental disability'.

243 [2012] EWHC 3129 (QB).

244 See *IAM Group Plc v Chowdrey* [2012] EWCA Civ 505, [2012] 2 P & CR 13 (CA), discussed in para 15.45.

245 Rule 194 provides that any person who has an interest in a registered estate which would be prejudiced by the application may apply to be registered as a person to be notified.

246 Rule 188A lists additional parties to be notified if the registered proprietor may be a dissolved company; r 17 (which gives the registrar a broad discretion to request further evidence) is also relied upon as giving authority to notify.

247 LRA 2002, Sch 6, para 2(2).

which gives the options of consenting to the application, objecting and requiring the application to be dealt with under Sch 6, para 5 or of listing other grounds of objection.[248] In *Hopkins v Beacon*,[249] Vos J cautioned against undue technicality in analysing the content of a Form NAP and held that an application must be dealt with under Sch 6, para 5 if the grounds of objection indicate that this is what is really being sought, even if that box is not ticked on the form. Notice is sent by the Land Registry to the address for service held by the Land Registry under r 198 of the LRR 2003, which makes the continued accuracy of this address vitally important. Rule 189 requires the counter-notice (ie the completed Form NAP) to be served on the Land Registry by 12 noon on the sixty-fifth working day after the date of issue of the application. If no counter-notice is filed, and the registrar is satisfied that the applicant satisfies Sch 6, para 1(1), the applicant will be registered as proprietor of the registered estate free from any registered charge affecting the estate,[250] but subject to any other interest affecting the estate.[251]

15.48 The effect of an unopposed application is thus that the applicant squatter becomes the successor in title of the previous registered proprietor by virtue of a statutory assignment,[252] in like manner as had been the case under s 75 of the Land Registration Act 1925.[253] If the 65-business day time limit is missed, the registered landowner may subsequently apply under Sch 4 of the LRA 2002 to rectify the register on grounds of mistake. Two relevant mistakes may be thought to arise: first, that the registered landowner missed the time limit due to a mistake on his part, and secondly, that the Land Registry made a mistake in acceding to the squatter's application as he did not satisfy the statutory preconditions to registration. In *Baxter v Mannion*,[254] the Court of Appeal gave a broad definition to the phrase 'correction of a mistake' in Sch 4, paras 1 and 5 and held that only the latter type of mistake need be established. It also held that a requirement to prove it would be 'unjust' not to rectify is satisfied where the real landowner proves he would otherwise be dispossessed by an unjustified application. It held that parliament could not have intended that an official error in the course of examining the application need be established as, given the short time limit to oppose the application, this would be an invitation to fraud.

Test applied if counter-notice is served by party notified of application

15.49 If the registered landowner, or any other person notified, opposes the application by filing a completed Form NAP requiring the application to be dealt

248 Rule 190(2).
249 [2011] EWHC 2899 (Ch).
250 LRA 2002, Sch 6, para 9(1) and (3). Paragraph 9(4) makes clear that a registered charge is not extinguished where the squatter is registered as owner under para 5 but only where his application is unopposed.
251 LRA 2002, Sch 6, para 9(2).
252 A squatter who is registered as owner of a registered leasehold estate will thus become liable to perform the covenants in the lease: see Jourdan and Radley-Gardner at para 22-69.
253 See *Central London Commercial Estate Ltd v Kato Kagaku Ltd* [1998] 4 All ER 948.
254 [2011] EWCA Civ 120, [2011] 1 WLR 1594.

with under Sch 6, para 5, the Land Registry will then review the applicant's Form ADV1 to see whether it discloses an arguable case that he can satisfy one of the three conditions in para 5, namely:

1 that it would be unconscionable because of an equity by estoppel for the registered proprietor to seek to dispossess the applicant;[255]

2 that the applicant is for some other reason entitled to the estate;[256] or

3 that the applicant reasonably believed, for at least the last ten years prior to the application, that the land the subject of the application belonged to him and the exact boundary line for the property had not been determined under s 60 of the LRA 2002.[257]

The first ground for registration gives statutory effect to the principles of proprietary estoppel and must be read together with s 110(4) of the LRA 2002, which provides that the adjudicator is expressly empowered to award a lesser remedy than registration and that he must determine how the equity due to the applicant is to be satisfied. The second ground is curiously worded and would appear to apply where the applicant is both a squatter and possessed of a superior interest to the registered landowner, which leaves it having limited effect, although if it applies it will give an applicant a less costly alternative to court proceedings.[258] The third ground for registration in an opposed application is designed to deal with boundary disputes between neighbours and has been described as 'the only one of any real importance'.[259] Its effect was recently considered by the Court of Appeal in *Zarb v Parry*[260] and *IAM Group Plc v Chowdrey,*[261] in both of which the main issue was whether the squatter had a reasonable belief as to a boundary line. This necessitated a careful analysis of the actions of the parties, information conveyed to them by lawyers and surveyors, and the physical condition of the properties (and their boundaries) over a lengthy period of time, and was found to have been satisfied in both cases.

15.50 If satisfied that an arguable case has been made out that one of the three conditions is satisfied, the registrar will then invite the parties to enter into negotiations concerning their dispute, but if this offer is declined or proves fruitless, the dispute will be referred to an adjudicator for a decision.[262] The adjudicator may then list the dispute for hearing before him and decide the matter himself,[263] or he may direct a party to commence proceedings within a specified time in the

255 Schedule 6, para 5(2).
256 Schedule 6, para 5(3).
257 Schedule 6, para 5(4).
258 However, see the rueful comments of Arden LJ in *Zarb v Parry* [2011] EWCA Civ 1306, [2012] 2 All ER 320 at para 1 in relation to costs incurred in the boundary dispute registration application which was appealed to the Court of Appeal.
259 Jourdan and Radley-Gardner at para 22-81.
260 [2011] EWCA Civ 1306, [2012] 1 WLR 1240; see further Milne, 'Mistaken belief and adverse possession – mistaken interpretation?' [2012] The Conveyancer and Property Lawyer 342.
261 [2012] EWCA Civ 505, [2012] 2 P & CR 13 (CA).
262 LRA 2002, s 73(7).
263 LRA 2002, s 109.

court for the purpose of obtaining the court's decision on the matter.[264] A person aggrieved by a decision of the adjudicator may appeal to the High Court.[265] If successful in the contested application under Sch 6, para 5, the applicant will be registered as proprietor of the estate the subject-matter of the application, but subject to any registered charge affecting the estate and subject to any other interest affecting the estate.[266]

Right to make a further application for registration two years after rejection of first application

15.51 If an application for registration as owner of a registered estate in land by adverse possession under Sch 6, para 1 is unsuccessful, the registered landowner then effectively comes under an obligation to institute possession proceedings to evict the squatter. This obligation arises from the fact that if the squatter remains in adverse possession for a further period of two years, he may lodge a second application for registration as owner of the registered estate by adverse possession, on this occasion under Sch 6, para 6(1). Unless possession proceedings are pending or have led to judgment for possession having been given against him within the previous two years or he has been evicted pursuant to such a judgment,[267] he will then be entitled to be entered in the register as the new proprietor of the estate and does not have to satisfy the conditions set out in Sch 6, para 5.[268] Although generally a court judgment is enforceable for a minimum of six years,[269] s 98(2) of the LRA 2002 provides that a judgment for possession of land ceases to be enforceable two years after the date of the judgment if given in proceedings brought against a person entitled to make an application under Sch 6, para 1 (ie if they had been in adverse possession of the registered estate for ten years). Section 98(4) applies the same two-year time limit to the life of a judgment for possession of land if, at the end of that period, the person against whom judgment is given is entitled to make a second application for registration as proprietor of an estate in the land under Sch 6, para 6. Section 98(3) of the LRA 2002 provides that if the owner of the registered estate brings possession proceedings on a date after the squatter becomes entitled to lodge a second application for registration under Sch 6, para 6, this latter right provides the squatter with a defence to the possession proceedings. Section 98(5) provides that where in any proceedings the court finds that the defendant is entitled to a defence under s 98 then the court must order the registrar to register the defendant as proprietor of the estate in relation to which he is entitled to make an application under Sch 6.

264 LRA 2002, s 110(1).
265 LRA 2002, s 111(1).
266 Schedule 6, para 9(2)–(4).
267 Schedule 6, para 6(2)(a)–(c).
268 Schedule 6, para 7.
269 See generally Ch 4: no time limit applies to several methods of enforcing a judgment.

CHAPTER 16

Personal Property

INTRODUCTION

16.01 This chapter discusses the provisions in the Limitation Act 1980 ('LA 1980') relating to actions to recover money secured by a mortgage or charge over personal property and the special rules applicable to actions relating to the conversion of goods.[1] The limitation rules that govern personal injuries or financial loss caused by items of personal property are discussed elsewhere in the book.[2] The rules on disability,[3] acknowledgment and part payment,[4] fraud and deliberate concealment,[5] and the limitation periods governing causes of action against trustees,[6] will in some cases be relevant to actions concerning personal property and readers are referred to the chapters in the book where these matters are discussed in detail.

CONVERSION

The limitation period and the extinguishing of title to goods

16.02 An action for conversion of goods[7] is an action founded on tort, for which s 2 of the LA 1980 prescribes a six-year limitation period. If the owner of a chattel does not recover possession of it prior to the expiration of the six-year limitation period following its conversion, his claim for damages in respect of the conversion is statute barred. In addition, s 3(1) provides that no action shall be brought in respect of any further conversion of the chattel, even if the

1 Although the LA 1980, s 4 had no equivalent in the Limitation Act 1939, it is now so well established that in *City of Gotha v Sotheby's (No 2), The Times*, 8 October 1998, it was held that it would be contrary to public policy to allow a defendant to rely on a provision in a foreign limitation statute that allowed a thief to extinguish title to a chattel.

2 See the chapters on contract (Ch 8); general principles in tort (Ch 10); the Consumer Protection Act 1987 (Ch 11); the Latent Damage Act 1986 (Ch 12); and personal injuries (Ch 13).

3 See Ch 5.

4 See Ch 6.

5 See Ch 7.

6 See Chs 17 and 18.

7 See the Torts (Interference with Goods) Act 1977.

further conversion occurred within six years of the original conversation and if the action in respect of that conversion is brought within six years of it occurring. Secondly, s 3(2) provides that the title of the person to the chattel is extinguished. It should be noted that the words 'chattel' and 'goods' are used in s 3 of the LA 1980. The definition of 'goods' in s 14(1) of the Torts (Interference with Goods) Act 1977 states that it 'includes all chattels personal other than things in action and money'. Actions relating to intangible property fall outside s 3 and are only subject to the limitation period in s 2[8] (for any damages claim) and s 36(1) (where equitable reliefs are sought). A good example of an intangible property right (or chose in action) is an intellectual property right, such as the share in the copyright in the song 'Whiter Shade of Pale' that was asserted by the claimant in *Fisher v Brooker.*[9] Despite only issuing proceedings in 2005 in respect of a song written in 1967, which had been exploited without reference to his rights or entitlements in the intervening period, the defendant was unsuccessful in raising a limitation defence (or one based on *laches* or acquiescence) to a claim for declarations as to ownership of copyright in the song, although the claim for a share in historic royalties was subject to a six-year limitation period.

The running of time

16.03 A right of action for conversion will accrue on the date of the wrongful interference with the claimant's goods. In cases of wrongful taking of goods, the cause of action will accrue upon the taking of the goods.[10] In cases of wrongful detention, time will run from the date when the defendant refuses to deliver up the goods in response to a lawful demand for their return.[11] Although it would appear that a claimant can in some cases delay the running of time by not making a demand for return of the goods, it was held in *British Crane Hire Corporation Ltd v Ipswich Plant Hire Ltd*[12] that where goods are detained by a bailee beyond an agreed date for return, time runs from that agreed date. If goods have been converted and afterwards sold, and the claimant sues for money had and received, time still runs from the conversion and not from the receipt of the money.[13]

The relationship between conversion, fraud and deliberate concealment

16.04 In some, but not all, cases of conversion, a claimant may be able to argue that his right of action is based on fraud or that a fact material to his cause

8 If the infringement affects an entitlement to a sum of money due by virtue of an enactment, the limitation period, still six years, will be contained in the LA 1980, s 9.

9 [2009] UKHL 41, [2009] 4 All ER 789.

10 *Granger v George* (1826) 5 H & C 149.

11 *Philpott v Kelley* (1835) 3 Ad & El 106; but see now the Torts (Interference with Goods) Act 1977, ss 1 and 2 and *Schwarzschild v Harrods Ltd* [2008] EWHC 521 (QB), [2008] All ER (D) 299 (Mar).

12 [1975] QB 303.

13 *Denys v Shuckburgh* (1840) 4 Y & C Ex 42.

of action was deliberately concealed by the defendant. In *Eddis v Chichester Constable*,[14] the Court of Appeal held that the phrase 'person through whom he claims'[15] should be interpreted so as to include all antecedent owners of the property, as the defendant's claim to own the chattel was derived from them. In *Beaman v ARTS Ltd*,[16] it was held by the Court of Appeal that an action alleging 'fraudulent conversion' should not be treated as an action based upon the fraud of the defendant, as the use of the word in that context adds nothing to the pleaded case and is instead 'nothing more than an abusive epithet'[17]. In *RB Policies at Lloyd's v Butler*,[18] it was held that if no material fact is concealed by a thief in the course of stealing the goods, the claimant will not be able to rely on a plea of deliberate concealment so as to gain an extension to the limitation period. The result in this case is criticised elsewhere in the book[19] and the change in the wording of the concealment provision effected by s 32(1)(b) of the LA 1980 means that the basic premise of the case may be open for reconsideration if the issue arises again, although its effect has now been reversed by s 4 of the LA 1980.

Exception to conversion limitation provisions in cases of theft

16.05 Section 4 of the LA 1980 introduced a cumbersome exception to the limitation provisions for an action for conversion which involves the theft of the chattel.[20] There has been very little case law on the section, and it has been stated that '[o]ne wonders if any injustice formerly arising from s 3 of the Limitation Act could ever have been worth such a complicated measure to put it right'.[21] In attempting to work out the meaning of the section, the author respectfully adopts the statement contained in *Clerk & Lindsell* that it 'probably'[22] means that the owner of stolen property may sue the thief or any other person who converts the goods subsequently, other than a purchaser in good faith, without limitation of time and his title to the chattel is not extinguished by s 3(2) after the expiration of six years following the theft. The ordinary limitation period of six years for conversion will apply to the cause of action for conversion against any purchaser in good faith of the chattel or any subsequent purchaser from him.[23] Curiously, the section only applies if the theft gave rise to the claim for conversion and not if the chattel is converted (without theft) and is then subsequently stolen.[24]

14 [1969] 2 Ch 345; see also *Beaman v ARTS Ltd* [1949] 1 KB 550.
15 LA 1980, s 32(1).
16 [1949] 1 KB 550.
17 [1949] 1 KB 550 at 558, per Lord Greene MR; see further the discussion at para 7.09.
18 [1950] 1 KB 76.
19 See para 7.18.
20 'Theft' is defined in s 4(5) of the LA 1980 as including any conduct outside England and Wales which would be theft if committed within the territory and obtaining a chattel by blackmail or fraud.
21 *Clerk & Lindsell on Torts* (20th edn, London: Sweet & Maxwell, 2010) at p 2083, fn 146.
22 *Clerk & Lindsell on Torts* (20th edn, London: Sweet & Maxwell, 2010) at para 32-33.
23 LA 1980, s 4(2).
24 LA 1980, s 4(1).

16.06 The effect of s 4 was considered in the curious case of *Kurtha v Marks*,[25] where a claimant who was unable to state when certain paintings had been stolen from his possession between 1984 and 2005 sued a defendant who was unable to produce any documents evidencing payment by him (of cash) for the paintings and only meagre contemporaneous documentary evidence of purchase. The action was commenced in 2007 and Tugendhat J held that if the claimant could prove he owned the paintings and they were stolen then the burden of proof shifted to the defendant to prove they had been purchased in good faith more than six years prior to the action being brought. Although the evidence of the somewhat absent-minded owner of the paintings was firmly challenged, Tugendhat J found in his favour and clearly had little time for a 'dealer in valuable works of art who pays in large amounts of cash, keeps no records, and asks no questions as to provenance of his supplier'.[26]

Exception to limitation provisions in Proceeds of Crime Act 2002

16.07 Section 27A(5) of the LA 1980, as inserted,[27] applies to proceedings started under Pt 5, Ch 2 of the Proceeds of Crime Act 2002 for a recovery order in respect a chattel. It applies to a person who (but for the provisions of s 3(2)) would have a cause of action for conversion of the chattel. It provides that his title to the chattel shall be treated as not having been extinguished by s 3(2) of the LA 1980 if the court makes a declaration that the property belongs to him.[28] Section 27B(5) of the LA 1980, as inserted,[29] is worded in similar terms and applies to applications for a recovery order brought under art 192 of the Proceeds of Crime Act 2002 (External Requests and Orders) Order 2005 in respect of a chattel.

The Return of Cultural Objects Regulations 1994

16.08 Member States of the European Union have a right of action under the Return of Cultural Objects Regulations 1994[30] ('ROCOR 1994') against the possessor or holder of a cultural object which has been unlawfully removed from the territory for its return to that country.[31] Such a claim is not subject to the LA 1980[32] as the ROCOR 1994 contain their own time limits for applications, namely one year after the member state became aware of the location of the cultural

25 [2008] EWHC 336 (QB), [2008] All ER (D) 379 (Feb); see also *de Préval v Adrian Alan Ltd*, unreported, 6 February 1997, Arden J.

26 [2008] EWHC 336 (QB), [2008] All ER (D) 379 (Feb) at para 141.

27 Proceeds of Crime Act 2002, ss 288(1) and 458(1); SI 2003/120, art 2(1).

28 LA 1980, s 27A(6).

29 Proceeds of Crime Act 2002 (External Requests and Orders) Order 2005 (SI 2005/3181), art 201(1).

30 SI 1994/501, reg 6. The right of action only applies to objects unlawfully removed from a Members State after 1 January, 1993: see reg 1(3).

31 ROCOR 1994, reg 6(1).

32 ROCOR 1994, reg 6(9).

object and of the identity of its possessor or holder[33] and what is described as the 'special limitation period'.[34] This period is 75 years in the case of objects forming part of public collections and of ecclesiastical goods subject to special protection arrangements under the national law of the Member State,[35] and 30 years in any other case.[36] These time limits run from the date on which the object was unlawfully removed from the territory of the requesting Member State.[37]

MORTGAGES OF PERSONAL PROPERTY

The statutory provisions

16.09 Section 20(1)(a) provides that no action shall be brought to recover any principal sum of money secured by a mortgage or charge on personal property after the expiration of 12 years from the date on which the right to receive the money accrued. Section 20(2) provides that a 12-year limitation period also applies to the right to bring a foreclosure action in respect of personal property, but that if the mortgagee was in possession of the mortgaged property after the date the right of action accrued to him, time shall only run from the date on which his possession discontinued. Section 20(3) provides that the rights of action governed by s 20(1) and (2) shall not be treated as accruing so long as that property comprises any future interest or any life insurance policy which has not matured or been determined. Section 20 appears only to govern actions by a mortgagee or chargee of personal property and thus has no application to redemption actions by the mortgagor of the personal property or claims in relation to the failure to pay over the net proceeds of sale. Both of these are equitable actions and the former circumvents the application of any limitation provision by analogy by forcing the mortgagor to discharge all arrears of interest without limitation of time in order to secure the relief.[38]

Action for the principal sum

16.10 Time runs for an action in respect of the principal sum secured on personal property from the date on which the right to receive the money accrued.[39] In *Yorkshire Bank Finance Ltd v Mulhall*,[40] it was held that once a charging order is made under the Charging Orders Act 1979 that any subsequent steps taken to enforce that charge are not subject to s 20 of the LA 1980. In *Gotham v Doodes*,[41] it was held that, while a charging order made against the property of a bankrupt

33 ROCOR 1994, reg 6(6)(a).
34 ROCOR 1994, reg 6(6)(b).
35 ROCOR 1994, reg 6(7).
36 ROCOR 1994, reg 6(8).
37 ROCOR 1994, reg 6(7), (8).
38 See *Holmes v Cowcher* [1970] 1 WLR 834.
39 LA 1980, s 20(1)(a).
40 [2008] EWCA Civ 1156, [2009] 2 All ER (Comm) 164.
41 [2006] EWCA Civ 1080, [2007] 1 All ER 527.

under s 313 of the Insolvency Act 1986 created a charge in respect of a principal sum of money within the meaning of s 20(1), as the right to receive the money would not accrue until an order for sale was made in respect of the property (which had not yet occurred), no limitation issue arose in relation to the enforcement of the charge. In *West Bromwich Building Society v Wilkinson*,[42] it was held by the House of Lords that the characterisation of a claim upon its accrual is not altered by subsequent events, and thus a shortfall claim (brought after the sale of the mortgaged personal property) is still governed by s 20 rather than, for example, the six-year limitation period for a claim founded on contract.

Action for arrears of interest

16.11 Section 20(5) provides that a limitation period of six years applies to a claim to recover arrears of interest payable in respect of a sum of money secured by a mortgage or other charge on personal property. This section is curious in that it applies even if the obligation to pay interest is created by a deed, which would ordinarily be subject to a 12-year limitation period.[43] It will be a question of construction of the loan documents to determine whether the right to recover instalments of interest accrue as they fall due, or only at the end of the term of the loan, or at some other point in time (such as on an accelerated basis following a default).[44] Section 20(6) provides that if a prior mortgagee or other incumbrancer is in possession of the mortgaged property and an action is brought within one year of the discontinuance of that possession by the subsequent incumbrancer, he may recover in that action all arrears of interest that fell due during the period of possession of the prior incumbrancer, or damages in respect of those arrears. Section 20(7) provides that where the property subject to the mortgage or charge comprises any future interest or life insurance policy, and it is a term of the mortgage or charge that arrears of interest shall be treated as part of the principal sum of money secured, interest shall not be treated as becoming due before the right to recover the principal sum of money has accrued.

42 [2005] UKHL 44, [2005] 4 All ER 97; this decision followed *Bristol & West Plc v Bartlett* [2002] EWCA Civ 1181, [2003] 1 WLR 284.

43 LA 1980, s 8.

44 See, for example, *Barclay's Bank v Walters*, *The Times*, 20 October 1988 (CA) and *West Bromwich Building Society v Wilkinson* [2005] UKHL 44, [2005] 4 All ER 97.

PART V

Equity and Estates

CHAPTER 17

Breach of Trust and Breach of Fiduciary Duty

INTRODUCTION

17.01 The limitation periods for an action for breach of trust or breach of fiduciary duty can only be properly understood if one has regard to the history of the equitable jurisdiction. No statutory limitation period applied to any claims in equity prior to the passing of the Trustee Act 1888,[1] but the courts of equity responded to stale claims in two ways. The first of these was to apply common law limitation periods by analogy in certain cases,[2] and the second was to recognise the defences of *laches* and acquiescence.[3] The Limitation Act 1980 ('LA 1980') now provides that a six-year limitation period applies to an action for breach of trust[4] and that no[5] limitation period applies in the case of a fraud or fraudulent breach of trust to which the trustee was a party or privy[6] or for a claim alleging that a trustee has wrongfully retained or converted trust property.[7] The limitation periods relating to land held on trust are discussed in Chapter 15.[8]

17.02 Despite the attempts to codify the limitation provisions for causes of action historically arising in the equitable jurisdiction of the courts, the law in force prior to the passing of the Limitation Act 1939[9] remains relevant to proceedings seeking equitable relief and actions alleging breach of fiduciary duty, as there is no statutory limitation period in respect of the former,[10] and no reference to the latter in the LA 1980.[11] One must therefore still look to the nineteenth century case law when dealing with limitation issues relating to equitable causes of

1 51 & 52 Vict c 59.
2 See *Knox v Gye* (1872) 5 App Cas 656 and paras 17.22–17.24.
3 See Ch 18 and LA 1980, s 36(2).
4 LA 1980, s 21(3). If an express statutory provision provides a limitation period, the equitable defence of *laches* may not be raised: *Re Pauling's Settlement Trusts* [1961] 3 All ER 717 at 735, per Wilberforce J.
5 The defences of *laches* and acquiescence may still be raised: see *Re Loftus, decd* [2006] EWCA Civ 1124, [2007] 1 WLR 591, discussed in para 17.13.
6 LA 1980, s 21(1)(a).
7 LA 1980, s 21(1)(b).
8 LA 1980, s 18: see para 15.17.
9 The 1939 Act repealed the earlier legislation with effect from 1 July 1940.
10 LA 1980, s 36(2), discussed in Ch 18.
11 However, a statutory limitation period may apply by analogy: see s 36(1) and fn 2.

action. The complexities in the law on limitation in this area have led to strident calls for the modernisation and simplification of the law in this area.[12]

Ascertaining the limitation period

17.03 The issue of what, if any, limitation period applies to proceedings having an equitable element is not always straightforward. The following questions should provide assistance in helping parties to ascertain the applicable limitation period:

1 **Breach of trust**

Is the defendant a trustee? Do the proceedings allege a breach of trust? What is the nature of the breach of trust alleged and does it come within the ambit of s 21(1) or 21(3)? If coming within s 21(1), can the defendant establish a defence of *laches* or acquiescence?

2 **Breach of fiduciary duty**

Did the defendant owe the claimant fiduciary duties? Would the courts of equity have applied a limitation period by analogy in those circumstances? If no statutory limitation period is applicable by analogy, can the defendant establish a defence of *laches* or acquiescence?

ACTIONS FOR BREACH OF TRUST

Statutory provisions relating to actions against trustees

17.04 Section 21 of the LA 1980 contains the limitation periods for actions in respect of trust property, subsections (1) and (3) of which are worth setting out in full:

> '(1) No period of limitation prescribed by this Act shall apply to an action by a beneficiary under a trust, being an action –
>
> (a) in respect of any fraud or fraudulent breach of trust to which the trustee was a party or privy; or
>
> (b) to recover from the trustee trust property or the proceeds of trust property in the possession of the trustee, or previously received by the trustee and converted to his use.
>
> …
>
> (3) Subject to the preceding provisions of this section, an action by a beneficiary to recover trust property or in respect of any breach of trust, not being an action for which a period of limitation is prescribed by any other provision of this Act, shall not be brought after the expiration of six years from the date on which the right of action accrued.

12 *Cia de Seguros Imperio v Heath (REBX) Ltd* [2001] 1 WLR 112 at 124, per Sir Christopher Staughton.

> For the purposes of this subsection, the right of action shall not be treated as having accrued to any beneficiary entitled to a future interest in the trust property until the interest fell into possession.'

Section 21(2) provides that where a trustee who is also a beneficiary under the trust receives trust property or proceeds in excess of his entitlements, and if he acted honestly and reasonably, s 21(1)(b) shall only apply to any claim against him to recover the excess over his proper share that he received. Section 21(4) provides that any beneficiary in respect of whose claim there would be a good defence under the LA 1980 shall derive no greater benefit from a judgment or order obtained by any other beneficiary.

Definition of 'breach of trust' and the accrual of cause of action

17.05 In *Tito v Waddell (No 2)*,[13] Megarry V-C noted that the meaning of the expression 'breach of trust' had not received judicial consideration in any case of which he was aware and that it had not been the subject of extensive academic analysis.[14] Although he did not attempt to offer a comprehensive definition of what amounted to a breach of trust, he held that it was not merely a synonym for breach of fiduciary duty, and that a breach of the fair-dealing or self-dealing rules was not a breach of trust.[15] The general rule is that a cause of action for breach of trust accrues as soon as the breach of trust has been committed, and not, if different, when the beneficiary suffers loss.[16]

Persons who are trustees under the Limitation Act 1980

17.06 Section 38(1) of the LA 1980 provides that 'trust' and 'trustee' shall have the same meaning as in the Trustee Act 1925 ('TA 1925'). Section 68(17) of the TA 1925 contains a lengthy definition as follows:

> '"Trust" does not include the duties incident to an estate conveyed by way of mortgage, but with this exception the expressions "trust" and "trustee" extend to implied and constructive trusts, and to cases where the trustee has a beneficial interest in the trust property, and to the duties incident to the office of a personal representative, and "trustee" where the context admits, includes a personal representative, and "new trustee" includes an additional trustee.'

13 [1977] Ch 106.

14 [1977] Ch 106 at 247–249. He referred to the definition provided in two US texts: *Scott on Trusts* (3rd edn, Boston: Little Brown, 1967), Vol III at 1605 and Pomeroy, *Equity Jurisprudence* (3rd edn, San Francisco: Bancroft-Whitney, 1905), Vol III at 2086.

15 [1977] Ch 106 at 249. More recently, the Court of Appeal in *Gwembe Valley Development Co Ltd v Koshy (No 3)* [2003] EWCA Civ 1048, [2004] 1 BCLC 171 at paras 104–109 disagreed with Megarry VC's formulation, and held that the breaches referred to were in fact breaches of trust.

16 *Thorne v Heard & Marsh* [1895] 1 AC 95; *Somerset v Earl Poulett* [1894] 1 Ch 231.

The effect of this provision is that, in a limitation context, 'trust' and 'trustee' extend to implied and constructive trusts, to cases where the trustee has a beneficial interest in the trust property and to the duties incident to the office of a personal representative. It seems, however, that a trustee in bankruptcy is not a trustee for the purposes of section 21.[17] However, any thoughts that s 68(17) provides an all-encompassing definition of 'trustee' are sadly misplaced, as the question of whether an express trust exists at all may not be straightforward[18] and more importantly, the reference in the definition to 'constructive trustees' is apt to mislead as the meaning of this phrase appears to have changed over time such that only certain constructive trustees are trustees within the meaning of the LA 1980.[19]

17.07 While it is clear from the wording of s 68(17) of the TA 1925 that express trustees are trustees for limitation purposes, the question of when a person in a fiduciary relationship will be deemed to be an express trustee is not immediately apparent. An early decision on the definition of the word 'trustee' for limitation purposes is *Soar v Ashwell*,[20] where an action for breach of trust against the estate of a solicitor was brought nearly 12 years after his death. The solicitor had been given money by trustees of a fund for the purpose of investing it, but failed to return all the money to the trustees (or to pay it to the beneficiaries). The Court of Appeal unanimously held that the deceased was a trustee for limitation purposes. As he had received the money on account of the fiduciary relationship between the parties and as trustee for his clients, it was held that he should be treated as an express trustee of the monies for limitation purposes.[21] The judgments also discussed the situation where a stranger to a trust had assumed to act and had acted as a trustee and had received trust money under a breach of trust in which he concurred.[22] The court noted that this was one circumstance where a 'constructive trustee'[23] would be found to be a trustee for limitation purposes, a further example being where a stranger to a trust participated in the fraud of a trustee.[24]

17.08 However, care should be taken, as *Soar v Ashwell*[25] was decided prior to the introduction of a statutory definition of trustee in the TA 1925 and it has been noted that s 68(17) of the TA 1925 'has at least partly abrogated the gen-

17 *Re Cornish, Ex p Board of Trade* [1896] 1 QB 99 (CA).

18 *Norwegian Government v Calcultta Marine Eng Co Ltd* [1960] 2 Lloyd's Rep 431 and *Westdeutsche Landesbank Girozentrale v Islington LBC* [1996] AC 669.

19 See *Paragon Finance Plc v DB Thackerar & Co (a firm)* [1999] 1 All ER 400, *Gwembe Valley Development Co Ltd v Koshy (No 3)* [2003] EWCA Civ 1048, [2004] 1 BCLC 171 and the cases discussed below in the paragraphs that follow.

20 [1893] 2 QB 390.

21 [1893] 2 QB 390 at 394 and 396–397. This had the consequence that the cause of action was not subject to a limitation period (in modern terms, that it was governed by s 21(1)(b): trustee retaining trust property).

22 [1893] 2 QB 390 at 396 and 405. Liability under this heading includes liability for what is now referred to as 'knowing receipt', although the language may include other heads of liability.

23 See the judgment of Bowen LJ at [1893] 2 QB 390 at 396.

24 [1893] 2 QB 390 at 394–395, per Lord Esher MR, and at 396–397, per Bowen LJ. Liability under this heading is now referred to as 'dishonest assistance'.

25 [1893] 2 QB 390.

eral distinction between express and constructive trustees'.[26] This is undoubtedly true but unfortunately does not provide any guidance as to whether a particular class of quasi-trustee is a trustee for limitation purposes. This is complicated by the fact that two approaches to the limitation position of constructive trustees are evident at Court of Appeal level since 1999: that advanced by Millett LJ in *Paragon Finance Plc v DB Thackerar & Co (a firm)*[27] and that contained in the judgment of Aldous LJ in *James v Williams*.[28] As the judgment of Millett LJ in *Paragon Finance* has gained widespread acceptance as setting out the law in the area, it is proposed to quote from it *in extenso*. In his judgment, having noted that prior to the Trustee Act 1888[29] coming into force an action against a trustee was never barred by lapse of time as his possession of trust property was treated as the possession of the beneficiaries, Millett LJ continued as follows:

> 'The rule did not depend upon the nature of the trustee's appointment, and it was applied to trustees *de son tort* and to directors and other fiduciaries who, though not strictly trustees, were in an analogous position and who abused the trust and confidence reposed in them to obtain their principal's property for themselves. Such persons are properly described as constructive trustees.
>
> Regrettably, however, the expressions "constructive trust" and "constructive trustee" have been used by equity lawyers to describe two entirely different situations. The first covers those cases already mentioned, where the defendant, though not expressly appointed as trustee, has assumed the duties of a trustee by a lawful transaction which was independent of and preceded the breach of trust and is not impeached by the claimant. The second covers those cases where the trust obligation arises as a direct consequence of the unlawful transaction which is impeached by the claimant.
>
> A constructive trust arises by operation of law whenever the circumstances are such that it would be unconscionable for the owner of property (usually but not necessarily the legal estate) to assert his own beneficial interest in the property and deny the beneficial interest of another. In the first class of case, however, the constructive trustee really is a trustee. He does not receive the trust property in his own right but by a transaction by which both parties intend to create a trust from the outset and which is not impugned by the claimant. His possession of the property is coloured from the first by the trust and confidence by means of which he obtained it, and his subsequent appropriation of the property to his own use is a breach of that trust … In these cases the claimant does not impugn the transaction by which the defendant obtained control of the property. He alleges that the circumstances in which the defendant obtained control make it unconscionable for him thereafter to assert a beneficial interest in the property.
>
> The second class of case is different. It arises when the defendant is implicated in a fraud. Equity has always given relief against fraud by making any person sufficiently implicated in the fraud accountable in equity. In such a case he is traditionally though I think unfortunately described as a constructive trustee and said to be "liable to account as constructive trustee". Such a person is not in fact a trustee at

26 McGee, *Limitation Periods* (6th edn, London: Sweet & Maxwell, 2010) at para 14.022.

27 [1999] 1 All ER 400.

28 [2000] Ch 1 (CA), decided *per incuriam Paragon Finance;* see also *Newgate Stud Co v Penfold* [2004] EWHC 2993 (Ch), [2008] 1 BCLC 46.

29 51 & 52 Vict c 59.

> all, even though he may be liable to account as if he were. He never assumes the position of a trustee, and if he receives the trust property at all it is adversely to the claimant by an unlawful transaction which is impugned by the claimant. In such a case the expressions "constructive trust" and "constructive trustee" are misleading, for there is no trust and usually no possibility of a proprietary remedy; they are "nothing more than a formula for equitable relief" …'[30]

It is now proposed to analyse the modern case law on the three categories of constructive (or implied) trustees discussed in *Soar v Ashwell*[31] as persons who are treated as trustees for limitation purposes.

Persons receiving property on account of a pre-existing fiduciary relationship

17.09 If a person owes fiduciary duties prior to receiving money or property on behalf of another, he will be held to be a trustee for limitation purposes. The classes of persons who have been held to be a trustee in such circumstances include the following: a solicitor holding client money;[32] a person who receives money from others for the purpose of investment;[33] and a company director, in respect of his control of company property and assets,[34] but not if the action arising from the breach of fiduciary duty by the director does not seek to recover the specific property in respect of which he owed trustee-like duties.[35] The extent to which employees owe fiduciary duties to their employers remains a developing area of the law, although several recent cases have led to findings of breach of fiduciary duty leading to the imposition of a constructive trust arising out of a breach of fiduciary duty by an employee.[36]

17.10 If a person only owes fiduciary duties as a consequence of having received money or property and not as a result of a pre-existing relationship, he will not be held to be a trustee for limitation purposes, as was held in cases involving a trustee in bankruptcy,[37] a statutory insolvency inspector having a sim-

30 [1999] 1 All ER 400 at 408–409. The two types of constructive trustee mentioned by Millett LJ are often referred to as 'category 1' and 'category 2' constructive trustees respectively: see *Cattley v Pollard* [2006] EWHC 3170 (Ch), [2007] Ch 353 at para 61.

31 [1893] 2 QB 390.

32 *Burdick v Garrick* (1870) LR 5 Ch 233.

33 *North American Land and Timber Co v Watkins* [1904] 1 Ch 242.

34 *JJ Harrison (Properties) Ltd v Harrison* [2002] 1 BCLC 162 (company director purchasing asset from company having concealed information about its true value); this extends to de facto directors: *Statek Corporation v Alford* [2008] EWHC 32 (Ch), [2008] BCC 266, and auditor having control of a company's money: *GL Baker Ltd v Medway* [1958] 1 WLR 1216.

35 *Gwembe Valley Development Co Ltd v Koshy* [2003] EWCA Civ 1048, [2004] 1 BCLC 171 (secret profits earned on currency exchanges which did not involve improper payments from company money); see also *Halton International Inc v Guernroy Ltd* [2006] EWCA Civ 801, [2006] All ER (D) 302 (Jun) and *Newgate Stud Co v Penfold* [2004] EWHC 2993 (Ch), [2008] 1 BCLC 46.

36 See *Cobbetts LLP v Hodge* [2009] EWHC 786 (Ch), [2009] All ER (D) 156 (Apr); *Nottingham University v Fishel* [2000] IRLR 471; *Reading v Attorney General* [1951] AC 507 and Stafford and Ritchie, *Fiduciary Duties: Directors and Employees* (Bristol: Jordan Publishing, 2008) at 93 et seq.

37 *Re Cornish* [1896] 1 QB 99.

ilar role to a liquidator[38] and a receiver appointed by the court.[39] The question of whether fiduciary duties are owed in respect of the monies which were received can prove difficult to answer in practice. In *Nelson v Rye*,[40] the musician Willie Nelson sued his former manager and accountant for breach of fiduciary duty for failing to account to him in respect of monies received on his behalf. Laddie J held that no limitation period applied to the claimant's claim for breach of fiduciary duty and also that any monies wrongfully retained were held as a constructive trustee.[41] The case was held to have been wrongly decided by Millett LJ in *Paragon Finance Ltd v Thakerar Plc*[42] on grounds that fiduciary obligations were not owed in respect of the monies which the defendant had received, and that only contractual obligations were owed to the claimant. More recently, in *Seaton v Seddon*,[43] it was held by Roth J, on facts similar to those in *Nelson v Rye*, that the defendants, who were solicitors for a 1980s music band, were not 'category 1 constructive trustees' in relation to monies paid to them and thus that any claim relating to those monies was subject to the six-year limitation period in s 21(3).

Trustees de son tort, knowing receipt and dishonest assistance

17.11 The second and third categories of constructive trustees referred to in *Soar v Ashwell*[44] as persons who may be held to be trustees for limitation purposes were not precisely defined. They are discussed here by reference to the modern terminology of 'trustees *de son tort*' and persons who are guilty of 'knowing receipt' of trust property or 'dishonest assistance' in a breach of trust. The position of trustees *de son tort* would appear to indicate that they should be treated as trustees for limitation purposes as their trust obligations come into existence prior to the breach which leads to the imposition of the constructive trust.[45] However, the position of parties guilty of knowing receipt or dishonest assistance is less clear. In *Cattley v Pollard*,[46] a solicitor's wife was sued on grounds that she had dishonestly assisted her husband in relation to a fraudulent breach of trust he had committed. Richard Sheldon QC, sitting as a deputy High Court judge, held that as the defendant's obligation to account as a constructive trustee arose as a consequence of the unlawful transaction rather than as a result of the defendant having assumed the duties of a trustee, the defendant was not a trustee for limitation purposes. This decision was distinguished in *Statek Corporation v Alford*,[47] where Evans-Lombe J held that, even if the defendant

38 *Taylor v Davies* [1920] AC 636.

39 *Re Gallard* [1897] 2 QB 8.

40 [1996] 2 All ER 176.

41 As the defendant, as trustee, had retained those monies for himself in breach of trust, he held that no limitation period applied by reason of the LA 1980, s 21(1)(a). However, the claimant's claim was unsuccessful in part by reason of *laches*.

42 [1999] 1 All ER 400.

43 [2012] EWHC 735 (Ch), [2013] 1 All ER 29.

44 [1893] 2 QB 390.

45 See *James v Williams* [2000] Ch 1.

46 [2006] EWHC 3170 (Ch), [2007] Ch 353; *Sinclair Investment Holdings SA v Versailles Trade Finance Ltd* [2007] All ER (Comm) 993.

47 [2008] EWHC 32 (Ch), [2008] BCC 266.

was not a trustee by virtue of being a de facto director of the company,[48] no limitation period applied to the claimant's claim alleging dishonest assistance. Evans-Lombe J reached this finding on grounds that the wording of s 21(1)(a) of the LA 1980 was sufficiently broad to apply to an action where a defendant was implicated in the fraudulent breach of trust on the part of a third party, even if the defendant himself was not a trustee.

17.12 In *Peconic Industrial Development Ltd v Lau Kwok Fai*,[49] Lord Hoffmann, sitting as a judge of the Court of Final Appeal of Hong Kong, followed *Cattley v Pollard* in preference to *Statek Corporation* and held that (the equivalent section to) s 21(1)(a) of the LA 1980 did not apply to a non-fiduciary accessory to a fraudulent breach of trust. However, in *Williams v Central Bank of Nigeria*,[50] the Court of Appeal followed *Statek Corporation v Alford*[51] in preference to *Peconic Industrial Development Ltd v Lau Kwok Fai*[52] and held that a party who dishonestly assists another in a fraudulent breach of trust is subject to the extended limitation period in s 21(1)(a) of the LA 1980. Sir Andrew Morritt C added the *obiter* comments that the extended limitation period would also apply in a case where the third party was fraudulent but the trustee was not.[53] Given the marked differences of opinion on this point, it is to be hoped that the Supreme Court gives definitive guidance at some point.

No period of limitation for actions within s 21(1)

17.13 It was suggested by the Court of Appeal in *Gwembe Valley Development Co Ltd v Koshy (No 3)*[54] that a defence of *laches* could not be raised in cases of fraudulent breach of trust.[55] However, this dictum was not followed in *Re Loftus, decd*,[56] where the Court of Appeal held that the opening words of the section only precluded the application of any *other* limitation period contained in the statute and that they did not affect the operation of the doctrines of *laches* and acquiescence.

'In respect of the fraud' and 'party or privy': s 21(1)(a)

17.14 The wording of s 21(1)(a) has given rise to some difficulties of interpretation. The section applies to an action 'against a trustee or any person claiming through him', which has been held to cover any action in which the recipient will have to rely on a disposition or transfer from the fraudulent trustee as his source

48 The comments that follow are, strictly speaking, *obiter dictum*, as the court also held that the defendant was a de facto director of the company.
49 [2009] 5 HKC 135.
50 [2012] EWCA Civ 415, [2012] 3 WLR 1501.
51 [2008] EWHC 32 (Ch), [2008] BCC 266.
52 [2009] 5 HKC 135.
53 [2012] EWCA Civ 415, [2012] 3 WLR 1501 at para 14.
54 [2003] EWCA Civ 1048, [2004] 1 BCLC 171 at para 140.
55 LA 1980, s 21(1)(a).
56 [2006] EWCA Civ 1124, [2007] 1 WLR 591. The same conclusion was reached in *Nelson v Rye* [1996] 1 WLR 1878 and *Patel v Shah* [2005] EWCA Civ 157 at para 22.

of legal title to the property.[57] In *Statek Corporation v Alford*,[58] it was held that s 21(1)(a) also governs claims for dishonest assistance in a fraudulent breach of trust, in circumstances where the defendant is the dishonest third party and not the fraudulent trustee.[59] This conclusion was based on a finding that the phrase 'in respect of any fraud or fraudulent breach of trust' was wider than an action 'for' fraudulent breach of trust. The conclusion reached in *Statek Corporation v Alford* follows the comments of Millett LJ in *Paragon Finance Plc v DB Thackerar & Co (a firm)*,[60] where he stated that a principled system of limitation should treat a claim against an accessory as barred when the claim against the trustee was barred '… and not before'.[61] As against this line of authority it is worth noting that s 21(1)(a) only applies if the trustee was party or privy[62] to the fraud. Negligence or inadvertence in entrusting trust property to a person who perpetrates a fraud falls outside the section.[63] The decision in *Statek Corporation* was not followed by Lord Hoffmann, sitting as a judge of the Hong Kong Court of Final Appeal in *Peconic Industrial Development Ltd v Lau Kwok Fai*,[64] where he held that if the phrase 'in respect of ...' had been intended to include 'claims against dishonest assisters or other non-fiduciaries on the ground that they were accessories to the breach of trust, the language would have been a good deal clearer'.[65] This decision, in turn, was not followed by the Court of Appeal in *Williams v Central Bank of Nigeria*,[66] where it was held that this interpretation overlooks the contrast in wording between s 21(1)(a) and (b) and s 21(3).

The meaning of 'fraud' and 'fraudulent' in s 21(1)(a)

17.15 In discussing what must be proved by a claimant who wishes to rely on the provisions of s 21(1)(a), a useful starting point is the speech of Viscount Haldane LC in *Nocton v Lord Ashburton*:[67]

> 'In Chancery the term "fraud" thus came to be used to describe what fell short of deceit, but imported breach of a duty to which equity had attached its sanction.'[68]

57 *GL Baker Ltd v Medway* [1958] 1 WLR 1216 at 1221–1222. This finding may have been *obiter*, as Dankwerts J also found that there had been fraudulent concealment by the defendant.
58 [2008] EWHC 32 (Ch), [2008] BCC 266.
59 The section may appear to apply even when the defendant is innocent of the fraud: *GL Baker Ltd v Medway* [1958] 1 WLR 1216.
60 [1999] 1 All ER 400.
61 [1999] 1 All ER 400 at 414. The result in *Statek Corporation v Alford* [2008] EWHC 32 (Ch), [2008] BCC 266 is also endorsed by the authors of Stafford and Ritchie, *Fiduciary Duties: Directors and Employees* (Bristol: Jordan Publishing, 2008) at 416.
62 See the definition given by Lord Denning MR in *Compania Maritima San Basilio SA v Oceanius Mutual Writing Association (Bermuda) Ltd* [1976] 3 All ER 243.
63 *Thorne v Heard* [1895] 1 AC 95; *Somerset v Earl Poulett* [1894] 1 Ch 231.
64 [2009] 5 HKC 135.
65 [2009] 5 HKC 135 at para 25.
66 [2012] EWCA Civ 415, [2012] 3 WLR 1501. The authors of Goff and Jones, *The Law of Unjust Enrichment* (8th edn, London: Sweet & Maxwell, 2011) express a preference for the *Cattley v Pollard* line of case law: see 750–751 at fn 28.
67 [1914] AC 932.
68 [1914] AC 932 at 953; see further Spry, *Equitable Remedies* (8th edn, London: Sweet & Maxwell, 2010), at 424–431.

This was expanded upon by Millett LJ in *Armitage v Nurse*,[69] where he commented as follows:

> 'Breaches of trust are of many different kinds. A breach of trust may be deliberate or inadvertent; it may consist of an actual misappropriation or misapplication of the trust property or merely of an investment or other dealing which is outside the trustees' powers … By consciously acting beyond their powers (as, for example, by making an investment which they know to be unauthorised) the trustees may deliberately commit a breach of trust; but if they do so in good faith and in the honest belief that they are acting in the interest of the beneficiaries their conduct is not fraudulent … It is the duty of a trustee to manage the trust property and deal with it in the interests of the beneficiaries. If he acts in a way which he does not honestly believe[70] is in their interests then he is acting dishonestly. It does not matter whether he stands or thinks he stands to gain personally from his actions.'[71]

In *Gwembe Valley Development Co Ltd v Koshy (No 3)*,[72] it was held that fraudulent, in this context, included the deliberate concealment of a material interest which the defendant knew should be disclosed.

Allegation of fraud should be fully pleaded

17.16 An allegation of fraud must be distinctly alleged and distinctly proved.[73] Although it is not necessary to use the words 'fraud' or 'dishonesty' if the facts which make the conduct complained of fraudulent are pleaded, if the facts pleaded are consistent with innocence then it is not open to the court to find fraud.[74] An allegation that the defendant 'knew or ought to have known' is not a clear and unequivocal allegation of actual knowledge and will not support a finding of fraud. This is because it is not treated as making two alternative allegations, ie an allegation (i) that the defendant actually knew, with an alternative allegation (ii) that he ought to have known, but rather a single allegation that he ought to have known (and may even have known – though it is not necessary to allege this).[75] As was stated by Millett LJ in *Armitage v Nurse*:[76]

> 'In order to allege fraud it is not sufficient to sprinkle a pleading with words like "wilfully" and "recklessly" (but not "fraudulently"' or "dishonestly"). This may still leave it in doubt whether the words are being used in a technical sense or merely to give colour by way of pejorative emphasis to the complaint.'[77]

69 [1998] Ch 241.

70 Elsewhere in his judgment he makes clear that a trustee will not have an honest belief if he is recklessly indifferent as to whether his actions are in the best interests of the beneficiaries.

71 [1998] Ch 241 at 251.

72 [2003] EWCA Civ 1048, [2004] 1 BCLC 171, reversing in part [2002] 1 BCLC 478; followed in *Newgate Stud Co v Penfold* [2004] EWHC 2993 (Ch), [2008] 1 BCLC 46.

73 *Davy v Garrett* (1878) 7 Ch D 473 at 489, per Thesiger LJ; see further the general discussion in para 2.20 on the necessity to plead a limitation defence.

74 *Belmont Finance Corporation Ltd v Williams Furniture Ltd* [1979] Ch 250 at 268.

75 *Belmont Finance Corporation Ltd v Williams Furniture Ltd* [1979] Ch 250; *Armitage v Nurse* [1998] Ch 241 at 257; *Schulman v Hewson* [2002] EWHC 855 (Ch), [2002] All ER (D) 58 (May).

76 [1998] Ch 241.

77 [1998] Ch 241 at 257.

Overlap between fraudulent breach of trust and deliberate concealment

17.17 The same facts which give rise to a plea of fraud or fraudulent breach of trust within the meaning of s 21(1)(a) may also amount to deliberate concealment of a fact relevant to the claimant's cause of action within the meaning of s 32(1)(b).[78] In *Newgate Stud Co v Penfold*,[79] the claimant alleged a breach of the self-dealing rule by a fiduciary who had failed to obtain his principal's informed consent to a transaction in which he was interested. While a plea of fraudulent breach of trust was not established, a related plea of fraudulent concealment was made out. In *Cattley v Pollard*,[80] although the defendant, who had dishonestly assisted in a breach of trust, was held not be a 'trustee' for limitation purposes, she was found to have concealed her wrong from the claimant such that the claim was not statute barred.

Trust property or its proceeds still retained by the trustee or the proceeds thereof

17.18 As the essence of a trust is that the trustee will possess trust property on behalf of the beneficiaries, time can never run against him in respect of trust property in his possession. Section 21(1)(b) extends the ambit of this general principle to cover cases where a beneficiary is effectively pursuing a tracing remedy against a trustee who has sold or otherwise converted trust property to his own use. However, the trustee must have actually received the property for this section to apply. In *Thorne v Heard*,[81] a mortgagee's agent did not pass on surplus monies to the mortgagee following the sale of a property. The House of Lords held that the trustee had never had the trust property or its proceeds in his possession. A broad interpretation was given to the phrase, 'in the possession of the trustee' in *Re Howlett, decd*,[82] where a father had taken possession of lands as trustee for his son, but had remained in possession for 17 years after the time when his entitlement to possess as trustee had ended. After his death, the claimant sued the estate of his late father and was awarded rents and profits which he should have paid during his period of occupation, as the court held that he could not be heard to say that he had not received rents and profits, or effectively to rely on his own wrongdoing in not paying same during his lifetime.

78 See Ch 7 and *GL Baker Ltd v Medway* [1958] 1 WLR 1216. *Gwembe Valley Development Co Ltd v Koshy (No 3)* [2003] EWCA Civ 1048, [2004] 1 BCLC 171 was a case where the claimant successfully established a fraudulent breach of trust on the part of the defendant, but in *Halton International Inc v Guernroy Ltd* [2006] EWCA Civ 801, [2006] All ER (D) 302 (Jun), Carnwath LJ (who was a member of the court in *GVDC v Koshy*) commented that the case should properly be viewed as a case involving a fraudulent concealment.

79 [2004] EWHC 2993 (Ch), [2008] 1 BCLC 46.

80 [2006] EWHC 3170 (Ch), [2007] Ch 353.

81 [1895] AC 595.

82 [1949] Ch 767.

Charitable trusts

17.19 The limitation provisions in s 21 of the LA 1980 are stated to apply to actions brought by a 'beneficiary'. The usual claimant in an action to enforce the terms of a charitable trust will be the Attorney General and not one of the beneficiaries of the trust. In *Attorney General v Cocke*,[83] it was held by Harman J that an application by the Attorney General for the taking of an account was not subject to any limitation period contained in the LA 1980 and was allowed to proceed more than 25 years after the accrual of the cause of action.

Future interests and accrual of claim

17.20 The right of action of a beneficiary entitled to a future interest in trust property is not deemed to have accrued until his interest falls into possession.[84] In *Re Pauling's Settlement Trust*,[85] it was held that invalid advances of capital do not cause a future interest to fall into possession and that, notwithstanding that the beneficiary had consented to the advance, this was not the equivalent to her consenting to the release of her life interest.

Effect of barring of a beneficiary's interest

17.21 Section 21(4) governs the situation where one beneficiary's right of action has become statute barred pursuant to s 21(3), but another's claim is not barred. This could occur in a case where a life tenant's claim has become statute barred but time has not begun to run against the remainderman's future interest by reason of s 21(3). This section prevents the life tenant from benefitting from a claim brought by the remainderman once his interest falls into possession, such as by claiming income which would otherwise have been payable to him by the life tenants but for his claim being statute barred.[86] So long as a statute barred beneficiary will not benefit from the action, this section does not affect the rights of those whose claims are not statute barred.[87]

BREACH OF FIDUCIARY DUTY

17.22 The LA 1980 contains no reference to actions for breach of fiduciary duty. A breach of fiduciary duty is a *cause of action* in equity rather than an equitable *relief*, but as the reliefs sought in action for breach of fiduciary duty will be

83 [1988] Ch 414.

84 LA 1980, s 21(3); *Russell v Crowley* [1907] 1 IR 275; *Armitage v Nurse* [1998] Ch 241; *Johns v Johns* [2004] NZCA 42.

85 [1961] 3 All ER 717 at 735; see also *Cattley v Pollard* [2006] EWHC 3170 (Ch), [2007] Ch 353.

86 See *Re Fountaine* [1909] 2 Ch 382.

87 *Cattley v Pollard* [2006] EWHC 3170 (Ch), [2007] Ch 353 at para 97.

equitable reliefs including equitable compensation, s 36(1) of the LA 1980 will still apply. This has the result that no limitation period will apply to an action for breach of fiduciary duty unless the courts would have applied a limitation period by analogy prior to 1 July 1940.[88] The leading case on when the courts of equity would apply a statutory limitation period by analogy is *Knox v Gye*,[89] a case concerning the taking of an account, in which Lord Westbury set out the law in the following terms:

> 'The general principle [is] that where a Court of Equity assumes a concurrent jurisdiction with Courts of Law no account will be given after the legal limit of six years, if the statute be pleaded. If it could be doubted whether the executor of a deceased partner can, at Common Law, have an action of account against the surviving partner, the result will still be the same, because a Court of Equity, in affording such a remedy and giving such an account would act by analogy to the Statute of Limitations. For where the remedy in Equity is correspondent to the remedy at Law, and the latter is subject to a limit in point of time by the Statute of Limitations, a Court of Equity acts by analogy to the statute, and imposes on the remedy it affords the same limitation. This is the meaning of the common phrase, that a Court of Equity acts by analogy to the Statute of Limitations, the meaning being, that where the suit in Equity corresponds with an action at Law which is included in the words of the statute, a Court of Equity adopts the enactment of the statute as its own rule or procedure. But if any proceeding in Equity be included within the words of the statute, there a Court of Equity, like a Court of Law, acts in obedience to the statute.'[90]

17.23 It can prove difficult to ascertain whether the common law limitation rules should be applied by analogy in any particular case. For example, in *Cia de Seguros Imperio v Heath (REBX) Ltd*,[91] the Court of Appeal held that as the facts giving rise to the claim for dishonest breach of fiduciary duty were the same as those relied on in alleging breach of contract and breach of duty in tort, the limitation period for the latter would be applied to the former. In *Coulthard v Disco Mix Club Ltd*,[92] the claimant brought an action against his former manager whom he alleged had underpaid him in breach of fiduciary duty and in breach of contract. It was held that the alleged breaches of the defendant's simple duty to account were not breaches of fiduciary duty, but instead only gave rise to a claim in contract.[93] Although the allegation of deliberate underpayment of royalties involved an allegation of disloyalty which did amount to a breach of fiduciary duty, as the factual allegations were the same as the common law claim for breach of contract it was held that the courts of equity would have applied

88 This date is chosen as the Limitation Act 1939 replaced the limitation provisions then in force from that date.

89 (1872) 5 App Cas 656.

90 (1872) 5 App Cas 656 at 674; see also Spry, *Equitable Remedies* (8th edn, London: Sweet & Maxwell, 2010) at 416–423, where it is also stated that a limitation period will not be applied by analogy if there are special circumstances rendering this position unjust.

91 [2001] 1 WLR 112.

92 [1999] 2 All ER 457.

93 See *Bristol and West Building Society v Mothew (t/a Stapley & Co)* [1998] Ch 1.

the limitation period by analogy.[94] In *Seaton v Seddon*,[95] the claimants, former members of a music band, brought proceedings in 2010 in which they alleged that their solicitors in the 1980s had dishonestly and fraudulently acted in breach of fiduciary duty and retained monies that were due to them. Their action was unsuccessful, with Roth J finding that the pleaded case of fraudulent behaviour was unsustainable and that the claim for damages for negligent breach of fiduciary duty was subject to the six-year contractual limitation period by analogy and thus statute barred. He held that the defendant was at most a 'category 2 constructive trustee' and thus that the claim relating to trust monies was subject to s 21(3) and also statute barred.

17.24 No limitation period will apply to an action for breach of fiduciary duty if the breach complained of is one for which there is no equivalent common law action, and also if the courts of equity[96] would not have imposed a limitation period by analogy in such a case. Fiduciary duties which have no common law equivalent include breach of the self-dealing or fair-dealing rules and breach of the obligations of loyalty and fidelity.[97] It would appear that a six-year limitation period should be applied by analogy in all such cases[98] unless the breach was fraudulent[99] or related to the misapplication of trust property which was in the possession of the defendant as trustee.[100] In *Gwembe Valley Development Co Ltd v Koshy (No 3)*,[101] the defendant's breach of fiduciary duty in deliberately and dishonestly failing to disclose the secret profits which he was going to earn on a contract was held to be subject to the limitation period applicable to a fraudulent breach of trust (ie no limitation period). In *JJ Harrison (Properties) Ltd v Harrison*,[102] a director obtained company property for himself by the misuse of his powers as a director in respect of that property. The action against him for breach of fiduciary duty was not subject to any limitation period, by analogy with the limitation period contained in s 21(1)(b) of the LA 1980.

94 [1999] 2 All ER 457 at 477–478, applying *Knox v Gye* (1872) LR 5 HL 656.

95 [2012] EWHC 735 (Ch), [2013] 1 All ER 29.

96 The courts of equity in this context means a court exercising its equitable jurisdiction prior to the coming into force of the Limitation Act 1939: see *Cia de Seguros Imperio v Heath (REBX) Ltd* [2001] 1 WLR 112.

97 See *Bristol and West Building Society v Mothew (t/a Stapley & Co)* [1998] Ch 1 at 16–17, per Millett LJ.

98 By analogy with the limitation period contained in the Trustee Act 1888, s 8(1)(b), now contained in the LA 1980, s 21(3): see *Gwembe Valley Development Co Ltd v Koshy (No 3)* [2004] 1 BCLC 171 at para 111.

99 Section 21(1)(a); see para 17.14 et seq.

100 Section 21(1)(b); see para 17.18.

101 [2003] EWCA Civ 1048, [2004] 1 BCLC 171; see also *Newgate Stud Co v Penfold* [2004] EWHC 2993 (Ch), [2008] 1 BCLC 46.

102 [2002] 1 BCLC 162.

CHAPTER 18

Claims for Equitable Relief; Laches and Acquiescence

INTRODUCTION

18.01 The previous chapter dealt with the history and development of the time limits governing claims in equity and the question of whether different causes of action having an equitable element are subject to a fixed period of limitation contained in the Limitation Act 1980 ('LA 1980') or the equitable defences of *laches* and acquiescence as retained in effect by s 36(2) of the LA 1980. Section 21(1) of the LA 1980 excludes causes of action in respect of a fraudulent breach of trust by a trustee or the wrongful retaining of trust property from the periods of limitation prescribed by the Act, and thus by implication those actions are instead subject to the defences of *laches* and acquiescence.[1] For all other actions relating to a breach of trust, s 21(3) imposes a six-year limitation period and, in *Re Pauling's Settlement Trusts*,[2] it was held that if an express statutory limitation provision provides a limitation period, the equitable defence of *laches* and acquiescence may not be raised. The following claims are subject only to the equitable defences and not the statutory limitation provisions:

(a) actions by a beneficiary in respect of any fraud or fraudulent breach of trust to which the trustee was a party or privy;[3]

(b) actions by a beneficiary to recover from the trustee trust property or the proceeds of trust property in the possession of the trustee, or previously received by the trustee and converted to his own uses;[4]

(c) actions in respect of a breach of fiduciary duty where no statutory limitation period is applied by analogy;[5]

(d) actions for an account where the claim which is the basis of the duty to account is governed by the defences of *laches* and acquiescence;[6] and

1 *In re Loftus, decd* [2006] EWCA Civ 1124, [2007] 1 WLR 591 at para 40, per Chadwick LJ, disapproving of the comments of Mummery LJ in *Gwembe Valley Development Co Ltd v Koshy (No 3)* [2003] EWCA Civ 1048, [2004] 1 BCLC 131 at para 140.
2 [1961] 3 All ER 718 at 735, per Wilberforce J.
3 LA 1980, s 21(1)(a).
4 LA 1980, s 21(1)(b).
5 LA 1980, s 36(1).
6 LA 1980, s 23.

(e) claims for equitable relief, whether sought on an interlocutory basis or as a final relief in the proceedings, including claims for an injunction, specific performance, relief against forfeiture, rescission or rectification, unless the courts would have applied a statutory limitation period by analogy prior to the passing of the Limitation Act 1939.[7]

This chapter considers the defences of *laches* and acquiescence, which may be raised in defence of the above claims.

LACHES, ACQUIESCENCE AND ESTOPPEL

18.02 Section 36(2) of the LA 1980 provides that nothing in the Act 'shall affect any equitable jurisdiction to refuse relief on the ground of acquiescence or otherwise'. The 'or otherwise' contained in this section refers to the related defences of *laches* and estoppel which, it has been noted, 'are often used interchangeably'.[8] The three doctrines are best seen as a continuum linking unconscionable behaviour, detriment, the avoidance of stale claims and the need for finality in people's affairs in the context of inaction, knowledge and the passage of time.[9] At one end of the spectrum, the doctrine of *laches* applies where the claimant's delay in bringing proceedings makes it impossible for a fair trial of the action to take place, eg because of the loss or destruction of evidence. At the other end of the spectrum, the doctrine of *laches* applies where the claimant's delay induces the defendant to act on the basis that his claim will not be asserted or pursued. In that context, *laches* overlaps considerably with the doctrines of affirmation, acquiescence and estoppel.[10]

18.03 In *Fisher v Brooker*,[11] the claimant brought proceedings in 2005 in which he sought a declaration that he was a co-author of the Procul Harum song 'A Whiter Shade of Pale', which had been written in 1967. In considering how the courts should approach a defence of *laches,* estoppel and/or acquiescence raised in response to the 38-year period of delay by the claimant in asserting his rights, Lord Neuberger stated as follows:

> 'The classic example of proprietary estoppel, standing by whilst one's neighbour builds on one's land believing it to be his property, can be characterised as acqui-

7 LA 1980, s 36(1). See the well-founded criticisms of Sir Christopher Staughton in *Cia de Seguros Imperio v Heath (REBX) Ltd* [2001] 1 WLR 112 at 124 calling for modernisation and simplification of this area of the law.

8 Bean, *Injunctions* (10th edn, London: Sweet & Maxwell, 2009) at para 2.20.

9 See Majumdar, 'The Burden of History' (2007) 157 NLJ 1186 and the judgment of Nourse LJ in *Goldsworthy v Brickell* [1987] 1 Ch 378 at 410.

10 For a discussion of acquiescence, see *Archbold v Scully* (1861) 9 HLC 360; *Jones v Stones* [1999] 1 WLR 1739; and Spry, *Equitable Remedies* (8th edn, London: Sweet & Maxwell, 2010) at 438–444.

11 [2009] UKHL 41, [2009] 4 All ER 789; see also *John v James* [1991] FSR 397, where a defence of *laches* was successfully raised in proceedings brought by Elton John to set aside various contracts.

escence – see per Oliver J in *Taylor Fashions Ltd v Liverpool Victoria Trustees Ltd* (Note) [1982] QB 133 at 151. Similarly, laches, failing to raise or enforce an equitable right for a long period, can be characterised as acquiescence.'[12]

18.04 A number of recent judgments have seen the courts adopt an approach to the defences of *laches,* acquiescence and estoppel which does not require an exhaustive inquiry into whether the facts of a case fit within principles established in previous cases, but instead asks whether it would be unconscionable for a party to be permitted to enforce his rights by reason of his delay and the matters which have occurred in the interim. In *Frawley v Neill,*[13] having discussed instances of the doctrines of *laches*, acquiescence and estoppel, Aldous LJ offered the following comments:

> 'In my view, the more modern approach should not require an inquiry as to whether the circumstances can be fitted within the confines of a preconceived formula derived from earlier cases. The inquiry should require a broad approach, directed to ascertaining whether it would in all the circumstances be unconscionable for a party to be permitted to assert his beneficial right. No doubt the circumstances which gave rise to a particular result in decided cases are relevant to the question whether or not it would be conscionable or unconscionable for the relief to be asserted, but each case has to be decided on its facts applying the broad approach.'

In a similar vein, it was stated by Laddie J in *Nelson v Rye* that:

> 'It can be misleading to approach the equitable defences of laches and acquiescence as if they consisted of a series of precisely defined hurdles over each of which a litigant must struggle before the defence is made out.'[14]

18.05 Notwithstanding the judicial *dicta* which point to the overlap in practice between the doctrines of *laches*, acquiescence and estoppel, each has its own separate elements when looked at separately as abstract legal concepts. A useful definition of *laches* is that contained in Snell's *Principles of Equity*, which states that '*laches* essentially consists of a substantial lapse of time coupled with the existence of circumstances which make it inequitable to enforce the claim'.[15] Acquiescence has been stated to arise '[i]f a party, who could have objected, lies by and knowingly permits another to incur an expense in doing an act under the belief that it would not be objected to, and so a kind of permission may be said to be given'.[16] Estoppel involves a representation (whether expressly or by silence) coupled with reliance and detriment such that it would be unconscionable to allow a party to rely upon their strict rights or act in a certain manner.

12 [2009] UKHL 41, [2009] 4 All ER 789 at para 62. This echoes the comments of Andrews LCJ in *McCausland v Young* [1949] NI 49 at 89, where he referred to acquiescence as 'an element in *laches* operating by way of estoppel'.

13 [2000] CP Reports 20, *The Times*, 5 April 1999. This passage has been quoted with approval on several occasions, including by Chadwick LJ in *In re Loftus, decd* [2006] EWCA Civ 1124, [2007] 1 WLR 591 at para 42; see also *Gafford v Graham* (1998) 77 P & CR 73.

14 [1996] 2 All ER 186 at 200.

15 Snell's *Principles of Equity* (31st edn, London: Sweet & Maxwell, 2005) at 101; to similar effect, see Spry, *Equitable Remedies* (8th edn, London: Sweet & Maxwell, 2010) at 431.

16 *Archbold v Scully* (1861) 9 HLC 360 at 383 per Lord Wensleydale.

Laches involves unreasonable delay *after* the infringement of the rights has taken place, whereas acquiescence and estoppel involve inaction *while* the infringement is taking place. *Laches* in its purest sense focuses primarily on delay (while taking acute cognisance of the effect this has on the defendant and third parties), whereas acquiescence and estoppel focus on the conduct of a claimant (and its affect on the parties). For this reason, the primary focus of this chapter is on the former doctrine, although the increasing prominence of an inquiry into whether the granting of relief would be unconscionable should be borne in mind at all times.

APPLICATION OF STATUTORY LIMITATION PROVISIONS BY ANALOGY

18.06 The principles by which the courts of equity decided whether or not to apply a common law[17] limitation period by analogy prior to the enactment of the Limitation Act 1939[18] arise for consideration in modern times most frequently in actions concerning breaches of fiduciary duty. The issues arising are accordingly discussed in the section of the previous chapter dealing with actions for breach of fiduciary duty,[19] but as the issue has recently come before the Court of Appeal in the context of a claimant seeking equitable relief, it is appropriate to discuss the issue in this chapter as well. In *P&O Nedlloyd BV v Arab Metals Co*,[20] it was held that no limitation period should be applied by analogy to actions seeking specific performance. Although this decision has been described as being 'incorrect' in the most recent edition of *Equitable Remedies*,[21] it is far from clear that the decision is unfair given the measure of discretion it leaves in the hands of a judge hearing the claim for relief. The existence of this broad discretion will lead to the imposition of a shorter limitation period in many, but not all, specific performance claims than the six-year limitation period which applies to a claim for damages for breach of contract. It should also be noted that the defences of *laches* and acquiescence can be raised in cases where an injunction is being sought in support of either legal or equitable rights.[22] However, in *Fisher v Brooker*,[23] it was held that if what is being sought is a declaration as to ownership of a property right recognised by statute (such as ownership of copyright), without an injunction or other equitable relief being sought as well, then the defence of *laches* may not be raised.

17 This phrase is used interchangeably with 'statutory limitation period' as historically the statutory limitation provisions only applied to claims brought at common law.

18 This is the test contained in s 36(2) of the LA 1980.

19 Paragraphs 17.22–17.24.

20 [2006] EWCA Civ 1717, [2007] 2 All ER (Comm) 401.

21 Spry, *Equitable Remedies* (8th edn, London: Sweet & Maxwell, 2010) ('Spry') at 245.

22 *Habib Bank Ltd v Habib Bank AG Zurich* [1981] 1 WLR 1265; *Gafford v Graham* (1998) 77 P & CR 73.

23 [2009] UKHL 41, [2009] 4 All ER 789 at para 79, per Lord Neuberger.

THE ELEMENTS OF THE DEFENCE OF LACHES

18.07 Notwithstanding the recent case law which has considered the doctrine of *laches*, the classic statement of the law remains that of Lord Selborne in *Lindsay Petroleum Co v Hurd*:[24]

> '[T]he doctrine of *laches* in Courts of Equity is not an arbitrary or a technical doctrine. Where it would be practically unjust to give a remedy, either because the party has, by his conduct, done that which might fairly be regarded as a waiver of it, or where by his conduct and neglect he has, though perhaps not waiving that remedy, yet put the other party in a situation in which it would not be reasonable to place him if the remedy were afterwards to be asserted, in either of these cases, lapse of time and delay are most material. But in every case, if an argument against relief, which otherwise would be just, is founded upon mere delay, that delay of course not amounting to a bar by any statute of limitations, the validity of that defence must be tried upon principles substantially equitable. Two circumstances, always important in such cases, are, the length of the delay and the nature of the acts done during the interval, which might affect either party and cause a balance of justice or injustice in taking one course or the other, so far as relates to the remedy.'[25]

In discussing the factors that the court will consider in a case where *laches* is raised as a defence, Laddie J in *Nelson v Rye*[26] stated as follows:

> 'Those factors include the period of the delay, the extent to which the defendant's position has been prejudiced by the delay, and the extent to which that prejudice was caused by the actions of the claimant. I accept that mere delay alone will almost never suffice, but the court has to look at all the circumstances, including in particular those factors set out above, and then decide whether the balance of justice or injustice is in favour of granting the remedy or withholding it. If substantial prejudice will be suffered by the defendant, it is not necessary for the defendant to prove that it was caused by the delay. On the other hand, the claimant's knowledge that the delay will cause such prejudice is a factor to be taken into account.'[27]

A more recent statement of the elements of *laches* is that given by Mummery LJ in *Fisher v Brooker*,[28] where he stated as follows:

> '[*L*]*aches* looks to undue delay, to any change of position by the defendants resulting from the delay and to the unreasonableness and injustice of stopping the defendants from carrying on doing what they have been doing for very many years. The concept of unconscionability, which, as I shall explain, underpins the doctrine of proprietary estoppel, also appears in formulations of the defences of *laches* and acquiescence. The change of position aspect of acquiescence and *laches* is less stringent than the requirement of detrimental reliance in cases of proprietary estoppel. Undue delay by the claimant and the defendant's intervening activities

24 (1873–74) LR 5 PC 221.
25 (1873–74) LR 5 PC 221 at 239–240.
26 [1996] 2 All ER 186.
27 [1996] 2 All ER 186 at 201.
28 [2008] EWCA Civ 287, [2008] EMLR 18.

over a long period may suffice to make it unjust to disturb the situation, especially if it is impossible to return the defendants to their original position without some injustice to them.'[29]

CONSEQUENCES OF LACHES

18.08 In cases where a defence of *laches* is established, this will in most instances lead to the court dismissing the claimant's claim,[30] or refusing an injunction but ordering a remedy in damages.[31] However, the court has a wide discretion as to how to respond to a finding of *laches* and in *Nelson v Rye*[32] it led to Laddie J limiting the period during which a party had to account to his principal to six years rather than the ten years claimed. This is consistent with the comments of Spry that even if prejudice or unfairness has been caused by the delay, 'the claimant may nonetheless succeed if he accepts relief that is restricted or modified so as to reduce prejudice or unfairness'.[33]

UNREASONABLE DELAY

18.09 The principle of 'reasonable diligence' depends on the circumstances of the case. A short delay preceding an application for an interim injunction or specific performance may be fatal to the application,[34] but a longer delay may not be excessive in other cases.[35] Lengthy delays have been found not to be fatal in a number of rectification cases.[36] A claimant must have been aware of all of the relevant facts which constitute the grounds for his claim before he can be regarded as having delayed.[37] If inadequate legal advice concerning the effect of a document is given then a claimant may not be fixed with knowledge of its contents.[38] So long as any undue influence persists, a claim may be brought whatever the length of time since the transaction, but once the claimant is no longer under the defendant's influence, a claim to set the transaction aside must be brought within a reasonable time.[39] The reasons for the delay must be examined, and if the reasons excuse or at least explain most of the delay, this may be an answer to an allegation of *laches*.

29 [2008] EWCA Civ 287, [2008] EMLR 18 at para 55.
30 *Gafford v Graham* (1998) 77 P & CR 73.
31 *Shaw v Applegate* [1977] 1 WLR 970; however, see also *Neylon v Dickens* [1987] 1 NZLR 402.
32 *Nelson v Rye* [1996] 2 All ER 186.
33 Spry, *Equitable Remedies* (8th edn, London: Sweet & Maxwell, 2010) at 232.
34 See the discussion of these two areas in paras 18.13 and 18.14.
35 *Fisher v Brooker* [2009] UKHL 41, [2009] 4 All ER 789.
36 See *M'Cormack v M'Cormack* (1877) 1 LR Ir 119 and *Burroughes v Abbott* [1922] 1 Ch 86.
37 *Lindsay Petroleum v Hurd* (1874) LR 5 PC 221 at 241.
38 *Humphreys v Humphreys* [2004] EWHC 2201 (Ch), [2005] 1 FCR 712.
39 *Humphreys v Humphreys* [2004] EWHC 2201 (Ch), [2005] 1 FCR 712; *Allcard v Skinner* (1887) 36 Ch D 145.

MERE DELAY AND ABSENCE OF PREJUDICE

18.10 Mere delay is not of itself sufficient to constitute *laches*,[40] but this must be qualified by saying that a delay in vindicating one's rights may give rise to an inference that the other party has changed its position[41] or that the delay constitutes acquiescence or confirmation of the challenged conduct or actions.[42] For example, in *Kuppusami v Kuppusami*,[43] Rimer J held that a property had been held by the defendant on a resulting trust for the claimant since 1977 and that the mere passage of time until proceedings were brought in 2000 was insufficient to make out a defence of *laches*. Delay may also cause prejudice to a defendant in defending an action.[44] Secondly, while it has been stated that there is no requirement of detrimental reliance for the application of acquiescence or *laches*,[45] the better view is that, while it is not an immutable requirement, 'some sort of detrimental reliance is usually an essential ingredient of *laches*'.[46] In *Fisher v Brooker*,[47] the claimant issued proceedings in 2005 in which he sought declarations as to his authorship of the song 'Whiter Shade of Pale' in 1967 and consequential royalties. In the absence of any prejudice having been suffered by the defendants by reason of his delay, the lapse of time on his part was not fatal to the House of Lords finding in his favour.

DETRIMENT AND CHANGE OF POSITION

18.11 The crucial factor which a court must consider in any case where a defence of *laches* is raised is whether the defendant acted to his detriment by reason of the claimant's delay in instituting suit. In *Nelson v Rye*,[48] it was held that the musician Willie Nelson was guilty of *laches* in bringing an action for breach of fiduciary duty against his manager in which he sought an account of all monies due to him for ten years prior to the date of issuing of the writ. Laddie J accepted that the passage of time had dimmed memories and that relevant receipts and vouchers were no longer available, by reason of which the defendant

40 See *Fisher v Brooker* [2008] EWCA Civ 287, [2008] EMLR 18 at para 53, per Mummery LJ; *KM v HM* (1992) 96 DLR (4th) 289 at 334, per La Forest J; *Hughes v La Baia Ltd* [2011] UKPC 9, (2011) 79 WIR 303.

41 *Allcard v Skinner* (1887) 36 Ch D 145 at 188–189.

42 *Allcard v Skinner* (1887) 36 Ch D 145.

43 [2002] EWHC 2758 (Ch); see also *Eastern Services Ltd v No 68 Ltd* [2006] NZSC 42 and *Re Oxford Pharmaceuticals Ltd* [2009] EWHC 1753 (Ch), [2009] 2 BCLC 485.

44 *Schulman v Hewson* [2002] EWHC 855 (Ch), [2002] All ER (D) 58 (May).

45 *Fisher v Brooker* [2008] EWCA Civ 287, [2008] EMLR 18 at para 85, per Mummery LJ. It would appear that fiscal prejudice may be more readily inferred in cases which seek the return of monies, such as proceedings seeking to set aside a gift, as occurred in *Allcard v Skinner* (1887) 36 Ch D 145.

46 *Fisher v Brooker* [2009] UKHL 41, [2009] 4 All ER 789 at para 64, per Lord Neuberger.

47 [2009] UKHL 41, [2009] 4 All ER 789.

48 [1996] 2 All ER 186. Although the aspects of this case dealing with the limitation period for breach of fiduciary duty and constructive trusts were overruled in *Paragon Finance v DB Thakerar & Co* [1999] 1 All ER 400, Laddie J's comments on *laches* would appear to remain good law.

would suffer real prejudice if an account was ordered without limitation of time. For this reason, the account to be taken was limited to six years prior to the date of issuing of the writ.

DELAY BY BENEFICIARY IN CLAIMING TRUST PROPERTY

18.12 In general, *laches* on the part of a beneficiary will not make it inequitable or unreasonable to grant relief in proceedings for the enforcement of an express trust in relation to property in the possession of the trustee.[49] Mummery LJ noted in *Patel v Shah*[50] that this accurately states the law in relation to 'orthodox, *inter vivos* and testamentary trusts, in which a beneficiary is not expected by anyone to do anything other than to receive the gift'.[51] However, in the case of commercial trusts arising out of partnerships, joint ventures and similar arrangements, if one partner leaves and allows the other partner do all the work and years later returns and brings proceedings in respect of his beneficial entitlements, a defence of *laches* may arise. A delay in excess of ten years prior to bringing proceedings was found to be fatal to the claimant's claim in *Patel v Shah* in circumstances where the defendants had borne the commercial risks during that period of delay.

LACHES AND INJUNCTIONS

18.13 It is sometimes said that an applicant for interlocutory relief must be especially prompt in seeking relief from the court and that a short period of delay may prove fatal to his application.[52] For example, in *Kenitex Chemicals Inc v Kenitex Textured Coating Ltd*,[53] a delay of three months was considered fatal and, in *Bravingtons Ltd v Barrington Tenant*,[54] an unexplained period of three months' delay was considered fatal. One reason for this approach was given by Jacob J in *Newport Association Football Club Ltd v Football Association of Wales Ltd*,[55] in the following terms: 'Normally a party who has delayed two years or more before applying for an interlocutory injunction will have it refused on the grounds of delay. After all, he could have had the final trial within that period.'[56] However, despite the existence of a particularly lengthy delay preceding an application for interlocutory relief in the *Newport Association FC* case, the claimant could point to apprehended harm of a terminal nature if the injunction were to have been refused and for this reason the delay was not fatal to the application for an injunction. An insightful and thorough discussion in Spry comments that it may be that

49 *Mills v Drewitt* (1855) 20 Beav 632 at 638; *Orr v Ford* (1989) 167 CLR 316 at 341.
50 [2005] EWCA Civ 157.
51 [2005] EWCA Civ 157 at para 30.
52 Spry, *Equitable Remedies* (8th edn, London: Sweet & Maxwell, 2010) at 489, referring to *Societe Francaise v Electronic Concepts Ltd* [1975] 3 All ER 425 at 429.
53 [1965] 2 FSR 109.
54 [1975] RPC 183.
55 [1995] 2 All ER 87.
56 [1995] 2 All ER 87 at 99.

the test in relation to *laches* is the same but any delay may affect the balance of convenience or weaken an argument that irreparable harm may be suffered.[57] In each case, the questions have to be asked as to whether the delay has caused prejudice or detriment.

LACHES AND SPECIFIC PERFORMANCE

18.14 A party seeking an order of specific performance must move with haste. In a phrase which was described by the Court of Appeal as having 'passed into Chancery folklore',[58] Lord Alvanley MR in *Milward v Earl Thanet*[59] stated that 'a party cannot call upon a Court of Equity for specific performance, unless he has shewn himself ready, desirous, prompt, and eager'.[60] A defence of *laches* was raised in somewhat unusual circumstances in *P&O Nedlloyd BV v Arab Metals Co*,[61] where the claimant delivered two containers to the third defendant in 1998 which the latter had refused to accept due to the presence of some low level radioactive material. Following a lengthy period during which the claimant sought to decontaminate the containers, in 2004 it issued proceedings in which it sought specific performance of the agreement whereby the third defendant had agreed to accept the containers. The Court of Appeal held that the claimant's claim was not statute barred, as no limitation period applied, and that the defendant could raise a defence of *laches* notwithstanding that proceedings had been brought less than six years after the breach of contract had occurred. Although the court did not have to express a concluded view on the defence of *laches*, its comments indicated that the defence might not be successful when the matter came to trial, given the explanations for some of the delay and the absence of significant prejudice. In more commonplace actions, a period of delay of over a year led to the court refusing relief in *Guerin v Heffernan*,[62] whereas in *Lazard Brothers & Co Ltd v Fairfield Properties Co (Mayfair) Ltd*,[63] a delay of two years was found not to disentitle the claimant to relief. However, each case depends on its facts and sometimes a much longer period of delay will not give rise to a defence of laches. The decision in *P&O Nedlloyd BV* was recently considered and approved by the Privy Council in *Hughes v La Baia Ltd*,[64] in a case in which the claimant sought and was granted an order of specific performance of a contract for the sale of land entered into in 1986 in proceedings commenced in 2001. The important factors that lessened the effect of the delay were that the claimant was held to have acted reasonably in relying on its equitable title to the property after payment of the

57 Spry, *Equitable Remedies* (8th edn, London: Sweet & Maxwell, 2010) at 488–493.

58 *P&O Nedlloyd BV v Arab Metals Co* [2006] EWCA Civ 1717, [2007] 2 All ER (Comm) 401 at para 50, per Moore-Bick LJ.

59 (1801) 5 Ves 720n.

60 (1801) 5 Ves 720n.

61 [2006] EWCA Civ 1717, [2007] 2 All ER (Comm) 401.

62 [1925] 1 IR 57.

63 (1977) 121 SJ 793, noted in Farrand, 'Speedy Performance' [1978] Conv 184.

64 [2011] UKPC 9, (2011) 79 WIR 303 at para 36, approving the statement of the test set out in the judgment of Moore-Bick LJ in *P&O Nedlloyd BV v Arab Metals Co* [2006] EWCA Civ 1717, [2007] 2 All ER (Comm) 401 at para 61.

purchase monies against a backdrop of unadministered estates of those beneficially entitled to the vendor's interest and proceedings concerning the land that were issued in 1998 which the claimant had defended and which were abandoned and struck out in 1999. For these reasons it was held by Lord Walker, giving the advice of the Privy Council, that the defendants had not established any reasons which made it inequitable for the court to order specific performance.

CHAPTER 19

Claims Involving the Estates of Deceased Persons

INTRODUCTION

19.01 The limitation provisions governing claims involving the estates of deceased persons are spread across several sections of the Limitation Act 1980 ('LA 1980'). The starting point is s 22 of the LA 1980, which provides that, subject to 21(1) and (2) of the Act:

(a) no action in respect of any claim to the personal estate[1] of a deceased person or to any share or interest in any such estate (whether under a will or on intestacy) shall be brought after the expiration of 12 years from the date on which the right to receive the share or interest accrued; and

(b) no action to recover arrears of interest in respect of any legacy, or damages in respect of such arrears, shall be brought after the expiration of six years from the date on which the interest became due.

While s 22 of the LA 1980 might appear to contain the applicable limitation periods for most claims involving estates, on closer inspection it becomes apparent that many claims relating to estates fall outside this section. First and expressly referred to are claims under s 21(1) or (2) of the LA 1980 (actions relating to a fraud or fraudulent breach of trust by a trustee[2] and actions for the recovery of trust property or its proceeds from a trustee[3]), where the trust limitation provisions are expressly given precedence.[4] Secondly, s 22 only applies to claims to the personal estate of a deceased and the 12-year limitation period contained in s 18 of the LA 1980 will apply to claims to recover an interest in land (unless factors exist which bring the claim within s 21(1)).[5] Thirdly, claims by creditors against an estate and *devastavit* claims (which arise where the estate pays out money to beneficiaries without having first discharged estate creditors)

1 The phrase 'personal estate' is defined in s 38(1) as excluding chattels real.
2 LA 1980, s 21(1)(a).
3 LA 1980, s 21(1)(b) and 21(2).
4 These provisions are discussed in Ch 17.
5 All pecuniary legacies, even if charged on land, are governed by s 22(1): *Sheppard v Duke* (1839) 9 Sim 567, (1839) 59 ER 477.

fall outside s 22 and are discussed below. Fourthly, in *In re Loftus, decd*,[6] it was held by the Court of Appeal that an application to remove an administrator falls outside s 22(1) as it does not involve a claim to the personal estate of a deceased.

DISCUSSION OF S 22 AND THE QUESTION OF WHEN A PERSONAL REPRESENTATIVE ACTS QUA TRUSTEE

19.02 In *In re Diplock; Diplock v Wintle*,[7] it was held that (the predecessor to) s 22(a) applies to claims by beneficiaries against personal representatives as well as to claims against parties who wrongly receive a distribution from the estate. The initial clause in s 22, which makes s 22 subject to s 21(1) and (2), is awkwardly phrased. However, when read together with the fact that personal representatives are trustees, it has the effect that a 12-year limitation period applies in respect of any claim by a beneficiary to the personal estate of the deceased, that a six-year limitation period applies if the beneficiary alleges that the personal representative has committed an ordinary breach of trust[8] and that no limitation period[9] applies if the personal representative is guilty of fraud (or fraudulent breach of trust) or has retained trust property (ie part of the estate or its proceeds) for himself. The logic underlying this distinction was explained by Patten J in *Davies v Sharples*[10] as follows:

> 'The provisions of s 22 are not intended in my judgment to deal with breaches of trust committed by trustees long after the period of administration has come to an end. They are intended (as their origins in s 8 of the Real Property Limitation Act 1874 makes clear) to cater for failures by a personal representative properly to administer the estate. This can include payment of legacies or the distribution of a residuary estate when it is to be subject to immediate division and no successive interests are involved. But in cases where the acts complained of take place after the trusts have come into effect that is a matter, which in my judgment, falls to be regulated by the provisions of s 21(3) and not by s 22(a).'[11]

WHEN DOES TIME BEGIN TO RUN UNDER S 22(1)?

19.03 Section 22(1) states that time begins to run for a claim to the personal estate of a deceased person 'from the date on which the right to receive the share or interest accrued' and in like manner, s 22(2) states time runs in respect of any action to recover arrears of interest in respect of any legacy, or damages in

6 [2006] EWCA Civ 1124, [2007] 1 WLR 591.
7 [1948] Ch 465, affd *sub nom Ministry of Health v Simpson* [1951] AC 251.
8 LA 1980, s 21(3).
9 The defences of *laches* and acquiescence can still be raised: *In re Loftus, decd* [2006] EWCA Civ 1124, [2007] 1 WLR 591; see further para 17.13.
10 [2006] EWHC 362 (Ch), [2006] WTLR 839. This case is also of interest for the lengthy extension to the limitation period which arose by reason of deliberate concealment of material facts within the meaning of the LA 1980, s 32(1)(b).
11 [2006] EWHC 362 (Ch), [2006] WTLR 839 at para 45.

respect of such arrears from the time the interest fell due. It was held in *Waddell v Harshaw*[12] that the right to receive a share in the estate accrues on death, notwithstanding that no action can be brought during the 'Executor's Year' to compel payment.[13] However, in *In re Loftus, decd,*[14] it was stated *obiter* that time only runs under s 22(1) from when the administrator has paid the costs, funeral and testamentary and administration expenses, debts and other liabilities properly payable out of the assets in his hands and provided for the payment of any pecuniary legacies.[15] While these comments were directed at the situation of a person named as a beneficiary of the residuary estate, logically the same approach would appear to apply in the case of pecuniary legacies also, as these rank in priority after creditors and administrator's expenses.

CLAIMS BY CREDITORS AGAINST AN ESTATE AND DEVASTAVIT CLAIMS

19.04 There are no special limitation rules which distinguish claims by creditors[16] against the estate of a deceased person from equivalent claims advanced against a living person, as the debts of a deceased do not die with him.[17] However, if a debtor (ie the deceased) charges his estate to secure payment of a debt, s 20 of the LA 1980 will govern the creditor's action to enforce the charge. Section 20(1) provides that no action shall be brought to recover a principal sum of money charged on land, or the proceeds of the sale of the land, after the expiration of 12 years from the date when the right to receive the money accrued. In *Re Oliver,*[18] where the deceased debtor created a trust of funds for the payment of his debts, it was held that (the equivalent of) s 21 governed the creditor's action. However, a general instruction to pay debts is not sufficient to create a trust, although it may create a charge.[19] If a personal representative distributes the estate to the beneficiaries without first satisfying the claims of creditors, his breach is termed *devastavit* and an unsatisfied creditor has a cause of action against him personally. In *Re Hyatt,*[20] it was held by Chitty J that *devastavit* is a tort and accordingly it is governed by the six-year limitation period contained in s 2 of the LA 1980. In *Lacons v Warmoll,*[21] it was held that time runs from the date of the wrongful

12 [1905] 1 IR 416; to similar effect is *Hornsey Local Board v Monarch Investment Building Society* (1889) 24 QBD 1. This view appears to have received support in *In re Diplock; Diplock v Wintle* [1948] Ch 465.

13 Administration of Estates Act 1925, s 44.

14 [2006] EWCA Civ 1124, [2007] 1 WLR 591.

15 Lawrence Collins J in the High Court in *Re Loftus (decd)* [2005] EWHC 406 (Ch), [2005] 2 All ER 700 had suggested that time runs from the later of the end of the executor's year and the date when the relevant interest falls into possession.

16 LA 1980, ss 21 and 22 only apply to beneficiaries of an estate.

17 Law Reform (Miscellaneous Provisions) Act 1934, s 1; Proceedings Against Estates Act 1970, s 1.

18 [1927] 2 Ch 323.

19 *Re Raggi* [1913] 2 Ch 206.

20 (1883) 38 Ch D 609.

21 [1907] 2 KB 350.

distribution, even when the liability which the personal representative disregards was only a contingent liability at that time.

CAUSES OF ACTION AFFECTING AN ESTATE THAT ACCRUE AFTER THE DEATH OF A DECEASED

19.05 Some different considerations to those discussed in the previous paragraph arise in respect of causes of action which only accrue to or against the estate of a deceased person after his death. These arise by reason of the general limitation principle that time can only run from a date when there is a claimant in existence who could bring proceedings and one who could be named as defendant in proceedings.[22] This special rule is not engaged if a debt arose, or a tort was committed, or a period of squatting commenced, while the deceased was still alive as time, once it starts to run, will continue to run during a subsequent period of disability.[23] Equally, no special rule arises if an executor is named in the will of a deceased who does not renounce his executorship, as the estate of a deceased person vests in an executor from the date of death of the deceased.[24] However, if the deceased dies intestate and a person takes adverse possession of estate land after that date, two features of intestacies must be noted: first, that persons entitled to a property on an intestacy take their interest jointly, and thus as trustees, and the rule contained in Sch 1, Pt I, para 9 on land held by trustees applies.[25] Secondly, s 26 of the LA 1980 provides that administration dates back to the date of death for limitation purposes as if there had been no interval between that time and the grant of letters of administration. This creates an exception to the rule that time does not run against an administrator of an estate until he is appointed.[26]

RIGHT OF DEPENDENT TO REASONABLE FINANCIAL PROVISION FROM DECEASED: INHERITANCE (PROVISION FOR FAMILY AND DEPENDENTS) ACT 1975

19.06 Section 2 of the Inheritance (Provision for Family and Dependents) Act 1975 provides a right to a dependent of a deceased person to apply to court for relief on grounds that the will of the deceased or their entitlements on an intestacy do not make sufficient provision for them. Section 4 of the Act states that an application under s 2 of the Act 'shall not, except with the permission of the court, be made after the end of the period of six months from the date on which representation with respect to the estate of the deceased is first taken out'. The statutory time limit was considered by Megarry J in *In re Salmon, decd*,[27] in a case where the widow of the deceased, from whom he had been separated for

22 See para 1.20.
23 *Prideaux v Webber* (1661) 1 Lev 31.
24 *Woolley v Clark* (1822) 5 B & Ald 744.
25 See *Earnshaw v Hartley* [2000] Ch 155 and paras 15.19–15.20.
26 *Atkinson v Bradford Third Equitable Building Society* (1890) 25 QBD 377 at 383, per Lopes LJ.
27 [1981] Ch 167.

many decades, had been left out of his will. While she instructed solicitors to act on her behalf and an application for legal aid was made within six months from when representation was taken out, no correspondence was sent intimating that a claim might be brought until four and a half months after the time limit had expired, and an application was brought one month later, the estate having been administered in the interim. Megarry J held that the onus lay on a claimant to establish sufficient grounds for taking the case out of the time limit; that all of the circumstances must be considered; including whether any negotiations had been commenced within the time limit, whether the estate had been distributed before any claim had been made or notified, and whether a refusal to extend time would leave the applicant without redress against anybody. He was plainly unimpressed by the reasons for the delay and commented that her solicitors might have a case to answer, and was influenced by the fact that the widow might only have a modest financial claim under the 1975 Act and refused to extend time.[28] An extension of time was granted in *Re W (a minor) (claim from deceased's estate)*,[29] where the eight-year-old illegitimate child of the deceased was blameless for the delay which had been caused by her mother's reluctance to become involved in litigation. Wilson J was clearly influenced by the fact that if an extension of time were to be refused, the infant would not have had any claim against the solicitors involved whereas it was conceded that the child would be entitled to substantial provision out of the estate, and in addition there had been no distributions out of the estate prior to the application being brought.

RECTIFICATION OF WILLS: ADMINISTRATION OF JUSTICE ACT 1982

19.07 Section 20 of the Administration of Justice Act 1982 ('AJA 1982') gives the court jurisdiction to rectify a will so as to carry out the testator's intentions, if it fails to carry these out in consequence of a clerical error or a failure to understand his instructions. Section 20(2) provides that an order under that section shall not, except with the permission of the court, be made after the end of the period of six months from the date on which representation with respect to the estate of the deceased was first taken out.[30] This statutory time limit was considered in *Chittock v Stevens*,[31] in a case where probate was granted on 2 October 1996 and the widow of the testator issued a writ on 22 July 1997 in which she sought to rectify the will of the deceased. The judgment records that this was the first case to have considered the effect of s 20(2) of the AJA 1982 and that counsel in the action agreed that the application to extend time was governed by the same factors as those considered relevant in an application to extend time under

28 An extension of time was also refused in *Escritt v Escritt* [1982] 3 FLR 280, in circumstances where a widow had been promptly informed of her rights and decided not to claim but then changed her mind and sued four years later.

29 [1995] 2 FCR 689, [1995] 2 FLR 24.

30 Section 20(4) states that, in deciding on when representation was first taken out, a grant limited to settled land or to trust property shall be left out of account, and a grant limited to real estate or to personal estate shall be left out of account unless a grant limited to the remainder of the estate has previously been made or is made at the same time.

31 [2000] All ER (D) 239, *Times Law Reports*, 5 April 2000.

the Inheritance (Provision for Family and Dependents) Act 1975.[32] This being the case, David Donaldson QC, sitting as a deputy High Court judge, granted an extension of time, as 'the delay was only a minor factor in the equation of justice' in this instance, in circumstances where the estate had not been administered, the beneficiaries did not know that the matrimonial home was in the sole name of the testator and as the mistake appeared reasonably clear to the extent that he commented that a claim would have arisen against the solicitors who had drafted the will. While this alternative remedy would have been open to the widow, it was held that this was only one factor to be considered and that it did not preclude the granting of an extension of time.

32 The judge adopted the approach set out in *In re Salmon, decd* [1981] Ch 167 and *Escritt v Escritt* [1982] 3 FLR 280.

PART VI

Miscellaneous Other Limitation Provisions

CHAPTER 20

Actions on a Specialty

THE HISTORICAL PERSPECTIVE

20.01 The word 'specialty' has been described as 'an archaic word of somewhat imprecise meaning'[1] which in modern usage covers deeds, contracts under seal and provisions in a statute.[2] It would appear that this dual meaning originates from the fact that, historically, a statute bore the Royal seal and was treated as 'the highest form of specialty'.[3] Universal, or near universal, literacy is a modern phenomenon. In the days before most people could sign their names, the usual way of authenticating a document was to 'seal' it by pouring molten wax on it and impressing one's crest or coat-of-arms on the wax.[4] No limitation period applied to contracts under seal until the passing of the Civil Procedure Act 1833, which imposed a 20-year limitation period. The limitation period for an action on a specialty was reduced to 12 years by the Limitation Act 1939. The longer limitation period for specialties recognises the additional level of formality involved in executing such contracts and its retention is justified to allow for situations where there is a risk that damage consequent upon a breach of contract will not become manifest until some years after the breach. The fact that a longer limitation period applies to an action arising under statute seeking non-monetary relief[5] than to an action seeking to recover a sum of money[6] due by virtue of an enactment is something of a historical anomaly which is not easy to justify in modern times.[7]

1 Franks, *Limitation of Actions* (London: Eastern Press Ltd, 1959) at 188.
2 See *Collin v Duke of Westminster* [1985] 1 QB 581 at 601–602, per Oliver LJ. *Halsbury's Laws of England* (5th edn, LexisNexis 2008) vol 68, para 976 also includes bonds and covenants within the definition of a 'specialty'.
3 *Central Electricity Board v Halifax Corporation* [1963] AC 785 at 799, per Lord Reid. See further *Cork and Bandon Rly Co v Goode* (1853) 13 CB 826 at 835, per Maule J and Oughton, Lowry and Merkin, *Limitation of Actions* (London: LLP Reference Publishing, 1998) at 212.
4 See *Stromdale & Ball Ltd v Burden* [1952] Ch 223 at 230, per Danckwerts J; *Santander UK Plc v Parker (No 2)* [2012] NICh 20.
5 LA 1980, s 8(1).
6 LA 1980, s 9(1).
7 See *Lievers v Barber, Walker & Co* [1943] 1 KB 385 at 397, per Goddard LJ.

THE LIMITATION PERIOD, THE MEANING OF 'SPECIALTY' AND THE RUNNING OF TIME

20.02 Section 8(1) of the Limitation Act 1980 ('LA 1980') provides that an action upon a specialty shall not be brought after the expiration of 12 years from the date on which the cause of action accrued, with s 8(2) adding that this shall not affect any action for which a shorter limitation period is prescribed by statute. The main actions on a specialty falling outside s 8(1) are actions to recover a sum recoverable by virtue of any enactment,[8] claims for contribution,[9] actions for rent arrears (or damages in respect of the arrears)[10] and actions for arrears of mortgage interest (irrespective of whether the lease or mortgage was created by deed).[11] Conversely, a statute might contain a declaration that a particular obligation takes effect as a specialty.[12] The absence of any obvious statutory limitation provision expressly stating that it applied to a non-monetary statutory claim led, until recently, to the occasional *dictum* to the effect that no limitation period applied to a particular statutory right of action.[13] However, the law in this regard is now relatively settled and, for example, in *Nolan v Wright*,[14] it was held that an application to reopen a loan as an extortionate credit bargain contrary to the Consumer Credit Act 1974 was an application upon a specialty.[15] More difficulty is still encountered where the right of action, although primarily aimed at a non-monetary result, also seeks monetary reliefs. This was the situation in *Hill v Spread Trustee Co Ltd*,[16] where a trustee in bankruptcy applied to set aside a transaction as having been entered into by the bankrupt at an undervalue. The Court of Appeal held that this was an action upon a specialty which was subject to a 12-year limitation period in respect of the primary relief sought, namely the setting aside of transactions.[17]

THE RUNNING OF TIME FOR AN ACTION ON A SPECIALTY

20.03 Despite there being a number of different classes of specialty, an action on a specialty is regarded as a type of contract action,[18] with the result that time

8 LA 1980, s 9(1).
9 LA 1980, s 10: see Ch 25.
10 LA 1980, s 19; *Romain v Scuba TV Ltd* [1997] QB 887.
11 LA 1980, s 20(5).
12 Companies Act 1985, s 14 (as enacted). However, s 33 of the Companies Act 2006 now provides that money payable by a member to the company is in the nature of an ordinary contract debt.
13 See *Halls v O'Dell* [1992] QB 393 at 405 (CA).
14 [2009] EWHC 305 (Ch), [2009] 3 All ER 823.
15 However, an action to recover sums already paid would be subject to the six-year period in s 9(1).
16 [2006] EWCA Civ 542, [2007] 1 WLR 2404. To similar effect is the judgment of John Randall QC in *Re Priory Garage (Walthamstow) Ltd* [2001] BPIR 144.
17 Arden LJ left open the issue of whether some aspects of the claim were primarily to recover money due by virtue of an enactment and thus subject to s 9(1): see [2007] 1 WLR 2404 at 2434.
18 Oughton, Lowry and Merkin, *Limitation of Actions* (London: LLP Reference Publishing, 1998) at 211.

will run from the date of breach. In *Nolan v Wright*,[19] this led to a finding that the time for the claimant to apply to set aside a loan as an extortionate credit bargain ran from the date of the loan. In *Hill v Spread Trustee Co Ltd*,[20] it was held that the limitation period for a trustee in bankruptcy to apply to set aside a transaction as having been entered into at an undervalue ran from the date of the bankruptcy, not the date of the transaction. Ordinary principles of contract law apply in relation to the running of time for actions on a specialty, including the issue of whether a demand on a guarantee is necessary for time to run,[21] whether a breach of covenant (eg a covenant to repair) is a continuing breach giving rise to a new cause of action each day[22] or a breach (eg to give good title) which gives rise to a single breach.[23] Another possibility arises in the case of a breach of a covenant of quiet enjoyment, where the breach only occurs when there is an interference with the purchaser's quiet enjoyment of the property.[24]

SEALING AN INSTRUMENT

20.04 It is not common for the full formality of sealing to occur in practice and, instead, a small red wafer is usually attached to a deed where execution under seal is intended.[25] Section 1(1)(b) of the Law of Property (Miscellaneous Provisions) Act 1989 now provides that a seal is no longer required for a deed executed by an individual, although it is still necessary for corporations sole and aggregate. In cases where a seal is still theoretically necessary, despite some *dicta* suggesting to the contrary,[26] it has been stated on a number of occasions that some mark or impression must be put on the deed 'even if only one caused by the end of a ruler'.[27] By way of exception to the need to use a seal at all, a circle enclosing the letters 'LS' (*locus sigilli*) was held to be sufficient in *First National Securities Ltd v Jones*[28] and no seal is required if a party is estopped from denying that an instrument was sealed.[29]

ACTION 'UPON' A SPECIALTY

20.05 Both contracts of service and debt obligations are capable of being 'specialties' and a claim on a specialty is not limited to a claim for specific

19 [2009] EWHC 305 (Ch), [2009] 3 All ER 823.
20 [2006] EWCA Civ 542, [2007] 1 WLR 2404.
21 *Re Brown's Estate, Brown v Brown* [1893] 2 Ch 300.
22 *Maddock v Mallet* (1860) 12 ICLR 173.
23 See *Bowling & Co Solicitors v Edehomo* [2011] EWHC 393 (Ch), [2011] 1 WLR 2217 for a discussion of some issues that can arise, in the context of a tort claim.
24 *Spoor v Green* (1874) LR 9 Exch 99.
25 The Law Commission in its Working Paper No 93, *Transfer of Land: Formalities for Deeds and Escrows* (1985) at para 42, described this practice as 'a meaningless exercise'.
26 See *Re Sandilands* (1871) LR 6 CP 411 at 413 per Bovill C.
27 *Re Smith* (1892) 67 LT 64.
28 [1978] Ch 109.
29 *Stromdale & Ball Ltd v Burden* [1952] Ch 223; *TCB Ltd v Gray* [1986] Ch 621; *Santander UK Plc v Parker (No 2)* [2012] NICh 20.

performance but also includes a claim for damages for breach of a contract which was created under seal.[30] However, an action will fall outside s 8(1) of the LA 1980 if the obligation is merely 'acknowledged or evidenced by an instrument under seal'.[31] For example, s 14 of the Companies Act 1985 stated that the memorandum and articles of association of a company bound the members as if signed and sealed by each member.[32] In *Re Compania de Electricidad de la Provincia de Buenos Aires Ltd*,[33] Slade J held that a six-year limitation period applied to an action brought against the company for the payment of monies due to a member as dividends or the return of capital. He held that while the share certificate evidenced title to the shares to which it related, it did not create or secure any debt. Accordingly, the action for unclaimed dividends and unclaimed capital was not an 'action upon a speciality' and the six-year limitation period applied.

30 *Aiken v Stewart Wrightson Members' Agency Ltd* [1995] 1 WLR 1281.

31 See *In re Compania de Electricidad de la Provincia de Buenos Aires Ltd* [1980] Ch 142 at 186, per Slade J.

32 Companies Act 2006, s 33 now provides that the obligation of the members is in the nature of a contract debt in this circumstance.

33 [1980] Ch 142 at 186. See *contra Re Artisans' Land and Mortgage Corp* [1904] 1 Ch 796 and *Smith v Cork and Bandon Railway Co* (1870) IR 5 Eq 65.

CHAPTER 21

Actions to Recover Any Sum Recoverable by Virtue of Any Enactment

INTRODUCTION

21.01 Section 9(1) of the Limitation Act 1980 ('LA 1980') provides that an action to recover any sum recoverable by virtue of any enactment is subject to a six-year limitation period. Excluded from this six-year period by s 9(2) are claims for contribution, for which a two-year limitation period is prescribed by s 10(1) of the LA 1980. This six-year limitation period was first introduced by the Limitation Act 1939[1] as an exception to the 12-year limitation period for actions upon a specialty, all actions on a statute having theretofore been considered actions on a specialty.[2] The word 'action' is given a broad definition in the LA 1980 and 'includes any proceeding in a court of law, including an ecclesiastical court'[3] and in *China v Harrow Urban District Council*[4] it was held to include the issuing of a distress warrant to recover arrears of rates. Certain sums are declared by statute to be specialty debts[5] or simple contract debts,[6] although in the latter case the limitation period is unaffected by their re-designation.

'SUM' OF MONEY RECOVERABLE

21.02 Section 9(1) refers to a 'sum' recoverable by statute. This has the effect that this limitation period only applies if a money claim is created by statute. For example, in *Collin v Duke of Westminster*,[7] it was held that the right of a

1 Section 2(1)(d).
2 The history of the phrase 'action on a specialty' is discussed in para 20.01; see further *Cork and Bandon Rly Co v Goode* (1853) 13 CB 826 at 835 and *Lievers v Barber, Walker & Co* [1943] 1 KB 385 at 397.
3 LA 1980, s 38(1).
4 [1954] 1 QB 178.
5 See eg the Insolvency Act 1986, s 80 (as enacted) and the Companies Act 1985, s 14 (as enacted), the predecessor to the latter of which was discussed in *Re Compania de Electricidad de la Provincia de Buenos Aires Ltd* [1980] Ch 142. The Companies Act 1985, s 14 has since been replaced by the Companies Act 2006, s 33 which provides that money payable by a member to the company is in the nature of an ordinary contract debt.
6 See eg the Land Registration Act 2002, Sch 8, para 8(a) and the Companies Act 2006, s 33.
7 [1985] QB 581.

tenant to purchase his landlord's interest falls outside the scope of s 9(1). In *Child Maintenance and Enforcement Commission v Mitchell*,[8] an application to commit the defendant to prison for failure to pay ordered[9] child maintenance was held by the Court of Appeal not to be an action to recover a sum of money, notwithstanding the fact that a payment would likely be tendered to avoid the unpleasant consequences of non-payment.

21.03 In *Bolsover DC v Ashfield Nominees Ltd*,[10] a winding up petition based on a council tax liability order was held not to constitute an action to recover a sum of money recoverable under an enactment, which is in line with the treatment by the courts of winding up petitions as being a *sui generis* procedure for winding up insolvent companies and not a form of action upon a judgment for the purposes of s 24(1) of the LA 1980.[11] However, the underlying council tax liability is a sum due by virtue of an enactment and the council must commence civil proceedings or an application for a council tax liability order within six years of the sum falling due or the debt will be statute barred by virtue of s 9(1).[12]

21.04 The 'sum' which is recoverable can include unliquidated damages which have to be assessed by the court. In *Re Farmizer (Products) Ltd*,[13] wrongful trading proceedings were brought by a liquidator against the directors of an insolvent company, in which a contribution towards the losses suffered by the company was claimed. It was held that this action was for a sum recoverable under statute. Similarly, in *Hillingdon London Borough Council v ARC Ltd*,[14] it was held that the right to claim compensation for lands which had been compulsorily acquired was a right to claim a sum recoverable under statute.

CAUSE OF ACTION ARISING 'BY VIRTUE OF' ANY ENACTMENT

21.05 For an action to be governed by s 9(1), it must be a type of action which could not be brought in the absence of the statutory provision. Thus, if the statute merely implies obligations into a contract (such as under the Sale of Goods Act 1979), the limitation period applicable to an action for breach of contract will apply.[15] By way of contrast, where the statute creates the contractual situation

8 [2010] EWCA Civ 333, [2010] 2 FCR 526. It was also held not to constitute an action upon a judgment.
9 An application for a child maintenance liability order was once expressly governed by a six-year time limit, which period ran from the date the payment fell due. The Court of Appeal refrained from commenting on whether an application for a liability order is now governed by s 9(1), although this would appear to be the case.
10 [2010] EWCA Civ 1129, [2011] 2 BCLC 42.
11 See *Ridgeway Motors (Isleworth) Ltd v ALTS Ltd* [2005] EWCA Civ 92, [2005] 1 WLR 2871, discussed in para 4.15
12 *Re Karnos Property Co Ltd* [1989] BCLC 340.
13 [1997] 1 BCLC 589.
14 [1998] 3 WLR 754.
15 *Aylott v West Ham Corporation* [1927] 1 Ch 30; *Gutsell v Reeve* [1936] 1 KB 272.

between the parties, the action will be classified as a claim on the statute.[16] In the case of a statute which imposes a duty but gives no remedy for its breach, an action for breach of statutory duty is a tort to which the tort limitation period will apply.[17] However, if the statutory provision provides the direct source of the obligation to pay the compensation, such as in the case of proceedings seeking compensation for reckless or fraudulent trading,[18] the proceedings will be governed by s 9(1). The dividing line may sometimes prove hard to identify, and will in most cases be a distinction without a difference as a six-year limitation period applies to claims governed by each of ss 2, 5 and 9(1). For example, in *Green v Eadie*[19] it was held by Mark Cawson QC sitting as a High Court judge that a claim for damages under s 2(1) of the Misrepresentation Act 1967 was subject to the tort limitation period in s 2 and not that contained in s 9(1) on grounds that the wrong created by the 1967 Act 'can properly be regarded as a statutory extension of the law of deceit'.[20]

ACCRUAL OF THE CAUSE OF ACTION

21.06 The date of accrual of a cause of action arising under statute will depend on the wording of the statute in question. If a cause of action vests in a liquidator or assignee in bankruptcy, it will be a question of construction as to whether the cause of action accrued prior to their appointment or only upon their appointment, notwithstanding the fact that the events giving rise to the claim occurred some time previously.[21] Difficulties may arise in cases where the statute requires a complaint to be referred at first instance to a particular official for determination or where a notice must be served prior to the bringing of proceedings. The question will then arise as to whether this requirement is a constituent element of the cause of action or whether it is merely a procedural condition precedent which does not affect the running of time from the date of the occurrence of the facts giving rise to the notice or referral.[22] In *Central Electricity Board v Halifax Corporation*,[23] a dispute arose as to the ownership of a fund of money which it was alleged should have been transferred to the claimant following the nation-

16 *The Cork and Bandon Railway Co v Goode* (1853) 13 CB 826, 138 ER 1427; *Re Cornwall Minerals Railway Co* [1897] 2 Ch 74; and *Pratt v Cook, Son & Co (St Paul's Ltd)* [1940] AC 437.

17 A claim for patent infringement was classified as a tort in *Sevcon Ltd v Lucas CAV Ltd* [1986] 1 WLR 462, although for criticism of this decision see McGee, 'Patent Nonsense' (1986) 49 MLR 650.

18 *Re Farmizer (Products) Ltd* [1997] 1 BCLC 589. The position is otherwise if reliance on the Companies Act is merely procedural and does not create the cause of action: see *Re Eurocruit Europe Ltd (in liquidation)* [2007] EWHC 1433 (Ch), [2007] All ER (D) 229 (Jun).

19 [2011] EWHC B24 (Ch), [2012] Ch 363.

20 [2011] EWHC B24 (Ch), [2012] Ch 363 at para 35.

21 See *Re Farmizer (Products) Ltd* [1997] 1 BCLC 589; *Re Yates (A Bankrupt)* [2005] BPIR 476; and *Re Eurocruit Europe Ltd (in liquidation)* [2007] EWHC 1433 (Ch), [2007] All ER (D) 229 (Jun).

22 See *Jarvis v Surrey County Council* [1925] 1 KB 554 and *Legal Services Commission v Henthorn* [2011] EWCA Civ 1415, [2012] 2 All ER 439.

23 [1963] AC 785.

alisation of the electricity industry by the Electricity Act 1947. Notwithstanding the fact that this Act imposed an obligation to refer all disputes to the Minister of Health (who had decided the dispute in favour of the claimant), the House of Lords held that the cause of action accrued on the date from which the defendant had wrongfully retained the money. In *Hillingdon London Borough Council v ARC Ltd*,[24] it was held that the limitation period for a landowner to claim compensation for lands compulsorily acquired ran from the date on which the council had acquired the lands, and not the date on which the amount of compensation had been assessed or agreed. In *R (on the application of Sutherland) v Secretary of State for Work and Pensions*,[25] it was held that a cause of action to recover child support ran from the date of assessment of the sum to be paid. Fine distinctions are frequently drawn in this area and it is instructive to compare *Legal Services Commission v Rasool*,[26] where the right to recover costs after a legal aid certificate was revoked was held to have accrued on date of revocation and not the date on which the costs were taxed, with *Legal Services Commission v Henthorn*,[27] where the claimant's cause of action to recover sums overpaid to a barrister on account of legal aid work was held to have accrued only when the assessment of the sums due had been completed.

24 [1998] 3 WLR 754; see also *Halstead v Manchester City Council* [1998] 1 All ER 33 and *West Riding County Council v Huddersfield Corporation* [1957] 1 QB 540.

25 [2004] EWHC 800 (Admin), [2004] All ER (D) 492 (Mar); see also *Regentford v Thanet District Council* [2004] EWHC 246 (Admin), *The Times*, 4 March 2000, where it was held that the right to sue on an assessment of liability to council tax accrues on the date of demand.

26 [2008] EWCA Civ 154, [2008] 3 All ER 381.

27 [2011] EWCA Civ 1415, [2012] 2 All ER 439.

CHAPTER 22

Admiralty Actions and the Carriage Statutes

INTRODUCTION

22.01 The Merchant Shipping Act 1995 ('MSA 1995') contains the limitation provisions for admiralty (or maritime) claims, which are considered in this chapter together with the collection of Acts of Parliament, International Conventions and European Regulations that govern the international carriage of passengers and goods (including luggage) by sea, air, road and rail. While these provisions ('the Carriage Statutes') were initially only applicable in cases of international carriage, with the expansion of European law, domestic transport is increasingly governed by the same rules. These provisions contain a variety of limitation periods, several of which are shorter than the equivalent provisions in the Limitation Act 1980 ('LA 1980'), so care should be taken when advising on issues relating to the carriage of persons and goods.

ADMIRALTY ACTIONS

Limitation provisions in the MSA 1995

22.02 Section 190 of the MSA 1995 (which replaced s 8 of the Maritime Conventions Act 1911[1]) provides for a general limitation period of two years for all claims in respect of damage to or loss of a ship, her cargo or freight or property on board, and for damages for loss of life or personal injuries suffered by any person on board,[2] caused by the fault of another ship. In *Gold Shipping Navigation Co SA v Lulu Maritime Ltd*,[3] it was held that this two-year period also applies to counterclaims. This limitation period may be extended by the court pursuant to a general discretion,[4] or on mandatory terms if satisfied that there has not, during the period, been a reasonable opportunity of arresting the defendant ship within the jurisdiction of the court, or within the territorial waters of

1 1 & 2 Geo 5, c 57.
2 Personal injuries claims by passengers are subject to the two-year limitation period contained in the Athens Convention, art 16(1): see MSA 1995, s 183, discussed in para 22.06 et seq.
3 [2009] EWHC 1365 (Admiralty), [2010] 2 All ER (Comm) 64.
4 MSA 1995, s 190(5): see para 22.04.

the country to which the claimant ship belongs or in which the claimant resides or has his principal place of business.[5] Where this two-year limitation period applies, including to a claim for personal injuries or fatal injuries, the LA 1980 has no application to the claim.[6]

Types of vessel and accident governed by s 190 of the MSA 1995

22.03 Section 190 of the MSA 1995 only applies in respect of damage to a ship, to cargo or freight on board, or to personal injuries suffered by persons on board, caused by the 'fault of another ship'. The case law on s 8 of the Maritime Conventions Act 1911 continues to be relevant and, for example, in *Curtis v Wild*,[7] it was held that a sailing dinghy used for pleasure purposes was not a vessel used in navigation and thus a personal injuries action arising out of a collision between dinghies was subject to the three-year limitation period in s 11 of the LA 1980. Similarly, in *Steedman v Scolfeld*,[8] it was held that a jet-ski is not a vessel within the meaning of this provision. Only accidents caused by the fault of another ship are governed by the section and in *The Niceto de Larrinaga*,[9] it was held that if an accident on board a ship was caused by the owners of that ship and not a collision with another ship it is governed by the ordinary limitation provisions and not what is now s 190 of the MSA 1995.

Principles on which discretion to extend time is exercised

22.04 The rule allowing an extension of time if there was not a reasonable opportunity to arrest the ship during the two-year limitation period requires a claimant to prove that he comes within the section. The general discretion to extend time in s 190 of the MSA 1995 has been the subject of much case law and the leading case is *The Al Tabith and The Alanfushi*,[10] where the Court of Appeal held that, in deciding on an application to extend time, the court must first consider whether good reason for the extension has been demonstrated by the claimant, and only then should it proceed to exercise its discretion by taking into account the balance of hardship as between the parties. Something more than mere oversight must be established to gain an extension of time.[11] Matters which have been found to justify an extension of time being granted include where correspondence from the defendant induced the claimant to delay while awaiting settlement of liability.[12]

5 MSA 1995, s 190(6). The Crown Proceedings Act 1947, s 30 states that s 190(6) does not apply to the Crown.

6 LA 1980, s 39; *The Caliph* [1912] P 213; *The Alnwick* [1965] P 357, [1965] 2 All ER 569.

7 [1991] 4 All ER 172.

8 [1992] 2 Lloyd's Rep 163.

9 [1966] P 80, [1965] 2 All ER 930; see also *The Norwhale* [1975] QB 589.

10 [1995] 2 Lloyd's Rep 336 (CA).

11 *The Al Tabith and The Alanfushi* [1995] 2 Lloyd's Rep 336.

12 *The Vadne* [1959] 2 Lloyd's Rep 480; see further the cases discussed in McGee, *Limitation Periods* (6th edn, London: Sweet & Maxwell, 2010) at 533–536.

Salvage claims

22.05 Salvage claims were formerly governed by s 8 of the Maritime Conventions Act 1911, but s 224 of the MSA 1995 now provides that such claims are governed by the Salvage Convention,[13] which is set out as Sch 11 to the MSA 1995. It provides a limitation period for a salvage claim of two years commencing on the date on which the salvage operations are terminated.[14] This period may be extended by the defendant making a declaration to the claimant to this effect.[15] A claim for indemnity by a person liable may be instituted even after the expiration of the limitation period so provided, if brought within the time allowed by the law of the state where proceedings are instituted.[16]

CARRIAGE OF PASSENGERS AND LUGGAGE BY SEA

22.06 The Convention relating to the Carriage of Passengers and their Luggage by Sea ('the Athens Convention') applies to any contract for the carriage of passengers[17] and their luggage by sea[18] and has force of law in England by virtue of s 183 of the MSA 1995.[19] For contracts having a European element, this has now been superseded by Regulation 392/2009 on the liability of carriers of passengers by sea in the event of accidents,[20] which incorporates the Athens Convention into European Union law, together with the 1976 and 2002 Protocols to the Convention.[21] Annex 1 of Regulation 392/2009 contains the consolidated text of the Athens Convention 1974 and the later protocols. Article 16(1) imposes a time limit of *two years* for a party to bring a claim for damages for personal injuries or for loss or damage to luggage. Article 16(2) states that the limitation period shall be calculated as follows:

(a) in the case of personal injury, from the date of disembarkation of the passenger;

(b) in the case of death occurring during carriage, from the date when the passenger should have disembarked, and in the case of personal injury occurring during carriage and resulting in the death of the passenger after disembarkation, from the date of death, provided that this period shall not exceed three years from the date of disembarkation; and

13 International Convention on Salvage (London, 28 April 1989); Cmnd 1526.
14 Salvage Convention, art 23(1).
15 Salvage Convention, art 23(2).
16 Salvage Convention, art 23(3).
17 Article 1(4) defines 'passenger' as 'any person carried in a ship, (a) under a contract of carriage; or (b) who, with the consent of the carrier, is accompanying a vehicle or live animals which are covered by a contract for the carriage of goods not governed by this Convention'.
18 For a more detailed discussion of the contracts covered by the Athens Convention, see Hill, *Maritime Law* (6th edn, London: Informa Publishing, 2003) at 450–451.
19 It had originally been incorporated into English law by the Merchant Shipping Act 1979.
20 Official Journal of the European Union on 28 May 2009: OJ L131/24.
21 It was implemented into English law by the Merchant Shipping (Carriage of Passengers by Sea) Regulations 2012 (SI 2012/3152).

(c) in the case of loss of or damage to luggage, from the date of disembarkation or from the date when disembarkation should have taken place, whichever is later.

22.07 Article 16(3) provides that 'the law of the court seized of the case shall govern the grounds for suspension and interruption of limitation periods', but that in no case shall an action under this Convention be brought after the expiration of any one of the following periods of time:

(a) a period of five years beginning with the date of disembarkation of the passenger or from the date when disembarkation should have taken place, whichever is later; or, if earlier,

(b) a period of three years beginning with the date when the claimant knew or ought reasonably to have known of the injury, loss or damage caused by the incident.

22.08 A final provision dealing with time limits is art 16(4), which states that the period of limitation may be extended by a declaration of the carrier or by agreement of the parties after the cause of action has arisen. However, in *Higham v Stena Sealink Ltd*,[22] it was held that art 16 does not leave the court with a residual discretion to disapply the personal injuries limitation period under s 33 of the LA 1980.

BILLS OF LADING AND THE HAGUE-VISBY RULES

22.09 The Hague-Visby Rules, which govern the international carriage of goods by sea in relation to the loading, handling, stowage, carriage, custody, care and discharge of goods from the time of loading to discharge,[23] were incorporated into English law by the Carriage of Goods by Sea Act 1971.[24] Article III, r 6 provides that an action for loss or damage to cargo must be brought within one year of their delivery[25] or the date when they should have been delivered. If a suit is not brought within that period, the carrier and the ship are discharged from all liability whatsoever in respect of the goods.[26] This period may be extended if the parties so agree, after the cause of action has arisen. In *The Stolt Loyalty*,[27] an

22 [1996] 3 All ER 660 (CA).

23 The Rules do not cover actions for hire or freight, and the loss must be loss or damage which is related to the cargo owner's goods. Nor do the Rules apply to charterparties (see Hague-Visby Rules, art V), but it is open to the parties to incorporate the Rules into a charterparty by inserting a Clause Paramount.

24 The UNCITRAL Convention on Contracts for the International Carriage of Goods Wholly or Partly by Sea 2008, more commonly known as the 'Rotterdam Rules', will replace the earlier Conventions if incorporated into English law.

25 See *Trafigura Beheer BV v Golden Stavraetos Maritime Inc; The Sonia* [2003] EWCA Civ 664, [2003] 4 All ER 746.

26 Article III, r 6; in *Aries Tanker Corporation v Total Transport Ltd* [1977] 1 WLR 185, it was held by the House of Lords that the expiry of this limitation period bars both the right and the remedy and that the claim can no longer be raised even by way of set off or counterclaim.

27 [1995] 1 Lloyd's Rep 598.

extension of time arose in circumstances where the court held that the defendant was estopped from objecting to the extension of time. Article III, r 6 *bis* provides that an action for indemnity against a third party may be brought despite the expiration of the period of one year referred to above, provided that it is brought within the time allowed by the law of the court seized of the case.[28]

22.10 The rules are capable of operating particularly inflexibly in several circumstances; actions brought by the wrong claimant,[29] brought against the wrong defendant (following a change in ownership of the vessel),[30] or brought in breach of an arbitration clause[31] have all been found not to constitute the 'bringing' of an 'action' within the meaning of Article III, r 6. By contrast, in *The Nordglimt*,[32] it was held by Hobhouse J that the bringing of proceedings before the courts of Belgium (which had jurisdiction to hear those proceedings) was sufficient to stop the running of time for any further proceedings that were brought between the parties in England. Similarly, in *Transpetrol Ltd v Ekali Shipping Company Ltd ('The Aghia Marina')*,[33] it was held that the nomination of an arbitrator, who initially accepted but subsequently had to decline his appointment, was sufficient to constitute the bringing of a suit. In cases governed by the Hamburg Rules,[34] the applicable limitation period is two years from the date of delivery of the goods or the date when they should have been delivered. If a bill of lading provides for a shorter limitation period than that contained in the Hague-Visby Rules, it is a matter of construction as to which time limit takes precedence.[35]

CARRIAGE BY AIR

22.11 The Carriage by Air Act 1961 (the 'CAA 1961'), as amended,[36] incorporates into English law the Warsaw Convention 1929 and the Montreal Convention 1999[37] on international air transport. It was held by the House of Lords in *Sidhu*

28 See Ch 25; see also *China Ocean Shipping Co v Andros* [1987] 1 WLR 1213.

29 *Transworld Oil (USA) Inc v Minos Compania Naviera SA ('The Leni')* [1992] 2 Lloyd's Rep 48.

30 *The Jay Bola* [1992] 2 Lloyd's Rep 62.

31 *Thyssen Inc v Calypso Shipping Corp SA* [2000] 2 Lloyd's Rep 243.

32 [1988] QB 183. However, the decision in *The Nordglimt* was overruled by the House of Lords in *Republic of India v India Steamship Co Ltd (No 2)* [1998] AC 878 on abuse of process grounds, leaving the point referred to in the text somewhat circumscribed in its utility.

33 [1989] 1 Lloyd's Rep 62.

34 See the United Nations Convention on the Carriage of Goods by Sea, adopted in Hamburg on 31 March 1978 ('The Hamburg Rules'); although not incorporated into English law, the Hamburg Rules may still apply by agreement or where foreign law governs the dispute.

35 *Finagra (UK) Ltd v OT Africa Line Ltd* [1998] 2 Lloyd's Rep 622.

36 In particular by the Carriage by Air Acts (Implementation of the Montreal Convention 1999) Order 2002 (SI 2002/263). Similar provisions are contained in the Carriage by Air Act (Application of Provisions) Order 2004 (SI 2004/1899) for cases where the CAA 1961 and EU legislation does not apply.

37 The Montreal Convention 1999 was already in force for all European airlines and their passengers through Council Regulation (EC) No 2027/1997 as amended by Council Regulation (EC) No 889/2002 prior to the amendment to the CAA 1961.

v British Airways Plc[38] that the Warsaw (now Montreal) Convention provides an exclusive cause of action in respect of actions for personal injury, damage, delay or loss arising out of the international carriage of passengers, cargo and baggage by air. In *Laroche v Spirit of Adventure (UK) Ltd*,[39] the claimant was a passenger in a domestic hot air balloon flight which crashed causing injury. His personal injuries action was held to be subject to the two-year limitation period in art 29 of the Warsaw Convention.

22.12 The Montreal Convention 1999 (which is included as Sch 1B to the CAA 1961) imposes time limits in relation to the notification of complaints and the bringing of actions against carriers, as follows:

(i) Notification of complaints

In the case of damage to baggage, the person entitled to delivery must complain to the carrier within seven days from the date of receipt of the baggage, or 14 days from the date of receipt of cargo.[40] In the case of delay, the complaint must be made at the latest within 21 days from the date on which the baggage or cargo was returned.[41] If no complaint is made within the above-listed times, 'no action shall lie against the carrier, save in the case of fraud on its part'.[42]

(ii) Limitation period

Article 35 of the Montreal Convention 1999[43] provides that the limitation period for bringing a claim for compensation under the Convention is two years from the date of accrual of the cause of action.[44] The date of accrual of the cause of action is stated to be 'the date of arrival at the destination, or from the date on which the aircraft ought to have arrived, or from the date on which the carriage stopped'.[45]

22.13 A number of features of the above provisions are noteworthy. First, art 29 provides that the claimant's right to damages is extinguished upon the expiration of the two-year limitation period. This is in common with several other carriage statutes but is different to ordinary tort actions, where the expiry of a limitation period merely bars the remedy and a limitation defence must be

38 [1997] AC 430.

39 [2009] EWCA Civ 12, [2009] QB 778; see also *Hall v Heart of England Balloons Ltd* [2010] 1 Lloyd's Rep 373, where leave to amend to substitute the correct defendant outside the two-year time limit was refused.

40 Article 31(2).

41 Article 31(2).

42 Article 31(4).

43 This provision replicates the time limit contained in the Warsaw Convention 1929, art 29, which is included as the CAA 1961, Sch 1.

44 The Warsaw and Montreal Conventions have been held not to apply to third party actions: see Goldhirsch, *The Warsaw Convention Annotated: A Legal Handbook* (The Hague: Kluwer Law International, 2000) 190–192; at 199 the same author notes that carriers have been held to be estopped from relying on the limitation period in certain cases.

45 Montreal Convention 1999, art 35; see further Goldhirsch, *The Warsaw Convention Annotated: A Legal Handbook* (The Hague: Kluwer Law International, 2000) 194–196.

specifically pleaded. Secondly, neither the Montreal Convention 1999 nor its predecessors makes any reference to the claimant being able to rely on the fact that he was under a legal disability to extend the limitation period or to whether a discoverability test applies in any circumstances or to whether s 33 of the LA 1980 has any application.[46] In light of *Sidhu v British Airways Plc*,[47] it is submitted that a claimant is not entitled to the benefit of an extended limitation period on any of these grounds. While a complaint must be made within the short time limits listed above for claims relating to baggage, this does not obviate the need to bring proceedings if no satisfactory response is received and it would appear that the making of a complaint does not affect the running of time for the bringing of proceedings.

CARRIAGE OF GOODS BY ROAD

22.14 The Carriage of Goods by Road Act 1965 incorporates into English law the Convention on the Contract for the International Carriage of Goods by Road (the 'CMR').[48] It applies to every contract for the carriage of goods by road in vehicles for reward where the place of taking over of the goods and the place designated for delivery (as specified in the contract) are situated in different countries, of which at least one is a party to the Convention.[49] Any stipulation in a contract which derogates from the provisions of the Convention is null and void.[50] The date from which time runs depends on the nature of the claim. Article 32 states that the day on which the period of limitation begins to run shall not be included in the period, and continues by stating that time begins to run:

(a) in the case of partial loss, damage or delay in delivery, from the date of delivery;

(b) in the case of total loss, from the thirtieth day after the expiry of the agreed time for delivery or, where there is no agreed time, from the sixtieth day from the date on which the goods were taken over by the carrier; and

(c) in all other cases, on the expiry of a period of three months after the making of the contract of carriage.

22.15 The limitation period for an action arising out of carriage under the CMR is one year.[51] In cases of 'wilful misconduct',[52] which would appear to include

46 See Goldhirsch, *The Warsaw Convention Annotated: A Legal Handbook* (The Hague: Kluwer Law International, 2000) at 197–198, for a discussion of the case law from international jurisdictions.

47 [1997] AC 430.

48 Convention on the Contract for the International Carriage of Goods by Road signed at Geneva on 19 May 1956, as amended by the Protocol signed at Geneva on 5 July 1978; see Wetter, 'The time-bar regulations in the CMR Convention' [1979] LMCLQ 504.

49 It does not apply to traffic between the United Kingdom and the Republic of Ireland: see the Protocol to the Convention.

50 Article 41(1).

51 Article 32(1).

52 See *Laceys Footwear (Wholesale) Ltd v Bowler International Freight Ltd* [1997] 2 Lloyd's Rep 369 (CA).

fraud and concealment,[53] an action must be brought within three years.[54] A written claim suspends the period of limitation until such date as the carrier rejects the claim by notification in writing and returns the documents attached thereto.[55] If part of a claim is admitted, the period of limitation shall start to run again only in respect of that part of the claim still in dispute. The burden of proof of the receipt of the claim, or of the reply and of the return of the documents, shall rest with the party relying upon these facts. Article 32(3) provides that, subject to the rules on suspension of the running of time following the making of a complaint,[56] the extension of the period of limitation shall be governed by the law of the court or tribunal seized of the case. This would to appear to incorporate by reference the provisions in the LA 1980 dealing with disability, acknowledgment, part payment and mistake. Although the Convention does not state whether the expiry of the limitation period bars the right or merely the remedy, art 32(4) provides that a right of action which has become barred by lapse of time may not be exercised by way of counterclaim or set-off.

22.16 An extended period of limitation applies in relation to claims 'between carriers'.[57] In essence, this provision covers contribution actions where the carrier who contracted to carry the goods sub-contracts the actual carriage (or some of it) to the performing carrier, who is alleged to be responsible for the loss. It provides that in such a case, although the period of limitation is still governed by art 32, time will not begin to run until:

> '[T]he date of the final judicial decision fixing the amount of compensation payable under the provisions of this Convention, or, if there is no such judicial decision, from the actual date of payment.'

This provision was considered in *Ulster Swift Ltd v Taunton Meat Haulage Ltd*,[58] where the Court of Appeal held that the claimant was still a 'carrier' even though it had sub-contracted all of the carriage to other parties, as it had contracted to perform the carriage.

CARRIAGE BY RAIL

22.17 The liability of railway operators arising in the course of carriage by rail is governed by the Convention concerning International Carriage by Rail (the 'COTIF Convention'), which is incorporated into English law by the Railways (Convention on International Carriage by Rail) Regulations 2005[59] and into

53 McGee, *Limitation Periods* (6th edn, London: Sweet & Maxwell, 2010) at para 26.020.
54 Article 32(1).
55 Article 32(2); see *ICI Fibres Ltd v MAT Transport Ltd* [1987] 1 Lloyd's Rep 354.
56 Article 32(2).
57 Article 39(4).
58 [1977] 1 Lloyd's Rep 346.
59 SI 2005/2092. The 2005 Regulations repealed the International Transport Conventions Act 1983, ss 1–8, which had formerly incorporated the COTIF into English law.

European Union law by Regulation 1371/2007[60] on rail passengers' rights and obligations.[61] The rules governing the carriage of passengers by rail are contained in the 'CIV Convention', which is contained in Appendix A to the COTIF Convention, and the rules governing the carriage of goods are contained in the 'CIM Convention', which is Appendix B to the COTIF Convention. The provisions on limitation take two forms in the Regulation: notification requirements and limitation periods proper.

Notification requirements in cases of death or personal injury

22.18 Article 58(1) of the CIV Convention provides that any right of action in the case of death or personal injury to a passenger shall be extinguished if notice of the accident is not given to one of the carriers to whom a claim may be addressed within 12 months of becoming aware of the loss or damage.[62] The right of action is not extinguished if, within the period of 12 months, the carrier who is liable became aware of the accident to the passenger in some other way;[63] if notice of the accident was not given, or was given late, as a result of circumstances not attributable to the person entitled;[64] or if the person entitled proves that the accident was caused by fault on the part of the carrier.[65]

Extinction of right of action arising from carriage of luggage

22.19 The general rule set out in art 59 of the CIV Convention provides that the acceptance of luggage by the person entitled shall extinguish all rights of action against the carrier arising from the contract of carriage in case of partial loss, damage or delay in delivery. However, the right of action is not extinguished:

(a) in case of partial loss or damage, if the loss or damage was ascertained in accordance with art 54 before the acceptance of the luggage by the person entitled, and the ascertainment which should have been carried out in accordance with art 54 was omitted solely through the fault of the carrier;

(b) in case of loss or damage which is not apparent whose existence is ascertained after acceptance of the luggage by the person entitled, if he asks for ascertainment in accordance with art 54 immediately after discovery of the loss or damage and not later than three days after the acceptance of the luggage, and, in addition, proves that the loss or damage occurred between the time of taking over by the carrier and the time of delivery;

60 The Regulation came into force on 3 December 2009.

61 SI 2970/2009 has exempted domestic British rail services from the provisions of Regulation 1371/2007 until 3 December 2014 at the earliest.

62 Article 58(1) of the Convention also provides that where the person entitled gives oral notice of the accident to the carrier, the carrier shall furnish him with an acknowledgment of such oral notice.

63 Article 58(2)(b).

64 Article 58(2)(c).

65 Article 58(2)(d).

(c) in case of delay in delivery, if the person entitled has, within 21 days, asserted his rights against one of the carriers specified in art 56(3); or

(d) if the person entitled proves that the loss or damage was caused by fault on the part of the carrier.

Limitation of actions

22.20 Article 60(1) of the CIV Convention provides that the limitation period for actions for damages based on the liability of the carrier in case of death of, or personal injury to, passengers shall be:

(a) in the case of a passenger, three years from the day after the accident; and

(b) in the case of other persons entitled to bring an action, three years from the day after the death of the passenger, subject to a maximum of five years from the day after the accident.

22.21 Article 60(2) states that the period of limitation for other actions arising from the contract of carriage shall be one year. A limitation period of two years applies in the case of actions for loss or damage resulting from an act or omission committed either with the intent to cause such loss or damage, or recklessly and with knowledge that such loss or damage would probably result. The day indicated for the commencement of the period of limitation is not included in the time period[66] and the suspension and interruption of periods of limitation shall be governed by national law.[67] The period of limitation set out in art 60(2) runs from the following dates:

(a) for compensation for total loss, from the fourteenth day after the expiry of the period of time provided for in art 22(3);[68]

(b) for compensation for partial loss, damage or delay in delivery, from the day when delivery took place;[69] and

(c) in all other cases involving the carriage of passengers, from the day of expiry of validity of the ticket.[70]

66 Article 60(3).
67 Article 60(6).
68 Article 60(3)(a).
69 Article 60(3)(b).
70 Article 60(3)(c).

CHAPTER 23

Arbitration, Mediation and Adjudication

23.01 The Arbitration Act 1996 ('AA 1996') contains the limitation provisions that govern arbitrations.[1] Its starting point is that the Limitation Act 1980 ('LA 1980') and other Limitation Acts apply to arbitral proceedings as they apply to proceedings before a court.[2] While arbitration clauses sometimes state that an award is a condition precedent to the bringing of legal proceedings, s 13(3) of the AA 1996 states that any clause of this nature shall be disregarded when determining when a cause of action accrued for limitation purposes. Accordingly, a defendant may plead a limitation defence in a dispute which is heard before an arbitrator. If proceedings are brought in breach of an arbitration clause, which are then struck out or abandoned and an arbitration commenced, time will continue to run until the arbitration is validly commenced, as the issue 'is whether the action before the court, and not some other action, has been instituted within the relevant limitation period'.[3] Other forms of alternative dispute resolution are also available to litigants, such as adjudication and expert determination, and limitation issues arising in those contexts are also considered in this chapter. Although generally the participation of parties in a mediation will have no effect on the running of the limitation period, this will not be the position for mediations governed by the Cross-Border Mediation (EU Directive) Regulations 2011,[4] whose effect on the limitation period for the underlying dispute is considered at the end of the chapter.

COMMENCEMENT OF ARBITRATION

23.02 The limitation period for a right of action litigated in arbitral proceedings only ceases to run when there is a valid commencement of the arbitration.

1 AA 1996, Sch 4 repealed LA 1980, s 34 (which dealt with arbitral proceedings) for any arbitration commenced after 31 January 1997.
2 AA 1996, s 13(1).
3 *Cia Colombiana de Seguros v Pacific Steam Navigation Co* [1965] 1 QB 101 at 126, per Roskill J, commenting on the analogous situation where two sets of proceedings are brought; the position may be otherwise if the Hague-Visby Rules apply and the substantive rights of the claimant are extinguished upon the expiry of the relevant limitation period: see *The Nordglimt* [1988] 2 All ER 531.
4 SI 2011/1133.

For this reason, the ascertainment of when the arbitration commenced is of considerable importance from a limitation perspective. The parties are free to specify when arbitral proceedings are to be regarded as having commenced,[5] and if this simply requires the giving of notice of a claim then one must consider whether a claimant identified the claim to the defendant and gave a definite indication that a claim was being made (rather than considered).[6] If there is no such agreement then s 14(3)–(5) of the AA 1996 apply,[7] which state as follows:

> '(3) Where the arbitrator is named or designated in the arbitration agreement, arbitral proceedings are commenced in respect of a matter when one party serves on the other party or parties a notice in writing requiring him or them to submit that matter to the person so named or designated.
>
> (4) Where the arbitrator or arbitrators are to be appointed by the parties, arbitral proceedings are commenced in respect of a matter when one party serves on the other party or parties notice in writing requiring him or them to appoint an arbitrator or to agree to the appointment of an arbitrator in respect of that matter.
>
> (5) Where the arbitrator or arbitrators are to be appointed by a person other than a party to the proceedings, arbitral proceedings are commenced in respect of a matter when one party gives notice in writing to that person requesting him to make the appointment in respect of that matter.'

23.03 In *Nea Agrex SA v Baltic Shipping Co Ltd*,[8] the claimant sent a letter to the defendant within one year after the delivery of goods it alleged were damaged, which stated as follows: 'Please advise your proposals in order to settle this matter, or name your arbitrators. Expecting your reply.' The defendant ignored the letter and subsequently sought to argue that the arbitration had not commenced within the applicable limitation period of one year.[9] The Court of Appeal held that the arbitration had been commenced by service of the notice, even though the letter was somewhat equivocal and did not name any particular arbitrators. All that was required to commence an arbitration was a simple notice requiring the difference to be submitted to arbitration, as, in the words of Lord Wright in *Hillas & Co Ltd v Arcos Ltd*,[10] '[b]usiness men often record the most important agreements in crude and summary fashion ... It is, accordingly, the duty of the court to construe such documents fairly and broadly, without being too astute or subtle in finding defects'.[11]

23.04 Although the judgments referred to above were based on the wording of statutory provisions in force at different times prior to the passing of the AA 1996, they provide illustrations of a non-technical approach still adopted when the question arises as to whether (and when) a party commenced arbitration

5 AA 1996, s 14(1).
6 *A/S Rendal v Arcos Ltd* [1937] 3 All ER 577, [1937] 58 Lloyd's Rep 287 (HL).
7 AA 1996, s 14(2).
8 [1976] 2 All ER 842; see also *Surrendra Overseas Ltd v Government of Sri Lanka* [1977] 1 WLR 565 at 570. However, whether this approach still represented the law was questioned in *Vosnoc Ltd v Transglobal Projects Ltd* [1998] 2 All ER 990 at 995–999.
9 Article III, r 6 of the Hague-Visby Rules.
10 [1932] 147 LT 503, [1932] All ER Rep 494.
11 [1932] 147 LT 503, [1932] All ER Rep 494 at 503.

proceedings. In *Seabridge Shipping AB v AC Orssleff's Eftf's A/S*,[12] it was stated by Thomas J that:

> '[In] cases where a party has given a notice to the other party, making it clear objectively that it is a reference of the matter to arbitration, that it is likely that these will be met by the construction of s 14 which is broad enough to include an implied request to appoint an arbitrator.'[13]

However, the test to be applied in any individual case will be fact specific, as evidenced by *Taylor Woodrow Construction Ltd v RMD Kwikform Ltd*,[14] where the claimant wrote to the defendant stating that it intended to issue court proceedings and asked whether the defendant was going to rely upon an arbitration clause. The court found that the letter in question did not make it objectively clear that the claimant was referring the dispute to arbitration or requesting the defendant to commence the process of agreeing an arbitrator. It also found that the purported unilateral appointment of an arbitrator by the claimant was not authorised by the arbitration clause and that it was of no effect.

23.05 Section 76 of the AA 1996 gives guidance on when a notice shall be treated as effectively served. As an initial matter, it states that the parties are free to agree on the manner of service of any document given or served in pursuance of the arbitration agreement or for the purposes of the arbitral proceedings.[15] To the extent that there is no prior agreement on the manner of service, it provides that a notice or other document may be served on a person by any effective means.[16] In addition to this, a statutory presumption of effective service arises if a notice or other document is addressed, put in a pre-paid envelope and delivered by post to the addressee's last known principal residence or (if applicable) his last known principal business address,[17] or where the addressee is a body corporate, to the body's registered or principal office.[18] As the statutory presumption arising under s 76(4) requires proof that the notice or document was 'delivered', the broader discretion contained in s 76(3) ('any effective means') is likely to be relied upon more frequently in practice. If service is 'not reasonably practicable' in accordance with the procedure agreed by the parties (or the default provisions contained referred to above),[19] s 77 of the AA 1996 provides that 'the court may[20] make such order as it thinks fit, for service in such manner as the court may direct, or dispensing with service of the document'.[21]

12 [2000] 1 All ER (Comm) 415.

13 [2000] 1 All ER (Comm) 415 at 423; he also added, 'Section 14 should, in my view, be interpreted broadly and flexibly. A strict and technical approach to this section has no place in the scheme of the 1996 Act': *ibid*.

14 [2008] EWHC 825 (TCC), [2009] 1 All ER (Comm) 770; see also *Atlanska Plovidba v Consignaciones Asturianas SA ('The Lapad')* [2004] 2 Lloyd's Rep 109.

15 AA 1996, s 76(1).

16 AA 1996, s 76(3).

17 AA 1996, s 76(4)(a).

18 AA 1996, s 76(4)(b).

19 AA 1996, s 77(1).

20 Any procedure within the arbitral proceedings for resolving a dispute about service must be exhausted prior to an application to court being brought: s 77(3).

21 AA 1996, s 77(2).

EXTENSION OF TIME FOR COMMENCEMENT OF ARBITRATION PROCEEDINGS

23.06 Many arbitration clauses provide that a party who wishes to refer a dispute to arbitration must do so within a period of time far shorter than the applicable limitation period for the underlying cause of action. Section 12 of the AA 1996 allows the court to extend the time limit for the commencement of an arbitration in restricted circumstances.[22] Any order made under s 12 cannot extend the limitation period for the claim but only the time limit for commencing an arbitration.[23] The court must be satisfied that either of two conditions set out in s 12(3) is satisfied in order to have jurisdiction to consider extending time:

(a) that the circumstances are such as were outside the reasonable contemplation of the parties when they agreed the provision in question, and that it would be just to extend the time, or

(b) that the conduct of one party makes it unjust to hold the other party to the strict terms of the provision in question.

23.07 In *Harbour and General Works Ltd v The Environment Agency*,[24] a builder referred a dispute to a conciliator outside the time limit provided for this by the contract but just inside the time limit for referring a dispute to arbitration. The employer was aware of the latter time limit but failed to inform the builder. The employer then opposed the builder's application to extend time to commence the arbitration, which had been brought under both s 12(3)(a) – relying on a procedural mishap which it was alleged was outside the reasonable contemplation of the parties) – and s 12(3)(b) – alleging that the conduct of the employer made it unjust to hold the builder to strict terms of the time limit. Waller LJ held that the failure by the builder to read the time limit clause was a failure which was quite likely outside the reasonable contemplation of the parties. However, despite this finding, he adopted a purposive interpretation to the section and held that the legislative intent, when narrowing the situations in which a time limit to commence an arbitration could be extended, required the court to approach the matter from the perspective of 'party autonomy' and ask what the parties would have said about the clause if considering it at the time they signed the contract. This reasoning is somewhat circular and mostly intuitive (the builder would quite likely have said when signing the contract that any time limits affecting him should be construed liberally) but reflects the judicial preference for a narrow interpretation for the section.[25] This approach has been followed in a number of cases where various mistakes by legal advisers were held to be insufficient for

22 The earlier case law should be treated with care as the Arbitration Act 1950, s 27 afforded a wider measure of discretion to the court in deciding whether to grant an extension of time.

23 AA 1996, s 12(5).

24 [2000] 1 All ER 50.

25 Colman J in the High Court gave what is perhaps a more coherent reason for refusing the extension of time, finding that 'a negligent omission to comply with a time bar could not, without more, constitute circumstances outside the reasonable contemplation of the parties': see [1999] 1 All ER (Comm) 953 at 962.

the claimant to obtain an extension of time.[26] If the error was within the control of the party seeking the extension of time, Waller LJ noted that this will usually preclude that party from an extension of time, though not in all cases such as where the notice to arbitrate was put into the wrong letterbox.

23.08 The attempt to rely on s 12(3)(b) in *Harbour and General Works Ltd v The Environment Agency*[27] was dismissed summarily, with Waller LJ noting that '[t]here was no obligation on the respondent to advise the appellant that time was about to expire or that it appeared that the appellant had failed to read the relevant provisions'.[28] In *William McIlroy Swindon Ltd v Quinn Insurance Ltd*,[29] it was held by Edwards-Stuart J that 'in the absence of unusual circumstances, the conduct of the party resisting the application must have been such as to have in some way caused or contributed to the failure of the applicant to comply with the relevant time bar'.[30] Despite expressing 'justifiable criticism' of the conduct of the respondent in raising spurious grounds of defence and delaying in responding to correspondence as this had not caused the claimant to miss the time limit for commencing arbitration, he refused to extend time pursuant to s 12(3)(b). One case in which an extension of time was granted under s 12(3)(b) was *Lantic Sugar Ltd v Baffin Investments Ltd*,[31] where some confusion (at best) on the part of the defendant's agent as to whether it had authority to accept service of a notice of arbitration which had been served on it rendered it unjust for its principal to rely upon the expiry of a time limit for commencing arbitration.

23.09 Given the restrictive interpretation that has been given to s 12(3) of the AA 1996, it is perhaps unsurprising that little consideration has been given to s 12(4), which provides that any application to extend time shall be at the discretion of the court. In *SOS Corporacion Alimentaria SA v Inerco Trade SA*,[32] Hamblen J held that the claimant had established that the reason why the time limit for part of its claim had been missed was outside the reasonable contemplation of the parties within the meaning of s 12(3)(a). However, he refused to extend time because subsequent delays on the part of the claimant had caused prejudice to the defendant in that samples of the defective goods had been destroyed and a potential claim by the defendant against its supplier had become time-barred.

26 See *Thyssen Inc v Calypso Shipping Corp SA* [2000] 2 All ER (Comm) 97, where an arbitration was preceded by ineffectual court proceedings, and *Monella v PizzaExpress (Restaurants) Ltd* [2003] EWHC 2966 (Ch), [2004] 1 EGLR 43 where a change in the law (whether time was of the essence for a rent review) was held not to have been outside the reasonable contemplation of the parties and also that it had not caused the time limit to be missed.

27 [2000] 1 All ER 50.

28 [2000] 1 All ER 50 at 59.

29 [2010] EWHC 2448 (TCC), (2010) 133 ConLR 181. The Court of Appeal allowed an appeal from the judgment of Edwards-Stuart J on grounds that the claimant was in time to commence the arbitration, without expressing any comment on the approach taken to s 12(3)(b): see [2011] EWCA Civ 825, [2012] 1 All ER (Comm) 241.

30 [2010] EWHC 2448 (TCC) at para 98.

31 [2009] EWHC 3325 (Comm), [2010] 2 All ER (Comm) 1170.

32 [2010] EWHC 162 (Comm), [2010] 2 Lloyd's Rep 345.

DELAY IN THE CONDUCT OF THE ARBITRATION

23.10 Until the passage of the AA 1996, the law on the effect of delays in progressing an arbitration was governed by the decision of the House of Lords in *Bremer Vulkan v South India Shipping Corp Ltd*,[33] which held that an arbitrator did not have the power to dismiss arbitral proceedings for want of prosecution. Although this may seem harsh, the underlying principle was not without merit, as it imposed an obligation on both parties to proceed with due dispatch rather than acquiesce in a period of delay and subsequently seek to dismiss the claim on grounds of delay. Section 41(3) of the AA 1996 now gives an arbitrator the express power to dismiss a claim if satisfied that there has been inordinate and inexcusable delay by the claimant in pursuing his claim and that the delay either, (i) gives rise, or is likely to give rise, to a substantial risk that it is not possible to have a fair resolution of the issues in that claim, or (ii) has caused, or is likely to cause, serious prejudice to the respondent. In *James Lazenby & Co v McNicholas Construction Co Ltd*,[34] Rix J applied the decision of the House of Lords in *Birkett v James*[35] to an application to dismiss for want of prosecution and held that an arbitrator had the power to dismiss a non-statute barred claim for want of prosecution, but only if 'exceptional circumstances' existed, which he found not to have been established in evidence.

POWER OF COURT TO EXTEND LIMITATION PERIOD IF AWARD SET ASIDE

23.11 If a court orders that an award be set aside (in whole or in part) or declares it to be of no effect, s 13(2) of the AA 1996 provides that in such a case:

> '[T]he court may order that in computing the time prescribed by the Limitation Acts for the commencement of proceedings (including arbitral proceedings) in respect of [the] dispute ... the period between the commencement of the arbitration and the date of the order [setting aside the arbitration or declaring it to be of no effect] shall be excluded.'

This section gives the court a broad discretion in cases where an award is set aside (or declared to be of no effect) to make a supplemental order that the parties' position from a limitation perspective be re-set to that which pertained on the date the original arbitral proceedings were commenced.

TIME LIMITS FOR ENFORCEMENT OF AWARD

23.12 Section 7 of the LA 1980 imposes a limitation period of six years 'from the date the cause of action accrued' for bringing an action to enforce an award

33 [1981] AC 909.
34 [1995] 3 All ER 820.
35 [1978] AC 297.

where the arbitration clause is not contained in an instrument under seal. By implication, the limitation period is 12 years if the clause is contained in an instrument under seal as it will in those circumstances be treated as a specialty.[36] Although the limitation period depends on the nature of the arbitration agreement, the cause of action only accrues when an award is made.[37] In *Agromet Motoimport Ltd v Maulden Engineering Co (Beds) Ltd*,[38] Otton J held that time did not run from the date of the award, but instead ran from the date on which the award should have been performed. In some cases, the contract or award may stipulate the period of time within which the award must be performed, but in other cases it will be a matter of evidence as to the length of a 'reasonable period' within which the award should have been performed.

23.13 There are two methods of enforcing an arbitral award. The first is where leave of the court is obtained to enforce the award in the same manner as a judgment or order of the court to the same effect.[39] The second means of enforcing an award is by bringing a new action upon the award. In *National Ability SA v Tinna Oils & Chemicals Ltd*,[40] the Court of Appeal held that the same limitation rules apply whether a party applies to enforce an award as a judgment or by bringing an action on the award. In deciding that the phrase 'action to enforce an award' should not be given a narrow interpretation by analogy with the approach adopted by the House of Lords to the phrase 'action upon a judgment' in *Lowsley v Forbes*,[41] Thomas LJ expressed an obvious preference for adopting an interpretation of s 7 of the LA 1980 which was 'free from technicalities [and] readily comprehensible to the layman'.[42]

ADJUDICATION OF DISPUTES ARISING UNDER CONSTRUCTION CONTRACTS

23.14 Section 108 of the Housing Grants, Construction and Regeneration Act 1996 provides that a party to a 'construction contract'[43] has the right to refer a dispute arising under the contract for adjudication under a procedure complying with that section. This right is additional to other avenues that are open to a party to a construction contract to litigate their dispute, and for example, the bring-

36 LA 1980, s 8; see *Bremer Oeltransport GmbH v Drewry* [1933] 1 KB 753.

37 *Bremer Oeltransport GmbH v Drewry* [1933] 1 KB 753.

38 [1985] 1 WLR 762. In *Good Challenger Navegante SA v Metalexportimport SA ('The Good Challenger')* [2003] EWCA Civ 1668, [2003] All ER (D) 320 (Nov), it was held that the limitation period may be extended by reason of a part payment or acknowledgment of the award.

39 AA 1996, s 66.

40 [2009] EWCA Civ 1330, [2009] All ER (D) 109 (Dec).

41 [1999] 1 AC 329; see further Ch 4.

42 [2009] EWCA Civ 1330, [2009] All ER (D) 109 (Dec) at para 20.

43 This phrase is defined in the Housing Grants, Construction and Regeneration Act 1996, s 104. The requirement that the contract be in writing was removed by the Local Democracy, Economic Development and Construction Act 2009, s 139.

ing of concurrent proceedings is not an abuse of process.[44] Section 108(2)(a) states that a construction contract governed by the Act shall include a provision in writing so as to enable a party to give notice 'at any time' of his intention to refer a dispute to adjudication. The meaning of the words 'at any time' arose for determination in *Connex South Eastern Ltd v MJ Building Services Group Plc*,[45] in circumstances where the defendant sought to refer a dispute to adjudication in February 2004 which had been simmering between the parties since December 2001. The claimant brought these proceedings in which it sought declarations that the referral to adjudication was an abuse of process, which was rejected, and that it had occurred outside the time limits governing a referral. In ruling on the latter point, Dyson LJ noted that the words 'at any time' were used in s 108(2) and that accordingly no time limits applied, although a party could lose the right to refer a construction dispute to adjudication if this right was waived or if an estoppel arose. However, he continued by stating that if a party referred a dispute to adjudication after the expiry of the relevant limitation period, he 'runs the risk that, if the limitation defence is taken, the adjudicator will make an award in favour of the respondent'.[46]

EXPERT DETERMINATION OF DISPUTE ARISING UNDER TERM IN CONTRACT

23.15 If a contract provides the parties with the right to appoint an 'expert' (howsoever described) to make a 'determination' in relation to a matter in dispute, the question arises as to whether (and if so, to what extent) the LA 1980 applies to that right. In *Braceforce Warehousing Ltd v Mediterranean Shipping Company (UK) Ltd*,[47] Ramsey J offered some interesting *obiter dicta* on this issue in circumstances where he held that the 'expert determination' clause had been invoked within the limitation period. He doubted the assumption of the parties that the LA 1980 applies to the commencement of an expert determination,[48] although he also noted counsel's concession that the expert would have to take account of any limitation defence in exercising his jurisdiction. Although the comments of Ramsey J on the question of whether the LA 1980 applies to an expert determination were brief and *obiter dictum*, they would appear to be correct as the invoking of an 'expert determination' clause is not the bringing of proceedings[49] and it is somewhat different to the commencement of an 'arbitration'.[50] However,

44 *Connex South Eastern Ltd v MJ Building Services Group Plc* [2004] EWHC 1518 (TCC), (2004) 95 ConLR 43. The limitation period for any concurrent proceedings runs from the date of completion of the works and not the date of the adjudicator's decision: see *Aspect Contracts (Asbestos) Ltd v Higgins Construction Plc* [2013] EWHC 1322.

45 [2005] EWCA Civ 193, [2005] 2 All ER 870.

46 [2005] EWCA Civ 193, [2005] 2 All ER 870 at para 39. Judge Richard Havery QC had gone further in his judgment in the High Court and had stated that if an adjudicator failed to take into account a limitation defence 'then any payment made pursuant to his award would give rise to a claim for restitution': [2004] EWHC 1518 (TCC), (2004) 95 ConLR 43 at para 34.

47 [2009] EWHC 3839 (QB), [2009] All ER (D) 101 (Jun).

48 [2009] EWHC 3839 (QB), [2009] All ER (D) 101 (Jun) at para 16.

49 LA 1980, s 38(1).

50 AA 1996, s 13.

for the expert to act consistently with the contractual rights of the parties, as they are commonly understood, it would appear appropriate for him to be compelled to act subject to an implied term in the contract limiting the definition of 'dispute' to those disputes that are not statute barred.

THE CROSS-BORDER MEDIATION (EU DIRECTIVE) REGULATIONS 2011

23.16 The Cross-Border Mediation (EU Directive) Regulations 2011[51] ('2011 Regulations') apply to cross-border disputes in which at least one of the parties is domiciled or habitually resident in a Member State other than that of any other party on the date on which the parties agree or are ordered by a court (or otherwise come under an obligation) to use mediation.[52] The Directive and the Regulations apply to civil and commercial matters except as regards rights and obligations which are not at the parties' disposal under the relevant applicable law; specifically excluded from its ambit are revenue, customs or administrative matters and claims relating to the liability of the State for acts and omissions in the exercise of State authority.[53] Section s 33A was inserted into the Limitation Act 1980 ('LA 1980') by reg 26 and provides that in cases where the 2011 Regulations apply and a mediation in relation to the dispute starts before the time limit expires and (if not extended by s 33A) that time limit would expire before the mediation ends or less than eight weeks after it ends, the limitation period shall expire instead 'at the end of eight weeks after the mediation ends'.[54] It also provides that where more than one time limit applies in relation to a dispute, any extension of time afforded by s 33A(3) of one of those time limits does not affect the others. A mediation is stated to start 'on the date of the agreement to mediate that is entered into by the parties and the mediator'.[55] A mediation is stated to end in any of the circumstances set out in s 33A(10), which in essence will occur if the dispute is settled, if the mediation ends under the terms of the agreement, or if one of the parties or the mediator withdraws expressly or by conduct. The Regulations also make consequential amendments to a number of other statutes in similar terms to the amendments to the LA 1980, in particular by the following newly inserted sections: the Sex Discrimination Act 1975, s 76ZA; the Foreign Limitation Periods Act 1984, s 1A; the Employment Rights Act 1996, s 207A; the Land Registration Act 2002, s 16 and the Equality Act 2010, s 140A.

51 SI 2011/1133. This Statutory Instrument implements Directive 2008/52/EC of the European Parliament and of the Council of 21 May 2008 on certain aspects of mediation in civil and commercial matters.

52 Directive 2008/52/EC, art 2(1). 'Mediation' is defined in art 3(a) of the Directive.

53 Directive 2008/52/EC, art 1(2).

54 LA 1980, s 33A(3).

55 LA 1980, s 33A(6).

CHAPTER 24

Company, Partnership and Insolvency Law

24.01 The Limitation Act 1980 ('LA 1980') does not contain any provisions which specifically refer to company, partnership or insolvency proceedings. While the limitation issues which arise in company, partnership and insolvency proceedings will, in many cases, involve the application of the general principles that govern torts, breaches of contract and breaches of fiduciary duty, unusual issues arise in relation to, *inter alia*, the restoration of companies to the register, applications for a disqualification order against a director, misfeasance and unfair prejudice proceedings, the legal attributes of a partnership and the legal effects of a winding up or bankruptcy, which justify separate consideration being given to these areas of law.

COMPANY LAW

Proceedings by company or liquidator against directors: general principles

24.02 In proceedings where a company (including a company in liquidation) sues a director for negligence, breach of trust or breach of fiduciary duty, the ordinary principles of the law on limitation will apply to the proceedings. A good example of issues which can arise is contained in the judgment of the Court of Appeal in *Gwembe Valley Development Co v Koshy (No 3)*.[1] In this case, the claimant brought proceedings against a former director in excess of six years after the latter had earned undisclosed profits in breach of fiduciary duty from currency exchange transactions involving the company's money. The Court of Appeal held that while personal claims against a fiduciary are normally subject to time limits by analogy with claims in tort or contract, in this case no limitation period applied as the applicable limitation period was that for fraudulent breach

1 [2003] EWCA Civ 1048, [2004] 1 BCLC 131. See the useful discussion of this case in Gower and Davies, *Principles of Modern Company Law* (8th edn, London: Sweet & Maxwell, 2008), at 601–602. Related limitation issues arose in *Re Pantone 485 Ltd; Miller v Bain* [2002] 1 BCLC 266 and *Re Oxford Pharmaceuticals Ltd; Wilson v Masters* [2009] EWHC 1753 (Ch), [2009] 2 BCLC 485.

of trust,[2] and accordingly, the proceedings were not statute barred. Deliberate concealment on the part of the defendant was also pleaded in the *Gwembe Valley Development Co* case,[3] which is an issue that can often arise in claims against delinquent directors. In *Re Eurocruit Europe Ltd (in liquidation); Goldfarb v Poppleton*,[4] the liquidator of a company claimed compensation from a former director for breach of his duty of care and skill, and for breach of fiduciary duty. The court held that the limitation period for an action in tort applied and that the claim was statute barred as it had not been brought within six years of the date when the loss was suffered. The fact that the application[5] had been brought within six years of the claimant being wound up did not extend the limitation period in any way.

Debts due by members to a company

24.03 Section 14 of the Companies Act 1985 (now repealed) provided that the memorandum and articles of association of a company bound its members to the same extent as if they had been signed and sealed by each member. In *Re Compania de Electricidad de la Provincia de Buenos Aires Ltd*,[6] Slade J held that while money owed by members to the company (eg uncalled share capital) was a specialty debt to which a 12-year limitation period applied, money owed to the members (eg as dividends or return of capital) was a simple contract debt for which the limitation period was six years, although in several older cases it had been held that a 12-year limitation period applied in both cases.[7] This issue is now of historic interest only as s 33 of the Companies Act 2006 has replaced the earlier provisions and provides that money payable by a member to the company is in the nature of an ordinary contract debt.

Unfair prejudice proceedings

24.04 No specific limitation period governs proceedings brought under s 994 of the Companies Act 2006 ('unfair prejudice proceedings') (formerly s 459 of the Companies Act 1985). Although the nature of the cause of action is *sui generis* and does not fit neatly into a heading of tort, contract or fiduciary duty, it was held in *Re a Company (No 005134 of 1986), Ex p Harries*[8] that the defence of *laches* may be raised in such proceedings, although on the facts of that case no inexcusable delay was made out such as would render it inequitable for relief

2 LA 1980, 21(1)(a).

3 See also the comments of Carnwath LJ in *Halton International Inc v Guernroy Ltd* [2006] EWCA Civ 801, [2006] All ER (D) 302 (Jun) on the proper characterisation of the cause of action in *GVDC* and his suggestion that it should more properly be viewed as a case involving deliberate concealment: see further the discussion in para 17.17.

4 [2007] EWHC 1433 (Ch), [2007] All ER (D) 229 (Jun).

5 Under IA 1986, s 212.

6 [1980] Ch 146.

7 *Smith v Cork and Bandon Railway Co* (1887) IR 5 Eq 65; *In re Drogheda Steam Packet Co Ltd* [1903] IR 512.

8 *Re a Company (No 005134 of 1986), Ex p Harries* [1989] BCLC 383 at 397–398.

to be granted. Delay and *laches* did prove fatal to the petitioner's case in *Re Grandactual Ltd*,[9] where a petition was issued in July 2004 which complained of matters which had occurred between 1995 and 1997. In striking out the petition as having no chance of success, Sir Donald Rattee stated as follows:

> 'Petitions under s 459 are always a very burdensome form of litigation. I understand that s 459 is not subject to any period of limitation, but relief under s 461 is always within the discretion of the court. I do not consider that the court should countenance such proceedings in the circumstances that I have described nearly ten years after the event.'[10]

24.05 While the result in *Re Grandactual Ltd* was undoubtedly correct given the very lengthy delays and acquiescence by the petitioners in that case, a more robust approach to delay is evident from the judgment of Warren J in *Re Southern Counties Fresh Foods Ltd*.[11] He held that *Re Grandactual Ltd* is not authority for the proposition that conduct in the remote past can never be brought into account, in particular if a course of conduct starting in the remote past has continued to the present time. In such a case, he held that the entire history of the conduct was relevant to the court's assessment of whether the conduct as a whole was unfairly prejudicial. He continued as follows:

> 'Of course, the fact that it may have continued without protest for a long period may show that there has been acquiescence and no unfair prejudice; but if the conduct has met with regular objection, or even resignation but with clear non-acceptance, it is not to be rejected *a priori* as incapable of being entertained by the court as part of the basis for a petition.'[12]

He held that the respondent in *Re Southern Counties Fresh Foods Ltd* could not in any sense have been lulled into a false sense of security or into thinking that the petitioner was happy with the way things were being dealt with, and the *laches* defence was not made out.

Limitation consequences of the dissolution and restoration of a company to the register

24.06 A company may be dissolved or struck off the register of companies for a number of reasons. Once this occurs then, in legal terms, it ceases to exist. An application to restore a company to the register by administrative action may be made under s 1024 and by order of the court under s 1029 of the Companies Act 2006. A time limit of six years from the date of dissolution applies to an applica-

9 [2005] EWHC 1415 (Comm), [2006] BCC 73.

10 [2005] EWHC 1415 (Comm), [2006] BCC 73 at para 20.

11 [2008] EWHC 2810 (Ch), [2008] All ER (D) 195 (Nov)

12 [2008] EWHC 2810 (Ch), [2008] All ER (D) 195 (Nov) at para 72. By contrast, a defence of *laches* was successfully raised in *Shah v Shah* [2005] EWHC 2237 (Ch). For the approach of the Canadian courts, see *Ford Motor Co v Ontario Municipal Employees Retirement Board* (2006) 263 DLR (4th) 450 and *Incorporated Broadcasters Ltd v Canwest Global Communications Corp* (2008) 300 DLR (4th) 577.

tion to restore a company to the register,[13] save where the application is being brought so as to allow a party to institute personal injuries proceedings against the company, in which case no time limit applies.[14] If the company is restored to the register, it is 'deemed to have continued in existence as if it had not been dissolved or struck off the register'.[15] In addition, the court may give such directions and make such provision as seem just 'for placing the company and all other persons in the same position (as nearly as may be) as if the company had not been dissolved or struck off the register'.[16] In *Smith v White Knight Laundry Ltd*,[17] it was held that a party who may be prejudiced by the terms of such an order has the right to be heard on the application to impose terms. Under the restoration provisions contained in the Companies Act 1985,[18] a distinction was drawn between the effect of an order restoring a company obtained under ss 651 or 653. In *Joddrell v Peaktone Ltd*,[19] it was held that the effect of the changes effected by the Companies Act 2006 mean that all restoration orders, whether administrative orders or court orders, should be treated alike (and effectively in like manner as applications under s 323 of the Companies Act 1948 and s 653 of the Companies Act 1985). Accordingly, once restored to the register, the company is deemed to have continued in existence as if it had never been struck off, with the effect that prima facie the limitation period will have been running even while the company ceased to exist. A company which is dissolved may not be sued in proceedings, but the effect of the provisions in the Companies Act 2006 is that any proceedings (invalidly) issued or continued against the company while dissolved are retrospectively validated once it is restored.[20] The predecessor to s 1032(3) was the subject of some case law which should remain valid under the Companies Act 2006. In *Re Donald Kenyon Ltd*,[21] an order was made restoring a company to the register to allow it to claim and distribute to its members certain monies to which it was entitled. In making the restoration order, Roxburgh J further ordered that in the case of creditors whose debts were not statute barred at the date when the company was dissolved, the period between the date of dissolution and the date when the name of the company was restored to the register should not be counted for the purposes of the Limitation Acts. The provision inserted in the order in *Re Donald Kenyon Ltd* was routinely made when a company was restored;[22] the same situation should pertain under the Companies Act 2006 provisions. However, in *Re Huntingdon Poultry Ltd*,[23] where a creditor applied to restore a company to the register and the court was not made aware of any other creditor who might benefit from the insertion of a special provision in the order

13 CA 2006, ss 1024(4) (administrative application) and 1030(4) (court application).
14 CA 2006, s 1030(1); the administrative procedure is available only to directors and members and thus there is no personal injuries exception to the six-year time limit.
15 CA 2006, s 1028(1) (administrative application) and s 1032(1) (court application).
16 CA 2006, s 1028(3) (administrative application) and s 1032(3) (court application).
17 [2001] 2 BCLC 206.
18 Prior to that, see the similarly worded Companies Act 1948, ss 322 and 323.
19 [2012] EWCA Civ 1035, [2013] 1 All ER 13.
20 *Tymans Ltd v Craven* [1952] 2 QB 100.
21 [1956] 3 All ER 596.
22 See, for example, *Re Advance Insulation Ltd* (1989) 5 BCC 55, Hoffmann J.
23 [1969] 1 All ER 328.

relating to limitation, Buckley J refused to make any such order on the ground that it was not necessary.

PARTNERSHIP

24.07 While two or more individuals remain in partnership, the relationship of debtor and creditor does not arise between them.[24] No right of action can exist until the partnership is dissolved (including where one partners leaves and the others remain in partnership) or until there is a binding settlement of the accounts.[25] However, the right to claim a share of profits may be lost to a partner by *laches*.[26] A partner owes fiduciary duties to the partnership and if these are breached the partnership may seek an account of profits from him, such as arose in *Lindsley v Woodfull*,[27] where the Court of Appeal held that compensation was payable until the date of the taking of a final account. In such circumstances, issues of deliberate concealment[28] and fraudulent breach of trust may extend the applicable limitation period, although on the facts of *Lindsley v Woodfull* it was not necessary for the claimants to raise any such arguments. Once a partnership is dissolved, a partner has six years within which to seek the taking of an account,[29] or 12 years if the partnership agreement is under seal.[30]

24.08 In *Marshall v Bullock*,[31] the Court of Appeal held that it was settled law of some antiquity[32] that the six-year limitation period, running from the date of dissolution, applied even if the former partner sued in relation to an asset which had been received by the partnership within the previous six years and after the dissolution of the partnership. A possible exception exists in cases where the taking of an account would have served no purpose upon dissolution (eg if the partners all knew the partnership had no assets at that date) but an asset is received subsequently.[33] But if, after the affairs of the partnership have been wound up and its accounts settled, an asset is received by one of the former partners which was not included in those accounts, time will only start to run as

24 *Miller v Miller* (1869) LR 8 Eq 499; *Noyes v Crawley* (1878) 10 Ch D 31.

25 *Meyer and Co v Faber* (No 2) [1923] 2 Ch 421 (CA); *Hopper v Hopper* [2008] EWCA Civ 1412, but see the discussion of the latter case in *Lindley & Banks on Partnership* (19th edn, London: Sweet & Maxwell, 2010) at para 23.32 as having overlooked the restrictions on re-opening an account.

26 See *Sherman v Sherman* (1692) 2 Vern 276, *Patel v Shah* [2005] EWCA Civ 157 and *Lindley & Banks on Partnership* (19th edn, London: Sweet & Maxwell, 2010) at paras 23.20–23.27.

27 [2004] EWCA Civ 165, [2004] 2 BCLC 131.

28 *Betjemann v Betjemann* [1895] 2 Ch 474.

29 LA 1980, ss 5 and 23.

30 LA 1980, ss 8 and 23.

31 Unreported, 27 March 1998 (CA); this decision was followed in *Manning v English* [2010] EWHC 153 (Ch), [2010] Bus LR D89.

32 *Knox v Gye* (1872) LR 5 HL 656; *Chetty v Vijayaraghavachariar* [1922] 1 AC 488 at 496, per Lord Phillimore.

33 See *Brown v Rivlin*, unreported, 1 February 1983 (CA), discussed in *Marshall v Bullock*, unreported, 27 March 1998 (CA).

regards the other partners' entitlement in respect of that asset with effect from the date of its receipt.[34] The reasons for this rule were well stated by Peter Gibson LJ in *Marshall v Bullock*[35] as follows:

> 'There are good policy reasons why this should be so. When a partnership comes to an end, there is an obligation on the partners to agree, or to have determined by the court, their respective liabilities and their respective entitlements. Once partners have dissolved the partnership, each should after six years be free of the risk of any claims being made by another partner.
>
> It would be unfortunate if the court were to encourage partners who have failed to obtain an account or who have allowed the time for an action for an account to be brought to expire, to rely years later on an individual item which would and should have featured in that account to make it the subject of a separate action for recovery. As I have already said, that is simply not fair, because, in ascertaining what is due from one partner to another, one has to look at both sides of the balance sheet, both sides of the account.'

CORPORATE INSOLVENCY

Debts relied upon in a winding up petition

24.09 The question of whether one can petition to wind up a company by relying on a judgment debt which is more than 12 years old came before the Court of Appeal in *Ridgeway Motors (Isleworth) Ltd v ALTS Ltd*,[36] where it was held that a judgment debt could be relied upon without limitation of time to ground a petition to wind up the judgment debtor. This result was reached on grounds that the bringing of a petition (to bankrupt an individual or to wind up a company) does not constitute the bringing of an 'action' and thus was not an 'action upon a judgment' within the meaning of s 24(1) of the LA 1980. Instead, in the words of Mummery LJ in *Ridgeway Motors (Isleworth) Ltd*, an application to wind up a company:

> '… is *sui generis*, being in the nature of a wider legal proceeding available for the collective enforcement of the admitted or proved debts of the company for the benefit of the general body of creditors on a *pari passu* basis'.[37]

By contrast, in *Re Karnos Property Ltd*, it was held that local authority rates which were more than six years old[38] could not be relied upon to ground a winding up petition. The primary finding of Mervyn Davies J was that the petition was an action, which has now been overruled (by *Ridgeway Motors*) and he placed less weight on the fact that the debt was statute barred and in fact discounted entirely

34 *Lindley & Banks on Partnership* (19th edn, London: Sweet & Maxwell, 2010) at para 23.41.
35 Unreported, 27 March 1998 (CA).
36 [2005] EWCA Civ 92, [2005] 1 WLR 2871; this case overruled *Re a Debtor (No 50A/SD/95)* [1997] 2 All ER 789 and *Re Karnos Property Ltd* (1989) 5 BCC 14.
37 [2005] EWCA Civ 92, [2005] 1 WLR 2871 at para 29.
38 Thus statute barred under the LA 1980, s 9 as a sum due by virtue of an enactment.

the fact that certain distress warrants remained available for execution. In the Australian case of *Motor Terms Co Pty Ltd v Liberty Insurance Ltd*,[39] it was held that a contract debt may not be relied upon to ground a winding up petition once it is statute barred, as the petitioner will not be a 'creditor' at that time, although it might be more correct to say that the company will have a full defence to any action on the debt.

Effect on limitation period of company being placed in liquidation

24.10 It was held in *Re General Rolling Stock Co*[40] that periods of limitation cease to run once a company is wound up. The rights of those claiming in the liquidation therefore crystallise at the commencement of the winding up, which has a undeniable logic in the case of claims on a company's assets which are the subject of a proof of debt in the liquidation, though the further one moves from this starting point of the analogy the more strained it becomes. In *Re Taff Wells Ltd*,[41] it was held that time ceased to run against a petitioning creditor from the date of presentation of his petition, but that a petitioning creditor did not act on behalf of all the other creditors of a company and therefore time did not stop running as against them until the order was made winding up the company. While the rule in *Re General Rolling Stock Co* applied originally in court-ordered liquidations, in *Re Mixhurst Ltd*[42] it was held that the same rule should apply in voluntary liquidations, as no sensible distinctions justified a different treatment. The Court of Appeal gave detailed consideration to this interesting and somewhat obscure issue in *Financial Services Compensation Scheme Ltd v Larnell (Insurances) Ltd (in liquidation)*,[43] holding that the rule applied whether the corporate assets the subject of a claim were within the liquidation or available under a policy of insurance and whether the claim was brought by proof within the liquidation or in litigation. In *Laroche v Spirit of Adventure (UK) Ltd*,[44] it was held that the rule in *Re General Rolling Stock Co* could not be relied upon to extend a two-year limitation period contained in art 29 of the Warsaw Convention. It held that this common law rule had been abrogated by the terms on which the convention had been implemented into law and that the Convention did not permit an extension of time being afforded on these grounds.

Effect on limitation period of administration or receivership

24.11 Neither the making of an administration order or the appointment of a receiver over the assets of a company prevents time running under the LA 1980. In *Re Maxwell Fleet and Facilities Management Ltd (in administration)*,[45] the

39 (1967) 116 CLR 177.
40 (1872) LR 7 ChApp 646 (CA).
41 [1992] Ch 179.
42 [1994] 2 BCLC 19.
43 [2005] EWCA Civ 1408, [2006] QB 808.
44 [2009] EWCA Civ 12, [2009] 2 All ER 175.
45 [2000] 1 All ER 464.

rule in *Re General Rolling Stock Co* was held not to apply to administrations on grounds that they lacked the essential feature of liquidations, namely that the administration did not impose on the company's available assets a statutory scheme of rateable division among creditors. However, the employees whose claims were before the court in *Maxwell* succeeded in their action, as by virtue of s 19(5) of the Insolvency Act 1986 their claims were charged on the property of the company in the administrator's custody when he ceased to be administrator. This had two consequences: first, that time only ran from the end of the administration (which was still ongoing) and secondly, that their claims were subject to the 12-year limitation period contained in s 20 of the LA 1980 as debts charged on property. The same result was reached in *Re Cosslett (Contractors) Ltd,*[46] where it was held by Patten J that if the administration lasts more than six years and the unsecured creditors have taken no action to have their debts acknowledged within that time, the creditors will lose the right to claim their debts in the administration. In *Re Joshua Shaw & Sons,*[47] the company went into receivership and it appeared unlikely that there would be any money available for the unsecured creditors. However, after nine years of receivership, it became clear that there would be a substantial surplus after the secured and preferential creditors were paid in full. Hoffmann J held (in the course of the subsequent liquidation of the company) that all of the claims except the Crown debts were statute barred.

Proof of statute barred debts in a liquidation

24.12 In *Re Art Reproduction Co Ltd,*[48] Wynn Parry J held that it is not open to a liquidator to discharge a debt which was statute barred at the commencement of the winding up, although in a voluntary liquidation where the company is solvent, they may, it seems, be admitted if all contributories consent. The same rules were held to apply in the case of an administration in *Re Leyland Printing (in administration).*[49] The judgment of Judge Hodge QC is of particular interest in discussing what is required for an entry in an administrator's progress report to constitute an acknowledgment of debt and the proofs necessary for the court to be satisfied that payment of a statute barred debt has received the unanimous approval of the shareholders of the company (and any other creditors having a valid claim).

Proceedings against directors for misfeasance, reckless trading and impugning transactions

24.13 The Companies Act 2006 (and earlier legislation) contains several statutory causes of action together with provisions which govern the exercise (in

46 [2004] EWHC 658, [2004] All ER (D) 241 (Mar); this decision was followed in *Re Leyland Printing (in administration)* [2010] EWHC 2105 (Ch), [2010] All ER (D) 114 (Oct), a decision which considered the law in force prior to the changes effected by the Enterprise Act 2002.

47 [1989] BCLC 362, (1989) 5 BCC 188.

48 [1951] 2 All ER 984.

49 [2010] EWHC 2105 (Ch), [2010] All ER (D) 114 (Oct).

particular by a liquidator) of various common law causes of action. While certain *obiter dicta* of the Court of Appeal in *Halls v O'Dell*[50] were to the effect that no limitation period applies to misfeasance proceedings, in *Re Farmizer (Products) Ltd*[51] it was held that wrongful trading proceedings brought by a liquidator against the former directors of a company under s 214 of the Insolvency Act 1986 are proceedings brought 'to recover any sum recoverable by virtue of any enactment', as the cause of action is created by that enactment, and are thus subject to s 9(1) of the LA 1980. The limitation period of six years, which applies in such cases, was held to run from the date the company was wound up. By contrast, in *Re Eurocruit Europe Ltd (in liquidation)*,[52] it was held by Blackburne J that the statutory provisions which allow a liquidator to bring misfeasance proceedings[53] are procedural in nature and do not create a new cause of action.[54] This finding had the consequence that the claim in *Re Eurocruit Europe Ltd* was held to be subject to the six-year limitation period for an action founded on tort[55] and that time ran from the date the company suffered loss and not the date the company was wound up.[56] In *Hill v Spread Trustee Co Ltd*,[57] it was held that the limitation period for a trustee in bankruptcy to apply under s 423 of the Insolvency Act 1986 to set aside a transaction at an undervalue is subject to the 12-year period contained in s 8(1) of the LA 1980 for an action upon a specialty, and that time runs from the date of the bankruptcy not the date of the transaction. In *Hill v Spread Trustee Co Ltd,* Arden LJ left open the issue of whether some aspects of the claim were primarily to recover money due by virtue of an enactment and thus subject to section 9(1).[58] The findings in *Hill v Spread Trustee Co Ltd* are relevant to the limitation issues arising in the course of similar applications by a liquidator, though the question of whether the applicable limitation period should run from the date of the winding up of the company or the transaction being challenged would have to be considered in light of the cases discussed above.

Delays in prosecuting misfeasance proceedings

24.14 Delays on the part of an applicant liquidator in prosecuting misfeasance proceedings have led to applications being brought to dismiss the proceedings in a number of cases. In *Re Farmizer (Products) Ltd*,[59] the Court of Appeal dismissed the proceedings and held that if prejudice is caused by the late commencement of proceedings, and if there is inordinate and inexcusable delay in prosecuting those proceedings, they should be dismissed if the respondent will suffer more than minimal prejudice by reason of the additional delays. The additional prejudice

50 [1992] QB 393 at 405.
51 [1997] 1 BCLC 589.
52 [2007] EWHC 1433 (Ch), [2007] All ER (D) 229 (Jun).
53 IA 1986, s 212.
54 See [2007] EWHC 1433 (Ch) at paras 24–26.
55 LA 1980, s 2.
56 An allegation of fraudulent concealment was not established.
57 [2006] EWCA Civ 542, [2007] 1 WLR 2404.
58 [2006] EWCA Civ 542, [2007] 1 WLR 2404 at 2434.
59 [1997] 1 BCLC 589; see also *Halls v O'Dell* [1992] QB 393.

that was established involved the dimming of witnesses' memories as a result of the delays as, while many documents were still available, these would still have to be explained at trial. This is now unlikely to occur as frequently given the increased role of case management under the CPR.

Time limit for bringing an application for a disqualification order

24.15 The Company Directors Disqualification Act 1986 ('CDDA 1986') gives the Secretary of State the power to apply to the court for a disqualification order against a director (or other appropriate party) in the period of two years from when the company became insolvent, or thereafter with leave of court.[60] Where an application is made under s 7(2) for leave to bring proceedings outside the aforementioned period, the Secretary of State or official receiver must show a good reason for the extension of time.[61] Relevant factors include the length of the delay, the reasons for the delay,[62] the strength of the case against the director and the degree of prejudice caused by the delay.[63] In *Secretary of State for Trade and Industry v Davies*,[64] the Court of Appeal took into account the seriousness of the charges and the public interest in having the charges determined, as well as the fact that the delay had caused no prejudice, in granting leave to issue proceedings out of time despite the inadequacy of the reasons offered for the delay. Similarly, in *Re Instant Access Properties Ltd; Secretary of State for Business, Innovation and Skills v Gifford*,[65] Floyd J granted leave to commence proceedings out of time in circumstances where the Secretary of State was able to establish a coherent and, on provisional assessment, reasonably strong case which required an explanation. As the facts underlying the claim were reasonably complex, the court had regard to the level of investigation that had been required and was not overly critical of the lack of urgency in progressing the investigation. The application for leave must be made prior to issuing the proceedings and it has been held that it is not open to the court to ratify proceedings which were issued without leave.[66]

Delays in prosecuting disqualification proceedings

24.16 After an application for a disqualification order is brought, the applicant remains under an obligation to progress the proceedings. However, a party seeking to dismiss disqualification proceedings for want of prosecution must be able to establish that the delay has affected his right to a fair trial.[67] In *Re Blackspur*

60 CCDA 1986, s 7(2).

61 *Re Crestjoy Products Ltd* [1990] BCLC 677, [1990] BCC 23.

62 *Secretary of State for Trade and Industry v Davies* [1996] 4 All ER 289.

63 *Re Probe Data Systems Ltd (No 3), Secretary of State for Trade and Industry v Desai* [1992] BCLC 405 at 416, per Scott LJ.

64 [1996] 4 All ER 289.

65 [2011] EWHC 3022 (Ch), [2012] 1 BCLC 710.

66 *Re Crestjoy Products Ltd* [1990] BCLC 677, [1990] BCC 23; contra *Re Probe Data Systems Ltd (No 2)* [1990] BCLC 574, [1990] BCC 21.

67 *Re Manlon Trading Ltd* [1996] Ch 136.

Group Plc (No 2); Secretary of State for Trade and Industry v Eastaway,[68] Sir Andrew Morritt V-C refused to dismiss the proceedings despite a delay of ten years since the events in question in circumstances where a criminal trial occurred during that period as well as a number of court challenges by the respondents. In *Davies v United Kingdom*[69] and in *Eastaway v United Kingdom*[70] (which followed the decision of the Vice-Chancellor referred to above), the United Kingdom was found to be in breach of the ECHR by reason of the failure by the State to ensure that the disqualification proceedings concluded within a reasonable time and the complainants were awarded modest damages by the court. However, an attempt by the same parties to then re-open their disqualification proceedings was rejected in *Re Blackspur Group plc (No 4); Eastaway v Secretary of State for Trade and Industry*,[71] with Lightman J essentially finding that the application was misconceived as there was no right to re-open the proceedings and as the modest damages awarded to the errant former directors were all they were entitled to by reason of the finding of the European Court.

BANKRUPTCY

Effect of bankruptcy on claims against the bankrupt

24.17 The effect of a bankruptcy order is that time ceases to run in respect of provable debts due by the bankrupt from the date of the adjudication under the same principle recognised in *Re General Rolling Stock Co*[72] for companies in liquidation.[73] In *Tanner v Everitt*,[74] it was suggested by Mann J that the same rule applies to creditors who agree to an individual voluntary arrangement with a debtor, with the judge noting that a finding to the contrary 'would be a surprising and unattractive conclusion ... [t]he reason they have not sued is because they entered into an arrangement with the debtors'.[75] The basis for this finding was stated to rest on the implied contractual agreement by the parties that the limitation period would not continue to run during the period the claimant agreed not to sue on the debt. A number of exceptions to the general rule in bankruptcies that time ceases to run in respect of debts owed by the bankrupt were discussed by the Court of Appeal in *Financial Services Compensation Scheme Ltd v Larnell (Insurances) Ltd (in liquidation)*,[76] although they are more properly seen as examples of debts that are not provable within the bankruptcy,[77] to include

68 [2001] 1 BCLC 653.
69 (Application No 42007/98) [2006] 2 BCLC 351.
70 (Application No 74976/01) [2006] 2 BCLC 361.
71 [2006] EWHC 299 (Ch), [2006] 2 BCLC 489.
72 (1872) LR 7 Ch App 646 (CA).
73 Time continues to run against a bankrupt's rights of action.
74 [2004] EWHC 1130 (Ch), [2004] All ER (D) 192 (May).
75 [2004] EWHC 1130 (Ch), [2004] All ER (D) 192 (May) at para 74.
76 [2005] EWCA Civ 1408, [2006] QB 808.
77 See the discussion of cases such as *In re Benzon* [1914] 2 Ch 68 and *In re Guedella* [1905] 2 Ch 331 at [2005] EWCA Civ 1408, [2006] QB 808 at paras 20–28, per Lloyd LJ, and 58–60, per Moore-Bick LJ.

claims by secured creditors relating to assets that fall outside the bankruptcy.[78] A further situation also discussed in *Larnell* arose in *Anglo Manx Group Ltd v Aitken*,[79] which involved a debt that was still enforceable despite a discharge from bankruptcy. In this case, the claimant relied on s 281(3) of the Insolvency Act 1986 ('IA 1986') and argued that the discharge from bankruptcy of the defendant did not release him from liability for a pre-bankruptcy loan which he alleged had been procured by fraudulent misrepresentations. In order for that claim not to be statute barred, he also argued that the limitation period ceased to run during the period the defendant was a bankrupt, by reason of the rule in *Re General Rolling Stock Co*. It was held by John Jarvis QC sitting as a High Court judge that time ran during the three years of the bankruptcy as this claim fell within the category of 'other remedies in respect of which time continues to run' during the bankruptcy.

Limitation period for applications by trustee in bankruptcy

24.18 The main class of action which it is open to a trustee in bankruptcy to take is to apply to set aside a transaction under s 423 of the IA 1986 which was entered into with the intention of defrauding creditors. In *Hill v Spread Trustee Co Ltd*,[80] it was held by the Court of Appeal that an action by a trustee in bankruptcy to apply to set aside a transaction under s 423 is subject to the 12-year period contained in s 8(1) of the LA 1980 for an action upon a specialty, and that time runs from the date of the bankruptcy not the date of the transaction. This period will in many cases be further extended, as it was held by the Court of Appeal in *Giles v Rhind*[81] that deliberate concealment is a matter which can be relied upon to secure an extension to the limitation period for applications under s 423. The foregoing gives rise to a situation where there are different limitation periods for different applicants under s 423 (ie the victim and the trustee in bankruptcy) even though there is only one cause of action,[82] which is a surprising result. It allows a liquidator to circumvent the five-year limitation period in s 341(1) of the IA 1986 for application to set aside a transaction at an undervalue under s 339. In *Hill v Spread Trustee Co Ltd*, Arden LJ left open the issue of whether some aspects of the claim (to set aside a transaction) were primarily to recover money due by virtue of an enactment and thus subject to s 9(1).[83] Section 283A of the IA 1986 provides that an interest in a dwelling house which is at the date of bankruptcy the bankrupt's home (or that of his current or former spouse or civil partner) will cease to form part of the bankrupt's estate and will vest in him unless, within a period of three years following his bankruptcy, an application is made for possession, sale or charge of the interest in the house. This provision was considered in

78 *Cotterell v Price* [1960] 1 WLR 1097.

79 [2002] BPIR 215.

80 [2006] EWCA Civ 542, [2007] 1 WLR 2404; see also *Cohen v Selby* [2001] 1 BCLC 176, *Re Priory Garage (Walthamstow) Ltd* [2001] BPIR 144 and *Re Yates (a bankrupt)* [2005] BPIR 476, which are to like effect.

81 [2008] EWCA Civ 118, [2009] Ch 191.

82 [2006] EWCA Civ 542, [2007] 1 WLR 2404 at para 112, per Arden LJ.

83 [2006] EWCA Civ 542, [2007] 1 WLR 2404 at para 118.

Stonham v Ramrattan,[84] although as the bankrupt had not informed his trustee in bankruptcy of his interest in the property within three months of his bankruptcy,[85] the longer limitation period contained in s 283A(5) of three years from the date the trustee became aware of the property was relied upon in response. However, the Court of Appeal held that s 283A did not apply to the action at all as the section has no application to a situation where an asset is transferred to a third party. This still left the problem of the lapse of time between the date of the impugned transfer in 1990 and the bringing of proceedings in 2007. The reasoning of the court thereafter is not easy to follow as it found that a 12-year limitation period running from the date of the bankruptcy order[86] applies to claims under s 339 of the IA 1986, apparently following a concession from counsel,[87] notwithstanding the reference to a five-year limitation period[88] for claims to set aside a transaction at an undervalue under s 339(2). While the result in the case might be correct, as there may have been grounds to extend time under s 32(1)(b) of the LA 1980, certain of the findings on limitation in *Stonham* should be treated with care. In *Gotham v Doodes*,[89] the Court of Appeal ruled on a challenge to the enforcement of a charging order obtained by a trustee in bankruptcy under s 313 of the IA 1986. Although the court held that an order under s 313 creates a charge over land and is subject to the 12-year limitation period in s 20(1) of the LA 1980, as the right to receive the amount payable would not accrue until an order for the sale of the property was made by the court (which had not occurred in *Gotham*) the trustee's rights in respect of the charge obtained under s 313 were not statute barred, notwithstanding the passage of in excess of 12 years between the date of the charging order and the application for an order for sale of the property.

84 [2011] EWCA Civ 119, [2011] 1 WLR 1617.
85 IA 1986, s 183A(5).
86 Lloyd LJ at para 25 suggested that time only started to run from the date on which a trustee in bankruptcy is first appointed or when the official receiver becomes a trustee.
87 See [2011] EWCA Civ 119, [2011] 1 WLR 1617 at para 25, per Lloyd LJ.
88 IA 1986, s 341(1)(a).
89 [2006] EWCA Civ 1080, [2007] 1 WLR 86.

CHAPTER 25

Contribution

INTRODUCTION

25.01 The Civil Liability (Contribution) Act 1978 ('CLCA 1978') provides a right of action to a defendant to proceedings (or intimated proceedings) to claim contribution from any person liable in respect of the same damage.[1] Section 10 of the Limitation Act 1980 ('LA 1980') provides that no action to recover contribution by virtue of s 1 of the CLCA 1978 shall be brought after the expiration of two years from the date on which that right accrued.[2] In an unusual case where the claim for contribution is advanced independently of the CLCA 1978, such as the claim from a co-surety for contribution following payment of the entirety of a guaranteed debt advanced in *Hampton v Minns*,[3] the limitation period contained in s 10 will not apply[4] either directly or by analogy as the claim is not advanced by virtue of s 1 of the CLCA 1978. Similarly, where the claim at issue is one seeking an indemnity based on the terms of a contract, an express indemnity agreement or an implied indemnity, the cause of action will not be governed by s 10 of the LA 1980.[5] The provisions on disability,[6] fraud, concealment and mistake,[7] mediations coming within the Cross-Border Mediation (EU Directive) Regulations 2011[8] and new claims in pending actions[9] apply to actions to recover

1 Civil Liability (Contribution) Act 1978, s 1; CPR Pt 20. The definitive interpretation of the phrase 'the same damage' is contained in the decision of the House of Lords in *Royal Brompton NHS Trust v Hammond* [2002] 1 WLR 1397.

2 LA 1980, s 9(2) states that the time limit for contribution claims in s 10 exists as an exception to the six-year limitation period contained in s 9(1), which applies to all other actions to recover any sum recoverable by statute.

3 [2002] 1 All ER (Comm) 481, [2002] 1 WLR 1.

4 The *obiter* finding of the court was that the six-year contract limitation period contained in the LA 1980, s 5 applied to this equitable cause of action by analogy (pursuant to the LA 1980, s 36(1)).

5 See *Telfair Shipping Corporation v Indersea Carriers SA: The Caroline P* [1985] 1 WLR 553.

6 LA 1980, s 28.

7 LA 1980, s 32.

8 SI 2011/1133 inserted a new s 33A into the LA 1980 which provides that if a time limit would otherwise expire while the parties are engaged in mediation or within eight weeks of the mediation concluding, the time limit shall be extended for a further period of eight weeks after it concludes: s 33A(3).

9 LA 1980, s 35.

contribution.[10] Noticeably, no reference is made to an acknowledgment or part payment extending the limitation period for claiming contribution.

THE 'RELEVANT DATE' FROM WHICH THE TWO-YEAR LIMITATION PERIOD RUNS

25.02 The date on which a right to recover contribution shall be deemed to have accrued is ascertained by reference to the matters set out in s 10(3) and (4) and is described as 'the relevant date' in s 10.[11] If a person is held liable for that damage by a judgment given in court proceedings or an award made in an arbitration, the relevant date is the date of the judgment or award and no account is taken of any judgment or award on appeal unless it varies the amount of damages awarded against the person in question.[12] This latter provision has the potential to operate unfairly and effectively creates an obligation to commence contribution proceedings after a first instance decision, notwithstanding the lodging of an appeal, or else to take one's chances in relation to any appeals. The date of assessment of the damages payable is the relevant date, if different from the date of the judgment on liability.[13] If the person claiming contribution settles his claim with the (potential) claimant, the relevant date is the date that the amount to be paid by him to the other person (or each of the persons, as the case may be) is agreed.[14] In *Knight v Rochdale Healthcare NHS Trust*,[15] it was held that even though a settlement was subsequently the subject of a consent court order, the limitation period ran from the date of firm agreement between the parties and not from the date of the consent order. Reference to the 'amount to be paid' was held in *Baker & Davies Plc v Leslie Wilks Associates*[16] to include payments in kind and that it should more properly be described in that case as a reference to the 'value of the payment in kind'. Judge Richard Havery QC also held that time ran from when the full amount of the payment in kind (ie remedial works) was determined rather than each item of expense setting time running separately.

CASES WHERE CLAIMANT'S RIGHT OF ACTION STATUTE BARRED AGAINST DEFENDANT OR THIRD PARTY

25.03 In cases where the defendant's claim for contribution against a third party is not statute barred under s 10, the claim for contribution will still fail as being time barred if the tortfeasor against whom contribution is sought has ceased to be liable to the claimant by virtue of the expiry of a limitation period which extinguished the right on which the claim against him in respect of the damage

10 CLCA 1978, s 10(5).
11 CLCA 1978, s 10(2).
12 CLCA 1978, s 10(3).
13 *Aer Lingus Plc v Gildacroft Ltd* [2006] EWCA Civ 4, [2006] 1 WLR 1173.
14 CLCA 1978, s 10(4).
15 [2003] EWHC 1831 (QB), [2004] 1 WLR 371.
16 [2005] EWHC 1179 (TCC), [2005] 3 All ER 603.

was based.[17] The reference to the claimant's claim having been 'extinguished' limits the scope of this provision to cases involving actions for the recovery of land[18] and the long-stop period contained in s 11A(3) of the LA 1980 in respect of claims under the Consumer Protection Act 1987. However, it would not appear to refer to the overriding time limit of 15 years within which negligence claims not relating to personal injuries must be brought by virtue of s 14B of the LA 1980.[19] It does not matter if the defendant's liability to the claimant is statute barred at the date the contribution action is brought so long as the defendant was under a legal liability to the claimant on the relevant date when judgment was entered or an agreement to pay the claimant was reached.[20]

PROCEDURE FOR CLAIMING CONTRIBUTION

25.04 The provisions in the CPR containing the procedural requirements for claiming contribution are quite forgiving and do not contain any obligation to seek contribution 'as soon as is reasonably possible' as is contained, for example, in the Irish Civil Liability Act 1961.[21] If the person against whom the defendant wishes to make a claim for contribution is one of a number of claimants, a claim for contribution may be made by way of counterclaim. A claim by way of set-off or counterclaim is deemed to be a new claim and to have been commenced on the same date as the claim in which the set-off or counterclaim is pleaded,[22] thus making the ability to rely on this deemed commencement date important in cases where a separate action would be statute barred, as was the case in *Law Society v Wemyss*.[23] If the person from whom contribution is sought is a co-defendant in the proceedings, the claim may be made by filing a notice of contribution under CPR 20.6(1).[24] If the person from whom contribution is sought is not already a party to the proceedings, the claim should be made by filing an additional claim form, which may be done without leave of court if done prior to filing a defence,[25] and thereafter with leave of the court.[26] An additional claim is made when the court issues the appropriate claim form.[27]

17 CLCA 1978, s 1(3); *George Wimpey & Co Ltd v British Overseas Airways Corpn* [1955] AC 169.
18 LA 1980, s 15(1).
19 *Financial Services Compensation Scheme v Larnell* [2005] EWCA Civ 1408, [2006] QB 808.
20 CLCA 1978, s 1(2).
21 See *ECI Ltd v MC Bauchemie Muller GmbH* [2006] IESC 16, [2007] 1 IR 156, where it was held by the Irish Supreme Court that if a defendant's third party notice is struck out for failure to issue and serve it as soon as reasonably possible, absent exceptional excusing factors, it will be an abuse of process for him to claim contribution in separate proceedings.
22 LA 1980, s 35(1), (2).
23 [2008] EWHC 2515 (Ch), [2009] 1 All ER 752.
24 Notice of contribution may be filed without leave of court if filed at the same time as a defendant files his defence or 28 days thereafter: CPR 20.6(2)(a), or at any time thereafter with the court's permission: CPR 20.6(2)(b).
25 CPR 20.7(3)(a).
26 CPR 20.7(3)(b).
27 CPR 20.7(2).

CHAPTER 26

European Union Law

INTRODUCTION

26.01 Limitation issues which arise in actions against the State alleging a breach of European Union law and in cases where it is argued that European Union law gives rise to an obligation to disregard a domestic limitation provision can pose certain conceptual difficulties. These issues together with the time limits applicable to proceedings before the European Court of Justice are considered in this chapter.

ACTIONS AGAINST THE STATE FOR BREACH OF EUROPEAN LAW

26.02 Proceedings may be brought against the State claiming damages for a serious breach of European law under the principle established by the European Court of Justice in *Francovich v Italian Republic.*[1] In *R v Secretary of State for Transport, Ex p Factortame (No 7),*[2] it was held by Judge John Toulmin QC that an action of this type is a tort and is subject to the six-year limitation period contained in s 2 of the Limitation Act 1980 ('LA 1980') which runs from the date the losses were suffered. That decision was followed in *Phonographic Performance Ltd v Department of Trade and Industry,*[3] where the breach in question was a failure to implement a directive correctly, which was held to give rise to a continuing tort for which damages could be recovered for losses suffered during the period of six years prior to proceedings being brought. However, in many cases, such as *Poole v HM Treasury,*[4] the breach will give rise to a single tort, which will be statute barred six years after the first loss is suffered. In *Poole,* the claimants brought proceedings in 2002 in respect of an alleged failure by the defendant to

1 (C-6/90 & C-9/90) [1991] ECR I-5357. These principles have been developed in subsequent cases, including in *Brasserie du Pêcheur SA v Federal Republic of Germany* (C-46/93 & C-48/93) [1996] ECR I-1029.

2 [2001] 1 WLR 942 at 967.

3 [2004] EWHC 1795 (Ch), [2004] 1 WLR 2893.

4 [2006] EWHC 2731 (Comm), [2007] 1 All ER (Comm) 255; see also *Spencer v Secretary of State for Work and Pensions* [2008] EWCA Civ 750, [2009] QB 358, the facts of which are set out in para 26.04.

implement correctly an insurance directive in 1975, which they said caused them to suffer losses between 1980 and 1996. They argued that the six-year period should only start to run from the date the directive was correctly implemented or the date they were in a position to know of the failure of the defendant to transpose the insurance directive (relying both on the effectiveness principle of European law and s 14A of the LA 1980). Langley J held that the cause of action, while recognised as a tort, did not arise in the tort of negligence and thus s 14A was inapplicable, and held that European law did not require any modification of the general rules on limitation.[5] An argument that the failure to transpose the directive correctly gave rise to a continuing tort was regarded as irrelevant to the facts of this case as the last breach that caused damage had occurred by 1993, although losses continued to be suffered thereafter, meaning that all claims were statute barred.

EUROPEAN LAW AS A REASON TO DISREGARD A LIMITATION PROVISION

26.03 The principle of national procedural autonomy governs the procedures that national courts must follow when a party attempts to rely on rights conferred under European law.[6] This principle is subject to two conditions, known as the condition of equivalence[7] and the condition of effectiveness,[8] with a requirement of legal certainty featuring as an aspect of the latter. Where breach of the condition of equivalence leads to a breach of European law, the proceedings challenging the breach must still be brought within the applicable limitation period.[9] The effectiveness condition provides that procedural circumstances (which includes limitation provisions) imposed by national law must not make it impossible to exercise rights arising under European community law. In *Emmott v Minister for Social Welfare*,[10] the applicant brought judicial review proceedings in 1988 in relation to the failure by the Irish government to correctly implement a directive and its subsequent failure to make payments to her which she should have received from 1984 onwards. The government argued that her judicial review proceedings had not been brought in time. The European Court of Justice stated that time limits which preclude an applicant from bringing a claim could only apply from the date when a directive had been fully implemented. However,

5 The claimants' argument based on *Emmott v Minister for Social Welfare* (C-208/90) [1991] ECR I-4269 was rejected: see further para 26.03 et seq.

6 See *Rewe-Zentralfinanz v Direktor der Landwirtshaftskammer Westfalen-Lippe* (C-39/73) [1973] ECR 1039.

7 See *Palmisani v INPS* (C-261/95) [1997] ECR I-4025, in which the applicant challenged the shorter limitation period which Italian law applied to claims for compensation against the State arising out of an incorrectly implemented Directive.

8 See Chalmers *et al*, *European Union Law* (Cambridge: Cambridge University Press, 2006) at 391.

9 See *Byrne v Motor Insurers' Bureau* [2008] EWCA Civ 574, [2008] 4 All ER 476, where the claimant's action was found not to be statute barred as he was under a disability and thus subject to an extended limitation period.

10 (C-208/90) [1991] ECR I-4269.

the European Court of Justice has proven to be less interventionist in subsequent decisions, with one academic text commenting that 'during the course of 1993, the Court of Justice seems to have suffered a crisis of confidence'[11]. In *Steenhorst-Neerings*,[12] it refused to apply the *Emmott* principle to national provisions which, rather than limiting the right to bring an action, limited the length of time for which a claim could be backdated. In *Johnson II*,[13] the ECJ then stated that the ruling in *Emmott* had been justified by the particular circumstances of that dispute including the steps taken by the State department to dissuade the claimant from enforcing her EU rights within the limitation period.

26.04 The retreat from *Emmott v Minister for Social Welfare*[14] continued in *Fantask A/S v Industriministeriet (Erhvervsministeriet)*,[15] where the European Court of Justice held that a time limit could begin to run before a directive had been properly implemented. This caused Langley J in *Poole v HM Treasury*[16] to state as follows:

> 'It would, I think, be difficult to find a case which, whilst never being overruled, has been more emasculated by subsequent decisions than *Emmott*'s case. "Unqualified *Emmott*" is, beyond doubt, now of no authority. National limitation periods can and do bite before a directive is implemented in respect of claims for non-transposition. The claimants in this case cannot therefore succeed in their primary submission on the limitation issue.'[17]

In *Spencer v Secretary of State for Work and Pensions*,[18] the claimants alleged that they had suffered loss by reason of the failure of the English government to implement two directives correctly, which resulted in one claimant recovering an inadequate sum as compensation and the other claimant's claim being dismissed. Their actions against the tortfeasors having concluded, the claimants brought proceedings against the State for breach of European law. The Court of Appeal held that their respective causes of action for breach of European law accrued when they had suffered personal injury. The fact that accurate measurement of the damage at that date might have been difficult and that they had to exhaust their domestic remedies before suing the State did not stop the running of time.

26.05 Although subsequent decisions have greatly restricted the scope of the *Emmott* decision, the requirements of effectiveness, equivalence and legal

11 Wyatt and Dashwood, *European Union Law* (6th edn, Oxford: Hart Publishing, 2011) at 299.

12 *Steenhorst-Neerings v Bestuur van de Bedrijfsverengiging voor Detailhandel* (C-338/91) [1993] ECR I-5475.

13 *Johnson v Chief Adjudication Officer* (C-410/92) [1994] ECR I-5483.

14 (C-208/90) [1991] ECR I-4269.

15 (C-188/95) [1997] ECR I-6783.

16 [2006] EWHC 2731 (Comm), [2007] 1 All ER (Comm) 255.

17 [2006] EWHC 2731 (Comm), [2007] 1 All ER (Comm) 255 at para 228. In his judgment in the Irish High Court in *TD v Minister for Justice* [2011] IEHC 37, Hogan J expressed some polite criticism of the analysis of the ECJ of the Irish judicial review time limits in *Emmott* and, at para 16, commented that 'the true basis for Emmott appears to have been that of quasi-estoppel'.

18 [2008] EWCA Civ 750, [2009] QB 358.

certainty have featured in a number of recent judgments of the ECJ and UK Supreme Court. The decision in *Commission v Ireland*[19] arose out of a challenge to a tender for the construction and maintenance of national roads by the Irish government. On 14 October 2003 the National Roads Authority ('NRA') informed the tenderers that it had selected Celtic Roads Group ('CRG') as its 'preferred tenderer' although it said that this did not mean that CRG was guaranteed to win the tender. On 9 December 2003 the NRA decided to award the contract to CRG and on 5 February 2004 the parties signed a contract. Proceedings were commenced on 8 April 2004 challenging the award of the tender, in which the claimant argued that time ran from 5 February, but the Irish High Court held that time ran from 14 October 2003 and dismissed the proceedings as having been brought outside the three-month time limit for public procurement challenges.[20] The European Commission pursued a complaint against Ireland, leading to the decision of the ECJ of 28 January 2010 that the Irish legislation containing the time limits for public procurement challenges breached the principle of legal certainty and effectiveness as it '[gave] rise to uncertainty as to which decision must be challenged through legal proceedings and as to how periods for bringing an action are to be determined'.[21] The ECJ approved of the comments of Advocate General Kokott that it was only if it was 'clear beyond doubt' that time ran from the earlier date that this would have satisfied the requirement of legal certainty.[22] It is important to note that the result of the decision in *Commission v Ireland* was that the State was found liable, not that the time limit was disapplied.

26.06 Issues relating to equivalence and effectiveness came before the Supreme Court on three occasions in 2012. In *BCL Old Co Ltd v BASF Plc (No 2),*[23] the Supreme Court heard an appeal directed solely at the question of whether the interpretation and legal effect of the two-year limitation period in s 47A of the Competition Act 1998 for follow-on claims in competition cases was sufficiently foreseeable and clear to satisfy the principles of effectiveness and legal certainty in the protection of the EU rights in question.[24] The facts of the case are set out in detail later in the book[25] but the salient feature of the facts was that the Court of Appeal in *BCL Old Co Ltd v BASF SE (No 1)*[26] and the Competition Appeal Tribunal ('CAT') in *BCL Old Co Ltd v BASF Plc (No 2)*[27] had suggested that the CAT and court had jurisdiction to extend time to bring claims under s 47A, whereas the Court of Appeal in *BCL (No 2)*[28] held that no such power exists. Despite the evident difference of opinion among judges in the lower courts as to

19 (C-456/08) [2010] ECR I-859, [2010] 2 CMLR 1138; see also *Uniplex (UK) Ltd v NHS Business Services Authority* (C-406/08) [2010] ECR I-817.
20 See further paras 29.07–29.08.
21 (C-456/08) [2010] ECR I-859, [2010] 2 CMLR 1138 at para 83. A specific ground of complaint, relevant only to public procurement challenges, that the decision which started time running had not been notified to the unsuccessful tenderer in good time was also upheld.
22 (C-456/08) [2010] ECR I-859, [2010] 2 CMLR 1138 at para 57.
23 [2012] UKSC 45, [2012] 1 WLR 2922.
24 See *Courage Ltd v Crehan* (C-453/99) [2001] All ER (EC) 886, [2002] QB 507.
25 Paragraphs 31.03–31.04.
26 [2009] EWCA Civ 434, [2009] Bus LR 1516.
27 [2010] Comp AR 1.
28 [2011] EWCA Civ 1258, [2011] Bus LR 428.

the correct interpretation to be given to s 47A, the Supreme Court held that the time limit in question was certain and its effects were reasonably foreseeable. In reaching this conclusion, Lord Mance looked at the language of the French text of the decision in *Commission v Ireland*[29] and found that the test of whether the meaning of the provisions containing the time limits was 'clear beyond doubt' did not represent an accurate translation of what the ECJ had intended to convey in its judgment, as otherwise 'any reasonably arguable question' as to the correct interpretation of a time limit would lead to a breach of EU law.[30] He stated that it was unfortunate if the decisions of the CAT and Court of Appeal had been erroneous but noted that '[a]n appellate system is there to remedy error and to establish the correct legal position. I do not accept that its ordinary operation is the hallmark of a lack of legal certainty or effectiveness'[31] and held that it should have been obvious to BASF of the risks involved in delaying the issue of proceedings beyond a particular date. He had little difficulty in rejecting a standalone argument that the two-year time limit made it excessively difficult for BASF to bring proceedings. He proceeded to consider the position that would have arisen if BASF had succeeded in arguing that the time limit breached EU law. In such a circumstance, Lord Mance stated that it was 'impossible to think that European law requires the setting aside as between civil parties of a limitation defence',[32] although the analogy he drew with the result of *Commission v Ireland*[33] is somewhat strained, as the defendant to that complaint was Ireland and as public procurement challenges are brought against an award of a contract by the State. In addition, if the claimant in *BASF* had established that the limitation period breached EU law, the result would presumably have been to provide it with a statute barred cause of action against the State. It remains to be seen whether these *obiter* comments are revisited in a future case where a party succeeds in the underlying claim that a time limit breaches EU law, although it should be noted that Lord Mance in *BASF (No 2)* was of the view that the legal principles expressed by him were *acte clair.* By contrast, in *Fleming (trading as Bodycraft) v Revenue and Customs Commissioners*,[34] the House of Lords, having held that a short time limit for certain claims for a refund of taxes breached EU law, held that no time limit applied to those claims and held that the time limit ceased to be of legal effect. A significant distinguishing factor between *BASF* and *Bodycraft* is that in the latter case the party seeking to rely on the time limit was, in effect, the State. However, it is possible to note some conflict between *BASF* and the judgment of Lord Walker in *Bodycraft*, which stated that in the case of directly enforceable Community rights breached by domestic legislation, '[s]ometimes, however, a conforming construction is not possible, and disapplication cannot be avoided'.[35]

29 (C-456/08) [2010] ECR I-859, [2010] 2 CMLR 1138; see also *Uniplex (UK) Ltd v NHS Business Services Authority* (C-406/08) [2010] ECR I-817.
30 [2012] UKSC 45, [2012] 1 WLR 2922 at para 20.
31 [2012] UKSC 45, [2012] 1 WLR 2922 at para 39.
32 [2012] UKSC 45, [2012] 1 WLR 2922 at para 45.
33 (C-456/08) [2010] ECR I-859, [2010] 2 CMLR 1138; see also *Uniplex (UK) Ltd v NHS Business Services Authority* (C-406/08) [2010] ECR I-817.
34 [2008] UKHL 2, [2008] 1 All ER 1061. See also *Marks and Spencer Plc v Customs and Excise Comrs* (C-62/00) [2003] QB 866, [2002] ECR I-6325.
35 [2008] UKHL 2, [2008] 1 All ER 1061 at para 25.

26.07 In *Test Claimants in the FII Group Litigation v Revenue and Customs Comrs*,[36] the Supreme Court had to rule on a number of issues in an appeal relating to a claim for a refund of taxes invalidly claimed by the State. The primary finding of the court was that the claimants were entitled to rely on the extended limitation period contained in s 32(1)(c) of the LA 1980 for an action seeking relief from the consequences of mistake, even though a statutory right to claim a refund having a shorter limitation period was also open to them. A second issue, on which the court divided, leading to the necessity for a reference to the ECJ, was whether the principles of effectiveness, equivalence, legal certainty or legitimate expectations precluded the State from enacting legislation[37] which sought to limit retrospectively the right of the claimants, or other taxpayers, from relying on s 32(1)(c) for their claims. A majority of the court held that this breached the principle of equivalence as it left the claimants with a remedy for breach of EU law that was less favourable than that available to them for other similar cases not involving a breach of EU law. Although the judgment of Lord Sumption was in the minority on the equivalence and effectiveness points, it contains a very detailed overview of the case law on the issue and a decision of the ECJ on the reference will be eagerly awaited. In *Birmingham City Council v Abdulla*,[38] Lord Wilson in the Supreme Court expressed some interesting *obiter* comments on what is required by the principle of equivalence for employment rights derived from EU law which may be prosecuted before either an employment tribunal or the civil courts. He noted that the House of Lords in *Preston v Wolverhampton Healthcare NHS Trust (No 2)*,[39] in ruling on the legality of a six-month time limit for certain pension claims when compared with the six-year contract limitation period, had 'with considerable hesitation'[40] held that it was not satisfied the six-month time limit was less favourable for an employee than the contract limitation period given other features of the two types of proceeding. Speaking in *Abdulla*, Lord Wilson noted that the decision of the House of Lords in *Preston v Wolverhampton Healthcare NHS Trust (No 2)* was one 'which some might now consider borderline but from which the court was not invited to depart'.[41] Given this invitation to raise this issue again before the courts, it may be expected that further litigation will follow on the point.

LIMITATION PROVISIONS FOR PROCEEDINGS BEFORE THE EUROPEAN COURT OF JUSTICE

26.08 The time limits for proceedings brought before the European Court of Justice have more in common with judicial review time limits than limitation provisions and in many cases what is being challenged is a legislative act. Importantly, however, a reference to the European Court of Justice made pursu-

36 [2012] UKSC 19, [2012] 2 AC 337.
37 Finance Act 2004, s 320 and Finance Act 2007, s 107.
38 [2012] UKSC 47, [2013] 1 All ER 649.
39 [2001] 2 AC 455, [2001] 2 WLR 448.
40 [2012] UKSC 47, [2013] 1 All ER 649 at para 33, per Lord Wilson.
41 [2012] UKSC 47, [2013] 1 All ER 649 at para 34, per Lord Wilson.

ant to art 267[42] of the Consolidated Treaty on European Union[43] is not subject to any limitation provision. For cases where a time limit applies, a general discretion exists to extend time in cases of 'unforeseeable circumstances'[44] and a distinct concept of 'excusable error' may also be relied upon to extend time. This latter concept may be invoked where the claimant's error arose from the conduct of the respondent institution.[45] In addition, time limits for all parties are extended by a uniform period of grace of ten days in order to take account of the distance between their habitual residence and the court.[46]

26.09 The following are the main limitation provisions which apply to actions brought before the European Court of Justice: An action for the annulment of legislation under art 263[47] must be brought within two months of the publication of the legislation in the Official Journal.[48] An action for failure to act under art 265[49] must be brought within two months of the failure of the relevant body to respond to a request to act. A request that the institution remedy its failure to act must occur within a reasonable time of it being clear that it is in breach.[50] An action against the European Community for damages under art 340[51] is subject to a five-year limitation period if the claim is non-contractual, which commences on the date of the occurrence of the events giving rise to the claim.[52] If the claim is contractual, it is governed by the law applicable to the contract and falls to be dealt with by the national courts.[53]

42 This article was formerly referred to as art 234.
43 The articles in the Treaty on European Union were renumbered with effect from the date of entry into force of the Lisbon Treaty: see OJ C 83, 30.3.2010.
44 Protocol on the Statute of the Court of Justice, art 45.
45 See *Bayer AG v European Commission* (T-12/90) [1991] ECR II-219.
46 Protocol on the Statute of the Court of Justice, art 45.
47 This article was formerly referred to as art 230.
48 See Vaughan and Robertson, *Law of the European Union* (Oxford: Oxford University Press, 2009) at para 105.
49 This article was formerly referred to as art 232.
50 See *Netherlands v Commission* [1971] ECR 639; Vaughan and Robertson, *Law of the European Union* (Oxford: Oxford University Press, 2009) at para.125.
51 This article was formerly referred to as art 288.
52 Protocol on the Statute of the Court of Justice, art 46.
53 See Vaughan and Robertson, *Law of the European Union* (Oxford: Oxford University Press, 2009) at para 148.

CHAPTER 27

Employment

THE CALCULATION OF TIME IN EMPLOYMENT CASES

27.01 The time limits for claims alleging breaches of the employment legislation are calculated differently to those governed by the Limitation Act 1980 ('LA 1980'), as periods of time under the employment legislation include both the start date and the end date in calculating the relevant period.[1] Thus, a claim which arises on 29 August and is subject to a three-month time limit must be presented to an employment tribunal by close of business on 28 November. A claim is 'presented' when it is delivered to the Central Office of Employment Tribunals. In *Birmingham Midshires Building Society v Horton*,[2] the employment appeal tribunal cautioned that it was not reasonable to expect first class post to arrive on the following day. In *Initial Electronic Security Systems Ltd v Avdic*,[3] the employment appeal tribunal (EAT) held that a claim form sent by email to the employment tribunal's email address which appeared to have been transmitted properly was sufficient to entitle the claimant to an extension of time in a case where the email subsequently appears not to have reached its intended target. If a claim is not made to an employment tribunal within the time limit provided by statute, it has been held in a series of cases since the 1970s that the employment tribunal will not have jurisdiction to hear the complaint as, unlike a limitation period properly so called, the temporal limitations on the bringing of employment claims are jurisdictional and not procedural in effect.[4]

PRIMARY TIME LIMITS FOR CLAIMS UNDER THE EQA 2010

27.02 The Equality Act 2010 ('EqA 2010') repealed and replaced a large number of anti-discrimination enactments such as the Equal Pay Act 1970 and the

1 *Pruden v Cundard Ellerman Ltd* [1993] IRLR 317; *Pacitti Jones v O'Brien* [2005] IRLR 188.
2 [1991] ICR 648; see also *Consignia Plc v Sealy* [2002] EWCA Civ 878, [2002] 3 All ER 801.
3 [2005] ICR 1598, [2005] IRLR 671.
4 *Dedman v British Building and Engineering Appliances Ltd* [1974] 1 All ER 205, [1974] ICR 53 (CA) and *Rogers v Bodfari (Transport) Ltd* [1973] IRLR 172, [1973] ICR 325. These decisions were most recently followed by the Court of Appeal in *Radakovits v Abbey National Plc* [2009] EWCA Civ 1346, [2010] IRLR 307; see further para 1.18.

Sex Discrimination Act 1975. As most of the legislation in this area is derived from European Directives, regard must be had to the underlying European Directive or Regulation when interpreting the English legislation.[5] Most of its provisions have been commenced,[6] although a change of government since its passing means that it is likely that not all of its provisions will be brought into force.[7] A number of enforcement options are open to an aggrieved party whose rights under the EqA 2010 are breached, depending on the precise nature of the breach alleged, and each has its own time limit. A complaint to an employment tribunal under s 120 must be brought within the period of time allowed by s 123, which is:

(a) the period of three months (claims under s 120) or six months (claims under s 121(1)) starting with the date of the act to which the proceedings relate, or

(b) such other period as the employment tribunal thinks just and equitable.[8]

Proceedings before the county court in respect of discrimination in other fields under s 114 must be brought within the period of time allowed by s 118, which is:

(a) the period of three months starting with the date of the act to which the claim relates, or

(b) such other period as the county court thinks just and equitable.[9]

The six-month period is extended to nine months for certain claims as referred to in s 118(3) and (4). Sections 118 and 123 also provide, in the same terms, that conduct extending over a period is to be treated as done at the end of the period[10] and the failure to do something is to be treated as occurring when the person in question decided on it.[11] In the absence of evidence to the contrary, a person is to be taken to decide on failure to do something:

(a) when he does an act inconsistent with doing it, or

(b) on the expiry of the period in which he might reasonably have been expected to do it.[12]

EXTENSIONS OF TIME UNDER THE EQA 2010 ON 'JUST AND EQUITABLE' GROUNDS

27.03 Sections 118 and 123 of the EqA 2010 allow the employment tribunal or the court, as appropriate, to extend the time limit for bringing a claim if this is

5 See Ch 26 and para 27.04 below.
6 See in particular the Equality Act 2010 (Commencement No 4, Savings, Consequential, Transitional, Transitory and Incidental Provisions and Revocation) Order 2010 (SI 2010/2317), which commenced the majority of the Act and repealed the prior legislation in force from 1 October 2010.
7 Deakin and Morris, *Labour Law* (6th edn, Oxford: Hart Publishing, 2012) at 615–616.
8 EqA 2010, s 123(1) and (2).
9 EqA 2010, s 118(1).
10 EqA 2010, ss 118(6)(a) and 123(3)(a).
11 EqA 2010, ss 118(6)(b) and 123(3)(b).
12 EqA 2010, ss 118(7) and 123(4)

'just and equitable'. The question whether it is 'equitable' to consider complaints out of time is one of fact and degree and in *British Coal Corpn v Keeble*[13] it was held that the exercise of the discretion may take into account factors similar to those relevant to the exercise of the discretion to disapply the limitation period for a personal injuries action in s 33 of the LA 1980. This requires the employment tribunal to consider the reasons for the delay, its effect on the cogency of the evidence and the nature of advice given to the complainant which may have contributed towards him missing the time limit. In *Aniagwu v Hackney London Borough Council*,[14] it was held just and equitable to extend time where the delay was caused by the fact that the applicant was attempting to resolve the grievance through an internal grievance procedure. In *Southwark London Borough v Afolabi*,[15] a lengthy extension of time was granted to the claimant who only discovered the evidence which led to his race discrimination claim nine years after his dismissal. In *Robertson v Bexley Community Centre*,[16] the claimant suffered one incident of racial abuse at work, following which a hearing was held at which the perpetrator apologised and then went on sick leave. Very soon after the perpetrator's return to work, six months after the first incident, he presented a claim to the employment tribunal, following which there was a second incident of racial abuse. At first instance an extension of time to the three-month time limit was refused, which was reversed on appeal, but the Court of Appeal restored the decision to refuse to extend time. Auld LJ noted that the applicant for an extension of time bears the burden of proof and that extending time should be the exception rather than the rule.[17] He held that the claimant was not entitled to rely on events after he had instituted his complaint in support of his application, and secondly, that there had been no 'course of conduct' which would have rendered the complaint in time. In light of those findings, he held that it was not just and equitable to extend time from April to October. In *Chief Constable of Lincolnshire Police v Caston*,[18] the employee's complaint was made within three months of a date when she alleged she decided that she had no option but to resign. In cross-examination at a pre-hearing review, she conceded that she had made the decision earlier, but the employment judge extended time for her claim and allowed it to proceed. The Court of Appeal upheld this decision and found that neither a liberal nor a strict approach should be taken for applications to extend time and Sedley LJ cautioned against 'distraction by a textbook comment of doubtful relevance or weight'.[19]

27.04 The area that has given rise to most difficulty in applications to extend time on just and equitable grounds is where the complainant alleges that as a result of a judicial decision the law, as previously understood, had changed and

13 [1997] IRLR 336 (EAT).

14 [1999] IRLR 303 (EAT); however, the rule is not universal: see also *Robinson v Post Office* [2000] IRLR 804 (EAT) and *Apelogun-Gabriels v London Borough of Lambeth* [2001] EWCA Civ 1853, [2002] IRLR 116.

15 [2003] EWCA Civ 15, [2003] IRLR 220.

16 [2003] EWCA Civ 576, [2003] IRLR 434.

17 [2003] EWCA Civ 576, [2003] IRLR 434 at para 25.

18 [2009] EWCA Civ 1298, [2010] IRLR 327.

19 [2009] EWCA Civ 1298, [2010] IRLR 327 at para 32.

he now realised that he had a claim worth pursuing. While in general the English courts are unsympathetic to an argument of this nature where domestic limitation legislation is at issue,[20] a complicating factor is the fact that this issue has arisen in several cases where either legislation transposing a European Directive, or the domestic case law interpreting that legislation, was found (sometimes by the ECJ) not to have afforded employees the rights they should have enjoyed. In *Foster v South Glamorgan Health Authority*,[21] the claimants presented a complaint alleging sex discrimination relating to their pension rights a lengthy period after the time limit for complaints of this nature, but soon after the ECJ in *Marshall v Southampton & South-West AHA*[22] had declared the relevant English legislation to be in breach of EU law. The employment tribunal found that it was just and equitable to extend time for their complaint. By contrast, the Court of Appeal in *Biggs v Somerset County Council*[23] found that the same argument could not be relied upon to extend a time limit where an extension depended on the applicant showing it was 'not reasonably practicable' to present a complaint in time, which is the wording used in what is now the Employment Rights Act 1996, discussed below. In *Mills v Marshall*,[24] the EAT distinguished *Biggs* and held that its approach is only applicable in cases that consider whether a misunderstanding of the law meant it was not reasonably practicable to present a complaint, and not to time limits that can be extended where this is just and equitable, such as those now contained in the EqA 2010. The effect of the EU law on limitation periods and time limits is considered further in Chapter 26.

CLAIMS OF BREACH OF AN 'EQUALITY CLAUSE OR RULE' BEFORE AN EMPLOYMENT TRIBUNAL OR THE COURTS

27.05 Section 127(1) provides that, except for complaints relating to service in the armed forces,[25] an employment tribunal has jurisdiction to determine a complaint relating to a breach of an equality clause or rule. Section 129(2) provides that '[p]roceedings on the complaint or application may not be brought in an employment tribunal after the end of the qualifying period'. The 'qualifying period' for a standard case is six months, which commences on different dates, the most important of which is the six-month period beginning with the last day of the employment or appointment.[26] A nine-month period governs complaints or applications relating to terms of service in the armed forces.[27] Section 127(9) of the EqA 2010 provides that '[n]othing in this section affects such jurisdiction as the High Court [or] a county court ... has in relation to an equality clause or rule'. However, s 128(1) provides that if it appears to a court in which proceedings are pending 'that a claim or counter-claim relating to an equality clause or rule could

20 See *Awoyami v Radford* [2007] EWHC 1671 (QB), [2008] 3 WLR 34, discussed in para 1.22.
21 [1988] IRLR 277, [1988] ICR 526.
22 (C-152/84) [1986] IRLR 140, [1986] ICR 335.
23 [1996] IRLR 203.
24 [1998] IRLR 494.
25 EqA 2010, s 127(6).
26 EqA 2010, s 129(3).
27 EqA 2010, s 129(4).

more conveniently be determined by an employment tribunal, the court may strike out the claim or counter-claim'. In *Abdulla v Birmingham City Council*,[28] the Supreme Court had to rule on the effect of the predecessor to s 128(1)[29] in the context of a claim brought by a number of employees before the High Court which would have been out of time if brought before an employment tribunal. The court held, by a majority,[30] in categorical terms, that a claim could never be more conveniently disposed of by the employment tribunal if it would be time-barred before the tribunal. However, proceedings brought before the courts could be struck out if they constituted an abuse of its processes, for example where a claimant had been invited to present a complaint in time to the tribunal but had spurned the invitation in order to secure an illegitimate advantage by bringing the claim before the court.[31] The court also commented that it retained a discretion to refuse a claimant costs in proceedings which could have been brought before an employment tribunal.[32]

PRIMARY TIME LIMITS UNDER THE ERA 1996

27.06 The Employment Rights Act 1996 ('ERA 1996') governs various employment rights including, *inter alia*, those relating to minimum notice, unfair dismissal and redundancy. Section 111 of the ERA 1996 contains the time limit within which a complaint of unfair dismissal must be made to an employment tribunal, which is either:

(a) three months from the 'effective date of termination',[33] or

(b) such further period as the tribunal considers reasonable in a case where it is satisfied that it was not reasonably practicable for the complaint to be presented within three months.[34]

The same time limit is also provided for complaints in relation to:

(i) the obligation to provide a statement in writing of employment particulars (which runs from the date on which the employment ceased),[35]

(ii) unauthorised deductions from wages (which runs from the date of the payment giving rise to the complaint);[36]

(iii) the right to time off work (eg for ante natal care) (which runs from the date the time off should have been allowed);[37]

28 [2012] UKSC 47, [2013] 1 All ER 649.
29 Equality Act 1970, s 2(3).
30 Lord Sumption and Lord Carnwath dissented.
31 [2012] UKSC 47, [2013] 1 All ER 649 at para 29, per Lord Wilson.
32 [2012] UKSC 47, [2013] 1 All ER 649 at para 30, per Lord Wilson.
33 ERA 1996, s 111(2)(a).
34 ERA 1996, s 111(2)(b).
35 ERA 1996, s 11(4).
36 ERA 1996, s 12(2) and (4).
37 ERA 1996, s 57(2). The ERA 1996, Pt VI lists several other circumstances in which time off work must be allowed; the three-month period applies in each case.

(iv) the right to parental leave (which runs from the date of the matters complained of);[38] or

(v) the right to compensation under Part XII from the Secretary of State in the case of employer insolvency (which runs from the date of refusal of the claim).[39]

An important right which is subject to a different time limit is the right to claim a redundancy payment, for which s 164(1) provides that the employee must apply to his employer for a redundancy payment[40] or refer a question as to his entitlements to an employment tribunal within six months of the date of dismissal. Section 164(2) provides that a late application may still be made if during the period of six months following that referred to in s 164(1) the employee submits a claim in writing to his employer for a redundancy payment or refers a question as to his entitlements to an employment tribunal, and it appears to the tribunal to be just and equitable that the employee should receive a redundancy payment. A small number of employment rights referred to in the ERA 1996, in particular the redundancy rights of public sector employees, are not circumscribed by a three- (or six-) month time limit and may be the subject of a referral to an employment tribunal during the contract limitation period of six years.[41]

EXTENSIONS OF TIME UNDER ERA 1996 IF NOT REASONABLY PRACTICABLE TO PRESENT COMPLAINT IN TIME

27.07 The jurisdiction to extend time under the ERA 1996 is more narrowly circumscribed than that contained in the EqA 2010. The approach adopted to the similarly worded provision in a predecessor to the ERA 1996 by Lord Denning MR in *Dedman v British Building & Engineering Appliances Ltd*[42] drew a sharp distinction between claimants who missed a time limit due to ignorance of their rights and those who engaged 'skilled advisers' who missed the time limit, with the latter class of person being unable to seek an extension of time and instead being left to a remedy against their adviser. Over time the courts and employment tribunals moved away from applying a strict rule of this nature, but in decisions such as *Camden & Islington Community Services NHS Trust v Kennedy*,[43] the EAT made clear that a solicitor who sought to argue that matters outside his control (such as post being mislaid) justified the EAT extending time would have to satisfy a stringent test of having taken all reasonable steps to check that documents had been received, which was not established to the satisfaction of the EAT in *Kennedy.* In *Biggs v Somerset County Council*,[44] the claimant was dismissed

38 ERA 1996, s 80(2).

39 ERA 1996, s 188(2).

40 The application must be sufficiently precise: see *Hetherington v Dependable Products Ltd* (1971) 6 ITR 1.

41 *Greenwich Health Authority v Skinner* [1989] ICR 220 (EAT).

42 [1974] IRLR 379.

43 [1996] IRLR 381.

44 [1996] 2 All ER 734.

from her part-time job in 1976 but English employment legislation appeared to preclude any claim being brought by her until a decision of the House of Lords in 1994 which favoured part-time workers. Within three months following this decision she made a claim for unfair dismissal and sought an extension of time within which to pursue her claim on grounds that she had only recently become aware of her rights. The Court of Appeal held that the test of whether it was 'reasonably practicable' to present a claim was directed to difficulties or impediments of a temporary nature, such as illness, faced by an individual claimant. Her mistake as to her rights was a mistake of law, not fact, and it would be contrary to the principle of legal certainty to allow past transactions to be reopened and limitation periods circumvented because the existing law at the relevant time had not yet been explained or had not been fully understood.

27.08 Other factors considered relevant include the fact that ignorance of time limits is often not considered a good ground for an extension of time,[45] although sometimes it justifies an extension of time;[46] bad advice from a legal adviser[47] is not normally a good ground to extend time, though bad advice from a trusted trade union official[48] or an official source[49] may be a good ground. In *Machine Tool Industry Research Association v Simpson*[50] and *Marley (UK) Ltd v Anderson*,[51] it has been held that the discovery of additional facts which revealed that a dismissal had been unfair may justify an extension of time being granted as it would not have been reasonably practicable to present a complaint in ignorance of those facts. While it was stated by Kilner Brown J in *Crown Agents for Overseas Governments and Administrations v Lawal*[52] that it would not in general be reasonably practicable to present a claim while a person is participating in a conciliation process, this was not followed by Browne Wilkinson J in *Bodha v Hampshire Area Health Authority*[53] or the Court of Appeal in *Palmer v Southend-on-Sea Borough Council*.[54] The same approach was adopted in the case of an employee awaiting the outcome of other proceedings, such as criminal proceedings.[55] However, in *Ashcroft v Haberdashers' Aske's Boys' School*,[56] Burton J held that the *Crown Agents v Laval* approach was to be preferred, in particular in light of the legislative intent in passing the Employment Act 2002,[57] and this

45 *Northamptonshire County Council v Entwhistle* [2010] IRLR 740 (EAT).
46 *Averns v Stagecoach in Warwickshire* [2008] All ER (D) 23 (Sep) (EAT).
47 *Dedman v British Building & Engineering Appliances Ltd* [1974] IRLR 379; *Northamptonshire CC v Entwhistle* [2010] IRLR 740 (EAT).
48 *Wright v Wolverhampton City Council* [2009] All ER (D) 179 (Feb) (EAT).
49 *Harvey's Household Linens Ltd v Benson* [1974] ICR 306; *Rybak v Jean Sorrelle Ltd* [1991] ICR 127.
50 [1988] ICR 558, [1988] IRLR 212 (CA).
51 [1996] ICR 728, [1996] IRLR 163 (CA).
52 [1978] IRLR 542.
53 [1982] ICR 200.
54 [1984] 1 All ER 945, [1984] IRLR 119.
55 *Union Cartage Co Ltd v Blunden* [1977] ICR 420; *Trevelyans (Birmingham) Ltd v Norton* [1991] ICR 488.
56 [2008] IRLR 375.
57 Since replaced by the Employment Act 2008.

has been followed in subsequent decisions.[58] If the employee is ill during part of the period for bringing a claim, such as the claimant in *Schultz v Esso Petroleum Ltd*[59] who suffered disabling depression, this is a factor which may justify an extension of time being granted.

58 *John Lewis Partnership v Charman,* UKEAT/0079/11/ZT; *Wandsworth Borough Council v Covent Garden Market Authority* [2011] EWHC 1245 (QB), but see contra *Shaw v Remploy Ltd* [2009] All ER (D) 294 (Jul) (EAT).

59 [1999] 3 All ER 338, [1999] ICR 1202 (CA).

CHAPTER 28

The Human Rights Act 1998 and the European Convention on Human Rights

CHALLENGES TO THE COMPATIBILITY OF LIMITATION PROVISIONS ON HUMAN RIGHTS GROUNDS

28.01 The very existence of limitation provisions *ipso facto* affects a claimant's right of access to the courts, more properly described as affecting his ability to obtain a remedy from the courts. In the case of real property (except if the claim is governed by the Land Registration Act 2002) and personal property their effect goes further, extinguishing the claimant's rights in the property upon the expiry of the applicable limitation period. An excessively short or unfair limitation period could be argued to violate the claimant's rights protected by the European Convention on Human Rights[1] ('Convention'). Equally, an excessively long limitation period could be argued to contravene a defendant's right to the quiet enjoyment of his property or to have potential claims against him determined within a reasonable time. Two articles are of particular relevance to limitation issues and have featured in recent challenges to the compatibility of sections in the Limitation Act 1980 with the Convention.

28.02 The article in the Convention having most relevance to the English limitation code is art 6, which provides that everyone has the right to a fair and public hearing within a reasonable time, ie a right of access to the courts. In *Stubbings v United Kingdom*,[2] the applicant alleged that her right of access to the courts had been unjustifiably impaired by the non-extendable six-year limitation period which was held by the House of Lords to apply to her claim for damages for sexual assault.[3] She argued that this was unreasonably short by reason of the nature of the psychological injuries that victims of child sexual abuse are caused to suffer, which inhibits them from bringing proceedings promptly. The European Court of Human Rights ('European Court') held that as the essence of her right of access to the courts was not impaired, and as the limitation period pursued a legitimate aim and was proportionate, there was no violation of art 6 of the Convention. Taking into account the margin of appreciation afforded to

1 Convention for the Protection of Human Rights and Fundamental Freedoms (Rome, 4 November 1950).

2 App No 22083/93; [1996] ECHR 44; (1996) 23 EHRR 213.

3 *Stubbings v Webb* [1993] AC 498.

contracting States in deciding how the right of access to the court should be circumscribed, and the lack of uniformity among Member States as to limitation periods, the European Court found there had been no violation of art 6.[4]

28.03 The second provision of particular relevance to limitation issues is art 1 of the First Protocol to the Convention, which provides that no one shall be deprived of his possessions except in the public interest and subject to conditions provided for by law, but that a State may control the use of property in accordance with the general interest. Following the decision of the House of Lords in *JA Pye (Oxford) Ltd v Graham*,[5] a case was taken to the European Court to challenge the law then in force in England and Wales, on grounds that the extinguishment of the claimant's title to land upon the expiry of the limitation period violated art 1 of the First Protocol as it allowed a squatter to take the land without payment of compensation.[6] The Fourth Chamber of the European Court held[7] that there had been a deprivation of the applicant's possessions which imposed a disproportionate burden on the applicant by reason of the lack of compensation. This decision was reversed on appeal by the Grand Chamber of the European Court in August 2007,[8] which held that the case did not involve the deprivation of possessions but instead the control of their use. The court held that the legislation pursued a legitimate aim and that it was proportionate, notwithstanding the absence of compensation and that it fell within the margin of appreciation given to States to regulate the control of use of land. Although the law on adverse possession had been in a state of flux between 2005 and 2007,[9] in light of the decision of the Grand Chamber of the European Court it has been held both by the European Court[10] and by the Court of Appeal[11] that the provisions in the LA1980 which govern actions relating to real property are compatible with the Convention.

LIMITATION PERIOD FOR PROCEEDINGS AGAINST A PUBLIC AUTHORITY UNDER THE HUMAN RIGHTS ACT 1998

28.04 Section 7(1) of the Human Rights Act 1998 ('HRA 1998') provides a right of action to a person who claims that a public authority has acted (or proposes to act) in a way which is incompatible with a Convention right. Section 7(5) provides

4 Subsidiary claims of breach of art 8 (failure to respect private life) and art 14 (discrimination) were also unsuccessful.

5 [2002] UKHL 30, [2003] 1 AC 419.

6 It should be noted that the Land Registration Act 2002 was enacted into law subsequent to the facts giving rise to the claim in *JA Pye (Oxford) Ltd v United Kingdom* and that, where the 2002 Act applies, the law is now quite different to that under consideration before the European Court; see further Ch 15.

7 [2005] ECHR 921; (2005) 43 EHRR 3.

8 App No 44302/02, judgment of 30 August 2007: [2007] ECHR 5559, (2008) 46 EHRR 45.

9 *Beaulane Properties Ltd v Palmer* [2005] EWHC 817 (Ch), [2006] Ch 79.

10 *Topplan Estates Ltd v United Kingdom,* App No 15642/05, [2008] ECHR 430.

11 See *Ofulue v Bossert* [2008] EWCA Civ 7, [2009] 1 Ch 1 (affirmed without reference to this point: [2009] UKHL 16, [2009] 1 AC 990) where the Court of Appeal held that the compatibility of the pre-2002 English law on adverse possession with the Convention could not be raised again, in the absence of special circumstances, which were not established.

that any such proceedings must be brought before the end of the period of one year beginning with the date on which the act complained of took place, or 'such longer period as the court or tribunal considers equitable having regard to all the circumstances' but also that any extension of time is 'subject to any rule imposing a stricter time limit in relation to the procedure in question'. Two aspects of s 7(5) appear relatively uncontroversial: the one-year time limit is clear on its face, and the reference to any extension of time being subject to a rule of procedure imposing a shorter time limit is presumably intended to refer to the judicial review time limits and is intended to avoid these being circumvented by the inclusion of a claim for relief under s 6 of the HRA 1998. The discretion to extend time if 'equitable' to do so has been the subject of a number of decisions of the courts, including two recent decisions of the House of Lords, which demonstrate the wide discretion granted to the courts to extend time by this subsection.

28.05 The claimant in *Dunn v Parole Board*[12] was released on licence having served part of a prison sentence but then had his licence revoked for breaching his terms. He sought an oral hearing to challenge the revocal of his licence but, due to delays on the part of the Parole Board, the hearing only occurred at the end of September 2001, approximately ten months after he was returned to prison. He issued proceedings in January 2006 seeking damages, *inter alia*, pursuant to the HRA 1998 and an extension of time to bring the proceedings pursuant to s 7(5)(b) of the Act. In dealing with this application, the Court of Appeal held, first, that the one-year time limit in s 7(5) is to be treated as a limitation period which can afford a defence to a claim, if pleaded, rather than as going to the jurisdiction of a court to hear a claim brought pursuant to s 7(1) of the HRA 1998. Secondly, it held that a claimant bears the burden of proving that there are circumstances which make it 'equitable' why the defendant should not be able to take advantage of the limitation provision. In discussing the factors to be taken into account in deciding on whether to extend time, Thomas LJ stated as follows:

> 'Parliament gave the court a wide discretion; I do not think it would be helpful to list the factors to be taken into account or to state which should have greater weight or lesser weight ... It is for the court to examine in the circumstances of each case all the relevant factors and then decide whether it is equitable to provide for a longer period. It may be necessary in the circumstances of a particular case to look at objective and subjective factors; proportionality will generally be taken into account. It is not in my view appropriate to say that one particular factor has as a matter of general approach a greater weight than others. The court should look at the matter broadly and attach such weight as is appropriate in each given case.'[13]

In deciding on whether it was 'equitable' to extend time in *Dunn*, the Court of Appeal noted that the Parole Board had suffered prejudice by reason of the delay as some files had been shredded in accordance with official policy prior to the

12 [2008] EWCA Civ 374, [2009] 1 WLR 728. Other judgments to have considered applications to extend time under s 7(5) include *Cameron v Network Rail* [2006] EWHC 1133, [2007] 1 WLR 163; *Weir v Secretary of State for Transport* [2004] EWHC 2772 (Ch), [2005] UKHRR 154 and *Dobson v Thames Utilities* [2007] EWHC (QB) 202.

13 [2008] EWCA Civ 374, [2009] 1 WLR 728 at paras 31–32.

claim being instituted, and that an assertion that the delay was explained in part by the claimant awaiting the result of certain litigation was not borne out on the facts. For these as well as other reasons an extension of time was refused.

28.06 The claimant in *A v Essex County Council*[14] was an autistic child with special educational needs who was born in 1989. His parents were asked to withdraw him from school in January 2002 pending the carrying out of a detailed medical assessment and decision on where his schooling should continue. Due to delays in carrying out the assessment and obtaining a suitable special school for him, he remained out of school until July 2003. Proceedings were issued on his behalf in May 2005 in which it was contended that the failure to provide him with special needs education in the 18-month period he was out of school breached his right of access to education. This argument was rejected, with the House of Lords finding that the relevant provision only prohibited discriminatory treatment of all students and not an entitlement on the part of the claimant to receive special needs schooling, which it was revealed cost the defendant £223,589 per annum from May 2005. A subsidiary issue then arose for consideration before the House, as to whether the claimant would still be entitled to claim damages in respect of the failure to provide him with basic non-special needs schooling between January 2002 and July 2003. As the proceedings were only brought in May 2005, the claimant was required to seek an extension of time to pursue this claim, which the House of Lords held it would refuse. Lord Nicholls gave the majority[15] speech on the limitation point and stated that, 'I do not think that it would be desirable to permit A an extension of time to pursue this alternative case, which, even if successful, would resolve no issue of principle and be unlikely to sound in significant damages'.[16]

28.07 The claimants in *Rabone v Pennine Care NHS Trust*[17] were the parents of a voluntary psychiatric inpatient who had committed suicide during a home visit. The defendant admitted negligence on its part and compromised the claim brought by them under the Law Reform (Miscellaneous Provisions) Act 1934. However, it denied liability in the second limb of the claim which sought compensation for their bereavement under s 7(1) of the HRA 1998 for breach of art 2 of the Convention by reason of the failure by the defendant to protect the right to life of the deceased. The proceedings were brought one year and four months after the death of the deceased and the defendant also opposed the claimant's application for an extension of time under s 7(5) of the HRA 1998 to enable them to pursue the claim. Having found that, limitation issues aside, the claimants

14 [2010] UKSC 33, [2011] 1 AC 280.

15 Baroness Hale dissented, noting that the delay was short, no prejudice had been caused to the defendant and that the approach adopted failed to vindicate the claimant's human rights. She identified the point that if a claimant has a strong case he is more likely to gain an extension of time, stating, 'I venture to speculate that, if he had thought that the case raised a triable issue, he would have had little difficulty in extending time so that it could be tried': [2011] 1 AC 280 at para 119.

16 [2011] 1 AC 280 at para 90. Lord Kerr added the following: 'a court may well have concluded that no award of damages was necessary in order to provide just satisfaction to A': *ibid* at para 169.

17 [2012] UKSC 2, [2012] 2 AC 72.

were entitled to succeed in their claims and that the Court of Appeal had correctly assessed the appropriate quantum of compensation at £5,000 per person, Lord Dyson proceeded to analyse the effect of s 7(5) of the HRA 1998, commenting as follows:

> 'The court has a wide discretion in determining whether it is equitable to extend time in the particular circumstances of the case. It will often be appropriate to take into account factors of the type listed in section 33(3) of the Limitation Act 1980 as being relevant when deciding whether to extend time for a domestic law action in respect of personal injury or death. These may include the length of and reasons for the delay in issuing the proceedings; the extent to which, having regard to the delay, the evidence in the case is or is likely to be less cogent than it would have been if the proceedings had been issued within the one-year period; and the conduct of the public authority after the right of claim arose, including the extent (if any) to which it responded to requests reasonably made by the claimant for information for the purpose of ascertaining facts which are or might be relevant. However ... the words of section 7(5)(b) of the HRA mean what they say and the court should not attempt to rewrite them. There can be no question of interpreting section 7(5)(b) as if it contained the language of section 33(3) of the Limitation Act 1980.'[18]

Having reversed the Court of Appeal[19] on the issue of liability, the House of Lords proceeded to reverse its decision on the application to extend the limitation period. The decision on liability was the most important factor,[20] with Lord Dyson noting that a number of other factors pointed in favour of granting the extension of time, namely that the required extension was short, that the defendant had suffered no prejudice by the delay, and as the claimants had acted reasonably in holding off proceedings in the hope that an investigative report promised to them by the defendant (but only delivered in 2007) might obviate the need for court proceedings.

28.08 The breadth of the discretion provided by s 7(5)(b) of the HRA 1998 was again emphasised in *R (on the application of D) v Metropolitan Police Commissioner*,[21] in proceedings in which the claimant alleged that art 3 of the Convention had been breached by the defendant in the manner in which her complaint of rape had been investigated. The focus of her claim was that defects in the efforts by the police to gather evidence for the criminal prosecution had contributed towards the acquittal of the accused by a jury in May 2006. The investigating Chief Superintendent subsequently apologised to the claimant for these defects and a report of the Independent Police Complaints Commission in March 2009 was critical of the investigation. Proceedings were launched by the claimant in February 2010. In assessing whether it was 'equitable' to extend time, Eady J took into account a number of factors, including the fact that she

18 [2012] UKSC 2, [2012] 2 AC 72 at para 75.
19 [2010] EWCA Civ 698, [2011] QB 1019.
20 The Court of Appeal in its judgment had stated that if it had found for the claimants on the issue of liability that it would have also afforded them an extension of time pursuant to s 7(5) to pursue their claim.
21 [2012] EWHC 309 (QB).

had problems with depression, drug taking and suicide attempts, what he characterised as a reasonable decision to await a grant of legal aid so that her legal advisers could apply for anonymity on her part in pursuing her claim, the fact that her legal advisers had apparently misunderstood the time limit contained in s 7(5) and the fact that the Strasbourg jurisprudence on the merits of her claim had advanced considerably in the period up to 2009. It is unclear why Eady J placed so much importance on receipt by the claimant of the IPCC report in March 2009, but the factors relied upon by the claimant can readily be seen to be stronger than those present in many cases.

TIME LIMIT FOR A COMPLAINT TO THE EUROPEAN COURT OF HUMAN RIGHTS

28.09 The European Court of Human Rights may only deal with a complaint after all domestic remedies have been exhausted[22] and if brought within a period of six months from the date on which the final decision was taken.[23]

22 See Van Dijk *et al* (eds), *Theory and Practice of the European Convention on Human Rights* (4th edn, Mortsel: Intersentia, 2006) at 125–161.

23 Article 35(1); Van Dijk *et al* (eds), *Theory and Practice of the European Convention on Human Rights* (4th edn, Mortsel: Intersentia, 2006) at 162–172.

CHAPTER 29

Judicial Review and Public Procurement Proceedings

INTRODUCTION

29.01 The procedural time limits contained in CPR Pt 54 and the Senior Courts Act 1981 for the bringing of judicial review proceedings are not technically a 'limitation provision' and neither are the time limits that govern public procurement challenges under the Public Contracts Regulations 2006 or the Utilities Contracts Regulations 2006. However, as these time limits perform an important role in regulating certain classes of proceedings, and as they serve an analogous role to that played by the Limitation Act 1980, they are discussed briefly in this chapter.

JUDICIAL REVIEW PROCEEDINGS

Time limit for commencing judicial review proceedings

29.02 The judicial review time limits in CPR 54 state that the claim form initiating an application for judicial review must be filed promptly, and in any event not later than three months after the grounds to make the claim arose.[1] This time limit may not be extended by agreement between the parties,[2] and if any other enactment specifies a shorter time limit for making the claim for judicial review then that shorter time limit applies.[3] These provisions must be read in conjunction with s 31(6) of the Senior Courts Act 1981, which provides that where there has been 'undue delay'[4] in making an application for judicial review, the court may refuse to grant leave for the making of the application or any relief sought on the application, if granting the relief 'would be likely to cause substantial hardship to, or substantially prejudice the rights of, any person or would be detrimental

1 CPR 54.5(1).
2 CPR 54.5(2).
3 CPR 54.5(3).
4 In *R v Dairy Produce Quota Tribunal for England and Wales, Ex parte Caswell* [1990] 2 AC 738, it was held by the House of Lords that if an application was not made promptly, or within three months, then undue delay for the purposes of s 31(6) was established, thus ensuring that the same analysis of the primary time limit applies to the test in both provisions.

to good administration'. The claim form and other documentation required to be served by CPR 54.6(2) and PD 54A must then be served on the respondent and the other interested parties within seven days after the date of issue.[5] The main difference between judicial review and other forms of proceedings is the next stage in the procedure, wherein the papers are then considered by a judge, generally without a hearing, who has to decide whether to grant the claimant permission to proceed with the proceedings.[6] The court will then serve an order on the claimant, defendant and other interested parties granting or refusing permission and notifying them of any other directions.[7]

The overriding requirement to move promptly

29.03 The overriding requirements that the application be made 'promptly' and without 'undue delay' mean that the three-month requirement has been described as 'the court's rule of thumb'[8] but that the court will 'listen to any argument or, if necessary, to take the point itself, that a lack of promptness renders it unfair or wrong to let an application proceed or succeed, albeit brought within the three months'.[9] In considering whether an application was made promptly, the court will take into account all the facts and circumstances including whether the claimant received prior warning of the decision complained of, and the length of time between the taking of the decision and its communication to the claimant. Time starts running when the grounds for application objectively first arose, whether or not that was known to the claimant. In *R (on the application of Berky) v Newport City Council*,[10] the second respondent was granted planning permission on 26 January 2011 and commenced building works on 26 March. The applicant commenced judicial review proceedings on 26 April, which the Court of Appeal noted was the last day of the three-month period prescribed by CPR 54.5(1).[11] However, it proceeded to find that the application had not been filed promptly and that the reliefs sought by reference to grounds of challenge based on domestic law[12] should be refused because of non-compliance with the requirement of promptness contained in CPR 54.5(1), as well as because the second

5 CPR 54.7.

6 CPR 54.4 and PD 54A, paras 8.4–8.5: this was formerly known as the 'leave application' and was made *ex parte* to the court. A claimant can request that the question of permission to proceed be considered at a hearing and that counsel be permitted to make submissions on his behalf. See, for example, *De Smith's Judicial Review* (6th edn, London: Sweet & Maxwell, 2007) at paras 16-041–16-049.

7 CPR 54.11.

8 *Crown Prosecution Service v City of London Magistrates' Court* [2007] EWHC 1924 (Admin) at para 21, per Sedley LJ.

9 *Crown Prosecution Service v City of London Magistrates' Court* [2007] EWHC 1924 (Admin) at para 21, per Sedley LJ.

10 [2012] EWCA Civ 378; see also *R (on the application of Burkett) v Hammersmith and Fulham LBC* [2002] UKHL 23, [2002] 1 WLR 1593; *Hardy v Pembrokeshire County Council* [2006] EWCA Civ 240, [2006] Env LR 28 and *R (on the application of MacRae) v Herefordshire District Council* [2011] EWHC 2810 (Admin).

11 *Pritam Kaur v S Russell & Sons Ltd* [1973] QB 336.

12 The law on judicial review time limits for grounds of challenge based on European Union law is discussed in para 29.04 et seq.

respondent would suffer prejudice consequent on the applicant's undue delay, namely that the construction works had been lawfully commenced but were now the subject of a court challenge.

Judicial review challenges based on EU law and Uniplex

29.04 In the important decision of the European Court of Justice in *Uniplex (UK) Ltd v NHS Business Services Authority*,[13] it was held, in the field of public procurement,[14] that an undefined test of 'promptness' offended the EU principles of certainty and effectiveness, and, accordingly, that only the express time limit could apply to such challenges. The CJEU put the matter in the following terms:

> '[41] A national provision such as Regulation 47(7)(b) of the 2006 Regulations ... gives rise to uncertainty. The possibility cannot be ruled out that such a provision empowers national courts to dismiss an action as being out of time even before the expiry of the three-month period if those courts take the view that the application was not made "promptly" within the terms of that provision.
>
> [42] As the Advocate General observed in point 69 of her Opinion, a limitation period, the duration of which is placed at the discretion of the competent court, is not predictable in its effects. Consequently, a national provision providing for such a period does not ensure effective transposition of Directive 89/665.'[15]

29.05 In *R (on the application of Buglife) v Medway Council*,[16] it was held that the *Uniplex* principle applies to judicial review proceedings challenging the absence or adequacy of other requirements of EU law, such as an Environmental Impact Assessment. In light of this decision it would appear to be settled law that only the three-month time limit contained in CPR 54.5 – and not the overriding obligation to move promptly *in addition* – applies to all judicial review challenges based on European Union law. In *R (on the application of Berky) v Newport City Council*,[17] it was stated *obiter* by the Court of Appeal that the impact of *Uniplex* may be that separate time limits now apply to judicial review grounds of challenge based on domestic and EU law, with the overriding obligation of promptness only applying to the former. More interestingly, Carnwath

13 (Case C-406/08) [2010] PTSR 1377, [2010] 2 CMLR 47 (ECJ). The same result and reasoning is evident in *Commission v Ireland* (Case C-456/08) [2010] 2 CMLR 1138, which involved a challenge to the public procurement time limits contained in the Irish rules of procedure which, though worded differently, were similar in effect to the time limits contained in the 2006 Regulations.

14 The challenge related to the Public Contracts Regulations 2006 (SI 2006/5), made to give effect in domestic law to the Procurement Directive 89/665. Following the decision in *Uniplex*, these Regulations and the Utilities Contracts Regulations 2006 (SI 2006/6) were amended by the Public Procurement (Miscellaneous Amendments) Regulations 2011 (SI 2011/2053) to ensure compliance with European Union law.

15 (Case C-406) [2010] ECR I-817, [2010] 2 CMLR 1255 at paras 41–42.

16 [2011] EWHC 746 (Admin), [2011] Env LR 27. This decision was followed in *R (on the application of U & Partners (East Anglia) Ltd) v Broads Authority* [2011] EWHC 1824 (Admin).

17 [2012] EWCA Civ 378.

LJ in *Berky* suggested that *Uniplex* may be capable of being distinguished and that it would not govern a situation where undue delay had caused prejudice to a respondent, in which case s 31(6) of the Senior Courts Act 1981 could still be relied upon to dismiss the proceedings. However, he was in the minority[18] in making these comments and it remains to be seen how the *Uniplex* principles will develop in future decisions.

Application to extend time in judicial review proceedings

29.06 CPR 3.1(2)(a) gives the court a general discretion to extend the time limit for filing a claim form. A 'good reason' for the delay is not the sole factor which will be considered by the court. Also relevant are the reasons for any delay and whether or not any extension of time would cause prejudice or hardship or would otherwise be detrimental to good administration. For example, an extension of time was granted in *R v Secretary of State for the Home Department, Ex p Ruddock*,[19] where the applicant was initially unaware of the decision, but once aware had acted quickly. However, a period of delay due to the fault of the applicant's lawyers was found not to provide a good reason to extend time in *R v Secretary of State for Health, Ex p Furneaux*,[20] in particular where the challenge affected third party rights. A more detailed analysis of the case law can be found in the practitioner textbooks on subject.[21]

PUBLIC PROCUREMENT CHALLENGES

Time limits applying to public procurement challenges

29.07 As discussed above, the ECJ in *Uniplex (UK) Ltd v NHS Business Services Authority*[22] held that an overriding requirement that an applicant for relief under the domestic legislation move 'promptly' was contrary to European Union law as it was impermissibly lacking in certainty. In light of this decision,[23] both the Public Contracts Regulations 2006 and the Utilities Contracts Regulations 2006 were amended by the Public Procurement (Miscellaneous Amendments) Regulations 2011.[24] Following their amendment, the Public

18 Moore-Bick LJ and Sir Richard Buxton did not think that *Uniplex* could be distinguished in this manner; all comments were *obiter* as the Court of Appeal was unanimous in dismissing the proceedings on their merits.

19 [1987] 1 WLR 1482.

20 [1994] 2 All ER 652.

21 See, for example, *De Smith's Judicial Review* (6th edn, London: Sweet & Maxwell, 2007) at para 16-054.

22 (Case C-406) [2010] ECR I-817, [2010] 2 CMLR 1255.

23 As well as the decision in the related case of *Commission v Ireland* (Case C-456/08) [2010] 2 CMLR 1138.

24 SI 2011/2053. The amended wording applies to all cases where the claimant's date of knowledge occurs on or after 1 October 2011. Transitional provisions applied to claimants whose date of knowledge was before that date but all such claims would by now have been concluded.

Contracts Regulations 2006 now provide in reg 47(6) that a challenge may be brought under the Regulations if:

> '[T]hose proceedings are brought within 30 days from the date of knowledge unless the Court considers that there is good reason for extending the period within which proceedings may be brought, in which case the Court may extend that period up to a maximum of three months from the date of knowledge.'[25]

The same wording is also used in the amended reg 45(5) in the Utilities Contracts Regulations 2006. Accordingly, after this amendment to the governing time limit, the only temporal issues to be considered are the date of the claimant's date of knowledge and whether a claimant who misses the initial 30-day time limit is entitled to an extension of time of up to three months from his date of knowledge.

29.08 In *Henry Brothers (Magherafelt) Ltd v Department of Education for Northern Ireland*,[26] the complainant commenced proceedings under the Public Contracts Regulations 2006 on 12 November 2007 in respect of a tender which had a deadline on 7 August 2007. The claimant argued that time should only be held to run from 17 October, when the tender was awarded, but that even if they were five days outside the three-month time limit,[27] time should be extended because the extension sought was so short as a standstill agreement had been in place for part of the period and there had been ongoing correspondence and exchange of information. Having analysed the recent case law in the area, the Court of Appeal for Northern Ireland offered the following helpful summary of the law:

> 'From these authorities we consider that we can draw three propositions which are material to this case.
>
> (i) The cause of action only arises where a breach of the regulations is alleged. Anticipation of a breach is not sufficient (see *Risk Management Partners Ltd v Brent London BC* [2009] EWCA Civ 490, [2010] LGR 99).
>
> (ii) The breach can consist of any infringement of the regulations which gives rise to the risk of loss or damage (see *Risk Management Partners* [2010] LGR 99 at paras 242 and 255; *Uniplex (UK) Ltd v NHS Business Services Authority* Case C-406/08 [2010] ECR I-817, paras 29–31; and *Sita UK Ltd v Greater Manchester Waste Disposal Authority* [2011] EWCA Civ 156, (2011) 134 ConLR 1 at para 22).
>
> (iii) Time runs from the date on which the claimant has the requisite knowledge that a breach of sufficient magnitude to justify proceedings has occurred (see *Uniplex (UK)* [2010] ECR I-817, paras 30–31).'[28]

In applying that summary of the law to the facts of the case, the court did not need to rule on whether time ran from 17 August or 17 October and was content

25 Regulation 47(7), as amended.
26 [2011] NICA 59, (2011) 142 ConLR 193.
27 Now reduced to 30 days by the Public Procurement (Miscellaneous Amendments) Regulations 2011 (SI 2011/2053), but now running from the claimant's date of knowledge: see para 29.07.
28 [2011] NICA 59, (2011) 142 ConLR 193 at para 33.

to find that even if time ran from the latter date that it would have extended time because of the strength of the reasons advanced by the claimant. As the time limits under the amended reg 47(6) of the Public Contracts Regulations no longer allow an extension of time of more than three months from a claimant's date of knowledge, there will be less scope for omnibus findings on time limit issues in future and defendants will have more reason to argue that time ran from before the tender being awarded.[29] However, the important point to note is that in assessing a claimant's date of knowledge, time starts to run from the date on which the claimant had sufficient knowledge to take an informed view as to whether there had been an infringement.[30]

29 See *Risk Management Partners Ltd v Brent London Borough Council* [2009] EWCA Civ 490, [2010] LGR 99; *Mears Ltd v Leeds City Council* [2011] EWHC 40 (QB).

30 *Sita UK Ltd v Greater Manchester Waste Disposal Authority* [2011] EWCA Civ 156, (2011) 134 ConLR 1.

CHAPTER 30

Proceeds of Crime

STATUTORY PROVISIONS: SS 27A AND 27B OF THE LA 1980

30.01 Sections 27A[1] and 27B[2] of the Limitation Act 1980 ('LA 1980') contain almost identically worded provisions which govern proceedings brought under the Proceeds of Crime Act 2002 ('POCA 2002') and the Proceeds of Crime Act 2002 (External Requests and Orders) Order 2005 ('2005 Order'). Section 27A applies to proceedings under Pt 5, Ch 2 of the POCA 2002 for the civil recovery of proceeds of unlawful conduct and s 27B applies to civil proceedings under the 2005 Order for the realisation of property to give effect to an external order. Subsection (1) in each of ss 27A and 27B provides that none of the time limits contained in the 'preceding provisions of this Act'[3] apply to any proceedings governed by the two sections. Subsection (2) in each case provides that proceedings governed by that section for a recovery order in respect of any recoverable property shall not be brought after the expiration of the period of 12 years from the date on which the relevant person's[4] cause of action accrued. Subsection (3) provides that proceedings are 'brought' when a claim form is issued, or an application is made for a property freezing order,[5] or an application is made for an interim receiving order, whichever is earliest. Subsection (4) states that the 'cause of action accrues in respect of any recoverable property':

(i) in the case of proceedings for a recovery order in respect of property obtained, or believed to have been obtained, as a result of or in connection

1 Section 27A was inserted into the LA 1980 by the Proceeds of Crime Act 2002, ss 288(1), 458(1) and SI 2003/120.

2 Section 27B was inserted into the LA 1980 by the Proceeds of Crime Act 2002 (External Requests and Orders) Order 2005 (SI 2005/3181), art 201(1).

3 The provisions on fraud and deliberate concealment contained in the LA 1980, s 31(1)(a) and (b) therefore apply to such claims: see the cases discussed in paras 30.03 to 30.04.

4 Section 27A(8) and 27B(8) define 'relevant person' as the Serious Organised Crime Agency, the Director of Public Prosecutions, the Director of Revenue and Customs Prosecutions or the Director of the Serious Fraud Office.

5 This clause was inserted by the Serious Organised Crime and Police Act 2005, s 109 and Sch 6.

with unlawful conduct[6] or criminal conduct,[7] when the property is so obtained, and

(ii) in the case of proceedings for a recovery order in respect of any other recoverable property, when the property obtained, or believed to have been obtained, as a result of or in connection with unlawful conduct[8] or criminal conduct[9] which it represents is so obtained.

CONVERSION OF CHATTELS: TITLE OF OWNER NOT EXTINGUISHED BY S 3(2) OF THE LA 1980

30.02 Section 3(2) of the LA 1980 provides that at the expiration of the limitation period for a person to bring an action in respect of the conversion of his chattel, his title to the chattel shall be extinguished. A significant modification of this rule exists in the case of theft[10] and ss 27A(5) and 27B(5) add a second major exception to s 3(2). They provide that if proceedings are started under Pt 5, Ch 2 of the POCA 2002 or Pt 5, Ch 2 of the 2005 Order for a recovery order in respect of the chattel, s 3(2) of the LA 1980 does not prevent the owner of the chattel from asserting on an application under s 281 of the POCA 2002, or art 192 of the 2005 Order, respectively, that the property belongs to him. If the court makes a declaration in his favour under the article, his title to the chattel is then treated as not having been extinguished by s 3(2) of this Act.[11]

CASE LAW ON S 27A: SZEPIETOWSKI AND GALE

30.03 The limitation provisions governing applications brought under the POCA 2002 appear only to have been the subject of two decisions to date. The interaction between the 12-year limitation period contained in s 27A(2) and the provisions on fraud and deliberate concealment in s 32(1) of the LA 1980 pose conceptual difficulties in the context of a cause of action and a claimant which have only been in existence since 2002. Section 316(3) of the POCA 2002 attempts to overcome these difficulties by providing that, 'for the purpose of deciding whether or not property was recoverable at any time (including times before commencement), it is to be assumed that this Part was in force at that time and any other relevant time'. In *Director of the Assets Recovery Agency v Szepietowski*,[12] it was held that the Assets Recovery Agency ('ARA') could rely

6 LA 1980, s 27A(4)(i). Section 27A(7) states that expressions used in the section and Pt 5 of the POCA 2002 shall have the same meaning in s 27A as in that Part.

7 LA 1980, s 27B(4)(i). Section 27B(7) adds that the phrase 'criminal conduct' is to be construed in accordance with the POCA 2002, s 447(8) and that other expressions used in s 27B which are also used in the 2005 Order, Pt 5 shall have the same meaning in this section as in that Part.

8 LA 1980, s 27A(4)(ii).

9 LA 1980, s 27B(4)(ii).

10 LA 1980, s 4.

11 LA 1980, ss 27A(6) and 27B(6).

12 [2007] EWCA Civ 766, *Times Law Reports*, 21 August 2007, [2008] Lloyd's Rep FC 10.

on acts of concealment which occurred prior to its existence, with Moore-Bick LJ stating that it could rely on acts which concealed the wrong from 'anyone who might be interested in discovering [the mortgage fraud]'[13] and Waller LJ adding that concealment of facts by the respondents from the defrauded mortgage lenders by the use of fictitious names and other dishonest conduct at the outset constituted concealment from the ARA.[14] Deliberate concealment from the ARA of facts relevant to the cause of action during the investigation was also found to trigger an extension of time under s 32(1)(b) until the concealment was discovered or with reasonable diligence could have been discovered, following the decision of the House of Lords in *Sheldon v Outhwaite*.[15] An argument that the ARA's cause of action was 'based on the fraud'[16] of the defendant was not accepted by the Court of Appeal,[17] on grounds that s 32(1)(a) only applies in the case of a fraud on the claimant and does not apply to a claim by a third party such as the ARA which arises by virtue of the fraud. It was also noted that the allegation of 'mortgage fraud' encompassed a number of causes of action where fraud was not a constituent element and as such fell outside the statutory provision.[18]

30.04 In *Serious Organised Crime Agency v Gale*,[19] the SOCA brought an application for an interim receiving order against the respondents on 28 July 2005 in which it was alleged that they had profited from drug trafficking over a lengthy period of time. Of relevance from a limitation perspective, £3 million of the monies claimed had been received by the respondents between 1989 and 1992; the respondents argued that any claim to recover this money was statute barred by reason of s 27A(2) of the LA 1980. The SOCA relied on s 32(1)(b) in response, pointing to the use of nominees, off-shore bank accounts and companies, the movement of money from country to country and the use of false names, although the respondents argued that the police were well aware from 1992 of the material now relied upon.[20] Based on these findings, Griffith Williams J in the High Court held that 'if there had been an Assets Recovery Agency in 1992, those [ie the concealed] facts would not have been known'.[21] He also made the rather surprising finding that the knowledge of the police in 1992 should not be attributed to the SOCA, which inverts the normal principles applicable to a concealment argument. On appeal, the Court of Appeal approached matters from an entirely different perspective and held that the respondents bore the burden of proof in raising a limitation defence, which required them to prove when the cause of action accrued. In reaching this conclusion, Carnwath LJ

13 [2007] EWCA Civ 766 at para 123, per Moore-Bick J.
14 See [2007] EWCA Civ 766 at para 59, per Waller LJ and para 85, per Wall LJ.
15 [1996] 1 AC 102.
16 LA 1980, s 32(1)(a).
17 Moore-Bick LJ dissented on this point.
18 See [2007] EWCA Civ 766 at para 46 and *Beaman v ARTS Ltd* [1947] 1 KB 550.
19 [2009] EWHC 1015 (QB), [2009] All ER (D) 119 (May) (HC); [2010] EWCA Civ 759, [2010] 1 WLR 2881 (CA). The limitation issues did not feature in the decision of the Supreme Court: [2011] UKSC 49, [2011] 1 WLR 2760.
20 Reference was also made to *Ezekiel v Lehrer* [2002] EWCA Civ 16, [2002] Lloyd's Rep PN 260, where it was held that a fact within the actual knowledge of a claimant cannot be concealed from him, even if he subsequently forgets the fact.
21 [2009] EWHC 1015 (QB) at para 152.

commented that 'there is nothing unreasonable in denying him a limitation defence, if his own conduct has made it practically impossible for anyone to discover the true source'.[22] It is to be noted that this approach to the interpretation of s 27A will limit the availability of a limitation defence in many applications under the POCA 2002 to cases where, limitation defence excepted, liability is admitted. Unfortunately no guidance was offered as to whether the approach of Griffith Williams J in the High Court should be followed in subsequent cases, meaning that the issues may arise for consideration again in future.

LIMITATION PROVISIONS GOVERNING EXPLOITATION PROCEEDS ORDERS

30.05 Part 7 of the Coroners and Justice Act 2009 ('CJA 2009') introduced statutory provisions to prevent criminals from profiting from publications about their crimes (ie criminal memoirs) by allowing the Serious Organised Crime Agency[23] to apply for an 'exploitation proceeds order' against the criminal so as to deprive them of any financial benefit from the publication. The limitation provisions for claims brought under Pt 7 of the CJA 2009 are contained in s 27C of the LA 1980.[24] The wording of s 27C is similar in several respects to the wording used in ss 27A and 27B and provides that none of the time limits contained in the preceding sections of the Act apply to proceedings under Pt 7 of the CJA 2009 for an exploitation proceeds order.[25] Section 27C(2) provides that proceedings for such an order are not to be brought after the expiration of six years from the date on which the enforcement authority's cause of action accrued. Subsection (4) adds that if the exploitation proceeds are obtained by a person from a relevant offence,[26] an enforcement authority's cause of action in respect of those proceeds accrues when the enforcement authority has actual knowledge that the proceeds have been obtained. Subsection (3) provides that 'proceedings', in the context of s 27C, are brought when an application is made to the High Court for an exploitation proceeds order.

22 [2010] EWCA Civ 759, [2010] 1 WLR 2881 at para 25.

23 CJA 2009, s 161(2)(a). Other 'enforcement authorities' may be prescribed by order made by the Secretary of State: *ibid*.

24 As inserted by the CJA 2009, s 171.

25 LA 1980, s 27C(1).

26 'Relevant offence' is defined in the CJA 2009, ss 155(3) and 159.

CHAPTER 31

Shorter Topics

ACTIONS FOR AN ACCOUNT

31.01 Section 23 of the Limitation Act 1980 ('LA 1980') provides that an action for an account shall not be brought after the expiration of the limitation period that is applicable to the claim which is the basis of the duty to account. Although an action for an account could at one time have been brought either in equity or at common law, the common law claim of account is obsolete[1] and only the equitable remedy of account is still in use.[2] *In Knox v Gye*,[3] it was held by the House of Lords that the common law limitation period should apply by analogy to an action seeking the equitable remedy of an account in any action involving the enforcement of legal rights not involving fiduciary duties. If no common law limitation period would have been applied by the courts of equity by analogy, the action was still subject to the defence *of laches*. Although the Limitation Act 1939 imposed a limitation period of six years for an action for an account, it was held by Megarry V-C in *Tito v Waddell (No 2)*[4] that this only applied to the obsolete action for an account at common law: s 23 of the LA 1980 has effectively codified the judgment of Megarry V-C. Accordingly, for example, the Court of Appeal in *Gwembe Valley Development Co Ltd v Koshy (No 3)*[5] held that the limitation period which applied to the claim for the taking of an account was the same as that for the underlying fraudulent breach of trust. It should be noted that the limitation period for an action for an account is subject to the provisions in the LA 1980 relating to disability, acknowledgment, part payment, fraud, concealment and mistake.[6]

1 See *Attorney General v Dublin Corporation* (1827) 4 ER 88 at 98; *Tito v Waddell (No 2)* [1977] Ch 106 at 250 and Oughton, Lowry and Merkin, *Limitation of Actions* (London: LLP, 1998) at 377.

2 See *Tito v Waddell (No 2)* [1977] Ch 106 at 250, per Megarry V-C.

3 (1872) LR 5 HL 656.

4 [1977] Ch 106 at 250: '[t]he law of limitation in relation to actions for an account seems to be in a very curious state'; see also *Attorney General v Cocke* [1988] Ch 414; *Mehra v Shah* [2003] All ER (D) 15 (Aug).

5 [2003] EWCA Civ 1048; [2004] 1 BCLC 171.

6 See *Friend v Young* [1897] 2 Ch 421 (part payment); *Betjemann v Betjemann* [1895] 2 Ch 474 (deliberate concealment) and *Mehra v Shah* [2003] All ER (D) 15 (Aug).

ADVOWSONS

31.02 Section 25 of the LA 1980 provided that an action to enforce a right to present or bestow any ecclesiastical benefice as patron of that benefice was subject to a limitation period of either:

(a) a period during which three clerks in succession have held the benefice adversely, or

(b) a period of 60 years during which the benefice has been held adversely to that right.

The Law Reform Committee in 1977 observed that the law on advowsons and benefices was 'of no practical importance in modern conditions'[7] and s 25 of the LA 1980 was repealed by s 4(3) of the Patronage (Benefices) Measure 1986, which now provides that a register of patrons is to be kept by the registrar of each diocese.

COMPETITION LAW

31.03 An action claiming damages for breach of the Competition Act 1998 may be treated for limitation purposes, depending on the precise facts, as an action claiming a sum due by virtue of an enactment,[8] an action founded on tort,[9] an action seeking restitution for unjust enrichment (subject to the contract limitation period)[10] or an action seeking relief from the consequences of mistake.[11] As breaches of competition law are often uncovered, investigated and publicised by competition enforcement agencies rather than the victims, in many cases the limitation period may already have expired prior to an injured party finding out about the infringement or their cause of action. To remedy this problem, ss 47A and 47B of the Competition Act 1998, as inserted,[12] created a right to claim damages in proceedings brought following on from a finding of infringement (a 'follow on claim') by the Office of Fair Trading, the Competition Appeal Tribunal ('CAT') or the European Commission. A claim for damages under these provisions is not subject to the provisions of the Limitation Act 1980 ('LA 1980') but must instead be made within two years from the 'relevant date',[13] which is defined as the date of the infringement decision or, if the infringing party appealed, from the date of the final appeal decision. However, the start of the two-year period will only be delayed by an appeal against liability, and in *BCL Old Co Ltd v BASF SE (No 1)*[14] it was held that an appeal against penalty only does not suffice to delay the start

7 Twenty-First Report, *Final Report on the Limitation of Actions,* Cmnd 6923, para 3.43.
8 LA 1980, s 10.
9 LA 1980, s 2.
10 LA 1980, s 5: see Ch 9.
11 LA 1980, s 32(1)(c).
12 Enterprise Act 2002, ss 18 and 19.
13 Competition Appeal Tribunal Rules 2003 (SI 2003/1372), r 31.
14 [2009] EWCA Civ 434, [2009] Bus LR 1516.

of the period. However, in *Deutsche Bahn AG v Morgan Crucible Company Plc*,[15] in an action in which, following a finding of multi-party infringement, it was held by the Court of Appeal that an appeal by one party will delay the start of the two-year period for claims against any infringing party. After the decision in *BCL Old Co Ltd (No 1)*, the proceedings returned to the CAT for a decision on whether the claimant was entitled to an extension of time within which to pursue its claim for damages under s 47A, as had been suggested by Richard LJ in his judgment in the case.[16] The CAT held that it had jurisdiction to extend time but declined to do so on the merits;[17] on appeal, the Court of Appeal reached the same result but held the CAT had no jurisdiction to extend time.[18]

31.04 On further appeal to the Supreme Court in *BCL Old Co Ltd v BASF SE (No 2)*,[19] solely on the question of whether the English provisions offended the European Union legal principles of effectiveness and legal certainty, it was held that once the two-year limitation period has expired, the CAT has no power to extend the time limit for follow-on claims and that this was consistent with EU law. Lord Mance, with whose judgment the other members of the Supreme Court agreed, expressed himself as having 'no doubt'[20] that the commencement of the two-year limitation period was foreseeable, although he also noted that, in certain circumstances, an appeal nominally directed against penalty only might in reality amount to an appeal against infringement.[21] While he noted the existence of a number of 'erroneous' decisions of the CAT, he robustly stated that this will be inevitable in a legal system having appellate courts.[22] Likewise, and notwithstanding the comments of Richard LJ in the Court of Appeal in *BCL Old Co Ltd v BASF SE (No 1)*,[23] he held that the absence of a jurisdiction to extend time was also reasonably foreseeable to the parties. If any breach of EU law had been established, it would appear as if the two-year time limit would have remained effective as between the parties but that the claimant would have had a (presumably statute barred) cause of action against the State. The decision in *BCL Old Co Ltd v BASF SE (No 2)* certainly clarifies certain aspects of the time limits for follow-on claims under s 47A of the Competition Act 1998 but the very definite judgment of Lord Mance downplays the complexities that have bedevilled the interpretation of the time limit provisions that govern follow-on claims brought under s 47A of the Competition Act 1998.

ENEMIES IN WARTIME

31.05 The effect of wartime on the running of the limitation period has not been the subject of any recent case law, but the law would appear to be that the

15 [2012] EWCA Civ 1055, [2013] Bus LR 125.
16 See [2009] EWCA Civ 434, [2009] Bus LR 1516 at paras 30, 31 and 34.
17 [2010] Comp AR 1.
18 [2011] EWCA Civ 1258, [2011] Bus LR 428.
19 [2012] UKSC 45, [2012] 1 WLR 2922.
20 [2012] UKSC 45, [2012] 1 WLR 2922 at para 29.
21 [2012] UKSC 45, [2012] 1 WLR 2922 at para 30.
22 [2012] UKSC 45, [2012] 1 WLR 2922 at para 39.
23 [2009] EWCA Civ 434, [2009] Bus LR 1516.

existence of a state of war does not prevent time from running or continuing to run.[24] An exception, which appears to have been codified rather than created by statute[25] is where the continued performance of a contract would involve dealings with, or benefit to, the enemy. In such a case, the contract becomes unenforceable for the duration of the war and time will not run so long as the right is suspended.[26] The effect on the running of the limitation period was codified by the Limitation (Enemies and War Prisoner) Act 1945, which suspends the running of the limitation period in certain circumstances. It only applies if a party is, or is deemed to be, an 'enemy' for the purposes of the Trading with the Enemy Act 1939, or if they were detained in 'enemy territory' as defined in the 1939 Act or the Defence (Trading with the Enemy) Regulations 1940. Section 1(1) of the 1945 Act provides that if, before the expiration of the limitation period for an action, any person who would have been a necessary party for that action was an enemy or was detained in enemy territory, the limitation period shall not run while he was an enemy or was so detained, and shall not expire before the end of 12 months from the date when he ceased to be an enemy or so detained. As the United Kingdom is not presently at war, the 1945 Act is only of historic interest and in any event did not give rise to much case law. Its effect appears only to have been considered in one reported decision[27] and it was only mentioned in a small number of other decisions.[28]

INTELLECTUAL PROPERTY

31.06 Actions for infringement of intellectual property rights arising at common law – such as those interests protected by the law on passing off, breach of confidence and the tort of privacy – are governed by the six-year limitation period for an action founded on tort[29] and the equitable principles of *laches* and acquiescence for any equitable reliefs sought.[30] Most intellectual property rights are now created by and governed by statute with the main pieces of legislation being the Patents Act 1977 ('PA 1977'), the Copyright, Designs and Patent Act 1988 ('CDA 1988') and the Trade Marks Act 1994 ('TMA 1994'). An action alleging patent infringement was conceded by the defendant in *Sevcon v Lucas CAV Ltd*[31] to be an action founded on tort within the meaning of s 2 of the LA

24 See *Prideaux v Webber* (1661) 1 Lev 31, *Bowring-Hanbury's Trustee v Bowring-Hanbury* [1943] Ch 104 at 110–111 (CA) and the discussion in *Halsbury's Laws of England* (5th edn, LexisNexis 2008) vol 68, paras 925, 1169 and 1232.

25 *Halsbury's Laws of England* (5th edn, LexisNexis 2008) vol 68, paras 925, 1169 and 1232.

26 Trading with the Enemy Act 1939.

27 *Société Dunkerquoise de Remorquage et de Sauvetage v Atlantic Scout (Owners), The Atlantic Scout* [1950] P 266, (1950) 84 Lloyd's Rep 22.

28 See *Chaplin v Chaplin* [1948] 2 All ER 408 (CA), *Heindal v Questier & Co Ltd* (1949) 84 Lloyd's Rep 452 and *Duncan v London Borough of Lambeth* [1968] 1 QB 747.

29 LA 1980, s 2.

30 LA 1980, s 36(1). See further *Fisher v Brooker* [2009] UKHL 41, [2009] 4 All ER 789 and the discussion of claims for equitable relief, *laches* and acquiescence in Ch 18.

31 [1986] 1 WLR 462.

1980,[32] in respect of which a limitation period of six years applies; if equitable reliefs had been sought, those would have been subject to s 36(1). A quirk of patent law gave rise to the dispute before the House of Lords in *Sevcon*, namely the inability of a party to bring proceedings alleging patent infringement prior to the grant of letters patent. It was argued by the claimant that the limitation period in those circumstances should only run from the date the letters patent were granted. This argument was rejected by the House of Lords, which held that time runs from the date of the infringement even though no action could have been brought at that time. Sections 113 and 203 of the CDA 1988 provide a six-year statutory limitation period (subject to extension on grounds of fraud, concealment or disability) for actions in respect of copyright and rights in performances, respectively. An order for delivery up of infringing material must be brought within the aforesaid limitation period.[33]

31.07 In the case of a registered trade mark, where the proprietor of an earlier trade mark (or other earlier right) has acquiesced for a continuous period of five years in the use of the registered trade mark, he ceases to have any right:

(a) to apply for a declaration that the registration of the later trade mark is invalid; or

(b) to oppose the use of the later trade mark,

unless the registration of the later trade mark was applied for in bad faith.[34] The concept of 'acquiescence' in this context was considered by the European Court of Justice in *Budejovicky Budvar v Anheuser-Busch Inc*,[35] where it was held that this will arise if a party 'knowingly tolerated' the use of a trade mark subsequent to his own for a substantial length of time and that it was not necessary to prove that the interests of the proprietor of the trade mark were inequitably prejudiced. When *Budejovicky Budvar* returned to the Court of Appeal for determination in light of the ruling of the ECJ, the court held that *Anheuser-Busch* was not entitled to object to *Budejovicky Budvar* using the registered mark in light of its delay and acquiescence in the latter using the name *Budvar*.[36] As a final matter, it is important to note that an intellectual property right is not a 'good' or 'chattel' that is extinguished at the expiration of the limitation period for actions relating to infringement of the right.[37]

32 It is arguable that certain statutory intellectual property rights are governed by s 9 if they give rise to a claim for a sum due by virtue of any enactment, but little turns on the point as the limitation period is six years in either case.

33 CDA 1988, ss 99 (copyright) and 195 (performance right).

34 TMA 1994, s 48(1); this provision should be read together with the First Council Directive (EEC) 89/104, art 9(1) to approximate the laws of the Member States relating to trade marks.

35 (Case C-482/09) [2012] IP & IT 160, [2012] RPC 12.

36 [2012] EWCA Civ 880, [2012] 3 All ER 1405.

37 See *Fisher v Brooker* [2009] UKHL 41, [2009] 4 All ER 789.

PROCEEDINGS INVOLVING THE CROWN[38]

General limitation principles for proceedings involving the Crown

31.08 Since the passing of the Crown Proceedings Act 1947 ('CPA 1947'), private law actions may be instituted against the Crown with the exception of two types of private suit which must still be brought by 'petition as of right'.[39] The word 'Crown' is defined in s 38 of the CPA 1947 (and s 37(3) of the LA 1980) as including the Duchy of Lancaster, the Duke of Cornwall, any government department or officer of the Crown and any person acting on behalf of the Crown. Section 37(1) of the LA 1980 provides that, save as otherwise provided by that Act or by another provision, the limitation provisions in the LA 1980 apply to actions by and against the Crown.[40] Section 37(2) of the LA 1980 provides that the 1980 Act shall not apply to:

(a) any proceedings by the Crown for the recovery of any tax or duty or interest on any tax or duty;

(b) any forfeiture proceedings under the customs and excise Acts; or

(c) any proceedings in respect of the forfeiture of a ship.

Section 37(6) adds that nothing in the LA 1980 shall affect the prerogative right of the Crown to any gold or silver mine, which means that no limitation period applies to the exercise of this prerogative right. Thus, in *Burmah Oil v Lord Advocate*,[41] it was held that no limitation period applied to a claim for compensation in relation to the expropriation of property during World War II, although the focus of the House of Lords was on the issue of whether the claim was barred by the Public Authorities Protection Act 1893 and the court did not consider whether any provisions in the Limitation Act 1939, such as those relating to trespass claims, applied.

Extended limitation periods for actions involving land

31.09 Schedule 1, Pt II of the LA 1980 modifies the limitation periods in s 15 of the LA 1980 for actions involving real property in cases where the Crown or a spiritual or eleemosynary corporation sole is the claimant. Subject to these modifications, both the Crown and a corporation sole may be a squatter, as was accepted by the Court of Appeal in *Roberts v Swangrove Estates Ltd*,[42] and may have their title

38 While judicial review proceedings nominally involve the Crown as a party, these are considered separately in Ch 29.

39 CPA 1947, s 40(1) and (2)(b). The two exceptions are actions against the Sovereign in a personal capacity and actions against the Crown with respect to matters arising outside the United Kingdom; the LA 1980, s 37(5) provides that a petition of right shall be treated as being commenced on the date on which the petition is presented.

40 This provision echoes the provisions of the Law Reform (Limitation of Actions etc) Act 1954, which abolished the special (shorter) limitation periods for actions against public authorities.

41 [1965] AC 75.

42 [2008] EWCA Civ 98,[2008] Ch 439.

to land extinguished. The phrase 'spiritual or eleemosynary corporation sole' is not defined in the LA 1980 but would appear to include the rector of a parish[43] (and similarly an archbishop, bishop or vicar) as well as Ecclesiastical Commissioners, but not corporations aggregate (such as the Church Commissioners).[44] The extended limitation periods arise in the following circumstances:

(i) Action to recover land: s 15(1) of the LA 1980

Paragraph 10 of Sch 1, Pt II provides that an action to recover any land by the Crown or by any spiritual or eleemosynary corporation shall be subject to a limitation period of 30 years. Paragraph 12 of Sch 1 further provides that where, for an action brought by a person other than the Crown or a spiritual or eleemosynary corporation sole, the right of action first accrued to the Crown or any such corporation sole through whom the person in question claims, the action may be brought at any time before the expiration of the shorter of –

(a) the period during which the action could have been brought by the Crown or the corporation sole; or

(b) 12 years from the date on which the right of action accrued to some person other than the Crown or the corporation sole.

In *Hill v Transport for London*,[45] it was held that 'first accrued to the Crown' means 'accrued to the Crown at some point' and that the extended limitation period arises even if the Crown was a successor in title to the party who originally had the right of action. This finding is in slight conflict with the general rule that the characterisation of a cause of action is fixed upon its accrual,[46] which might still be relied upon to prevent a landowner conveying to the Crown in order for a 30-year limitation period to apply to the claim.

(ii) Action to recover foreshore: s 15(1) of the LA 1980

An exception to the 30-year limitation period for an action by the Crown to recover land arises in the case of 'foreshore', which is defined as 'the shore and bed of the sea and of any tidal water, below the line of the medium high tide between the spring tides and the neap tides'[47]. Paragraph 11 of Sch 1 provides that a limitation period of 60 years shall apply to an action by the Crown to recover foreshore[48] and that if the land ceases to be foreshore, but remains in the ownership of the Crown, the limitation period shall be the shorter of 60 years from the date of accrual of the right of action or 30 years from the date when the land ceased to be foreshore.[49]

43 See *Hayward v Chaloner* [1968] 1 QB 107.
44 See *Ecclesiastical Commissioners v Rowe* (1880) 5 App Cas 736; *Re Armitage's WT* [1972] 1 Ch 438.
45 [2005] EWHC 856 (Ch), [2005] Ch 379.
46 *West Bromwich Building Society v Wilkinson* [2005] UKHL 44, [2005] 4 All ER 97.
47 LA 1980, Sch 1, Pt II, para 11(3).
48 LA 1980, Sch 1, Pt II, para 11(1).
49 LA 1980, Sch 1, Pt II, para 11(2).

(iii) Action in relation to adverse possession of an estate in reversion or remainder: s 15(2) of the LA 1980

Paragraph 13 of Sch 1 provides that where the Crown or a spiritual or eleemosynary corporation sole is entitled to the succeeding estate or interest, the limitation period shall be either 30 years from the date of accrual of the right of action or 12 years from the date the right of action accrued to the person entitled to the succeeding interest, whichever last expires.

(iv) Sch 1, para 6 on the effect of payment of rent to person not entitled does not apply to the Crown

Paragraph 6(1) of Sch 1 applies to leases in writing where the rent reserved is less than £10 and provides that if the rent is received by a person wrongfully claiming to be entitled to the land in reversion to that lease, a right to recover land arises immediately upon the payment of rent to a person not entitled. Paragraph 6(2) of Sch 1 states that para 6(1) shall not apply to cases where the Crown is the lessor. This has the result that a right of action by the Crown to recover the land will only accrue upon the determination of the term of the lease.

MISCELLANEOUS OTHER STATUTORY LIMITATION PERIODS

31.10 Section 39 of the LA 1980 states that the Act shall not apply where an alternative limitation period is prescribed under any other statute. It is not practicable to consider every other statutory limitation period or time limit, but the following constitute some of the main statutory limitation periods:

(a) Defective Premises Act 1972

An action under the Defective Premises Act 1972 for breach of the statutory warranty that dwellings are to be constructed in a workmanlike and professional manner and shall be fit for habitation when completed is six years from the date the building is completed.

(b) Land Compensation Act 1973

The limitation period for a claim arising out of noise nuisance from a public highway is seven years from the date the stretch of highway causing the nuisance opened to public traffic.[50]

(c) Rent Act 1977

Section 57 of the Rent Act 1977[51] imposes a limitation period on a claim by a tenant against a landlord for recovery of rent in excess of the recoverable

50 *Price v Caerphilly County Borough Council* [2005] 1 EGLR 157.

51 As substituted by the Housing Act 1980, s 69(3).

rent of two years for a claim for the recovery of that rent, or one year if the rent is recoverable by virtue of s 54 of the Act.

(d) Solicitors Act 1974

Section 70 of the Solicitors Act 1974 provides that a client has one year following receipt of a bill of costs within which to refer it to taxation. Following this period there is no provision whereby the bill may be referred to taxation, although this does not affect a client's right to make a complaint of overcharging to the Law Society.

(e) Taxes Management Act 1970

The Taxes Management Act 1970 ('TMA 1970'), as amended most recently by the Finance Act 2008, contains the time limits during which Her Majesty's Revenue and Customs may make assessments on a taxpayer and a taxpayer may make claims to the Revenue. The following are the main time limits: s 34(1) of the TMA 1970 provides that, subject to any provision of the Taxes Acts prescribing a longer or shorter period, 'no claim for relief in respect of income tax … may be made more than 4 years after the end of the year of assessment to which it relates'; s 36(1) provides that in cases where a loss of tax was brought about carelessly, an assessment may be made 'at any time not more than six years after end of the year of assessment to which it relates'; s 36(1A) provides that in cases where a loss of tax was brought about deliberately, an assessment may be made 'at any time not more than 20 years after end of the year of assessment to which it relates'. These time limits must be read in the light of the decision of the Supreme Court in *Test Claimants in the FII Group Litigation v Revenue and Customs Comrs,*[52] which confirmed that a taxpayer is still entitled to bring a restitutionary claim to recover monies overpaid by mistake in preference to a claim under the TMA 1970 so as to gain the benefit of the extended limitation period arising under s 32(1)(c) of the LA 1980.

52 [2012] UKSC 19, [2012] 2 AC 337.

APPENDICES

Table of Limitation Periods

APPENDIX 1

The Main Causes of Action: Contract, Unjust Enrichment, Tort, Personal Injuries, Real Property, Personal Property

Action	Statutory Provision	Limitation Period
Contract (see also Acknowledgment and Part Payment)		
Action on a simple contract not claiming equitable relief, except where the action claims damages in respect of personal injuries (including death)	LA 1980, s 5	Six years from date of breach of contract
Action in respect of a loan	LA 1980, ss 5 and 6	Six years from date loan fell due or date of demand
Action on a specialty (ie contract under seal) (except personal injuries actions)	LA 1980, s 8	12 years
Exceptions to 12-year period:		
– Action for rent	LA 1980, s 19	Six years
– Action for interest in respect of money secured by a mortgage or other charge	LA 1980, s 20(5)	Six years
Unjust enrichment/ Restitution		
Action for money had and received or in respect of unjust enrichment or claiming restitution (subject to exceptions)	LA 1980, s 5	Six years, but see further Ch 9 for exceptions
Action for relief from the consequences of mistake	LA 1980, s 32(1)(c)	Time runs from when the mistake was, or could with reasonable diligence have been, discovered
		contd

Action	Statutory Provision	Limitation Period
Unjust enrichment or restitution claim seeking equitable relief or seeking the return of trust property or its proceeds from a trustee	LA 1980, ss 21(1)(b) and 36	No limitation period applies, unless by analogy, but defences of *laches* and acquiescence may be raised
Tort (other than personal injuries)		
Action founded on tort (unless subject to one of the other limitation provisions listed below)	LA 1980, ss 2 and 14A	Six years from date of accrual of the cause of action
Action claiming damages for negligence where the 'starting date' (ie the claimant's 'date of knowledge') is after date of accrual of cause of action	LA 1980, ss 14A and 14B	The longer of six years from the date of accrual or three years from the starting date, subject to an overriding time limit of 15 years
Conversion by theft	LA 1980, s 4	No limitation period
Conversion by a sale of a chattel to a bona fide purchaser after initial conversion by theft (except where property converted by a trustee, in which case, see Trusts in App 2)	LA 1980, s 4(2)	Six years from the date of purchase of the converted goods by a bona fide purchaser
Defamation and malicious falsehood	LA 1980, ss 4A and 32A	One year from date of publication. This period may be disapplied if it is equitable to allow the action to proceed
Action claiming damages under Consumer Protection Act 1987, Pt 1, not including damages for personal injuries	LA 1980, s 11A	Three years from the date of damage or claimant's date of knowledge, subject to a ten-year long-stop
Action based on the fraud of the defendant, or his agent, or any person through whom the defendant claims	LA 1980, s 32(1)(a)	Six years from when the claimant discovered, or could with reasonable diligence have discovered the fraud
Personal injuries (including wrongful death actions)		
Action claiming damages for personal injuries caused by negligence, nuisance or breach of duty (whether the duty arises under contract, statute or otherwise) (see also the Carriage Statutes in App 2)	LA 1980, s 11(4); the date of knowledge provisions are in s 14	Three years from the date of accrual of the cause of action or the date of knowledge (if later)
		contd

Action	Statutory Provision	Limitation Period
Action claiming damages under Fatal Accidents Act 1976	LA 1980, s 12(2); the date of knowledge provisions are in s 14	Three years from the date of accrual of the cause of action or the date of knowledge (if later)
Discretion to disapply the limitation period for an action claiming damages for personal injuries or death	LA 1980, s 33	The court may disapply the limitation period if it is equitable to allow the action to proceed
Action claiming damages for personal injuries under Pt 1 of the Consumer Protection Act 1987	LA 1980, s 11A	Three years from the date of damage or claimant's date of knowledge, subject to a ten-year long-stop
Real property – Registered land		
Action to recover registered land (other than by a chargee) or to redeem registered land	LRA 2002, ss 96–98	The limitation periods in the LA 1980 do not apply
Right to apply for registration as owner of registered estate in land (unopposed)	LRA 2002, Sch 6, para 1(1)	Ten years' adverse possession
Right to apply for registration as owner of registered estate in land (opposed)	LRA 2002, Sch 6, paras 1 and 5	Ten years' adverse possession plus one of the conditions in para 5 satisfied
Right to apply for registration as owner of registered estate in land (second application, if first application unsuccessful due to para 5 not being satisfied)	LRA 2002, Sch 6, paras 1 and 6	Ten years' adverse possession plus remaining in possession for two years after first application
Real property – Unregistered land – Action to recover land (see also Acknowledgment and Part payment)		
Action to recover land (to include right to enter possession of land)	LA 1980, ss 15 and 38(7)	12 years from date on which the right of action accrued
Action to recover land by the Crown or any spiritual or eleemosynary corporation sole	LA 1980, Pt II, Sch 1, para 10	30 years from date on which the right of action accrued
		contd

Action	Statutory Provision	Limitation Period
Action to recover land by a person other than the Crown or any spiritual or eleemosynary corporation sole where the right of action first accrued to such person	LA 1980, Pt II, Sch 1, para 12	The shorter of 30 years from date of accrual to the Crown or 12 years from accrual to the other person
Action by the Crown to recover foreshore	LA 1980, Pt II, Sch 1, para 11	60 years or 30 years from when the land ceased to be foreshore
Special limitation period for the recovery of land where the adverse possession commenced before a future interest fell into possession	LA 1980, s 15(2)	The later of 12 years from the date the adverse possession commenced, or six years from when the future interest vested in possession
Fee tails	LA 1980, ss 15 and 27	See Ch 15
Action to recover settled land and land held on trust and adverse possession as between co-owners	LA 1980, ss 15, 18 and 21	See Ch 15
Real property – Unregistered land – Leasehold estates (see also Acknowledgment and Part payment)		
Action (or distress) to recover rent or rentcharge or damages in respect thereof	LA 1980, s 19	Six years
Action for damages in respect of a breach of a covenant in a lease (other than relating to the payment of rent)	LA 1980, ss 5 and 8	Six years, or 12 years if the lease was made by deed
Action seeking equitable relief in respect of a breach of a covenant in a lease (other than relating to rent)	LA 1980, ss 5 and 8	No limitation period applies but *laches* and acquiescence may be raised
Action for breach of commonhold duty	LA 1980, s 19A	Six years

Action	Statutory Provision	Limitation Period
Real property – Unregistered land – Mortgages, charges and debts secured on land (see also Acknowledgment and Part payment)		
Foreclosure action (unless the property includes a future interest)	LA 1980, ss 15 and 20(4)	12 years from date for legal redemption
Mortgagee's power of sale	LA 1980, s 15	See mortgagee's right to recover land
Action to recover any principal sum of money secured by a mortgage or charge on land (unless the property includes a future interest)	LA 1980, s 20(1) and (3)	12 years from the date on which the right to receive the money accrued
Action to recover arrears of interest payable in respect of a sum of money secured by a mortgage or charge on land (or in respect of the proceeds of sale)	LA 1980, s 20(5)	Six years from the date on which the interest became due (except for mortgagor seeking to redeem land)
Action by mortgagor to redeem land in the possession of the mortgagee	LA 1980, s 16	12 years from when the mortgagee entered into possession
Personal property (see also Tort: Conversion)		
Action to recover any principal sum of money secured by a mortgage or charge on personal property (unless the property includes a future interest)	LA 1980, s 20(1)(a) and (3)	12 years from the date on which the right to receive the money accrued
Action to bring a foreclosure action in respect of personal property (unless the property includes a future interest)	LA 1980, s 20(2) and (3)	12 years from the date the cause of action accrued or the date the mortgagee's possession discontinued
Redemption action by mortgagor of personal property	Common law and equitable rules	No limitation period
Action to recover arrears of interest payable in respect of a sum of money secured by a mortgage or other charge on personal property	LA 1980, s 20(5)	Six years from the date on which the interest became due

contd

Action	Statutory Provision	Limitation Period
Cause of action vested in the State to seek the return of a cultural object that was unlawfully removed	Return of Cultural Objects Regulations 1994 (SI 1994/501)	One year after the Member State became aware of the location of the cultural object and 30 or 75 years after removal

APPENDIX 2

Other Causes of Action

Cause of Action	Statutory Provision	Limitation Period
Account		
Action for an account	LA 1980, s 23	Subject to the same period as that applicable to the claim giving rise to duty to account
Admiralty and maritime		
Claims in respect of damage to or loss of a ship, her cargo or freight or property on board, and for damages for loss of life or personal injuries suffered by any person on board caused by the fault of another ship	Merchant Shipping Act 1995, s 190	Two years, subject to discretion to extend the limitation period
Salvage claim	Salvage Convention, art 23(1); MSA 1995, s 224 and Sch 11	Two years from the date the salvage operations are terminated
Proceedings in respect of the forfeiture of a ship	LA 1980, s 37(2)(c)	No limitation period
Arbitration		
Commencement of arbitration	Arbitration Act 1996, s 13(1) and 14	Same limitation period as if civil proceedings were issued: time runs until notice of arbitration served
Extension to a contractual time limit to commence an arbitration	Arbitration Act 1996, s 12	Limited jurisdiction to extend time
Action to enforce an award where agreement not under seal	LA 1980, s 7	Six years from when the award should have been performed
Action to enforce an award where agreement under seal	LA 1980, s 8	12 years from when the award should have been performed

Cause of Action	Statutory Provision	Limitation Period
Bankruptcy	See Ch 24	
Carriage by air		
Action for personal injuries or death, or for loss, damage or delay in relation to luggage or goods arising out of air transport	Montreal Convention 1999, art 35; Carriage by Air Act 1961 and Regulation 2027/1997 as amended by Regulation 889/2002	Two years from the date the aircraft arrived or ought to have arrived. There are also notification requirements; for damage: seven days for baggage and 14 days for cargo; for delay: 21 days from the date the baggage or cargo was returned
Carriage by rail		
Action for damages for personal injuries or for loss or damage to goods suffered in the course of rail travel	Convention on International Carriage by Rail (COTIF) of 9 May 1980, arts 54–60; Railways (Convention on International Carriage by Rail) Regulations 2005 and Regulation 1371/2007	Three years for personal injuries or death; one year for other actions or two years where intent can be proved. There is also a requirement that notification be given within 12 months of the incident
Carriage by road		
Claim in relation to loss or damage suffered in the course of the international carriage of goods by road in a vehicle for reward	Geneva Convention on the Contract for the International Carriage of Goods by Road, arts 35 and 39(4); Carriage of Goods by Road Act 1965	One year, except in the case of wilful misconduct, where the limitation period is three years. A written claim suspends the period of limitation until the carrier rejects the claim. The time limit for a claim for contribution runs from the date of the final judicial decision fixing the amount of compensation payable
Carriage by sea		
Claim for damages for personal injuries or for loss or damage to luggage	Athens Convention 1974, art 16; Merchant Shipping Act 1995, s 183 and Regulation 392/2009	Two years from the date of disembarkation or the date when disembarkation should have occurred *contd*

Cause of Action	Statutory Provision	Limitation Period
Claim for loss or damage to goods	Hague-Visby Rules, art III, r 6; Carriage of Goods by Sea Act 1971	One year from when the goods were delivered or should have been delivered
Commonhold		
Action for breach of commonhold duty	LA 1980, s 19A	Six years
Company law	See Ch 24	
Competition law		
Follow-on claim for damages following a finding of infringement	Competition Act 2002, ss 47A and 47B	Two years from the infringement decision or the final appeal on liability
Contribution		
Action claiming contribution	LA 1980, s 10	Two years after date of judgment or award or agreement to pay compensation
Counterclaim	LA 1980, s 35	An original counterclaim or set-off is deemed to have been brought on the same date as the action in which it is pleaded
Deceased person (see also Probate)		
Cause of action against the estate of a deceased person which was subsisting prior to his death	n/a	The limitation period runs from the date the cause of action accrued
Cause of action against the estate of an deceased person arising after his death	Common law rules	See Ch 19
Cause of action accruing to estate of deceased person after his death	LA 1980, s 26 and common law rules	See Ch 19
Employment legislation	See Ch 27	
Equitable relief	LA 1980, s 36	Unless a limitation period applies by analogy, no limitation period applies but a defence of *laches* may be raised instead
Estates (actions against)	See Deceased person as defendant and Probate	

Cause of Action	Statutory Provision	Limitation Period
European Union law	See Ch 26 and Tort (App 1)	
Fiduciary duty	See Equitable relief	
Gold or silver mine		
Prerogative right of the Crown to any gold or silver mine	LA 1980, s 37(6)	No limitation period
Human Rights Act 1998		
Action for compensation under HRA 1998, s 7(1)	HRA 1998, s 7(5)	One year or such longer period as the court considers equitable
Injunction	See Equitable relief	
Insolvency	See Ch 24	
Judgment (enforcement of)		
Action on a judgment	LA 1980, s 24(1)	Six years from the date the judgment became enforceable
Claim for arrears of interest in respect of a judgment debt (unless enforced by charging order)	LA 1980, s 24(2)	Six years from the date the interest became due
Execution on a judgment (except for order for possession of registered land: see Land Registration Act 2002, s 98)	RSC Sch 1 Ord 46, r 2(1)	Leave of court required for writ of execution if six years have elapsed since date of order
Enforcement of charging order	Charging Orders Act 1979	No limitation period
Third party debt orders	CPR 72	No limitation period
Minors	See Disability (App 3)	
Mistake		
Action for relief from the consequences of mistake	LA 1980, s 32(1)(c)	The limitation period does not run until the claimant has, or could by the exercise of reasonable diligence, have, discovered the mistake
Partnership	See Ch 24	
Person of unsound mind	See Disability (App 3)	

Cause of Action	Statutory Provision	Limitation Period
Probate		
Action by beneficiary in respect of any claim to the personal estate of a deceased person or to any share or interest in any such estate	LA 1980, s 22(a), subject to s 21(1) and (2)	12 years from the date when the right to receive the share or interest accrued, subject to extension if s 21 applies
Action by beneficiary to recover arrears of interest in respect of any legacy, or damages in respect of such arrears	LA 1980, s 22(b), subject to s 21(1) and (2)	Six years from when the interest became due, subject to extension if s 21 applies
Action by beneficiary against estate in respect of any claim to the real property of a deceased person	LA 1980, ss 15 and 18, subject to s 21(1) and (2)	Six years from when the cause of action accrued, subject to extension if s 21 applies
Challenge to a will or entitlements on an intestacy on grounds that it does not make sufficient provision for that beneficiary	Inheritance (Provision for Family and Dependents) Act 1975, s 4	Six months from the first taking out of representation, or a longer period with leave of court
Application to rectify a will so as to carry out the testator's intentions	Administration of Justice Act 1982, s 20(2)	Six months from the first taking out of representation, or a longer period with leave of court
Proceeds of crime		
Proceedings for a recovery order in respect of the proceeds of crime or to give effect to an external order	LA 1980, ss 27A, 27B	12 years from when the cause of action accrued
Proceedings for an exploitation order under Coroners and Justice Act 2009, Pt 7	LA 1980, s 27C	Six years from when the cause of action accrued
Revenue	LA 1980, s 37(2) and Taxes Management Act 1970	No limitation period applies; time limits contained in Tax Acts: see Ch 31
Set off	See Counterclaim	
Sexual abuse	See Personal injuries (App 1)	
Specialty	See Contract (App 1) and Statute	
Specific performance	See Equitable relief	

Cause of Action	Statutory Provision	Limitation Period
Statute		
Action to recover a sum recoverable by virtue of an enactment (other than a claim for contribution)	LA 1980, s 9(1)	Six years
Action on a statute where no other limitation period applicable (a claim on a specialty)	LA 1980, s 8	12 years, unless a shorter period is prescribed by any other provision
Trusts		
Action by a beneficiary to recover trust property or for breach of trust	LA 1980, s 21(3)	Six years
Action in relation to settled land and land held on trust	LA 1980, s 18(1)	Limitation period is the same as if no trust was involved, subject to s 21(1) and (2)
Action for breach of trust where trust property or proceeds thereof is retained by trustee or converted to his own use	LA 1980, s 21(1)(a)	No limitation period, but defence of *laches* may be raised
Action in respect of any fraud or fraudulent breach of trust to which the trustee was a party or privy	LA 1980, s 21(1)(b)	No limitation period, but defence of *laches* may be raised

APPENDIX 3

Extensions to the Limitation Period: Acknowledgment and Part Payment, Cross-Border Mediations, Deliberate Concealment, Disability, Enemies and Detainees in Wartime, and Mistake

Reason for Extension to the Limitation Period	Statutory Provision	Length of Extension to the Limitation Period
Acknowledgment and part payment		
Acknowledgment of title or debt or part payment of debt	LA 1980, ss 29–31; see further Ch 6	The right of action is deemed to have accrued on the date of the acknowledgment or payment
Cross-border mediation		
An extension of time arises if the limitation period would otherwise expire during the mediation or within eight weeks thereafter	LA 1980, s 33A	The limitation period instead expires at the end of eight weeks after the mediation ends
Deliberate concealment		
Any fact relevant to the claimant's right of action deliberately concealed by the defendant or his agent or of any person through whom he claims or his agent	LA 1980, s 32(1)(b)	The limitation period does not run until the claimant has discovered the concealed fact or could with reasonable diligence have discovered that fact
Disability		
Persons who were minors or lacking capacity (within the meaning of the Mental Capacity Act 2005) to conduct legal proceedings when a right of action accrued to them gain a general extension to the limitation period	LA 1980, s 29(1)	An action may be brought at any time before the expiration of six years from the date when the person ceased to be under a disability or died, whichever is earlier *contd*

Reason for Extension to the Limitation Period	**Statutory Provision**	**Length of Extension to the Limitation Period**
Main exceptions to the six-year extension of time:		
– Personal injuries action, including an action under the Fatal Accidents Act 1976	LA 1980, s 28(6)	Three years
– Libel and slander, slander of title or other malicious falsehood	LA 1980, s 28(4A)	One year
– Contribution action	LA 1980, s 28(5)	Two years
– Action under Consumer Protection Act 1987, Pt 1	LA 1980, s 28(7)	Three years
– Other exceptions to six-year extension	See Ch 5	
Enemies and detainees in wartime		
Suspension of time while a person is an 'enemy' within the Trading with the Enemy Act 1939 or while he was detained in enemy territory	Limitation (Enemies and War Prisoner) Act 1945, s 1(1)	The limitation period ceases to run and only starts to run again 12 months after he ceased to be an enemy or be detained
Mistake		
Action for relief from the consequences of mistake	LA 1980, s 32(1)(c)	The limitation period does not run until the claimant has, or could by the exercise of reasonable diligence, have, discovered the mistake

Index

All references are to paragraph number.